THE AUTHOR

FREDERICK RUDOLPH is Mark Hopkins Professor of History and Chairman of the American Civilization Program at Williams College. He taught at Williams in 1946–47, after four years of service in World War II and before attending graduate school; he has been a member of the Williams faculty since 1951. Rudolph received his Ph.D. in history from Yale in 1953 and has been the recipient of two Guggenheim Fellowships, 1958–59 and 1968–69. In 1960 and 1961 he was visiting lecturer in history and education at Harvard. His books include *Mark Hopkins and the Log* (1956), *The American College and University: A History* (1962), and *Essays on Education in the Early Republic* (1965).

CURRICULUM

*A History of the American
Undergraduate Course of Study
Since 1636*

PREPARED FOR THE CARNEGIE COUNCIL
ON POLICY STUDIES IN HIGHER EDUCATION

Frederick Rudolph

CURRICULUM

*A History of the American
Undergraduate Course of Study
Since 1636*

Jossey-Bass Publishers
San Francisco • Washington • London • 1977

CURRICULUM
A History of the American Undergraduate Course of Study Since 1636
    Frederick Rudolph

Copyright © 1977 by: The Carnegie Foundation
                      for the Advancement of Teaching

              Jossey-Bass, Inc., Publishers
              615 Montgomery Street
              San Francisco, California 94111

              Jossey-Bass Limited
              28 Banner Street
              London EC1Y 8QE

The Carnegie Council on Policy Studies in Higher Education,
2150 Shattuck Avenue, Berkeley, California 94704, has sponsored
preparation of this report as part of a continuing effort to
obtain and present information for public discussion.
The views expressed are those of the author.

Copies are available from Jossey-Bass, San Francisco,
for the United States, and Possessions, and for Canada,
Australia, New Zealand, and Japan.
Copies for the rest of the world are available from
Jossey-Bass, London.

Library of Congress Catalogue Card Number LC 77-84319

International Standard Book Number ISBN 0-87589-358-9

Manufactured in the United States of America

DESIGN BY WILLI BAUM

FIRST EDITION

Code 7754

The Carnegie Council Series

The Federal Role in Postsecondary
Education: Unfinished Business,
1975–1980
*The Carnegie Council on Policy
Studies in Higher Education*

More Than Survival: Prospects for
Higher Education in a Period
of Uncertainty
*The Carnegie Foundation for the
Advancement of Teaching*

Making Affirmative Action
Work in Higher Education:
An Analysis of Institutional and
Federal Policies with
Recommendations
*The Carnegie Council on Policy
Studies in Higher Education*

Presidents Confront Reality: From
Edifice Complex to University
Without Walls
*Lyman A. Glenny, John R. Shea,
Janet H. Ruyle, Kathryn H.
Freschi*

Progress and Problems in
Medical and Dental Education:
Federal Support Versus
Federal Control
*The Carnegie Council on Policy
Studies in Higher Education*

Faculty Bargaining in Public
Higher Education: A Report and
Two Essays
*The Carnegie Council on Policy
Studies in Higher Education,
Joseph W. Garbarino,
David E. Feller, Matthew W.
Finkin*

Low or No Tuition: The Feasibil-
ity of National Policy for the First
Two Years of College
*The Carnegie Council on Policy
Studies in Higher Education*

Managing Multicampus Systems:
Effective Administration in an
Unsteady State
Eugene C. Lee, Frank M. Bowen

Challenges Past, Challenges
Present: An Analysis of American
Higher Education Since 1930
David D. Henry

The States and Higher Education:
A Proud Past and a Vital Future
*The Carnegie Foundation for the
Advancement of Teaching*

Educational Leaves for Employees:
European Experience for
American Consideration
*Konrad von Moltke,
Norbert Schneevoigt*

Investment in Learning: The
Individual and Social Value of
American Higher Education
*Howard R. Bowen with the collabo-
ration of Peter Clecak, Jacqueline
Powers Doud, Gordon K. Douglass*

Selective Admissions in Higher
Education: Comment and Recom-
mendations and Two Reports
*The Carnegie Council on Policy
Studies in Higher Education,
Winton H. Manning, Warren W.
Willingham, Hunter M. Breland,
and Associates*

Curriculum: A History of the
American Undergraduate Course of
Study Since 1636
Frederick Rudolph

Contents

Foreword

It is impossible to think clearly about the curriculum of the American college or university without some sense of its past. In the final analysis, the curriculum is nothing less than the statement a college makes about what, out of the totality of man's constantly growing knowledge and experience, is considered useful, appropriate, or relevant to the lives of educated men and women at a certain point of time. If we hope to understand how much of that statement is an expression of enduring educational and national values, we need to know how much of it was considered relevant to the lives of students in the early New England colleges. If we hope to understand the relevance itself, we have to know something about the society to which students were expected to adapt themselves and about the ideas and technological developments that constantly change our world. And if we hope to understand why educators have never been totally satisfied with the curriculum, we have to realize that a college's course of study has been subjected to incessant, often conflicting, pressures and tensions from within and without the college since the founding of Harvard in 1636.

One effective way to describe any college curriculum, even today, is to compare it, say, to the highly prescribed curriculum of the first American colleges, to the classical curriculum defended by the Yale Report of 1828, to the elective curriculum adopted at Harvard in the 1870s and its modifications in 1909, to the comprehensive university created at Cornell in the 1860s and the research university created at Johns Hopkins in the 1870s, and to the many experiments with core courses, interdisciplinary education, and competency-based learning that have taken place in our present century.

When these institutional models fail to orient us, there are other historic dimensions that give us bearings. Most of these involve differences between conflicting or contrasting concepts—prescription versus free choice; general versus specialized education; elite versus egalitarian education; mass versus individualized instruction; autocratic versus bureaucratic administration; subject-based versus competency-based curricula; and many more. Only history can fully explain the origins of such concepts and the extent of the tensions that exist between them.

The importance of such historical perspectives was immediately recognized by the Board of Trustees of The Carnegie Foundation for the Advancement of Teaching and members of the Carnegie Council on Policy Studies in Higher Education when it was decided in 1974 to make the undergraduate curriculum a subject of special concern for both organizations. And we were very fortunate that our interest in the subject happened to be shared at that time by Frederick Rudolph, Mark Hopkins Professor of History at Williams College. His previous history of *The American College and University* had already become a standard reference, and one of the most insightful and enjoyable contributions that has been made to the literature in many years. To *Curriculum*, he brings the same sense of the significant moment, of the decisive event, and of the illuminating particular that made his previous history of the American colleges so outstanding. He binds these together with a sure comprehension of the broad influences and trends, the continuities and discontinuities in the national disposition, and the internal dynamics of the American college and university. The result is a contribution to our own studies and to those of future scholars and educational policy makers that is immense. We are very pleased to have his work represented among publications in our series.

CLARK KERR
Chairperson
Carnegie Council on Policy
Studies in Higher Education

Preface

When Clark Kerr and Verne Stadtman proposed the idea for this book to me, I did not instantly say no. I surprised myself, for I had once spent the better part of a year not writing a book that had been someone else's idea, and I did not want another year like that one. I am now glad that I lingered long enough over the invitation from the Carnegie Council on Policy Studies in Higher Education to say yes. I have enjoyed trying to give shape and focus to a subject and a concept that are fundamentally so elusive that I know that what I have caught and here called the *curriculum* cannot really be the same curriculum another would have found.

History is not a science, and I am grateful that my mentors at the Yale Graduate School, especially Ralph Gabriel, did not allow me to think that it was other than a rather sophisticated art. Also, a book long enough to say something and short enough to be read is bound to say too much and too little. Among the difficulties presented by the subject was the temptation to roam beyond the curriculum, but since I was in charge of defining it there was nothing to help me with the limits of my subject except a sure sense that I was not writing a history of American higher education. If, as I suspect the Carnegie Council had in mind, these chapters make their readers conscious of the dimensions of the curriculum and the influences and environments that have shaped it, then my errors and omissions and emphases will not be allowed to get in the way of my purpose: to give as clear an account as I am able of how this country, in the curriculum of its undergraduate colleges and universities, moved from 1636 to 1976.

Right here at the beginning I want to make clear what this history is not. It is not a detailed and definitive account of how various academic fields expanded, divided, and intruded on each other, although how that process defined the curriculum is made abundantly clear. It is not intended as a history of the internal state of learning. I have chosen to place the curriculum in a broad setting of time and place and to see it as an instrument of many purposes and persons (including students), rather than essentially as the reflection of college catalogues, curriculum committees, and faculty debates. The books that this is not would have delivered different and legitimate rewards. The subject is capable of many definitions. What is offered here is the definition that study, experience, and reflection led me to.

In this effort I have been beautifully encouraged by my wife, who, while having more faith in me than in the subject, sustained both while it and I regularly came to dinner together. In addition, she gave the manuscript a beneficial reading. Graham Hone, Juanita Terry, and Ann Williams-Dawe assisted me admirably in my researches. At the Williams College Library, Sarah McFarland and Lee Dalzell, reference librarians, kept embarrassingly ahead of my demands; they and the entire staff of the library made me grateful that I am a member of the Williams College faculty. My colleagues in the Department of History and in the American Civilization program, and the president and trustees of Williams College, allowed me to write this book; they did not have to; I thank them for the fun I have had. No one has been better served by his typists than I have been by Carol Watterson of Sanibel, Florida, who prepared the first draft, and Rosemary Lane and her staff of assistants in the faculty secretarial office at Williams College, who have sustained this project in countless helpful ways, including typing the final draft. And there is no question about whether I should also credit Florida's coldest and wettest winter in memory for keeping me at my desk.

Whatever its present shortcomings, this book has benefited enormously from the critical reading of the first draft by generous friends, colleagues, and fellow historians: Michael Bell, Williams College; Robert T. Blackburn, University of Michigan; Robert F. Dalzell, Jr., Williams College; Hugh Hawkins, Amherst College; Codman Hislop, Dorset, Vermont; Charles R. Keller, Williamstown, Massachusetts; David P. Livermore, San Rafael, California; David Riesman, Harvard University; Rhoda R. Ross, Williamstown, Massachusetts; Robert C. L. Scott, Williams College; Richard B.

Sewall, Bethany, Connecticut; and Laurence R. Veysey, University of California, Santa Cruz. I am grateful for their help.

The Carnegie Council, my sponsors in this project, deserve my appreciation for the generosity with which they licensed me to write my own book. Their only questions, as the work progressed, had to do with how they might help me. Philanthropic foundations and such offspring as the Carnegie Council are not in business to underwrite history, although this book is not the first instance in which a foundation has done so. If this work is a contribution to reform, which is what foundations are all about, it will only be because some historical understanding never did any reformer or good movement any harm. Among the publications of the Council, this history is a maverick: It is not a report, it makes no recommendations, it contains no summaries—these characteristics, appropriate as they are for almost everything the Council does, fall outside my sense of history as art.

My first chapter is not a preview of things to come, nor is the last chapter a review of what has gone before. I think of the first chapter as an invitation to the reader to confront, as I have had to, the curriculum as a concept. I think of the last chapter as an opportunity to consider the past fifty years against the almost three centuries of curricular history that are covered in the intervening chapters.

I have kept away from the future—from the controversies and issues that may or may not be those that either deserve our attention or may, deserving or not, demand it. Harvard is about to have another go at defining liberal education. Going to college itself is an idea that has recently been discussed as an option, by people who are not at all clear what the alternative is, either for the individual or for society. More young people are attending college, but the U.S. Army is enlisting a declining percentage of high school graduates. Career education, a new label attached to old habits, has entered the arena, just as progressive education, life adjustment education, and countless other movements have passed in and out of our experience. This is the stuff of which someone else sometime later will write another history of the curriculum.

Williamstown, Massachusetts　　　　　　　Frederick Rudolph
September 1977

For my students at Williams College,
past, present, and future

The Author

FREDERICK RUDOLPH is Mark Hopkins Professor of History and Chairman of the American Civilization Program at Williams College. He taught at Williams in 1946–47, after four years of service in World War II and before attending graduate school; he has been a member of the Williams faculty since 1951. His books include *Mark Hopkins and the Log* (1956), *The American College and University: A History* (1962), and *Essays on Education in the Early Republic* (1965).

He received the Ph.D. in history from Yale in 1953 and has been the recipient of two Guggenheim Fellowships, 1958–59 and 1968–69. In 1960 and 1961 he was visiting lecturer in history and education at Harvard. Among his many published articles is "Neglect of Students as a Historical Tradition," which appeared in *The College and the Student* (L. E. Dennis and J. F. Kaufman, editors, 1966).

CURRICULUM

*A History of the American
Undergraduate Course of Study
Since 1636*

PREPARED FOR THE CARNEGIE COUNCIL
ON POLICY STUDIES IN HIGHER EDUCATION

1

Frames of Reference

There is no way to make a history of the American college and university curriculum read like an account of the winning of the West or the collapse of the Old South. Martin Duberman's study of the history of sexuality in America, three years in the offing, has something going for it that curricular history does not. Even so, a puckish inspiration to entitle this book *The Harvard-Yale Game and Other Major Rivalries* was not altogether misleading. For the curriculum has been an arena in which the dimensions of American culture have been measured, an environment for certifying an elite at one time and for facilitating the mobility of an emerging middle class at another. It has been one of those places where we have told ourselves who we are. It is important territory.

There have been times and places where the curriculum was not taken seriously or should not have been. A little over 100 years ago fewer than two of every 100 Americans between the ages of eighteen and twenty-one were serious enough about it to enroll in a college or university, and many of those who did enroll were not serious. The approximately 700 pages of catalogue material required to describe the undergraduate courses of study for 1975 at Cornell are impressive evidence that Ezra Cornell did indeed, as he promised, "found an institution where any person can find instruction in any study." But can we take all 700 pages seriously?[1]

Thinking about the curriculum historically presents many problems and requires a willingness to accept surprise, ambiguity, and a certain unavoidable messiness. If the world does not always make sense, why should the curriculum? George W. Pierson, coming up for air after being long submerged in the history of Yale, gasped, "One is appalled at the incoherence of American higher education."[2] The inability of colleges to take common action, to speak or act with authority and a common voice, is surely more than a manifestation of the competitive nature of American life, but this inability or even unwillingness is a challenge to anyone who would view the curriculum with clarity. An elementary caution on the way to understanding the curriculum may be to assume, at the beginning anyway, that maybe there is no such thing as *the* curriculum.

An argument can be made for thinking of the curriculum as being about what students learn or about the body of organized knowledge at the command of teachers or about the courses that try to make some effective connection between learning and teaching. Certainly the curriculum cannot be understood without paying attention to all the elements that give it life—students, knowledge, teachers, and the courses where everything either falls together or falls apart. Also, the curriculum is both structure and substance, subject to measurement and judgment. In describing its structure, we compute courses, semesters, lectures, departments, majors, and so forth. In exploring the substance of the curriculum, the stuff of which the learning and teaching is made, we are in the presence of quality, whether good or bad.[3]

Judging quality requires some notion of what the curriculum is expected to do. If the design is to turn out clergymen and the performance delivers businessmen, has something gone wrong with the curriculum, or has society changed its mind? Even if it is easy to agree with William James's suggestion that the curriculum is intended to "help you know a good man when you see him," a few more particulars would be helpful. Because higher education is the habitat of the more verbal among us, there is, however, no shortage of particulars. A president of Smith College clarified curricular expectations with these demands: "Make a man or woman wiser, more sensitive, more compassionate, more responsible, more useful, and happier." A university professor may have been more or less saying the same thing when he assigned to the college the responsibility for developing in its students "such general attributes as freedom from prejudice, depth of interest, a humanized conscience, and eagerness for continued learning."[4] In any case, the curriculum is also a locus and transmitter of values.

Values change and so does the curriculum, as the more than 300 years since the founding of Harvard College clearly say. Since that time long ago, when a peculiarly self-demanding band of alienated Englishmen got themselves a college almost before they had built themselves a privy, change in the course of study has been constant, conscious and unconscious, gradual and sudden, accidental and intentional, uneven and diverse, imaginative and pedestrian. An earlier historian of the curriculum, writing in 1907, decided that "the process of alteration from the colonial type of curriculum to that of modern date has everywhere proceeded by cautious amalgamation and well-considered deliberation."[5] If that is so, the curriculum is the only institutional expression of social purpose to pass so gently through the dynamic and explosive decades of the nineteenth century. But of course it did not.

Patience is not one of the essential qualities of a reformer, and it must be from the collective frustration of curricular reformers that there has developed the "academic truism that changing a curriculum is harder than moving a graveyard."[6] The reasons for curricular rigidity are many, some simply being a function of organization. Assemble a cluster of professors in a country town, surround them with scenic grandeur, cut them off from the world beyond, and they will not have much trouble congratulating themselves into curricular torpor. Let someone knock at the door with a vision of change, he will discover that access is blocked by those within the gate. Let him argue in behalf of some perceived need or desire of the students, and he will soon discover his mistake: The institution is really not for the students, after all, but for the professors. Besides, that is not the way it is done, nor is the particular purpose or goal, however worthy, the only one that must be considered.

These are barriers to change in all institutions. Colleges and universities in addition have had some that are particularly characteristic. Their intentions are conservative—to preserve and to transmit that which has survived. Their friends and supporters are mostly among the more comfortable classes, those with an investment in stability. Colleges and universities are also in a way trapped between the schools that send them students and the graduate and professional schools to which they send their own graduates; the curriculum is necessarily responsive to and limited by these relationships. And then there are the professors, a highly organized and narrowly self-selected guild of professionals, each something of a law unto himself, collectively suspicious of efficiency and expert at obstruction. Each of these rather special academic barriers to change has a history of its own. Because the American "system" of education developed downward rather than upward, with the founding of colleges before there were schools sufficient to supply them, standards of all kind—including curricular standards—were from the beginning difficult to establish. On the other hand, social change has sometimes been more rapid than the capacity of the colleges to respond, and on occasion they have found themselves almost without any friends at all. And professors have not always been as firmly in charge of the curriculum as they now are. The changing fortunes of these characteristic sources of academic inertia are ingredients in the shaping of curricular history.[7]

Also, as life developed in British America in the years after the founding of Harvard College in 1636, a whole new set of social and economic expectations that had not been anticipated by the country's first settlers intruded themselves into defining what a curriculum could be. The college as an environment for the general education of a small governing elite found itself losing ground in the nineteenth century, as it became increasingly apparent that the new nation was going to be a country in which getting rich would be a good deal easier than at any time and any place elsewhere in human history. The consequences for the college course of study would be staggering. When the goal of worldly wealth and ease finally collided, as it did, with the more ascetic traditions of New England—traditions by then stretched across the country in hundreds of little colleges bearing the imprint of Yale and Princeton—the explosion was resounding. By 1900 the sons of the rich, the clumsy, awkward rich, were going to Yale for quite different reasons from those that had guided young men to Yale two centuries before, and the curriculum was required to acknowledge the difference.

The universities that were redefining the course of study in the late nineteenth and early twentieth centuries were recording more than the arrival on their campuses of sons and daughters of a confident bourgeoisie. The curricular remedies they developed—sometimes grossly utilitarian, sometimes purely scientific, occasionally romantically cultural—would make defining the American college and university curriculum forever after an exercise in intellectual juggling.[8]

Yale and Harvard really did wage a major battle over what that curriculum should be. The presidents of Harvard and Princeton engaged in public debate. The presidents of eight New England colleges placed themselves before the Harvard corporation as opponents of the Harvard president. By the time when these encounters took place, the curriculum as a focus of universal concern could not rival the football field, but great talent and great wisdom and sometimes great blindness were engaged. The friends of pure science and of scholarly research who identified the enemy as undergraduate teaching and utilitarian values; the friends of liberal learning who identified the enemy as the scientists, both pure and applied; and the friends of the useful for whom the enemy was everyone else—all were very much aware that the stakes were high and that if the consequences were not of great popular interest they were of tremendously greater importance than the outcome of all the football games ever played.

"The curriculum is the battlefield at the heart of the institution," JB Lon Hefferlin concluded after an exhaustive study of academic reform. "Complaints of institutional irrelevance, obscurantism, and ossification all aim here. . . . To leave the curriculum to its own devices and try to improve its periphery . . . is, in the vernacular of the religious fundamentalists, to whitewash the sepulcher."[9] Those who would understand the history of the college and university curriculum must, among everything else, see the sepulcher as a battleground.

The battle in which the contenders over the curriculum have been engaged in a sense has known no beginning and no ending, in large part because the curriculum is a remarkably vital organism, containing within itself and its environment seeds of change that only intuition might reveal. In 1848 Philip Lindsley, the brilliant young president of the college at Nashville, defined the ideal product of the curriculum: "Our graduates . . . betray no arrogance, pride or vanity. . . . They seem to think their education only just begun. . . . They do not think more highly of themselves than they ought to

think. . . . To bring youth to this point—to this modest correct self-
appreciation . . . is the crowning glory of a university education. . . ."[10]
Who could have imagined, hearing Lindsley in that year when
Europe was racked with revolution and his own country was playing
at war with Mexico, that only a half century later a whole new
vocabulary would be required by one college alumnus to describe the
process that formed the graduate in 1901? "The history of the Yale
curriculum," wrote John C. Schwab of the class of 1886, "is the story
of a medieval workshop, with its limited range of simple tools, all of
which the apprentice learned to master, developing into a modern
factory, well equipped with a large stock of tools and machinery, no
two of them alike in their construction or use, many of them delicate
and complicated, and few of them fully understood and manipulated
by all the employees of the shop."[11] Of course there were some in 1848
who made the imaginative leap to 1901, as there were some in 1901
who could make the no less difficult leap to 1848 or to any other
moment in the past or the future. But it was not easy. So much
changed.

All kinds of assumptions and certainties turned out to be peril-
ously unstable. If one generation found guidance in the stern morality of the Old Testament, another found a softer style in the love and
fellowship of the New Testament. Could a curriculum that was
appropriate for young men named Jedidiah, Ephraim, and Israel be
passed without change to their sons with names like Matthew, Mark,
Luke, and John? Wide as the Atlantic was, even before the American
Revolution it was no barrier to the importation of disruptive ideas: A
parcel of books threw eighteenth-century Yale into curricular disarray. A changed view of human nature threw Latin out of Yale's
requirements for the bachelor's degree 200 years later: The difficult,
disciplinary, testing study of impractical Latin may have been appropriate for a world that lived with the reality of Hell, but in a world
oozing with natural goodness Latin became an abomination.[12] Even
the origin of truth changed in the history of the curriculum, from
book (one book, at that) to process. Human psychology itself was
finally recognized as a bed of shifting sands.

The best way to misread or misunderstand a curriculum is from
a catalogue. It is such a lifeless thing, so disembodied, so uncon-

nected, sometimes even intentionally misleading. Because the curriculum is a social artifact, the society itself is a more reliable source of
curricular illumination. In his inaugural address as president of
Harvard in 1869, Charles William Eliot stated the relationship
clearly: "The university must accommodate itself promptly to significant changes in the character of the people for whom it exists. The
institutions of higher education . . . are always a faithful mirror in
which are sharply reflected the national history and character." In
1907 Louis Franklin Snow, pioneer historian of the curriculum,
agreed: "The ideals of the community have become the ideals of the
college. . . . That college becomes most truly national which reflects
and reproduces, in its curriculum, the national ideal."

More recently a historian of Indiana University went as far as to
describe the relationship between the curriculum and society as a one-
way connection: "The curriculum reflects the society . . . it does not
significantly affect or change that society." On the other hand, a
young historian of higher education sees the relationship in quite different terms: "The university has exerted a formative influence upon
society: as the matrix within which the culture of professionalism
matured; as the center to which practitioners trace the theoretical
basis of knowledge upon which they establish authority; as the source
of a usable history, economics, political science, and sociology for
individuals who in the course of rapid movement require instant
ideas." And as if that were not enough, "The university contained
and structured the culture of ideas in American life, as college football
stadiums contained and structured the culture of spectator recreation,
and home economics the culture of good housekeeping."[13] The traffic
between the society and the curriculum may essentially have been all
or mostly in one direction, whichever direction that was, but by any
useful definition of culture, the traffic necessarily flowed in both directions, the curriculum responding to the society and in turn shaping
that society, the relationship being sufficiently subtle sometimes even
to defy detection.

But it takes no great investigative imagination to see in the proliferation of colleges during the Jacksonian era at the same time that
their classical course of study was under wide public attack the reflection of a consistency rather than a conflict in Jacksonian society. The
Jacksonian temper was friendly to college founding as an act of cor-

porate enterprise and unfriendly to the course of study as a manifestation of class privilege. Nor should there be any mistake about whether
a new social demand was about to be placed upon the curriculum in
the late nineteenth century, when Chauncey M. Depew observed that
he had met many millionaires but none "who did not feel in the presence of cultured people a certain sense of mortification which no
money paid for."[14]

The absence of a strong federal interest or control in higher education in no way denied society's recognition of the college as a social
necessity. Society's claims and expectations were large, although the
federal interest was weak: The 1802 act that provided two townships
of federal land for the endowment of a university in each new state
carved out of the national land holdings was an act to promote settlement, not education, and the Morrill Land-Grant Act in 1862, which
endowed the beginnings of agricultural and mechanical colleges in
all the states, was an act as much for getting rid of land as for supporting education.[15] At one time the burden of the curriculum was to
facilitate the production of what society defined as a cultured gentleman; eventually a professional career in the United States would be
unthinkable without benefit of the college course, although in an earlier day, when most college graduates went into the learned professions, most who practiced these professions were not college graduates. Not until the twentieth century—and well into it—was the
professional education of a majority of doctors, lawyers, and clergymen a postcollegiate experience. Most professionals in those fields in
the nineteenth century entered practice by way of apprenticeship or
education in professional schools that were coequal with the colleges,
just as the elementary school teachers for a growing public school
movement were trained in normal schools that were coequal with
academies and high schools. The shifting technological focus of
society, from steam to electricity, from the railroad to the dynamo,
also meant a corresponding shift in the curriculum.

But if no course of study was as vulnerable as the American curriculum to social demand, nowhere else in the world (a 1911 Carnegie
Foundation report pointed out) did colleges compete for students,
nowhere else was education treated as a commodity.[16] Was there a
moment in the history of the curriculum when the individual overtook society as the client? Did the college, as an extension of the

society's agencies of value formation and nurture, withdraw, concede, regroup, and reorganize, and then fulfill a whole new set of demands that may have served individuals well but society poorly? The curriculum may have undergone some such experience between the Civil War and World War I.

Status was socially defined; the status of teaching was one determinant of what a curriculum was. In a society that respected and valued its professors the curriculum was not the same as in a society that was indifferent to professors. Moreover, the professors, whatever their status, if their concern was primarily intellectual rather than moral, thought of the course of study as serving the needs of an intellectual community as opposed to the needs of individual clients. But society's purpose cannot be denied, and in recent years, as society has redefined higher education from being a privilege to being a right and a duty, it has moved in on colleges and universities in a way that has made university and society almost inseparable. The California system of higher education *is* California. But even as universal access fulfills the democratic promise of American life and reshapes the course of study accordingly, at a place such as Harvard, since World War II extracurricular achievement has been no substitute in the status race among Harvard undergraduates for winning out "in the major meritocratic contest of the curriculum."[17] Who would resist the verdict of one historian, who concluded that the curriculum is "as irrational and confusing as society itself"?[18]

By 1960, 2,452 different kinds of degrees had been conferred by American institutions of higher education, 832 of which had been abandoned, casualties of changing academic fashion, curricular consolidation, or a revision of standards. Of the 1,620 degrees still being awarded in 1960, 43 percent were various kinds of bachelor degrees for four years' study in specific fields and 8 percent were associate degrees, generally for the work of two years in a junior or community college. Bachelor of arts degrees (108 varieties) and bachelor of science degrees (426 varieties) were being earned in agriculture, architecture, dentistry, education, forestry, nursing, public administration, social work, and almost any other vocation for which an organized body of knowledge existed. In addition, such degrees as bachelor of music, bachelor of music education, bachelor of fine arts, and bachelor of education revealed both the proliferation of knowledge and the disintegration of a common body of learning since the day in 1642 when Harvard awarded to nine young men the first American bachelor of arts degrees.[19] It is one thing to describe the curriculum under which Harvard for decade after decade awarded nothing but the B.A; it is almost an affront to the imagination to be expected to make sense of the 200 different degrees offered by the University of Illinois in 1960. Yet some sense must be made, for those degrees recorded, among other things, an explosion of knowledge, an accumulation of technical learning and scholarship that burst on the world in the nineteenth century as a result of the gathering prestige of empirical thought.

In the nineteenth century the great German universities were the centers from which spread a gargantuan appetite for research and scholarship as well as a profound regard for the scientific ethos that defined it. The consequences have generally and appropriately been described as both profoundly inventive and overwhelmingly destructive. The creation of new knowledge seeking a place in the course of study, the specialization of various areas of academic endeavor, the consequent tendency to view all subject matter as equal, and the disestablishment of "the conception of a liberal education as a definite body of knowledge"—these may be thought of as curricular fallout from the knowledge explosion.[20] While making room for new knowledge, therefore, became a baffling challenge for those responsible for the course of study as the nineteenth century progressed, the nature of knowledge and of the society in whose service it was created also led to the abandonment of substantial portions of the curriculum. Some knowledge that had appeared in the colonial curriculum as innovative and practical, such as navigation and surveying, lost utility. Some knowledge, such as Latin and Greek, could not be made popular, a fatal flaw for knowledge in the kind of country the United States was developing into. Some knowledge, such as arithmetic, English grammar, geography, and algebra, could be shoved into the secondary schools by brave colleges willing to raise their admissions standards as one way of making room for new knowledge. Some knowledge instead of being abandoned found new life by being synthesized into a new field of study; the biology and social science that became ecology may even be thought of as having benefited from blood transfusions.[21]

About some curricular developments it is never possible to be certain, but if professors became interested enough in something to focus their research on it, almost certainly that research would make its way into the course of study—as new subjects, new courses, or simply new lectures and texts; the extracurriculum played a similar role in being responsive to undergraduate interests and has even on occasion anticipated and guided the formal curriculum. The simplicity and sanctity of the old course of study were irreparably violated by the explosion of knowledge, but some of the dismay and unhappiness with the consequences that have been registered by curricular critics has bordered on the hysterical. The so-called Germanic influence has been a favorite target for those who needed a villain to explain what happened to the tightly ordered course of liberal studies with which Harvard College began. The Germans did not really ignite the knowledge explosion, an event that in no way could have been avoided. They did know what to do with it, and the example they set was much needed by an untried new nation tied to two charming but absurd conceits—the jack-of-all-trades and the self-made man.

The curriculum was in many ways whatever students made of it. Were they more responsive to "the rich financial reward of an early mastery of some practical branch of knowledge" than to "the advantage of a mental culture which they are too immature to appreciate"?[22] Were they to think of themselves, in the presence of the curriculum, as children with duties or as citizens with rights?[23] Were they mature or assumed to be? Did their chronological and psychophysical ages harmonize with the course of study or had they fallen out of balance? The answers to these and similar questions will clarify what the curriculum was at any given time. What could go on in an American college—contrasted with a German university—was in part a function of the entering age, which was much lower in the United States, and in part a function of the absence of a driving student motivation that, in Germany, recognized the vital relationship between university studies and the state-administered examinations that opened the way to professional careers. The openness of American society for a very long time militated against the importance of a college education and helped to undercut efforts to support a high level of intellectual rigor and achievement. Perhaps not until after World War II, in an environment that for the first time permitted colleges in any number to be selective in their admissions policies, were students who represented "the academic culture"—the curriculum, the intellectual life—setting the tone of undergraduate society, instead of that traditional turned-off or indifferent majority who found their purpose in the extracurriculum.[24]

Around 1900, college rooms all over the country were decorated with posters bearing the admonition: "Don't let your studies interfere with your education."[25] This motto placed constraints not only on what the curriculum could do but also on what it could be. What faculty could be expected to develop a course of study that treated students like young men and women when they insisted on behaving like boys and girls? And what faculty possessed the collective imagination to recognize the extent to which their students were often learning from life itself what was being denied in the classroom? Was there a classroom in the United States in 1845 that was advanced enough in the teaching of sociology and psychology to match the experience described that year by a student at Indiana University in a letter to his mother:

> On last Saturday evening . . . I went into a house and tried to make peace between a man and his wife. The man had been whipping her brutally. I tried to defend her, and she turned on me, and at length run me out of the house with some boiling water; but not until I had knocked her husband down with my cane. . . . She says since that she was very glad I came to her assistance, but she says she could not stand by and see me knock her husband down without throwing some hot water on me.[26]

Much can be made of the invigorating new directions in which the curriculum turned as induction and empiricism created new scientific studies—economics, sociology, political science—out of what had sometimes almost been only Biblical exegesis. It did sometimes seem as if real life, the real world, was not allowed access to the course of study until the late nineteenth and early twentieth centuries. Until then, however, and long after, students derived from the extracurricular fabric of clubs, athletics, libraries, and fraternities a kind of instruction and experience that anticipated their needs and their futures. If much that was first extracurricular in time became curricular—English literature, American history, fine arts, music—for a considerable period the intellectual and vocational interests of students were supported by the extracurriculum. The institutionalization of the extracurriculum gave students a source of strength in the academic power structure; it also both usurped some of the prerogatives and responsibilities of the caretakers of the curriculum, the professors, and gave them excuses for resisting curricular innovation.

The extracurriculum complemented the curriculum quite as much as it subverted it. The intensity of some students' attachment to the former was certainly subversive to the latter, but in another sense the extracurriculum was a kind of laboratory for nascent practical and vocational interests. On the curricular battlefields, for three centuries, one contender or the other has insisted on being recognized as the friend of the practical in the course of study. When both contenders knew what they were doing, both were claiming the practical label, for it should never be thought that any curricular reform was really ever advocated or any curriculum defended, at least on this side of the Atlantic, as being other than practical. The famous Yale Report of 1828 has been thought of as a dramatic last stand in defense of the impractical studies, but the Yale faculty in the report argued for the practicality of what others considered impractical.

The president of Bowdoin was making a point in his attack on elective studies in 1802, but he did not expect to be taken seriously when he said: "I declare . . . that in my opinion a youth had better be four years employed . . . in diligently doing what would be utterly useless to him in life, than in light reading which requires no thinking." And the president of the University of Alabama displayed a spectacular failure of imagination when, relying on the durability of the apprentice system in a craft society, he resisted demands in 1855 for a more vocational emphasis in the course of study: "While time lasts, the farmer will be made in the field, the manufacturer in the shop, the merchant in the counting room, the civil engineer in the midst of the actual operation of his science." The Hamilton College president who as late as 1904 insisted that his college educated "man, and not blacksmiths and farmers" did not really say what he meant; what he meant was that Hamilton College educated businessmen, clergymen,

and lawyers, and not blacksmiths and farmers. For the course of study
had always to some degree—except perhaps at St. John's since the
1930s and for a time at the University of Chicago—been relevant to
the practical affairs of men, intentionally oriented toward social
utility.[27]

There is something perniciously misleading about the interpretation of the American experience with the curriculum that argues
that "only students who could afford to be unconcerned about their
eventual employment and its economic rewards have been able to
enjoy an exclusively cultural or nonutilitarian higher education."[28]
Nothing could have been more cultural or nonutilitarian than the
Harvard education that was being experienced by the student who
responded to Henry Adams's question as to why he was at Harvard:
"The degree of Harvard College is worth money to me in Chicago."[29]
An exclusively cultural or nonutilitarian education is a concept contrary to experience. As Christopher Jencks and David Riesman put it,
"The question always has been *how* an institution mixed the academic with the vocational, not *whether* it did so."[30] And the question
has also been how much value society attached to the academic, the
cultural, and supposedly nonutilitarian.

The students who designed the extracurriculum as a testing
ground for skills and aspirations ignored by the curriculum were, on
the other hand, complementing the course of study as an instrument
of personality development. The language might not have been
understood by the founders of Harvard College but, in appropriate
translation, they would have agreed with the judgment of the psychologist Nevitt Sanford that "all curricula either favor or hamper
personality regardless of whether they were designed with such development in mind."[31] It is instructive that in the era when recitation,
the testing of memorized texts, dominated the college classroom, the
extracurriculum correspondingly dominated student life; the classroom style was hostile to imagination; literary societies and fraternities supported personality development by freeing the imagination.
And the students knew it.

The curriculum was a record of how the American people faced
such matters as who were to be their leaders, whether the society was
to be governed by an elite, and how far the concept of equality was to

be carried in the provision of courses of study appropriate not just for the few but for the many. These questions agitated the academic community in the United States long before they were recognized as pertinent to the concerns of higher education elsewhere in the Western world. By progressive steps the American people enlarged their commitment to mass education, on the primary level in the first half of the nineteenth century, on the secondary level in the first half of the twentieth century, and increasingly since World War II on the level not only of higher education[32] but also of that more accessible network of opportunities known as "postsecondary education."

The commitment to mass higher education was not made automatically; if it was implicit in the Declaration of Independence and the Constitution, even Thomas Jefferson, who designed an educational system for Virginia that would sift the talented from "the rubbish," did not know it. As late as 1845 in the democratic atmosphere of Jacksonville, Illinois, Julian M. Sturtevant, the president of the struggling little college there, argued for the appropriateness of a common school education for the majority and a college education for the minority. In Indiana nearly a decade later a professor at the state university made an extraordinary—and unheeded—plea: "Could my voice prevail with our American colleges I would say, 'Cut down your numbers without fear and thereby increase your power; sift, select, separate, purge out until you have only men, though but a select few—men who are fitted to do the highest work of society!' "[33]

Such intentions could be better fulfilled on the eastern seaboard than at a western college or university, and especially at both Johns Hopkins under Daniel Coit Gilman and Harvard under Charles William Eliot, where the course of study and the arrangements that implemented it were designed with regard for what Eliot called "the cravings of the select few as well as the needs of the average many." Gilman and Eliot were building for leadership, for an intellectual aristocracy, for, in Eliot's words, an "elite . . . those who, having the capacity, prove by hard work that they have also the necessary perseverance and endurance."[34]

But what was possible, or even worth trying, in one part of the United States was out of question in another. The problem was illustrated by the grading systems adopted at the University of Michigan and at Harvard in the late nineteenth century. Both were designed to encourage standards, but Michigan, sensitive to the need to avoid more "undemocratic" distinctions than necessary, provided in 1879 for a system that divided obvious failures into those who passed, those who were conditioned, and those whose work was incomplete. Ten years later Harvard adopted a system of degrees that encouraged distinctions and grades of superiority—an ordinary degree plus three degrees of distinction: *cum laude, magna cum laude,* and *summa cum laude.*[35] The curriculum for nurturing an elite would necessarily differ from a curriculum for everyone, even if only in expectations and standards. Could the United States choose between an elite and the mass? Could it have both? Could it make up its mind? Who should go to college? "I grow weary of the expression so often on the lips of men who call themselves educators that too many men and women go to college," said the president of the University of South Carolina in 1925. "Every potential leader . . . and no one else . . . should go to college," said the president of Oberlin College in 1927.[36]

In 1872 Richard Owen, son of Robert Owen, was elected the first president of Purdue. His "Plan of Education" presented to the board of trustees in 1873 omitted all reference to how the curriculum was to be organized, but it did recommend that "the free use of pork, meats, fried grease, rich pastry, and the like be avoided as being highly injurious to those having more work of the brain than of the muscle." Owen resigned in 1874, before Purdue opened, perhaps because the trustees wanted a curriculum *and* pork. Owen's importance is symbolic. He is a reminder of the extent to which eccentricity and diversity entered into the construction of the course of study. "How different might the teaching of French be with exclusive use of four rooms designed and furnished in Renaissance, Louis XIV, Louis XV, and Empire styles respectively!" fantasized a Wesleyan University professor in 1948. But these were deviations that did not occur. An important one that did was the persistence of the Catholic colleges in resisting curricular change, in standing outside the main curricular movements until well into the twentieth century. The 1905 catalogue at Holy Cross resembled Yale's catalogue for 1828.[37]

If eccentricity could be a characteristic of the curriculum, so could a flexibility of style and purpose that hid change even from its perpetrators. Thomas LeDuc has pointed out that geology and the classics were taught in the colleges for over a hundred years "for various purposes and with various results." Edward Hitchcock taught geology at Amherst in 1840 as a demonstration of divine benevolence, the geological state of the world being so "well adapted to a state of probation." Geology was still being taught at Amherst a hundred years later. Edward Hitchcock would have been shocked by what was going on.[38]

Purposes and results varied from time to time and place to place, but there was a consistent thread of concern with values and character, even, it might be said, at those institutions in the twentieth century that were willing to say that values and character were not their concern. In the early eighteenth century the Yale College laws put the matter directly: "Every student shall consider the main end of his study to wit to know God in Jesus Christ and answerably to lead a Godly sober life."[39]

The history of the American college curriculum may be the history of how a people departed from such a goal, but it is also a history of how the course of study has been laced with a concern for values, character, personality, a concern so enmeshed with everything else that was going on that, leaving aside the question of what happened to God, one asks without expectation of finding the answer, "What happened to man?" Such questions, however they are answered, chart the career of values in the curriculum. To evaluate the effectiveness of the college's concern with values is to assess the private and public lives of the American college and university graduate; that surely is another book, a book that might not go beyond the wisdom of William James's observation that "there is not a public abuse for which some Harvard advocate may not be found."[40] Be that as it may, in 1959 over half of Harvard's undergraduates professed to having had their political values changed while at Harvard, over a half of them by lectures and course reading.[41] Colleges also taught values absentmindedly. Can there be any question about whether Princeton was teaching values by not admitting black students until World War II?

Some young professor once said of the possibilities of curricular reconstruction at his institution: "The progress of this institution . . . will be directly proportional to the death rate of the faculty."[42] The professor was an optimist. College faculties by the late nineteenth and early twentieth centuries had developed an authority that made the course of study a jealously guarded compound of special interests. By then it seldom mattered who died. What the curriculum was has depended in greater measure on whether the institution has been an autocracy or a bureaucracy, the former being likely—at least in the hands of a reformer like Eliphalet Nott at Union—to be more innovative and receptive to change than a bureaucracy of self-serving, jealous, single-purposed, departmentalized professors. An experimental college at Fordham was possible because of the autocratic nature of the institution; on the other hand, autocracy, in the form of a president who was suspicious of psychology, delayed the development of that subject as a field of study at Notre Dame.[43]

When Eliot was in the process of reforming Harvard—it should not be forgotten that it took him forty years—an obstructionist faculty was remarkably adept at advancing "good" reasons for protecting its own interests: Electives would be too expensive, they would encourage attendance by students with base motives, they would require the appointment of inexperienced young instructors. Eliot prevailed in part because, knowing that his reforms were expensive, he raised enough money to keep everyone happy.[44]

The faculty stranglehold on the curriculum was a function of intellectual specialization and academic professionalization: With the Ph.D. went a kind of competence and authority and power that an earlier academic community did not have. With the explosion of knowledge that created the generations of trained professionals, there developed a curriculum that was a compound of courses subject to change, but to change that derived from faculties increasingly unable to make up their minds about how much election, how much prescription, how strong a major, how general an education there should be. What they could make up their minds about was what would advance or retard the interests of their own academic departments.

The curriculum was subject to accident, peculiarities of time and place, delayed reaction, and singularity of style. Western colleges often resounded with echoes of practices long since abandoned in the East, memories carried westward by graduates who grew up to be successful and adept at founding colleges. In 1888 a replica of an earlier

New England college was opened at Pomona in California; extracurricular literary societies were withering away in the East when Euphronia and Nestoria announced their presence on the opening of Stanford. As late as 1931 at Tusculum College, a small Presbyterian institution in Tennessee, the curriculum was required to adjust itself to Monday holidays, instituted to avoid the preparation of classes on Sundays.[45]

In any given state or region or locality the question of which institution or institutions shouldered the major curricular responsibility of training high school teachers—the state university, the land-grant college, the normal schools, or the liberal arts colleges—depended on political and socioeconomic considerations that defy simple generalization.

In the twentieth century, as college enrollments dramatically mounted, more and more thousands of young men and women went off to college to experience something called "freshman year." Esther Raushenbush described how different those freshman experiences were: Some courses of study were almost a repeat of senior year in secondary school; some were a mystifying and shattering embarkation into a curriculum for which students were in no way prepared; others were an invitation to intellectual excitement and growth. Every college and university delivered a freshman year appropriate to its own history; higher education in the United States necessarily delivered a whole range of freshman years.[46]

President Millar Upton of Beloit once said that "when a college is on the verge of oblivion, there is no problem in its achieving instant curricular revision." He could have been thinking of Brown in 1850, Antioch in 1921, and St. John's in 1937, where radical curricular transformations were necessary for survival. Each of these transformations can be identified with the dedicated advocacy of an inspired reformer. The imprint of creative and imaginative reformers has been so indelible that a kind of perverseness is required to think of the University of Virginia without Thomas Jefferson, Johns Hopkins without Daniel Coit Gilman, the University of Chicago without William Rainey Harper or Robert Maynard Hutchins.[47]

The takeover of Harvard by the Unitarians in 1805 has been considered a significant contribution to "the advance of a free intellectual climate at Harvard." The Unitarians were not of a sort to have designs on other colleges, with the result that the fresh air of inquiry and the hostility to intellectual parochialism with which they blessed Harvard were not generally shared during the first half of the nineteenth century. Harvard's Unitarian era may greatly explain why there was but one Harvard, why in 1910 an undergraduate socialist club could petition—with three hundred signatures—for a course on socialism and get it, and why early in the 1970s another student generation could apply pressure that led to the appointment of a Marxist professor and the inclusion of Marxist materials in economics courses.[48]

In an earlier time businessmen had as easy a time of it, even at Harvard, where, partly in response to pressure from Boston merchants and Massachusetts manufacturers, the course of study was redesigned to accommodate orthodox economics, the natural sciences, and the useful social sciences. At Union College in 1894 an expanded curriculum in electrical engineering was a gift of the General Electric Company.[49]

More subtle influences shaped the curriculum. Concern for university prestige and image called forth a rivalry in which university presidents used professorships and academic departments as part of the weaponry; competition meant expansion, growth, and curricular standardization.[50] At Yale in the 1930s and 1940s anti-Semitism in professional appointments restricted the development and health of scientific and humanistic study; the absence of a comparable anti-Semitism caused the sciences to flourish at Columbia and Princeton.[51] Humanistic studies were strengthened by the enrollment of women in the colleges, but there is no way of knowing what the curriculum would have been had women been welcomed into a more creative role in its shaping.

The curriculum was also sometimes a creature of convenience. Early in the twentieth century the University of Illinois, cramped for space, suddenly made all junior and senior courses elective in order "not to block the graduation of men who could not be given laboratory space" in previously required courses.[52]

The writing of curricular history runs the risk of making the irrational rational, of overlooking the significant while stressing the dramatic, and of emphasizing subject matter at the expense of style.

It may even take itself too seriously or not seriously enough.

Surely there was nothing unique about the officers of Yale College, who have been described by one historian as "not always sure what they believed, or agreed when they were sure, or able to blend the varied things on which they did agree." The verdict of Christopher Jencks and David Riesman would be difficult to refute: "American educators have seldom been able to give coherent explanations for what they were doing."[53] The curriculum makers and the curriculum itself were no more rational than the rest of us, and a history about them should not make them so.

The dramatic commands attention—a bold curricular statement such as distributed by the Yale faculty in 1828, Ezra Cornell's fantasy brought to life in Ithaca, William Rainey Harper's everything university in Chicago—but basically learning, change, the new moved slowly, surreptitiously, silently into the curriculum. As Edmund Morgan said of Ezra Stiles's Yale: "You could not close down the college while you retooled for the new model of learning." Change in the teaching of physics at Yale between 1701 and 1739 did not announce itself with new course titles but was registered by the abandonment of an out-of-date Aristotelian manuscript developed from 1688 Harvard class notes and its replacement by a "disguised Newtonian" treatise. A recent student of academic change has concluded: "Accretion and attrition are the most common means of academic change, primarily because they are the most simple."[54] That should not be news, but it often is.

"One cannot tell anything about the character of the training given by a certain course from its name or department," Edwin E. Slosson wrote in 1910. "Whether a study trains the eye, cultivates the memory, stimulates the imagination, improves the taste, or inspires the soul depends not so much on the subject matter as upon the way it is taught."[55] His stress on the style and spirit of instruction as being of more importance in the definition of what the curriculum was up to than subject matter itself has been widely shared. It found expression in Charles William Eliot's Harvard inaugural address in 1869, although he may not really have meant it. President Arthur Twining Hadley of Yale may have been apologizing for a deliberately sluggish course of study when he bluntly declared: "It does not matter so much what you teach as how you teach it." Eliot and Hadley have been echoed down the halls so long and so often that what may have been a sort of public relations defense for university and college presidents embroiled in curricular reform has now become more or less scientific truth. The ultimate dismissal of subject matter must have been James A. Garfield's celebrated aphorism: "The ideal college is Mark Hopkins on one end of a log and a student on the other." Laurence Veysey, whose understanding of the American university may be equaled by a few of his contemporaries but not surpassed by any, has concluded that while "the precise nature of the curriculum seems to be rather unimportant," what has been important is its "flavor and texture."[56]

There is supporting evidence. A 1957 survey of college graduates in the employ of General Electric gave subject matter a mere 2 percent edge over teaching personalities as the more long-term influence—and this among graduates of largely vocationally oriented courses of study. (The respondents listed engineering as the third most useful subject and as the third least useful subject.) David Riesman, a senior statesman on the frontier of figuring out what the curriculum is all about, has decided that "Harvard can make its greatest contribution to undergraduate teaching, less by revision of the undergraduate curriculum than by more serious efforts to introduce graduate students to problems of teaching as a regular part of their training."[57] Riesman's preference for better teaching rather than curricular reform has a long tradition; it may even be purely sentimental, but in 1977 it sounds revolutionary.

Antidotes to a posture of excessive solemnity toward the curriculum have rarely appeared in the literature, and, when they have, they have even more rarely been recognized. The great educational foundations had hardly begun their work, however, before one observer sensed how close to the edge of the ridiculous the curriculum could be urged: "If some educational revolutionist were to arise and assert that the whole curriculum should be inverted, that we should begin with metaphysics and ethics and end with geography and arithmetic, nobody could prove him a fool, and if he were given a few millions and a free hand, he might prove that he was not."[58] And today nothing is more sobering than a trip through the history of a great state university: A history of the University of California is not, cannot, be a curricular history, it has to be so much else; a curricular history of the University of California would be an excursion beyond reality; the University of California is a way of life, a multiversity, but it is not a curriculum.[59]

The intentions of *this* curricular history, as of all those that have come before it, are serious, but it does not intend to make more claims for the curriculum than the record allows. Who would reject the suggestion that "the paperback revolution did far more to improve academic quality in this country . . . than any curricular innovation of the last seventy years"?[60] Who would dispute the promoters of higher education in late nineteenth-century Colorado who, directing attention to malaria in Indiana and tuberculosis in the East, stressed the salutary role of the Colorado climate to a degree that left the impression that a Colorado college was not a curriculum but a sanitarium?[61] Who would deny the uncalculated influence of television in changing the perceptions and skills of students and in subtly challenging the primacy of the written word?

The curriculum began as an import, arriving in the intellectual baggage of the settlers of Massachusetts Bay. Over three hundred years of change have given it a thoroughly American character, reflecting the diversity and flexibility of the culture around it, lending itself to society's major purposes.

The shaping of the curriculum has had its heroes, perhaps even its villains. Were Jeremiah Day at Yale and James McCosh at Princeton, determined to hold the future at bay until the colleges could digest the changes being forced on them by a rapidly moving world, heroes or villains? Had the bottom dropped out of the world or of American democracy, or simply of Yale, or not even that, when a freshman might arrive in New Haven without entrance Greek and be welcomed? Did Samuel Eliot Morison take leave of his historical senses when he accused his distant cousin, Charles William Eliot, of "the greatest educational crime of the century against American youth—depriving him of his classical heritage"?[62] In the problem-oriented history curriculum of the 1940s and 1950s there existed a pamphlet text that asked, "John D. Rockefeller: Robber Baron or Industrial Statesman?"[63] Should William Rainey Harper, who staffed the University of Chicago by raiding the vulnerable faculties of eastern and midwestern universities, be subjected to similar treatment?

Curricular history is American history and therefore carries the burden of revealing the central purposes and driving directions of American society. As the curriculum has moved across time from being wholly prescribed to greatly elective, the loss of philosophic purpose and neatness has been repeatedly but unsuccessfully countered by structural devices designed to support some coherent, defensible general education. In the meantime the curriculum, in response to social demand and the financial support necessary to underwrite that demand, has been burdened with larger purpose than the provision of a general education for the native governing elite of a few frontier colonies of the British Empire. By the 1960s, indeed, the American college and university had arrived at a position of awesome power in the culture, having achieved—without quite knowing it—a near monopoly over entry to social and economic success. Except for skilled trades, entertainment, art, and professional athletics (and less so even there), a college education had become a necessity for all those seeking such success.[64] It may well be, as Christopher Jencks and David Riesman have argued, that "the majority of those who enter college are plainly more concerned with accumulating credits and acquiring licenses than with learning any particular skill while enrolled."[65] In this view the purpose of the curriculum is not education but certification. According to Clark Kerr, there is no organic university, as such, only a gathering of functions and discrete schools for carrying them out.[66] Perhaps there is no curriculum either, only an assumption of burdens and discrete programs for carrying them out: an accidental compromise between the only partially understood past and the unanticipated future.

2

The English College on the American Frontier

Hanover, New Hampshire, was an unlikely place for it to happen, but at one point in his sophomore year at Dartmouth, Ephraim Smedley of the class of 1793 recorded that he had read 7,913 pages since the beginning of the year and was still at it. He died before the year was over, in some degree probably a victim of his appetites.[1]

College was a serious business in the seventeenth and eighteenth centuries, so serious, in fact, that the official catalogue of the Yale library in 1734 listed the works of Shakespeare, Pope, and Spenser under the heading, "Books of Diversion."[2] In a world where Shakespeare was frivolous and a Dartmouth sophomore might kill himself from academic exertion, colleges did not run the risk of being popular. Going to college was one of the least likely things to happen to young men in the years before 1800—and for some years after, and it did not happen at all to young women.

Not until 1759 did the handful of colonial colleges graduate, among them, more than a hundred young men in any one year. On the eve of the American Revolution a directory of all the graduates, living and dead, of all the colleges—somewhat over 5,000—could have been listed in less space than twenty pages of an urban telephone directory 200 years later. The English colonies in North America entered upon independence with a college-educated population of approximately 2,500, some of whom were to become famous as

Founding Fathers. Many others passed into obscurity as exiles loyal to the Crown.[3]

The colleges were not popular, but they were important, and their importance was symbolized just as readily as degree statistics attested to their lack of popularity. Nassau Hall at Princeton was no Chartres, no sphinx or pyramid, nor did it carry within itself the promise of all the great buildings that would surpass it, but in 1756 it was the largest building in Britain's American colonies.[4] The society that built Nassau Hall may have had only a modest need for college graduates, but the need was vital and central enough to make the largest and most imposing structure in the colonies not a statehouse, not a church, nor a stock exchange, but a college.

In its initial impulse the American college grew out of the tradition in European Calvinist communities of founding new colleges or reshaping old ones "to preserve the purity and continue the propagation of the faith."[5] Harvard, Yale, and Princeton were the consequence of good Calvinists doing what they expected of themselves. William and Mary in Virginia and King's College in New York were similar in being the work of concerned Anglicans.

Harvard and the American colleges that came along later drew on the experience of the academies created by Calvinist nonconformists after they were excluded in 1662 from the colleges at Oxford and Cambridge. These dissenting academies, as well as the academies and universities of Calvinist Scotland and the Huguenot academies of France, contributed to the knowledge and educational philosophy of college leaders in the American colonies. The degree of their influence is difficult to assess. Colleges on both sides of the Atlantic, conformist and nonconformist, responded to intellectual currents with complex and diverse intentions and results. The colleges in New Jersey, Rhode Island, and New Hampshire were particularly influenced by the existence of the dissenting academies, but all the colonial colleges responded to practices and developments with which the English academies and Scottish universities were identified: the use of English as the language of instruction, a stress on science and politics, a friendliness to experimental inquiry.[6]

The first of the colonial colleges, Harvard, was founded long before the intellectual ferment of the eighteenth century. It arrived without benefit of the signals that suggested that the Enlightenment was on its way. Chartered by the General Court of Massachusetts in 1636, it served as a model for Yale, as Yale did for Princeton. All these colleges were shaped by the Calvinist commitment to a learned clergy and a literate people. The 1701 Connecticut act that led to the founding of Yale provided for a school "wherein Youth may be instructed in the Arts and Sciences who thorough [sic] the blessing of Almighty God may be fitted for Publick employment both in Church and Civil State." The curriculum of the colonial colleges was designed to fulfill this purpose. "The great End of all your Studies," the president of Yale admonished his students in 1743, "is to obtain the Clearest Conceptions of Divine Things and to lead you to a Saving Knowledge of God in his Son Jesus Christ."[7]

One trouble with this limited religious purpose, of course, was people. The impossibility of controlling a social institution—or a course of study—for purposes serving only an original narrow intention was demonstrated by the anguished complaints of a 1703 sermon against Harvard, which charged that it was "not worth the while for persons to be sent to the *Colledge* to learn to Complement men, and Court women; they should be sent thither to prepare them for Publick Service."[8] Learning could be put to many purposes. Harvard did not design the curriculum to be a course of instruction in flattery and seduction, but apparently little time passed before students discovered that it could be.

Yale's first forty years were an instructive demonstration of the extent to which colleges were beyond the control of those who planned for them. Because it was a liberal arts college, Yale incorporated in its curriculum ideas and attitudes that were new and yet that also were extensions of previous learning prompted by new inquiry. This "New Learning," although hardly anyone recognized it at the time, had a serious negative effect on the theological purposes of the college and the religious life of Connecticut. The "New Learning" changed man's concept of God as well as his understanding of himself; there was no way to hold to scholastic thought once Copernicus, Newton, and Locke had been unloosed. By 1740 the thrust of a Yale education had moved from medieval scholasticism to the "New Learning"; the courses looked essentially the same when listed in the college catalogue, but what was read or conveyed had changed profoundly.

The curriculum could not exclusively be an instrument in the service of God or of Church and State, as the founders of Harvard and Yale had intended. Because they were colleges, the tools for fulfilling their purposes were the liberal arts and sciences, that whole, inherited, vital body of learning that had a life and purpose of its own. Whether they liked it or not, the colonial colleges were burdened with perpetuating "the learning and culture of Europe."[9]

This purpose may have been gratuitous and even alarmingly ascendant in importance. It was not, however, allowed to be deflected, nor was it allowed to undermine the colleges' original purpose to qualify a governing elite for carrying forward the society that had created colleges in the first place as guarantees of their own permanence. But even the idea of permanence was a source of change. Every generation defined its own conditions for survival. When King's College opened in 1754 its president, Samuel Johnson, announced that the course of study would include husbandry and commerce, subjects that had not been thought of as being weighted with social purpose by the founders of Harvard College not much more than a hundred years earlier.[10]

The curriculum of the English college on the American frontier, whether in Cambridge, New Haven, or elsewhere, was conditioned by poverty, its distance from England, the lack of concentrated centers of population, the vast reaches of an unexplored and unsettled country. The first and most noticeable casualty of these conditions was standards. In the colonies professional preparation for the practice of law and medicine fell out from under the sway of the colleges. Apprenticeship—cheaper, more practical, more informal—was substituted for the "theoretical and systematic education" traditionally offered by higher faculties in institutions of higher learning. In New England professional training for the ministry assumed a college education, but as popular sects with their suspicion of an educated clergy found their way into American life, even the ministry had less use for the colleges.

Students found themselves being taught as groups of freshmen or sophomores or whatever, whereas instruction at Oxford and Cambridge, where both endowment and instructors were in greater supply, was an individual matter resting on the student-tutor relationship. In contrast, there was a time at Harvard when all of the instruction was done by the president. Poverty and lack of a population sufficient to justify or underwrite growth also meant that an English college in colonial America existed in parochial isolation, its curriculum unable to profit from the intellectual stimulation and diversity that the clustering of colleges permitted at Oxford and Cambridge.[11]

Even in Connecticut a suspicion of learning created an environment that regarded the course of study as an invitation to democratic excess. In 1721 the annual election sermon warned against "too great a spirit of learning in the land; more are brought up to it than will be needed or find improvement." Where population was sufficiently concentrated to support a college, the dropout rate was alarming; about a half of those who entered King's College gave up, usually by the end of the second year. Instead of providing a source of students, New York's urban location, with its opportunities in commerce and business and its easy access to apprenticeships in medicine and law, acted as an alluring alternative to the curriculum. A spokesman for the college in 1753 described King's as an institution intended for those whose "fortunes enable and inclinations induce them" to attend. While those few youths who did attend the colonial colleges, including King's, were drawn largely from upper and upper middle-class families, most of the sons of the colonial elite did not go to college at all.[12]

The course of study they found there may have had something to do with it. Yet what other course of study could have drawn these unenrolled sons of ministers, magistrates, and merchants into the embrace of the colleges? The curriculum was more or less what it had to be, and life in the American colonies abounded with challenges, opportunities, and even drudgery enough, for none of which the curriculum was an essential preparation.

The curriculum of the colonial college was basically the result of the collision in early sixteenth-century England of a traditional course of study with powerful new intellectual and social forces. The traditional course of study had been institutionalized by the middle of the thirteenth century in a dozen or so European universities, where the liberal arts as organized and propounded in ancient Greece were regarded as the sum of all learning and the most appropriate education for the highest of callings—theology. The medieval universities organized and divided seven liberal arts into the *quadrivium* (arithmetic, geometry, astronomy, music), which was of a lower order than the *trivium* (logic, grammar, and rhetoric). The trivium was essentially a program of studies in the meaning and use of the Latin language. These basic studies provided the intellectual equipment that allowed the medieval university student to move into a study of the three philosophies of Aristotle: natural philosophy (physics), moral philosophy (ethics), and mental philosophy (metaphysics).[13] To a considerable degree, as Samuel Eliot Morison described it, the medieval curriculum was "very nearly equivalent to a course on the works of Aristotle, in Latin translation."[14] And because the university existed to support and produce thinkers, the university curricular experience was permeated with the study of theology.

By the time that this course of study had moved out of the medieval university, passed through the universities of Renaissance and Reformation England, and landed in the American forest, much had happened. The Renaissance intruded into universities that had been narrowly religious in orientation a concern with the proper education of a gentleman and a concern with humanistic ideals of classical scholarship. A broadened view of letters and language, knowledge appropriate to the responsible use of leisure, and an interest in Greece and the Greeks before they fell into Latin translation entered into the university course of study. What had been a curriculum for theologians now carried the burden of training a governing class of gentlemen and men of action. A heightened respect for rhetoric and the addition of natural science, Greek, Hebrew, and ancient history to the traditional liberal arts had the effect of stretching the definition of liberal learning. New needs had appeared, new knowledge had knocked at the door.[15]

To the unsettling influence of the Renaissance and its insistence that the universities make themselves useful to a new governing class, the Puritan Reformation added its particular weight to strengthening the university as the place for training a learned clergy. In the great Puritan migration to New England in the seventeenth century at least 130 university men were among those who emigrated before 1646.[16] The idea of the university that they carried with them was part medieval, part Renaissance, part Reformation; the curriculum that they

delivered to Harvard carried old burdens and new burdens and perhaps also a burden of its own making in its need to accommodate the
not always compatible urgencies of scholastic philosophers, Renaissance gentlemen, and Westminster Calvinists. The English college
curriculum was now on its way to becoming the American college
curriculum.

In 1642 Henry Dunster, the young president of Harvard who
had been graduated from Magdalene College, Cambridge, in the very
year that Massachusetts Bay was founded, prepared for his board of
overseers a description of a course of study that would reproduce in
Massachusetts, as best he could manage it, an English college.[17] The
three-year course that he presided over was something of an anomaly.
Why he deviated from the four years characteristic of an English college is not clear. Were entering students sufficiently well prepared to
permit them to be admitted, in effect, with a year of advanced standing? Were three college classes all that Dunster, at first alone, and
later with the assistance of tutors, could possibly manage? Whatever
the reason for deviating from the English pattern, the three-year
course was extended to four in 1652, resulting in Harvard's class of
1652 graduating as an extra class of 1653. The shift from three to four
years did not change the subjects of instruction; it extended the
studies of the first year across two years.

The first year—and after 1652, the first two years—consisted of a
review of Latin and a continuation of the Greek that Harvard students offered for admission. The study of logic, Hebrew, and rhetoric
was begun in the first year and continued in the second year. Sometime after the adoption of the four-year curriculum, natural philosophy became an introductory experience in the second year. The third
year (originally the second year) confronted students with the three
philosophies—natural, mental, and moral—as well as geography, a
course that had its origins in the Renaissance. During their last year
Harvard students reviewed Latin, Greek, logic, and natural philosophy, and began the study of mathematics. Divinity (catechism) was a
study for all four years, during which small amounts of history and
botany further acknowledged Renaissance influence.

This curriculum was organized and structured with a fine dedication to logic and order. Morning classes were devoted to recitations:

Here students demonstrated whether or not they had learned their lessons. Afternoons were given over to disputations (debates): Here students demonstrated not only whether they could think but also whether they could think correctly. Monday and Tuesday were assigned to philosophy, Wednesday to Greek, Thursday to Hebrew, Friday to rhetoric, and Saturday to reciting the catechism in the mornings and history (winter) and botany (summer) in the afternoons. A striking quality of this early course of study was its provision for relief from the mornings of recitation in the active afternoons of debate, practice in grammatical construction and literary creativity, declamation, and argumentation. A student who journeyed through this curriculum and could demonstrate an ability to translate the Old and New Testaments from Hebrew to Latin and an understanding of natural and moral philosophy and who had attended classes regularly and deported himself with blameless character earned the right to receive the degree of bachelor of arts and be welcomed into the fellowship of educated men.

Dunster's 1642 curriculum was the model after which, with little variation, higher education in the English colonies was patterned. The particular place of some subject within the four years, greater or lesser emphasis on one subject or another, the appearance of a new subject—these matters of academic concern offered opportunities for disagreement and variety. Each college cut the cloth to fit its own requirements, but the style and the model did not vary appreciably until the appearance of new colleges in New York and Philadelphia near the end of the English period of the American college.

The Yale curriculum a hundred years later included all the same major subjects, although to some extent rearranged.[18] Freshmen were introduced to logic. It was no longer enough to translate the Bible from Hebrew to Latin; Yale freshmen took the Bible in English and made it Greek, sophomores and juniors took it in Hebrew and turned it to Greek, and the seniors translated from English and Latin into Greek. At Yale, Friday and Saturday, for all classes, were devoted to rhetoric, oratory, ethics, and divinity. As at Harvard a hundred years earlier, the Yale course of study in 1743 had an architectural unity. The first year established language skills—tools; the second year provided depth in the study of logic—a method, another tool; during the third and fourth years, these skills and method were turned on the advanced subjects—natural philosophy, mathematics, and meta-physics—one at a time. And during all four years, every Friday and Saturday, all Yale students recited and disputed the key subjects—divinity and ethics. On Sunday the college worshiped together, and what may have appeared to be a day off for the curriculum was really the day when the curriculum fell into place, with the assistance of prayer, sermon, and Biblical explication from the president of Yale College.

While remarkable stability was, therefore, a characteristic of the college course of study in the English colonies, the curriculum was responsive to European intellectual movements.[19] Mathematics was only indifferently included in the eighteenth-century Harvard curriculum, a slight remnant of the ancient quadrivium, considered perhaps of use to mechanics but of no value to gentlemen, scholars, and men of affairs. A little arithmetic and plane and spherical geometry, the latter read in English as if even further to reduce its importance, appeared in the senior year almost as an afterthought.

Mathematics experienced a significant change of fortune in the curriculum in 1714 as the result of a collection of over seven hundred books gathered in London by Jeremiah Dummer, colonial agent for Connecticut, and sent by him to Yale College. Dummer had solicited books from Isaac Newton and other leading figures of the Royal Society, an inspired moment in the history of philanthropy that led Yale's first two tutors, Samuel Johnson and Daniel Browne, both of the class of 1714, to insinuate Copernicus, Descartes, and Newton into the curriculum, so carried away were they by what they found themselves reading in the Yale library. Their lectures and conversations with their students soon made clear that the "New Learning," which had arrived in Dummer's parcels of books, could not be understood without more mathematics than the meager arithmetic with which students entered Yale. In 1718 algebra appeared in the Yale course of study, in 1720 astronomy was being studied in mathematical terms, and by 1723 Yale students were propounding the thesis: "In a musical progression the difference of the first and second numbers is proportional to the difference of the third and fourth according to the ratio of the first to the fourth."[20] In 1742 mathematics instruction began in the freshman year; three years later geometry appeared as a sophomore subject and mathematics was included in the junior year as well.

The growth of mathematical studies in the curriculum was unavoidable once Newtonian physics made its way into the course of natural philosophy.

With the effective advocacy of two students of Newtonian physics, Professor John Winthrop at Harvard (1738–1779) and Thomas Clap, the rector of Yale (1739–1766), mathematics made bold advances in a course of study in which a century earlier it had all but been ignored. Winthrop presided over the first laboratory of experimental physics in America and gave off some early signs of how a scientific laboratory could change society's notion of what a college was: In 1761 he prevailed on the General Court of Massachusetts to support an astronomical expedition to Newfoundland to observe the transit of Venus, and in proving that earthquakes were natural phenomena he brought down on Harvard the wrath of the orthodox clergy. Clap made Yale the first college to require some arithmetic for admission, reduced instruction in logic in order to expand the mathematical studies, and purchased and built Yale's first scientific apparatus.[21]

The teaching of natural philosophy (physics) was transformed by the "New Learning." As first taught at Yale by Rector Abraham Pierson, based on his own Harvard studies, physics included a section on angels, defined as spirits "not made of one of the elements, but of rare medium, endowed with reason and will, and ministers of God, having always existed from the beginning, of least materiality but of many forms."[22] This was the kind of physics that required no mathematics to understand. At Harvard a breakthrough in physics toward a Newtonian orientation occurred under the tutelage of Charles Morton late in the seventeenth century, but "the earliest generous recognition of the sciences in America came at William and Mary," which established the first scientific professorship in an American college in 1711, a professorship of natural philosophy and mathematics. Isaac Greenwood, the country's and Harvard's first scientist, became one by going to London in 1724 to study for the ministry and by there being so completely seduced by scientific lectures that he persuaded a wealthy London merchant to found a professorship at Harvard in mathematics and natural philosophy, a position he promptly filled in 1728. These early professors worked and taught on the edge of the unknown, developing ways of thinking and looking at nature that were unconsciously tearing away at the fabric of certainty and preordained truth on which the curriculum rested. Was it only accident and coincidence that William and Mary's and Harvard's first science professors, the first in America, had to be removed because of intemperance?[23]

Although Yale did not create a professorship of natural philosophy and mathematics until 1770, both subjects were being seriously studied on a respectable level by the 1730s, when Yale students were familiar enough with Copernicus and Newton to recognize in nature not so much an inspiration to contemplation as a challenge to experimental investigation. The distance that natural philosophy had traveled in the eighteenth century was the distance between Rector Pierson's discourse on angels and the remarks of a contributor to a Connecticut newspaper who in 1770 praised the college for establishing a professorship of mathematics and natural philosophy that would help to "dissipate superstitions, chimeras, and old women's fables, which are the natural attendants of ignorance, and the offspring of overheated imaginations."[24]

By 1776 six of the eight colonial colleges had professorships of mathematics and natural philosophy; by 1788, the remaining two had found the funds necessary to establish similar chairs, the first in all eight institutions of an essentially worldly rather than spiritual nature. Science was in the process of being organized into a number of discrete subjects, not just mathematics. Breaking loose from natural philosophy, from physics as it had long been taught, were such curricular departures as chemistry, geography, and natural history. And science was proposing a new way of looking at the world: The message that increasingly presented itself to the students of the colonial colleges was revolutionary: "The business of the mind [is] to discover things hitherto unknown."[25]

By 1788 at Princeton, President Walter Minto, welcoming science into the curriculum, proposed nonetheless not to allow it to get out of hand:

Natural philosophy . . . by leading us in a satisfactory manner to the knowledge of one almighty all-wise and all-

good Being . . . is the very handmaid of religion. . . . A student of that branch of science . . . [is] engaged in a continued act of devotion.[26]

One group of sciences—botany, chemistry, anatomy, and physiology—first appeared in those colleges that undertook to provide a
medical course as well as a bachelor's course. At the College of
Philadelphia, King's College in New York, and Harvard, an associated medical school offered courses that regular undergraduates
might take as supplements to the prescribed course. In 1789, in
Philadelphia, Benjamin Smith Barton became the first professor of
botany and natural history in an American college; at Princeton, in
1796, John Maclean became the first professor of chemistry in an arts
college without a medical program.[27] The significance of these developments in drawing attention to the world at the expense of the sub-
lime was not yet widely apparent, but the sciences had not only found
their way into the curriculum—they were also speaking a new language, rearranging old priorities, and changing the definition of a
college education.

In one sense the curriculum was a course in the learning and use
of language. The proper use of the language of divinity was held in
such high regard that at the time of the founding of Harvard the rules
of Cambridge and Oxford called for the use of Latin in ordinary conversation.[28] University authorities held their students to these rules
with some difficulty. The failure of similar rules in the American colleges can be assumed, although in 1653 Michael Wigglesworth, a
Harvard tutor, recorded in his diary his distress over having used
English in conversation, and as late as 1688 two students were admonished for using English within college precincts.[29] The Latin speaking requirement appeared in the Harvard laws of 1686 but not of 1692.
A similar requirement disappeared from the Yale laws of 1774, presumably long after the practice itself had disappeared. Historians of
the other colonial colleges have found no evidence that an effort was
made to hold to Latin as the language of conversation.[30]

In the meantime, on the highly sensible grounds that learning
proceeded best where understanding was most encouraged and facilitated, reforming schoolmasters eased the shift from Latin to English

as the language of instruction by introducing English textbooks into sixteenth-century English schools.[31] At seventeenth-century Harvard, however, most texts were still in Latin. English translations increased in use in the eighteenth century, apparently on the initiative of students seeking to avoid the Latin.[32]

The preparation of English textbooks or manuscripts in English, copied for their own use by students, was in part a response to new learning. Thomas Clap's ethics text, published in 1765, had before then been studied in manuscript. Yet, as late as 1731 at Harvard a foolish effort was made to force Latin out of the mouths of Harvard students at Saturday prayers, when the week's absences were announced in Latin and the students were required to respond with their excuses in Latin. The students turned the effort into a series of verbal pranks, and it was abandoned.[33]

In the disputations or debates in which the students tried out their learning, Latin was the indicated language. A 1653 Harvard commencement disputation in English was "a concession to the general public . . . not soon repeated."[34] A hundred years later, as a curricular innovation, Harvard in 1754 provided for a group of English debates at commencement, although until 1760 commencement exercises themselves were conducted entirely in Latin. Three years later, for the first time an English oration was part of the program. The ascendancy of English in the public exercises of the college, in instruction, and in the debates which were a vital part of academic intellectual life was in part a function of the substitution of forensic disputations for syllogistic disputations. The "New Learning" made itself felt throughout the curriculum, dignifying induction at the expense of deduction, ethics at the expense of theology, and English at the expense of Latin.[35]

The translating in and out of English, Latin, Greek, and Hebrew that was such a commanding part of the curricular experience gave undergraduates more than a knowledge of the Old and New Testaments. Their exposure to the classics of the ancient world— Plutarch, Cicero, Demosthenes, Plato, Aristotle—was on a scale that allowed Samuel Eliot Morison to exaggerate: "It was the classics that made Harvard men of that day effective in politics and statesmanship."[36] The ancient languages also had a usefulness in the professions: Lawyers, doctors, and clergymen used them as if they were indeed still living languages. And the knowledge of the past and of the human experience that accompanied all that reading and translating and reciting was in no sense trivial: It had its uses for a self-respecting cultured gentleman as well as for the effective man of public affairs. With it, he could *write* and *speak* with power. He knew *words*. And it complemented the rest of the curriculum and the regimen of religious exercises as a guide to character and moral conduct.[37]

Hebrew, as the original language of the Old Testament, was an essential study for a Puritan community. The Harvard curriculum included Hebrew from the beginning, but apparently only the compulsory nature of the course of study sustained it. Put on an elective basis in 1755, it lingered on, but by 1782, when students were permitted to choose French instead, Hebrew spoke to the needs of very few Harvard students. Until 1817 there was a Hebrew oration at commencement, and, although the language was studied only superficially at Yale, President Ezra Stiles delivered an address in Hebrew at commencement in 1781, and leading his senior students through Hebrew by way of the Psalms, he may even have convinced some of them that one of those Psalms was the first that they would hear sung in heaven.[38]

The language and literature of the future—English—began to find support in an environment that was emancipating itself from the past. Oratory, history, and poetry, the kinds of subjects that were peripheral in the curriculum, were peripheral precisely because they did not lend themselves to the old deductive logic and were, moreover, instruments of delight and emotion. Here were subjects and materials that went beyond the didactic to the esthetic and to a fuller definition and understanding of the human experience. The rise of such subjects was another measure of the decline of theological authority and of the shift to a concern with the nature of man. It was also an acknowledgment that English was the language of Englishmen and that the experience of the English people was not recorded in the language of the prophets nor the languages of the ancients.[39]

In 1756 Harvard provided for a system of undergraduate exhibitions in which English oratory was displayed. In 1767 English grammar and oratory entered the sophomore studies at Yale. In 1771 two new tutors, Timothy Dwight and John Trumbull, edged the study of belles lettres into their instruction, a "frivolous" departure that inflamed a public already unhappy with the stubbornness of Yale's clerical governors and the impracticality of its course of study. In 1776 the Yale corporation grudgingly acceded to a request from the senior class that they be allowed to receive instruction in rhetoric, history, and belles lettres—all in English—from Timothy Dwight. The revolutionary generation in effect asked to be equipped for the future, and, while the corporation did not turn them down, it refused to allow such instruction to be a part of the course of study, it refused to pay for it, and it required every student who chose to sit at Tutor Dwight's feet to get parental approval. At Princeton John Witherspoon, elected president in 1768, arrived with a fresh sense of what was happening in the Scottish and English universities and promptly introduced instruction in belles lettres. In 1785 Ezra Stiles welcomed into the Yale course of study *Hugh Blair's Lectures on Rhetoric and Belles-Lettres*, published in London two years before, the first textbook in English literature.[40]

In the meantime, while natural philosophy, which kept that Aristotelian label long after it might better have been called Newtonian physics, was spawning new subjects and encouraging the mathematical studies, moral philosophy (ethics) was moving into an ascendancy over the curriculum as a whole.[41] Developing into a kind of capstone course that was wonderfully reassuring in its insistence on the unity of knowledge and the benevolence of God, moral philosophy by mid eighteenth century had achieved a dominance over logic, divinity, and metaphysics in the course of study.

The course in moral philosophy grew out of the final year course in divinity, which had always been something more than recitations in the Westminster Catechism. At Harvard, Henry Dunster used Saturday afternoons to apply religious doctrine, argument, and opinion to the study of man, his relation with God, and his relations with his fellow man. At Yale the movement of ethics into a position of central concern was accomplished by a reduction in the study of divinity and metaphysics. Clearly what was happening was a shift in "the philosophical presuppositions of the New England mind."[42] Man was increasingly expected to learn about himself, nature, and God less through the Bible and philosophical speculation than through the use of reason and intuition and the study of nature, including human nature itself.

This shift in emphasis and in the locus of moral guidance was accompanied by a recognition among the ruling elders of the New England colonies that they needed something more than the Bible to hold their communities together. A fear of cosmic justice after death was in decline; a sometimes unruly and untamed popular will was on the loose; the appearance of sects and the breaking away of dissenting Puritans threatened the unity and the stability of society. An apprehensive awareness of these developments, according to Norman S. Fiering, led to "an urgent quest to investigate thoroughly the sources of moral behavior as well as the nature of virtue itself."[43] In the colleges this search resulted in a course that "was the bastion not only of duty and virtue, but also of religion," a course that systematically brought together, in the words of Samuel Johnson, who taught such a course at King's College, "not only the Objects, Boundaries, Ends and Uses of each of the Sciences; but at the same time, their Foundation in the nature of things."[44]

Clearly the course in ethics became the place where an effort was made to find a substitute for a declining "divine coercive authority."[45] If men could not be counted on to behave correctly because God said so, then reason and human nature—God's gifts to man—might be enlisted in the battle to bring them as near as possible to the side of the angels. To some extent the moral philosophy course was developed as an antidote to human arrogance, a quality that the New World tended to be particularly disposed to encourage and that was a threat to social and economic stability.

The course had come to America in a refined form from the dissenting academies of England and Scotland; in the colleges founded late in the colonial era at Princeton and Philadelphia the inspiration for the course in moral philosophy appears to have been the dissenting academies.[46] But, as Yale demonstrated, the course could have an organic growth out of the intellectual currents and social needs that sought expression in the curriculum. As taught, usually by the president to seniors, the course moved easily into a consideration of current events and questions of pressing practical concern to young men; it brought a mix—but a systematic mix—of ethics, science, and religion to bear on a very large question: How should man behave?

To arrive at a central position in the curriculum this question required, among other things, a declining Calvinist attachment to a belief in the efficacy of faith over works as a means of salvation. Ethics, after all, is a guide to good works, as Cotton Mather recognized in his complaint in 1716 against "employing so much time upon Ethik in College, a vile form of paganism."[47] His complaint, however, registered the awful truth: Faith might be enough as a guide to heaven; it was not enough, given the nature of the Englishmen who sought a worldly competence in North America, to guide a community in the ways of stability.

Appropriate texts were also necessary before the course in moral philosophy could become a standard capstone course either in the colonial colleges or in the rash of new colleges that developed during the first decades of the new American nation. At the College of Philadelphia in 1756 the moral philosophy course drew on the writings of Frances Hutcheson, Jean Jacques Burlamaqui, as well as of Pufendorf, Sidney, Harrington, and Locke. The views of these and other moral philosophers were incorporated into the textbooks, which, in a sense, by their appearance certified the course in moral philosophy as having made its way into a commanding position in the curriculum. The first of these, by Thomas Clap, appeared in 1765: *Essay on the Nature and Foundation of Moral Virtue and Obligations: Being a Short Introduction to the Study of Ethics, for the Use of the Students of Yale College.*[48] One of the first to appear after the Revolution, by which time King's College had become Columbia College, was the text used by John Daniel Gros in his course in moral philosophy there: *Natural Principles of Rectitude for the Conduct of Man in all States and Situations of Life demonstrated and explained in a systematic treatise on Moral Philosophy comprehending the Law of Nature—Ethics—Natural Jurisprudence—General Economics—Politics—and the Law of Nations.*[49] The first endowment for a professorship in moral philosophy created the Alford professorship at Harvard in 1789.

The course itself picked up subject matter and appropriate areas of concern as it developed. In moving from the idea of morality as deriving from God to morality as a function of reason and human nature, the course took side trips—into political morality on the eve of the Revolution, for example. And by 1796 textbooks on the subject were including sections on physiology.[50] The route and methods by which ethics as a separate discipline elevated reason, surpassed theology, invited deist thought into the course of study, and generated a secular approach to moral questions were circuitous and complex, but the course was well on the way there by the end of the colonial period.[51] In attempting to reconcile Lockean empiricism, Newtonian physics, and Christian revelation, the moral philosophy course may have been attempting the impossible, but between 1700 and 1850 it took its place in the curriculum as "the semisecular way station between the great era of theological dominance" of the Middle Ages and the twentieth century, "when objective science presses so hard on all other modes of experience."[52]

Yet, what was it like to be a student? At Yale, Thomas Clap conceived of the curriculum as an opportunity to give evening lectures, after prayers, on questions of law, agriculture, commerce, gunnery, and whatever else ignited undergraduate imagination. Ezra Stiles decided that as president of Yale one of his responsibilities was to steer his seniors toward books appropriate to their career intentions, however inappropriate for the formal course of study.[53]

At Harvard, Isaac Greenwood and John Winthrop and, at William and Mary, William Small discovered that the traditional use of recitations as a way of teaching and examining at the same time did not work. For them there were no textbooks; what they knew had not yet been organized and standardized; they lectured, their students took notes, and some of them sensed that they were on the edge of the unknown. Greenwood even used laboratory equipment to show his students what a principle in physics looked like. That had not happened before.[54]

Some professors, some tutors, consciously or not, were confident enough about what they were doing to be fascinated by the depth of their own ignorance and inspired by the vastness of their students' aspirations. Some of them tried out the style of Socrates, and it worked. There was a looseness of teaching arrangements that allowed King's College to have no classrooms at all—only a great hall where meals were served, lectures were delivered, and recitations heard. In 1766 Harvard built its first classroom.[55]

The student who wrote down the Latin dictations considered

appropriate by his tutor may have had his mind somewhere else, but if his notebooks survived, those dictations—to a son or grandson, a daughter or granddaughter—would look like guides to right conduct, pious encouragement to the faltering young, and gems of wisdom from great men. Latin grammar *could* be a course of ethics in disguise. The lectures, the declamations, the debates were the instruments of a culture for which the ears were more useful than the eyes. Professors on the frontier of specialized knowledge, possessing ideas that did not seem to fit, imbued with enough of the new learning to make their every remark an experience on the way toward skepticism, threw away texts and recitations in favor of lectures: Otherwise, they were tongue-tied. Yet, between 1750 and 1800, in the nineteen colleges then existing, only a few of the two hundred or so college professors— the entire professoriate for half a century—fell into a style that required such adventure. They did not know enough or, if they did, they lacked imagination or skill to articulate it.[56]

And there were tutors, young men just graduated, appointed to assist the president and the professors in instruction, about as young as the students, willing for a while, between college and career, to linger a little longer. Until 1755 Yale depended entirely on the president and young tutors for instruction; Yale's first professor was appointed that year. Until then for his first three years a Yale undergraduate was led through the course of study by a young recent graduate, a veteran of the curriculum who could be counted on to review the Latin and the Greek and to stir up the young men just enough to make them fit for a senior year of awesome instruction by the president.[57]

The tutors were in charge of the unstated curriculum. Edmund Morgan has said of the tutors under Ezra Stiles that they enjoyed complete freedom in conducting their classes and undoubtedly interrupted the routine of recitations to discuss with the students the lectures of the president and professors or to give their own views on some topic in the textbook that particularly interested them.[58] Tutors compensated for what there was not: In the absence of books, libraries, and urban intellectual communities, they sometimes, through conversations and lectures, brought their students into the presence of ideas that students at Oxford and Cambridge found in books.[59]

Whether the tutors were instruments of cultural lag and retardation or were really flexible young subversives is a matter of question.

Of course they were both. In the late eighteenth century Harvard tutors did not hold their students to the course of study. With tutorial permission and encouragement, what should have been Latin or Greek or Hebrew became French, mathematics, and Anglican theology.[60] The shipment of disruptive books sent from London to Yale in 1714 would not have been disruptive without the two young tutors set on fire by the presence—at Yale, in a book—of Isaac Newton.

On the other hand, the specialization and refinement of knowledge encouraged by the emergence of a scientific style meant that tutors with their lack of training and their youth, while they could teach everything, could not be expected to teach any one thing especially well. The attachment of a new seriousness and expectation to the tutorial role in the colonial college was a recognition of new practices at the Scottish universities in Edinburgh and Glasgow, where instructors with specialized competence were substituted for regents in 1708 and 1727 respectively.[61] In time the cultural lag and comfortable provincialism that may have supported most American tutors in a posture of rigidity, inflexibility, and a lack of adventure and imagination were bound to give way. In 1767 the tutors at Harvard College stopped being intellectual jacks-of-all-trades; they stopped teaching everything to one college class and began teaching one subject to all classes.[62]

The English college on the American frontier told about itself at the annual commencement exercises. There and then the curriculum went on display: Students exhibited, professors paraded, parents applauded. Commencement was an exercise in institutional public relations and a sort of social inquiry. The colleges were saying, "This is how and what we are doing." On the other hand, church, state, and neighborhood, all those assembled for what was sometimes a week-long holiday, made of commencement an investigation into how well the colleges were fulfilling the expectations of society.

The fundamental instruments for conveying to the public the work of the college were the commencement disputations or debates. These debates were also the means by which the public judged the quality of the college and received a sense of the intellectual drift, the movement of ideas, in the colleges. Commencement was a holiday with appropriate social diversions; attendance by public officials was a recognition of the "dependence of the college on civil authority," while prayers, sacred music, and attendance by the clergy in a body attested to the religious nature of the collegiate experience. But what gave the occasion a peculiarly collegiate character were the debates and orations that constituted an exhibition of the college's intellectual competence.[63]

Disputations, an inheritance from the medieval university, were a feature of the course of study during all four years; graduating seniors had had extensive experience in participating in debates as well as in practicing declamation. Confronted with a thesis, a statement of some universal truth, two students, one serving as disputant and one serving as questioner, would apply their powers of deduction to establish the validity of the thesis. For undergraduates the appeal of disputations as a curricular exercise derived from the extent to which they went beyond memorization and recitation; they invited creativity, drew on the imagination, and became instruments of self-definition and growth—as the basic course of study and the pedagogy on which it rested never did. "At their best," Samuel Eliot Morison concluded, "these exercises trained men in oratory and debate, taught them to think on their feet, stimulated the sluggard, and showed up the bluffer. At its worst, the disputation was a mere play on words, obscuring sound habits of thought and rewarding the superficially clever."[64]

The scholastic tradition of syllogistic argumentation lent itself to both the strengths and weaknesses cited by Morison, but increasingly, with its presupposition that all truth could be demonstrated only by deduction rather than induction, syllogistic disputation became a clumsy device for discovering truth in an environment receptive to the new learning. The history of debating both as a formal aspect of the curriculum and as a public relations gesture at commencement is the history of the replacement of Latin syllogistic debate by forensic debate in English. Syllogistic disputation had been an effective instrument for testing and mastering a prescribed course of study in a book-scarce environment that was friendly to the scholastic tradition, but it was absolutely useless as an instrument for "the advancement of free inquiry."[65] As Edmund Morgan has said of such syllogistic topics as whether animals think or whether man can sin while sleeping, "The difficulty with topics like these was that they presented issues so abstract or so remote from common experience that the arguments tended to be mere mental gymnastics."[66]

In the 1750s at Yale the forensic debate appeared and achieved equality with syllogistic argumentation. Its greater flexibility and its greater suitability for the consideration of secular content and the new learning made the forensic style more congenial to the scientific temper. It gave "a greater Scope to their Genius," observed Thomas Clap.[67] Each year the number of debates on practical learning increased. The syllogistic style continued to be the appropriate form for the consideration of theological topics, but the forensic debate, because it was not constricted by a prohibition against induction, experience, and intuition, the intellectual posture that was changing man's whole understanding of himself and his world, lent itself to topics that were inspired by making a connection between the curriculum and the real world. A 1767 debate at King's College asked "Whether a man ought to engage in war without being persuaded of the justness of his cause." A 1773 debate at Harvard argued the question of slavery. At Yale the commencement debates mirrored the movement of new subjects and new intellectual attitudes into the curriculum: "All physical knowledge is acquired from experimentation" (1730); "The movement of muscles arises from the intrinsic elasticity of fibriles" (1733); "Ethics is the art of living according to reason" (1733-1740).[68]

By 1779 Yale seniors were taking their commencement debates into the realm of current political controversy: "Which [would be] the most just and eligible mode of Taxation for paying the Continental Debt, that founded on *Estates,* or that on the *Number of Inhabitants,* or that on a Ratio and Valuation compounded or constituted of both?"[69] The scholastic style, the syllogism, the stress on deductive logic could not survive in an environment where Descartes, Berkeley, Newton, and Locke were in vogue. The new colleges at Philadelphia and New York revealed how far the spirit of induction had entered into the course of study. At Philadelphia in 1761 the graduating seniors considered the proposition that "mathematical truth can be demonstrated; therefore, to propose mathematical theses as if there could be any disputation over them is absurd." King's College chose not to have any syllogistic debates at all.[70]

At Yale by 1782 syllogistic Latin disputation had been reduced to one day a month; forensic English disputation had become a curricular ornament and delight every Tuesday and three Mondays a month. In 1789 syllogistic debate was abandoned altogether; it lasted until 1810 at Harvard. And commencement everywhere began to move away from debates toward orations as the more suitable means of putting the curriculum on display. Princeton added a mathematical oration to the annual commencement program in 1792, an oration in belles lettres the next year. At Yale the 1781 commencement program was peppered with orations, disputes, and colloquies in English. Nothing so clearly symbolized what had been happening to the college curriculum between the founding of Harvard and the Declaration of Independence than this downward movement of the syllogistic style and the ascendancy of empirical thought.[71]

Old colleges quietly and undramatically undertook the changes necessary to keep them responsive to shifting intellectual currents. New colleges could declare themselves free of much of the old intellectual baggage. King's College in New York and the College of Philadelphia both at mid century showed that a new eighteenth-century college did not have to be a replica of seventeenth-century Harvard. In 1754 a prospectus for the new King's College advised the New York press that King's would institute a course of study that included surveying, navigation, geography, history, husbandry, commerce, government, meteorology, natural history, and natural philosophy, in other words "the knowledge . . . of every thing *useful* for the Comfort, the Convenience and Elegance of Life . . . and everything that can contribute to . . . true Happiness."[72] These ambitious plans were far from fully realized, and while more than another century passed before Ezra Cornell and Andrew D. White created an institution as catholic and as widely useful as King's proposed to be, the King's prospectus pointed in the direction of the modern American university.

William Smith, a 1747 graduate of the University of Aberdeen, had hoped to be the first president of King's College, and to that purpose circulated among appropriate circles in 1753 a pamphlet containing a utopian vision of what a new-style American college curriculum might be. His *College of Mirania* owed much to his Scottish experience and something to Samuel Johnson's preface to Robert

Dodsley's *The Preceptor*, published in London in 1748, but it led him
not to King's but to the College of Philadelphia. There he presided
as provost from 1754 to 1779, designing a curriculum that was "the
earliest systematic arrangement, in America, of a group of college
studies not following medieval tradition and not having a specifically
religious object."[73] Smith's utopian vision for Mirania was a wonder-
ful mix of the traditional and the new: Xenophon and merchants'
accounts the first year; surveying, map making, and logic in the second; a stress on the vernacular, agriculture, and history in the final
year. The Philadelphia course of study was a forecast of the future:
Elective instruction was provided in German, Spanish, Italian, fenc-
ing, military science, and dancing. Religion was neither neglected
nor overpowering, but subtle and supported through the courses in
history, Sunday lectures in revealed religion, and the moral force and
character of the instructors.[74]

　　Philadelphia was not ready to become Mirania, but Smith tai-
lored a curriculum that fitted into the enterprising life of the city,
which sometimes seemed to be little more than the elaboration of the
imaginative dreams of Benjamin Franklin. Indeed, the College of
Philadelphia developed out of Franklin's academy, an earlier educational design intended to meet the needs of a rapidly changing
society. Smith's course of study for the College of Philadelphia eliminated the sophomore year: Americans, he said, have neither the time
nor the money, and, besides, the busy world cast its seductive eye on
the energetic and the aspiring. The high dropout rate at King's College verified the correctness of Smith's instincts. There were no electives in Smith's three-year curriculum, but it had a style of its own:
professors with specialized knowledge and responsibilities, great
amounts of science (fully 40 percent of classroom time in contrast to
Harvard's 9 percent of 1650), and long reading lists that supplemented the regular courses and that were to be read, studied, and discussed with the tutors and integrated with the formal course of
study.[75]

　　The last decades of the eighteenth century were an unsettled
time in the life of the colleges. The country went to war and took the
colleges along. War occupied them, loosened attachments, questioned certainties. The curriculum that had been incorporating all
the change that a leisurely pace required now had to listen to what the

American Revolution was all about. A certain dynamic, of no one's responsibility, was loose, the coming together of elements beyond the understanding of deduction or induction. After almost two centuries' experience as colonial Englishmen, the Americans now proposed to make a nation.

An observer in the 1770s could not have been sure whether the college curriculum was coming together or was falling apart. At King's private students were allowed to take the courses that interested them, pay the professors the indicated fees, and excuse themselves from the bachelor's degree. In the 1770s Robert Harpur taught navigation, surveying, and mathematics to fourteen students who were not enrolled in the college. At Yale Ezra Stiles came up with a design in 1777 that proposed to add professors of medicine and law to the college staff, as well as professors of ecclesiastical history, civil history, Hebrew and oriental languages, oratory, and belles lettres.[76]

The American Revolution is thought to have been fought on a terrain dictated by the movement of armies. Ezra Stiles's proposals of 1777 knew where the revolution really was. Ezra Stiles had a barometric sensitivity to the dynamic nature of American society; his lectures to Yale students toward the end of the century attempted to keep them abreast of everything that was going on in linguistics, geography, mathematics, natural philosophy, astronomy, oriental languages, moral philosophy, as well as the structure of the eye and the nature of vision. His one-man effort to fill all the curricular gaps of the eighteenth-century course of study included a series of three lectures on the learned professions.[77] The nervousness of colleges and universities about fulfilling society's expectations was an index to American culture; vocations and professions apparently were roaming around in search of clients, purpose, and rationale. In time the search would lead to the creation of a distinctively American university, but until then Ezra Stiles was a magnificent demonstration of what one man could do until the American university came along.

At the College of William and Mary in Virginia in 1779 Thomas Jefferson demonstrated what an imaginative member of the college's board of visitors could do to transform a provincial version of an Oxford college into a model American college appropriate to a new republic. Jefferson's reorganization of the college abolished the professorships of divinity and oriental languages, the two professorships that carried the weight of religious purpose at the college; added professorships in public administration, modern languages, and medical sciences; and added natural history to the professorship of mathematics and natural philosophy and natural and international law and fine arts to the professorship of moral philsophy. These reforms not only brought the college abreast of new learning but shifted the curriculum from a religious to a secular purpose.[78]

The extent to which the new William and Mary departed from traditional practices was described by the president of the college, the Reverend James Madison, to Ezra Stiles in a letter in 1780: "The Doors of ye University are open to all, nor is even a knowledge in ye ant. Languages a previous Re-quisite for Entrance. The Students have ye Liberty of attending whom they please, and in what order they please, or all ye difft. Lectures in a term if they think proper. . . . The time of taking Degrees . . . depends upon ye Qualifications of ye candidate."[79] With these departures from ancient practice William and Mary introduced the principle of electives into the curriculum, abandoned the idea of a prescribed course of study for all students, gave up Latin and Greek as admissions requirements, and invited prospective students to use the college as later generations of consumers would learn to use department stores and supermarkets.

For a while the reformed college at Williamsburg served as a model for postrevolutionary collegiate developments elsewhere in the South, where the founding of new colleges represented an effort of the southern gentry to provide instruction for a class of gentlemen in the classics, the new learning, and subjects appropriate as preprofessional training in law and medicine. Colleges founded to provide gentlemen with "a veneer of culture and the social graces" or transformed, as was William and Mary, from centers of piety to centers of culture, were unable to withstand the unleashing of dozens of small sectarian colleges that narrowed the purpose and lowered the quality of what a college needed to be to call itself one. The ascendancy of sectarian purpose would succeed in eliminating William and Mary, the new University of North Carolina, and others as the centers of culture and utilitarian emphasis that they had promised, for a short time, to be.[80]

In 1784 the regents of the University of the State of New York designed a prophetic, if premature, plan for the renamed Columbia

University. The new republic was intoxicated with national aspirations; the Columbia scheme was one of the more giddy consequences. It called for a faculty of over thirty professors; in 1750 there had only been ten in all the American colleges. The university was to be divided into four faculties—arts, law, divinity, and medicine. The professorships covered the entire world of knowledge—French, German, Dutch, oriental languages, civil history, architecture, commerce, agriculture, music, painting, law of nature and nations, Roman civil law, municipal law, and all the sciences and philosophies, languages and literatures that had been a part of the developing curriculum in the past. In 1787 a new charter and an internal reorganization threw out the scheme of 1784 and reduced Columbia from a paper university to an American college. At Princeton a less ambitious plan that would have greatly expanded instruction in the sciences and would have required no Greek or Latin after the freshman year was turned down by the trustees in 1796, although special scientific students were admitted, not as degree candidates, but as partial course students who received a "certificate of proficiency" for study in the shorter, inferior, less prestigious partial curriculum.[81]

Fad and fashion entered the making of the American college curriculum for the first time when during and after the Revolution the new nation carried on an affair with the French. In 1778 an offer from Silas Deane, then an American emissary in Paris, to raise from wealthy French friends funds for a professorship of French was spurned by the Yale corporation, which preferred to protect its reputation for sound and steady conservative practices. But French influence could not be denied. The regents of the University of the State of New York, who had designed Columbia's grandiose scheme, were organized as a nonteaching and nondegree-granting institution, supervisory in purpose and patterned on the French model.

French entered the formal course of study for the first time at an American college at Columbia in 1779 and at William and Mary at about the same time. For a few years Hampden-Sidney College in Virginia accepted French as a substitute for Greek in awarding the B.A. degree. In 1787 Harvard permitted the substitution of French for Hebrew. Williams allowed the substitution of French for Greek as an admissions subject during the period from 1793 to 1799; William and Mary required it for admission in 1793; in 1795 Williams made

French the subject of its first professorship, and Union College in New York, in addition to introducing American history and American constitutional history quite appropriately into the curriculum of a college so named, also permitted the substitution of four years of French for four years of Greek. The affair with French cooled in the American college as the French Revolution got out of hand and a conservative reaction among college authorities set in against French deism, but the flirtation was a demonstration, often repeated in the future, that the college curriculum could be manipulated by current events. One consequence of the reactionary mood that set in among college governors and others during the first decade of the nineteenth century was a general tightening of the curriculum and the collapse of programs such as those at the University of North Carolina and Princeton that offered students the option of a utilitarian education without the classics. Although Jefferson's curriculum survived at William and Mary, it became an anachronism preserved in a discredited institution, a monument to the liberal republican enthusiasm of the postrevolutionary era.[82]

As strong as English tradition had been and as compelling as the new purposes were, the college curriculum was not thoroughly standardized nor could it yet be said that there was an American system of higher education. King's began with a four-year course and stuck with it in the interest of standards but with a price in low enrollments and a reputation for favoring the wealthy; the College of Philadelphia began with a three-year course and held to it until well into the nineteenth century; after the Revolution both Princeton and Union adopted policies that encouraged the enrollment of students as nondegree candidates who were allowed to take whatever interested them. In the early years of William and Mary a B.A. degree was awarded for two years and an M.A. degree for four. At Yale most students took a four-year course, although a three-year accelerated course was possible.[83]

Preparation for college was diverse and admission practices were varied. Because the colonial colleges were founded before there existed any network of grammar schools and because the population of the colonies was widely scattered, most entering students were prepared privately, often by studying with the local minister. Ability to read Latin and Greek was long the only admissions requirement, until Yale added arithmetic in 1745.[84]

Louis Franklin Snow's 1907 history of the curriculum must be one source of the notion that the course of study was transmitted essentially unchanged from early Harvard to the era of the American Revolution. "Save that the students are divided into four classes, and that Arithmetic is required for entrance," he wrote, "the scheme in Princeton in 1764 has little to offer, as a means of culture and of training for the general student that has not already been included in the Laws and Orders of Harvard as prepared by President Dunster in 1642."[85] This judgment attributed a static quality to curricular history that was contrary to experience. The Enlightenment had enlarged the role of natural science and mathematics; the breakdown of natural philosophy into mathematics, chemistry, natural history, and geography had produced new texts, written in English and therefore subversive of the continuing usefulness of Latin as the language of instruction. Beginning in the 1760s the idea of the "man of letters" as a proper definition of the college graduate intruded into the curriculum the study of belles lettres—orations, history, poetry, literature. An emphasis on reason and observation, on rational moral behavior, replaced a reliance on divine law in the study of ethics. The God who inhabited Dunster's Harvard was a righteous and wrathful God; the God who inhabited Princeton in 1764 was the creator and source of all of nature's wonders. The curriculum had shifted from explaining the ways of God to exploring the ways of man. Professors replaced tutors, and tutors themselves became specialists. The syllogistic disputation and its reliance on deductive logic had all but disappeared.[86]

Much of "the change was both gradual and subtle, neither understood nor acknowledged by those who underwent it," while what from the point of view of the faculty looked like a systematic curriculum was often, as experienced by students, "something of a shambles."[87] The limited size of the faculties and the limited range of conventional knowledge may have delivered students over to a curricular experience that for every generation at whatever college was essentially the same, but at the Harvard of Henry Dunster and the Princeton of Samuel Finley the curriculum itself was in no sense the same. It was in the grips of a continuing, unfinished, and to some extent unacknowledged revolution. If Louis Franklin Snow could not sense that revolution in 1907, Harvard students of 1642 would have recognized it at the Princeton of 1764.[88]

3

The New American Curriculum

The history of higher education in the United States is full of moments of creative absentmindedness, but the action of the trustees of Columbia College in 1810 was not one of them. They knew what they were doing. In a burst of self-confidence and high ambition they urged the professors to see to it that their students' mental faculties were "kept on the stretch . . . employed in work demanding severer tension and more dauntless vigour." And to help the professors along, the trustees then adopted a four-year curriculum and dispensed with the somewhat innovative course of study with which the college had been identified.[1]

Twenty years later the Columbia trustees were in panic. They added an entirely new course of study to the curriculum—a "Scientific and Literary Course," without Latin and Greek but including almost everything else, which might be taken in whole or in part and rewarded by a certificate but not a degree. They drew up a program of tuition scholarships for citizens of the city, graduates of its high school, members of all the religious denominations, as well as members of the General Society of Mechanics and Tradesmen. They offered to relieve the United States Navy of the necessity of creating a naval academy by proposing a package of relevant scientific instruction for up to forty-three midshipmen for a group fee of $3,500 a year. For $1,000 any ordinary citizen could buy a perpetual scholarship, entitling the purchaser to free tuition for one person in perpetuity.

For every $20,000 given to Columbia, in cash or real estate, by any person or corporation in the city, the city government could appoint a trustee, at least as long as those so appointed did not outnumber the existing board. And in 1836 the trustees further revised the curriculum to help along the ambitions of would-be architects, engineers, and factory superintendents.[2]

From self-confidence and high ambition to panic and pandering in twenty years: What had gone wrong? Much, but it is not at all clear that the Columbia trustees knew either what or why. Was New York environmentally uncongenial to higher education? Was a great seaport and financial center an inappropriate setting for the muses? It almost seemed so, for the newly chartered University of the City of New York, which had prompted the trustees into their alarms and proposals of 1830, floundered even as Columbia's enrollments declined.

Columbia's difficulty in establishing an institutional identity and in settling on a curriculum that defined its purposes was not unique. Higher education in the United States had not yet been rationalized. Its character was disorderly, lacking in standards, without coherence. Institutionally it was located in liberal arts colleges, theological seminaries, medical schools, law schools, academies, technical institutes, even libraries and lyceums where society provided not simply diversions but opportunities in adult education.[3] American society had use for this diversity of educational experiences, but it had not yet sorted them out or put them together in any way that could be said to make sense. Even at the time, life in the United States during the first half of the nineteenth century looked like a free-for-all. Higher education behaved in harmony with a culture that built canals and railroads in seemingly endless number and for reasons that were often more consistent with the national psychology than with sound economic and engineering practice. The first half of the nineteenth century closed quite appropriately with the California Gold Rush, not the last American free-for-all by any means, but it did differentiate and certify losers as well as winners.

The colleges were essentially engaged in the same kind of experience, surely less dramatic and less appealing to the popular imagination but nonetheless important to a definition of what kind of society the new American nation would develop into. The colleges were somehow trying to make a statement, Columbia among them, and the curriculum seemed to be the most indelible way of saying it. They thought that they knew what had been holding society, fragile under the best of circumstances, together, at least since the pagans and the barbarians had been conquered, held at bay, but not extinguished. They could not help believing that whatever order and stability there were in the society around them owed much to them. Since the founding of Harvard College, that society had counted on the colleges to produce its leaders, and they had not failed. Of the eighty-nine signers of the Declaration of Independence and the Constitution, thirty-six were products of the colonial colleges—Adams, Hamilton, Jay, Jefferson, and Madison among them.[4]

But now everything was uncertain. Egalitarian impulses challenged the essentially elitist pretensions of the colleges. The agricultural-commercial world to which they had been attuned was undergoing strains that were moving it in the direction of a technological-industrial order. For years it had been possible to teach Greek without teaching Homer, and then along came James Luce Kingsley, who told President Timothy Dwight of Yale that he would like permission to use Homer as well as the New Testament in teaching Greek. The problem presented by Professor Kingsley was almost insurmountable, so challenging was it to the idea that Yale College had of itself. Greek was recited on Mondays, and Dwight would not allow Yale to be put in a position of requiring Yale students to study an infidel author on Sundays; Homer was made optional, but at the price of having raised doubts about the capacity of Yale to retain its Christian character.[5] In most early nineteenth-century colleges, Yale among them, religious revivals were promoted as "manifest, open, and direct" expressions of curricular purpose.[6] What could be expected from students who read Homer on Sunday? Or of a college that allowed it?

The answer had already been given as far as Harvard was concerned. The biggest patron of American higher education before the Civil War was the American Education Society, founded in 1815 by prominent Congregational and Presbyterian laymen to support promising ministerial students in the colleges. In 1836 the society subsidized 352 students in the New England colleges, including over half the student body at Amherst, but it could find only one student worthy of support at Harvard.[7] The intention was clear: There must be but one Harvard. But who could be sure?

Latin and Greek were in trouble. Whether it was President John Wheelock at Dartmouth early in the nineteenth century getting no results from the commencement band when he announced "Musica expectatur" (and in exasperation shouting "Play up!") or the faculty at Kenyon in 1836 having trouble deciding whether it or the board of trustees possessed control over the pronunciation of Greek and Latin vowels, the evidence abounded that Latin and Greek did not have much to do with the directions in which American society appeared to be heading.[8]

Latin and Greek as language tools and the classics of ancient literature as influences in the political education of the Founding Fathers could not be denied. Clergymen still found them useful, and they had a role to perform as models for an age in which oratory and the formal essay were characteristic forms of communication and persuasion. In the South the classics were regarded with special favor because in ancient Rome and Greece the South found justification for itself and slavery.

Progress was not an idea in which the South believed; it held off all that the word meant for as long as it could. Elsewhere in the United States, however, progress was inescapable, and it visited upon the colleges an alarming bundle of movements and tendencies that undermined the traditional prestige of classical learning. The ancient languages and the classics did not lend themselves to egalitarianism: their usefulness, while demonstrable, was limited to a narrow class; they were well suited, on the other hand, to the purposes of the commonsense school of antiintellectualism that simply had little regard for books in the first place, let alone dead ones. Graduates of the colleges, the liberally educated gentlemen, were themselves losing political influence to the rising West and the urban immigrant. Students appeared in the colleges whose sense of their own futures did not include careers in the traditional professions; young men, in larger numbers, who recognized in the rise of wealthy self-made businessmen a new path to status did not appear in the colleges at all. Science—the very instrument of progress, the intellectual attitude that did not receive truth from the past but from inquiry in the present—

made an insistent claim for attention, at the expense of the ancient languages.[9]

The manner in which a college was to go about defining or redefining itself in the presence of all these currents of contemporary life was not obvious. What was Amherst to do about the ancient languages and sciences at a time when a quarter of its annual income was being supplied by the American Education Society?[10] How did a college satisfy the needs of prospective clergymen among the students, of temperamental aspiring scholars among the professors, and of determined democrats and utilitarians in the state legislature? Could Dartmouth College afford to ignore the complaint of Governor William Plummer that American colleges had traditionally been "more anxious to please the priesthood than to pursue a manly and expedient course to fit men for the business and duties of this world"?[11] Certainly there was evidence enough that the new governing classes were ignoring the colleges. As one Bostonian confided to a foreign resident in the city: "I have brought up my sons to become merchants and manufacturers; only Sam, the poor boy who is a little hard of hearing, and rather slow of comprehension, shall go to college."[12]

It was no wonder that "the eighteenth-century American college curriculum had been far more adventurous for its time than was the curriculum of the early nineteenth-century college."[13] There was a certain clarity of purpose in the eighteenth century—the training of a governing class—that could not so easily be adhered to in the nineteenth century. Until the American Revolution the colleges, for all of their difficult times and uncertainties, had not been defensive and nervous about their own legitimacy, but in the unsettled context of a dynamic new nation, they stumbled around in search of some secure identity, lost momentum in the process, and sometimes behaved quite as bizarrely as the trustees of Columbia College.

Yet some kind of an anchor, some sense of continuity with an honorable tradition, was possible, and while the rationalization of higher education in the United States proceeded, the classics themselves provided that anchor in the myth of Hercules, who, confronting Virtue and Vice, chose Virtue and thereby passed on through time from fifth-century B.C. Athens into nineteenth-century A.D. Princeton, where a representation of the myth adorned the diplomas of the

American Whig Society, one of the undergraduate literary societies. The myth of the choice of Hercules, James McLachlan has convincingly demonstrated, was capable of supporting old curricular purpose, while at the same time it addressed itself to student ideals and calmed the nerves of unsettled college authorities.[14] "While the multitude of mankind are grovelling in the Earth," one Princeton alumnus wrote to a nephew at the college in 1816, "convince them . . . that your wish is not to live for yourself alone, but for the benefit of Society, and for the glory of that divine being who hath created you, and endowed you with superior mental faculties, to the end that you might improve them for valuable and important purposes."[15] In other words, make the choice of Hercules!

The choice of Hercules, the choice for Virtue, was encouraged by the undergraduate literary societies, where members were emboldened to aspire to the life of a responsible and virtuous man of learning —the social reformer, the orator-writer-poet, the leader who knew what was best and acted accordingly. The eighteenth-century curriculum had adjusted itself to new learning in the support of just such an ideal; the American Revolution had been fought and won by college graduates who fulfilled that ideal. With it the colleges in the nineteenth century might borrow time, hold off the threat of democratic values to talent and virtue. With it they might succeed in justifying themselves to themselves and to society, too. The question of whether they could do so would be decided in part by what happened to the course of study.

The absence of system in the educational arrangements of the new republic was particularly apparent in college preparation. A student might arrive at college by a variety of roads—prepared by a resident tutor in the South or by the local clergyman in the North, in a private day school or a Latin grammar school, in the preparatory departments of the colleges themselves, or increasingly in multipurpose academies that provided a terminal general education as well as college preparation.[16] This diversity of preparation was a challenge to the college curriculum: It set limits on what it could be and also created demands for what it had to be.

The academy movement generated in the first half of the century an increase in the numbers seeking a college education, but in numbers there was a demand for a course of study that went beyond the traditional classical course. Diversity in college preparation also encouraged a wide age range and therefore degrees of maturity and different levels of expectation in regard to the course of study.

Where a college did not run its own preparatory department—a device for catching students young and funneling them into the college in various stages of preparation—the evidence supports the impression that a well-prepared student usually skipped the freshman year and entered as a sophomore. If a college preparatory school did a particularly notable job, as did the Round Hill School at Northampton, Massachusetts, it sent its graduates sometimes into the junior or senior year. Round Hill was too good a school to survive in a world dominated by low-grade colleges; after sending 291 graduates on to college between 1823 and 1831, 50 of them to Harvard, it closed in 1834.[17]

In 1829 the freshman class at Harvard was drawn from the usual mixed preparation: 36 percent from academies, 26 percent from private proprietary schools, 21 percent from Latin grammar schools, 10 percent from private tutors, and 5 percent from college preparatory departments of other colleges.[18] The mix varied from college to college, and from section to section, but the meaning for the curriculum was almost everywhere the same: a freshman year that was often repetitive and often of secondary school level; a course of study that could not rely on any standards, on any pattern of preparation. College authorities, defining their own course of study, learned to restrain their expectations in deference to the preparation of the students who came their way.

Of course, the colleges were to a large degree responsible for their own difficulties. They could not increase their own expectations toward those who entered and those who prepared them unless they could establish some standards for themselves. In a rash of overbuilding they denied themselves that possibility. Between 1630 and 1800 only 25 colleges were chartered; almost twice that number, 44, were chartered in the first three decades of the nineteenth century; exactly seven times that number, 175, were chartered between 1860 and 1870. There were many reasons for all these colleges. Denominational rivalry, state rivalry, community pride, and grandiose dreams created some of them. Eastern fear of a barbarian West without colleges accounted for others. In a country spread across a wide continent, the persistence of the idea of the college as a necessary source of leaders made college founding a geographical necessity, while the reluctance of legislatures to support generously existing state institutions licensed ambitious competitors.[19]

The proliferation of colleges surely encouraged intellectual ambition and aspiration in young men and women who could not hope to attend distant institutions. And there must have been benefits for the society as a whole, given its open class system, in a movement that prevented the monopolization of talent and resources by a few favored institutions. The colleges, moreover, were agencies of social cohesion, and in the nineteenth century the United States needed all the cohesion it could get.

Even so, there were too many colleges for the population and too few colleges offering a course of study that the college-age population either needed or wanted. In 1830 approximately 5,400 young men were enrolled in college, spread so thinly that it would be another thirty years before the oldest college in the country graduated a class of 100.[20] Contemporary analysts of the colleges' problems gathered statistics that demonstrated a declining percentage of the population going to college.[21] In this climate the college course of study, even if authorities did not know what to do about it, was vulnerable.

Science continued to make inroads on the old course of study and even found dramatic encouragement in altogether new institutions, but an enlarged domain for science as well as recognition of the modern languages were not achieved without great struggle and bitterness. The appointment of Benjamin Silliman as professor of chemistry, geology, and mineralogy at Yale in 1802 revolutionized the American outlook on science. He combined a masterful sense of showmanship, a skill at popularization, and a deep religious faith that were irresistible. His textbooks in chemistry and geology; the *American Journal of Science and Arts*, which he founded in 1818; and his extensive involvement in the lyceum movement helped to create a wider public audience for scientific subjects.[22]

Silliman was such a master of the lecture demonstration that a member of the Yale corporation asked him: "Is there not danger that with these physical attractions you will overtop the Latin and the

Greek?"[23] Indeed there was, although religion was thought to be safe
in his care. When Yale required chemistry of seniors in 1802, it was
being taught not as a medical or premedical subject but as an exposure to divine creation. When Union, inspired by Silliman's course at
Yale, made chemistry a senior requirement in 1807, the purpose was
the same.[24] Chemistry quickly made its way into the required curriculum elsewhere, in part because it had been certified and popularized at
Yale. But science in the colleges could not be rushed. The University
of Pennsylvania in 1816 organized a four-man "Faculty of Physical
Science and Rural Economy" for the purpose of teaching a program
that emphasized botany, natural history, geology, zoology, mineralogy, practical chemistry, comparative anatomy, and veterinary science. In the absence of demand, it was abolished in 1828.[25]

Science did best where it was most welcome and where it did not
need to wrestle with entrenched interests and traditions. In establishing a military academy at West Point in 1802, Congress created the
first technical college in the United States.[26] Cadets studied moral philosophy in their last year, but in hardly any other way did the West
Point course of study resemble the ordinary American college curriculum. Advanced mathematics, chemistry, engineering, drawing,
and French were central in this curriculum; cadets were sectioned for
instruction by ability; their assignments were often in advanced
European texts freshly translated by their academy instructors. In
1829 twenty-four cadets formed themselves into the American Association for the Promotion of Science, Literature, and the Arts, a direct
forerunner of the American Association for the Advancement of
Science.[27]

The Rensselaer Polytechnic Institute (R.P.I.), founded at Troy,
New York, in 1824, was a noncollegiate institution in style and purpose, but until higher education was ready to accommodate the kind
of instruction and research that went on there, R.P.I. was the center of
applied science in the United States. Stephen Van Rensselaer conceived of the school as one that would train teachers who would go
out into the rural schools to instruct "the sons and daughters of farmers and mechanics . . . in the application of experimental chemistry,
philosophy, and natural history, to agriculture, domestic economy,
the arts, and manufactures." Van Rensselaer anticipated the land-   ·
grant college by forty years, and his first senior professor, Amos

Eaton, proceeded to make the school a demonstration of innovative practices and subjects.

The first systematic field work, the first chemistry and physics laboratories for the instruction of students, the first course of study in engineering occurred not in an American college but in the high school-level scientific institute at Troy. In 1835 a well-prepared student could master the R.P.I. course in a year; a college graduate, arriving with some theoretical grounding, could earn an R.P.I. degree in twenty-four weeks.[28]

In their origins these institutions on the Hudson, the military college at West Point and the scientific school at Troy, owed something to European models. The emphasis on French at West Point was a tribute to French military science; the school at Troy bore the influence of Sir Benjamin Thompson, Count Rumford, who in 1800 in London had founded the "Royal Institution of Great Britain for the Promotion, Diffusion, and Extension of Science and Useful Knowledge." But both institutions revealed a characteristically American bias in their stress on the experimental and applied sciences in the service of a democratic people. The designers and builders of the country's canals and railroads were overwhelmingly graduates of the military academy at West Point, R.P.I., and Union College, the one traditional liberal arts college in the first half of the nineteenth century to make a thoroughly uncompromising and effective place for applied science in the course of study. These institutions also were changing the civil engineer in the United States from a product of training on the job to a professional formally instructed in an educational institution.[29]

The modern languages—French, German, Spanish, Italian—drew on no such great reserve of popular and practical interest as did the sciences.[30] More than anything else, what favored the modern languages was dislike of the ancient languages. Where parallel courses of study leading to degrees developed, the substitution of the modern languages for the ancient languages made the parallel courses both palatable enough to attract students and respectable enough to justify awarding a degree, although not the B.A. degree.

An argument of practicality was made for the modern languages: They were alive, they were the native languages of many Americans, they were useful in foreign travel and the conduct of business, and they opened the door to some of the world's great literature. Such considerations entered into the founding of a professorship in modern languages at Harvard in 1816. George Ticknor, "the first American by birth of outstanding personality and accomplishment to enter the modern language field," was appointed to the chair in 1817 and began instruction in 1819.[31] The modern languages at Harvard flourished under Ticknor's tutelage, if only numbers mattered. But Harvard did not make the modern languages a requirement—they existed by sufferance, as electives that students could take in order to avoid more of the ancient languages than they could stomach, and, for all of Ticknor's efforts and success, French, German, and Spanish lacked curricular prestige and were not taken seriously by the large number of students who enrolled in them.

To be a part of the modern world, to ease the inevitable shift from the ancient languages, a professorship of modern languages became a collegiate necessity. In 1827 the Princeton Alumni Association pledged itself to raise funds for a professorship of modern languages. In 1830 Henry Wadsworth Longfellow became the first professor of modern languages at Bowdoin. As characteristic as the founding of these professorships, however, was the experience of modern languages at Wesleyan and Dartmouth. Between 1838 and 1842 at Wesleyan a professor of modern languages offered courses that added to a student's program but did not substitute for any of the required courses; this arrangement made taking French burdensome, and the professor was let go in 1842. Student initiative led to instruction in French at Dartmouth as early as 1830, but French did not get into the Dartmouth catalogue until 1851, and not under a professor of modern languages until 1860. In 1841 the arrangements for modern languages at Yale, whose policies carried great weight elsewhere, were succinctly stated in the college catalogue: "Gentlemen well qualified to teach the modern languages are engaged by the Faculty to give instruction in these branches to those students who desire it, at their own expense." Such instruction could be used for credit only by juniors who might substitute it for Plato's *Gorgias* or fluxions (differential calculus).[32]

If science was being advanced and required as essential to living in the modern world, no argument of indispensability came to the support of the modern languages. In the first half of the nineteenth century their professional usefulness was recognized only by the military and by civil engineers. They collided also with a certain national disdain for the foreign and a preference for things American. A people in the process of creating its own language and literature was not the most reliable sponsor of the study of foreign languages.

Inevitably, for a while anyway, the future of the American college, a definition of what should be going on there, and a stable sense of the curriculum would have to be determined by Yale. Harvard not only slipped away from the norm, whatever it was, first; it was absolutely uncomfortable doing the same as all the others. Tutors specialized at Harvard as early as 1767; they did not specialize at Yale until 1830.[33] Unitarians took over Harvard; the threat to Yale was from the Anglican right. Basil Hall, an Englishman traveling in the United States in 1827 and 1828, liked what he found in New Haven: "It was extremely agreeable to see so many good old usages and orthodox notions kept up as vigorously . . . as possible. . . . Every thing that came under my notice, seemed judiciously regulated."[34]

Hall's approval was widely shared. In 1829 Yale had the largest enrollment, the widest geographical distribution, and the largest living alumni roll of any of the American colleges. Of the seventy-five American colleges in existence in 1840, thirty-six were presided over by Yale graduates and another twenty-two by graduates of Princeton.[35] For most of its history Princeton had been much like Yale, only more so.

In 1828 the Yale course of study may have been as stable a statement of values and purpose as could be found anywhere in the United States. The Yale curriculum by then lacked some of the spontaneity that had characterized it in the century or so in which it had been developing; it represented, however, an honest and deep sense of commitment to where it had arrived. Yale did not see itself as accidental; it thought itself still in charge and acted accordingly. The Yale College catalogue for 1828 required but a page in which to reveal itself, about 199 fewer than would be required a century and a quarter later.[36] On that page were both a description of the Yale course of study for the forthcoming year and a summation of almost 200 years of American curricular history.

During the first three years Yale students took courses mostly in

Greek, Latin, and mathematics, but they also studied geography, history, science, astronomy, English grammar, and rhetoric. The senior year was a time for large questions and, to some extent, a final process of refinement: moral philosophy and metaphysics, English composition, and belles lettres. Each class experienced something special: Freshmen translated from the Latin, as if to prove that they had been fit to be admitted; sophomores and juniors were instructed in English composition; juniors received lecture demonstrations in experimental physics; seniors went out into the world with the most recent understanding of chemistry, mineralogy, geology, and theoretical physics. Juniors and seniors debated; all classes declaimed, were instructed by the professor of rhetoric and oratory, and heard lectures from the professor of ancient languages. The practice of curricular options had arrived: French in 1825—and, then later, Anglo-Saxon in 1839 and German in 1841. These noncredit options, simply courses available for those who thought that they mattered, were clearly unsatisfactory from the view of the students, but alarming from the view of the authorities. The arrival of Anglo-Saxon as an option prompted Yale's president, Jeremiah Day, to sigh: "It might soon be necessary to appoint an instructor in *whittling*."[37]

This curriculum and the practices that supported it prompted the students of Yale into ill-conceived adolescent rebellion in 1825 and the Connecticut legislature into the writing of a report critical of the impracticality and unprogressive nature of the curriculum.[38] The students appeared to be objecting to the style, the legislature to the content, but the Yale corporation took them both seriously, and on September 11, 1827, it appointed a committee of the corporation "to inquire into the expediency of so altering the regular course of instruction in this college, as to leave out of said course the study of the *dead languages*, substituting other studies therefor: and either requiring a competent knowledge of said languages, as a condition of admittance into the college, or providing instruction in the same, for such as shall choose to study them after admittance."[39] In April 1828, the corporation committee referred the resolution to the Yale faculty for an expression of opinion. With the concerned and sensitive and talented leadership of President Day and Professor James L. Kingsley, the Yale faculty prepared a report in two parts, "one containing a summary view of the plan of education in the college; the other, an inquiry into the expediency of insisting on the study of the ancient languages."[40]

Published separately in 1828 and in Silliman's *American Journal of Science and Arts* in 1829, the report was widely distributed and widely read. The first section, an exposition and explication of "the plan of education in the college," was prepared by President Day; the second section, attributed to Professor Kingsley, confronted the question of the future of the ancient languages at Yale; a final section, by Governor Gideon Tomlinson for the Yale corporation, confirmed the faculty's position as its own. The Yale Report, as it came to be known, provided a rationale and a focus for comprehending a course of study that was wandering somewhere in the no-man's land between inflexibility and disintegration. Henceforth the American college curriculum could not be understood without reference to this first major effort to spell out both a philosophy and the particulars of an American system of higher education.

President Day began by conceding a certain legitimacy to the enemy. Of course, he said, improvement is called for. The colleges must be sensitive to the needs and nature of the society they serve. They should know what is going on in the universities of Europe. But, he continued, the charge that the colleges were impervious to change was malicious and contrary to evidence. Even recent graduates returning to the campus expressed surprise at the changes they found, not only within courses and in methods of instruction but also in the arrival of entirely new subjects in the curriculum. Returning Yale alumni discovered more demanding admissions requirements than they themselves would have been able to meet.[41]

Whether to throw out the whole course, hold to it, or incorporate change gradually was not, Day argued, the question with which an inquiry on the college curriculum should begin. The first question should elicit a philosophy, a rationale. In the absence of the question, Day himself asked it: "What . . . is the appropriate object of a college?"[42] His answer, which took twenty-three more pages of the report, began:

> Its object is to lay the foundation of a superior education
> . . . at a period of life when a substitute must be provided
> for *parental superintendence*. The groundwork of a

thorough education must be broad, and deep, and solid.
. . . The two great points to be gained in intellectual culture, are the *discipline* and the *furniture* of the mind;
expanding its powers, and storing it with knowledge. . . . A
commanding object, therefore, in a collegiate course,
should be, to call into daily and vigorous exercise the faculties of the student.[43]

Day then proceeded to spell out in particulars where the prevailing educational philosophy and psychology had taken Yale and, per-
force, all American colleges. The mind as muscles with inherent
capacities required a variety of educational experiences. "In laying
the foundation of a thorough education," he argued, " it is necessary
that *all* the important mental faculties be brought into exercise."

If the student exercises his reasoning powers only, he will
be deficient in imagination and taste, in fervid and impressive eloquence. If he confines his attention to demonstra-
tive evidence, he will be unfitted to decide correctly, in
cases of probability. If he relies principally on his memory,
his powers of invention will be impaired by disuse. In the
course of instruction in this college, it has been an object to
maintain   such   a   proportion   between   the   different
branches of literature and science, as to form in the student
a proper *balance* of character.[44]

The uneducated democrat in the Connecticut legislature was
not impressed; a twentieth-century psychologist would be appalled;
even a Yale senior at the time might have demurred. But the faculty
psychology with which Day justified the Yale curriculum, subject by
subject, was the conventional wisdom of its time. In defining the road
to mental discipline, it took the reasonable position that training,
habit, routine, and plain hard work were sources of intellectual vigor.
In each subject inhered a special promise. Mathematics: demonstra-
tive reasoning. Physical sciences: facts, induction, probable evidence.
Ancient literature: taste. English reading: speaking and writing.
Logic and mental philosophy: thinking. Rhetoric and oratory:
speaking. Composition: copiousness, accuracy of expression. Extem-

poraneous discussion: promptness, fluency, animation.[45] Holding these skills together was a profound commitment to the idea that "eloquence and solid learning should go together." Day asked, "To what purpose has a man become deeply learned, if he has no faculty of communicating his knowledge? And of what use is a display of rhetorical elegance, from one who knows little or nothing which is worth communicating?" His answer was a resounding "Est enim scientia comprehendenda rerum plurimarum, sine qua verborum volubilitas inanis atque irredenta est."[46]

Day's concept of the role of the curriculum was anything but narrow. He asked that it "throw the student upon the *resources of his own mind.*" He was not excessively demanding in his expectations of what the curriculum could accomplish: "The scholar must form himself, by his own exertions. . . . A college . . . can do little more than stimulate and aid his personal efforts." He recognized the student as an unfinished quantity that somehow had to be brought to some sense of synthesis and analysis, some acquaintance with the wisdom of the ages, some command of his faculties; pushed, even, or enticed to the creative exercise of his imagination.[47] The faculty could only do so much.

And they were not doing nearly as badly as portrayed by their detractors. In his consideration of teaching methods Day applauded the use of lectures in imparting new knowledge, fanning the interest of students, and conducting scientific experiments, but he acknowledged that "they do not always bring upon the student a pressing and definite responsibility. He may repose upon his seat, and yield a passive hearing . . . without ever calling into exercise the active powers of his own mind." He defended daily recitations as the most effective means of securing the students' "steady and earnest efforts," and he defended the use of a single textbook over reading in a half dozen different books as being less likely to confuse students or furnish them with an excuse for sloppy thinking.[48]

Other arrangements of the curriculum, moreover, provided intellectual opportunities of an order different from the memorization and usually elementary study called for by recitations. In writing essays and participating in debates students experienced a deeper investigation of particular subjects than daily recitations allowed; semiannual examinations for all classes and the annual examination of the seniors occupied Yale students for twelve to fourteen days of "unceasing and strenuous exercise of the intellectual powers." And the division of the faculty into wise and knowledgeable professors and young but enthusiastic tutors created an environment in which expertness, affection, and parental concern combined to encourage in the students a seriousness toward the curriculum.[49]

Having defined the course of study appropriate for a college, Day then directed his attention to all the noncollegiate educational purposes that Yale refused to confound with its own undergraduate purposes—professional education, which it would provide in separate medical, law, and theological schools but not as programs in the college; formal education appropriate to careers in business, engineering, and agriculture, which were better prepared for on the job; university education, for which it lacked the resources; and a partial course program of essentially scientific courses, for which it lacked a philosophical justification.[50]

Yale College could not and would not try to do everything. Conscious of its own failings, it would attempt to improve the quality of what it did the best way it knew how: by raising admissions standards.[51] It would not be deflected from its essential obligation to the student: "The object is not to *finish* his education; but to lay the foundation. . . . If he acquires here a thorough knowledge of the principles of science, he may then, in a great measure, educate himself. He has, at least, been taught *how* to learn."[52] Yale's commitment could not be to everything and everyone: "Men of mere practical detail are wanted, in considerable numbers, to fill the subordinate places in mechanical establishments; but the higher stations require enlightened and comprehensive views."[53] Young men who could fill those higher stations were the college's special concern. For them "our prescribed course contains those subjects only which ought to be understood, as we think, by every one who aims at a thorough education."[54]

Day's tone and posture were neither defiant nor unbending. He would welcome changes adapted from the experience of European universities "as are suited to our peculiar situation and character."[55] If admissions standards could be raised, thus pushing down into the schools much of the elementary work of the college, the more advanced work of the college years could be put on an elective basis, permitting students to follow their tastes and peculiar capacities more than was possible in a prescribed course.[56] He asked that serious attention be given to upgrading the work of all the components of a young man's educational experience so as to make possible before the age of eighteen study "of all which is now required for admission into the college, in addition to the course [now] prescribed for the undergraduates," to be followed by three years of professional study.[57] He had no quarrel with the work of the high schools, academies, and lyceums; he described them as "valuable institutions" with curricular purposes of their own.[58]

In the end, Jeremiah Day's summary view of the college course was a plea for quality. Conscious of the democratic pressures against a thorough education and the readiness with which a shallow education could be translated into social and economic mobility, he was uneasy about the prospects of a nation at the mercy of superficially educated demagogues and uncouth millionaires.[59] Day saw Yale and the rest of the colleges as the ramparts of a free people.

To Professor Kingsley he left the defense of the ancient languages, those fundamental bastions with which the colleges had long identified themselves and their purposes. The professor was uncompromising. A college education without the classics was not a college education.[60] Who would think of omitting mathematics from the course of study simply because it was of no practical future use? Besides, mathematics was practical, as were the classics. No significant body of European literature could be discussed intelligently without a knowledge of classical learning; no sounder models of taste and merit existed outside the classics. To attempt a professional career without them, although possible, was to invite a life of inferiority: "The mere divine, the mere lawyer, or the mere physician, however well informed he may be in his particular profession, has less chance of success, than if his early education had been of a more liberal character."[61]

The ultimate strength of the classics, as it had to be argued in a report preceded by Jeremiah Day's masterful rationalization of the college course, was their superb effectiveness in strengthening and enlarging the mental faculties. "Study of the classics," Kingsley stated, "forms the most effectual discipline of the mental faculties. . . . Every faculty of the mind is employed."[62] As for the modern languages, they could not really be thought of in the same context or with the same seriousness: "Modern languages, with most of our students, are studied, and will continue to be studied, as an accomplishment, rather than as a necessary acquisition."[63]

President Day and Professor Kingsley left to Governor Tomlinson of the corporation the opportunity to use the report as an occasion to take high ground, and he took it. "The models of ancient literature, which are put into the hands of the young student," he claimed, "can hardly fail to imbue his mind with the principles of liberty; to inspire the liveliest patriotism, and to excite to noble and generous action. . . . The single consideration that divine truth was communicated to man in the ancient languages, ought to put this question at rest, and give to them perpetuity."[64] The committee of the corporation, therefore, had come "to the conclusion that it is inexpedient so to alter the regular course of instruction, at this college, as to leave out of the same, the study of the ancient languages," but it was ready to entertain, if the faculty should care to make it, a proposal to raise admission requirements in Latin and Greek.[65]

The report was widely read and just as widely heeded. It echoed across the land. Soon college audiences and the readers of leading journals of opinion could not avoid it if they would. Daniel D. Barnard gave an address at Williams College in 1831 that sounded like a skillful paraphrase. Alpheus Crosby in 1833 agreed with Professor Kingsley's claim that classical study was "best fitted to enlarge, discipline, and mature the whole mind."[66] Three essays in the *New-England Magazine* in 1833 admitted to substantial agreement with the Yale Report: "On most points . . . we consider the sentiments of the committee correct, their illustrations satisfactory, and their reasonings conclusive. And such we presume is the general opinion." The one point on which the author disagreed—"the *necessity* of a knowledge of Greek and Latin as an *element of a liberal education*"— immediately created a chasm between Boston and New Haven that could not be crossed. The *New-England Magazine* articles were an inspired expression of transcendental thought and a fulsome attack on the ancient languages.[67] Their influence, like that of transcendentalism itself, was probably limited to a small portion of eastern Massachusetts and the intellectual community centering around Boston and Harvard College.

When Middlebury College opened in 1839 the inaugural

addresses were a tribute to the strength of Yale. The classics, declared Professor Solomon Stoddard, "improve the memory, strengthen the judgment, refine the taste, give discrimination and point to the discerning faculty, confer habits of attention, reasoning, and analysis— in short, they exercise and cultivate all the intellectual powers." On the same occasion Professor John Hough provided a similar assurance: The classics "invigorate and enlarge the understanding, sharpen the powers of discrimination, chasten the taste, and elevate, refine and ennoble all the faculties of the mind."[68] They were not quoting each other. They had unquestionably read the Yale Report.

The influence of Yale on the course of study of other colleges was often direct and transparent. The 1836 inaugural address of the Reverend Elihu Baldwin, Yale, class of 1812, as president of Wabash was an echo of the Yale Report. Western Reserve adopted a curriculum avowedly in order to be "the Yale of the West"; a similar intention was claimed by the Yale men who founded Illinois College. In the South Yale-educated presidents and professors, with the help of like-minded graduates of Princeton, held southern colleges to the curricular faith as propounded in New Haven and staved off any effective influence from the innovative university launched at Charlottesville, Virginia, during the last years of Thomas Jefferson.[69] In 1854 the University of Alabama issued a report that had good reason to sound like the Yale Report of 1828: Its president, Frederick A. P. Barnard, had been a member of the Yale corporation that year. As late as 1860 the power of Yale was asserting itself on the Pacific coast, where the College of California opened with a course of study that required French and Spanish in the freshman and sophomore years; Sherman Day, a trustee and son of Jeremiah Day, protested, and the intruding languages were relocated—French into the sophomore year, Spanish into the senior year as an elective.[70] Sherman Day asserted his power for a while; the name, the Yale connection, subsidized his swagger; but was there any question about whether the ancient languages could experience revitalization in California? As foolish a conjecture as imagining that the Puritans had landed somewhere in the neighborhood of San Diego!

The Yale Report of 1828 may have been the last chance for the American *college*. It offered a rationale, even proposed certain actions —raising admissions requirements, invigorating the secondary schools, indulging in university activities if properly funded—but there was no way to keep it from being misconstrued as a defense of a fixed and fading moment in the history of the American people.

The college that Jeremiah Day and his supporters were trying to define and refine found itself in a most trying and embarrassing way in competition with the country itself. The emphasis of the report on the college as an environment for furnishing the mind with potentially useful and retrievable facts ran up against life itself. Without benefit of college at all, the likes of Benjamin Franklin and Andrew Jackson and later Abraham Lincoln suggested that the United States was a free furniture store. And it was not yet clear which furniture would be most useful. The curriculum, for all of Jeremiah Day's sympathies for creative impulse and the imagination, was more effective in suppressing the imagination than in encouraging it.[71] The Yale people said that they were not against new knowledge, new subjects. "As knowledge varies, education should vary with it," Professor Kingsley wrote in his part of the report.[72] He cannot be believed now; why should anyone have believed him then? The attachment of the Yale faculty and the Yale corporation to the psychology of mental faculties meant that they had too little room for the empirical, imaginative, even disturbing news that was erupting out of human experience and the observations of an arrogant school of American philosophy. The *New-England Magazine* in effect asked who the Yale professors thought they were fooling when they said that for taste people needed Latin and Greek: "Females excel in all sorts of taste, without any knowledge of ancient literature."[73]

The word was getting around: Man could be in charge if he would get out from under the authority, the traditions, the institutional arrangements that had held him in moral and intellectual, if not physical, slavery. There were those who thought that it was for this purpose that the American nation had been created. Jeremiah Day himself may have been one of them, yet history has cast him on the other side, so ambiguous have been the characteristics by which Americans have distinguished between freedom and slavery.

The Yale Report may have helped small denominational colleges in the provinces to justify their narrow outlook to grateful neighborhoods; it may have provided a veneer of educational philosophy to what in many places was a psychology of poverty. Very often, the curriculum was not what historians have said it was; the Yale Report allowed educational philosophy to be attached to what often was simply institutional poverty. At Yale the report was an assertion of self-respect: The business of Yale was the humanist tradition and the liberal arts; the report was not so much a call to arms as a kind of last gesture, a summoning of energy and purity and clarity of purpose appropriate to a tribe on the edge of extinction.

The colleges did promote "an ethos . . . uncharacteristic of the larger society." They shared with the upper class "alarm over rapid social and intellectual change." They may even have dug in their heels, courted unpopularity, and chosen "integrity at the price of a reduced influence." The classical course as rationalized in the Yale Report may have been designed to support "the maintenance of a numerically tiny social elite against the hostile pressure of a rising Jacksonian equalitarianism."[74] Certainly the tone of Jeremiah Day's statement of support for the classical curriculum was contrary to the buoyant, optimistic expansiveness of the age.[75]

The Yale Report argued persuasively for the importance of imagination—even to the point of asserting that "the sublimest efforts of genius consist in the creations of the imagination, the discoveries of the intellect, the conquests by which the dominions of science are extended"—and then the imagination of Jeremiah Day and the Yale corporation failed.[76] They embraced the uses of the past, but they withdrew from the uncertainties of the future. Trapped, perhaps even imprisoned, by the social and economic environment in which they had been reared, the authors of the Yale Report confronted the college course of study within a psychological framework that allowed them little room for imagination. Their respect for quality, for standards, for certain enduring definitions of human worth, was class bound. They were blinded to much that was insistent and already out of control in American life. The Yale Report was an effort to apply the brakes to a country that was showing how to exploit everything and everybody but that had not yet learned how to harness human wisdom. It was not enough.

The effort to devise an American alternative to the classical college engaged some of the country's greatest talents in the decades before the Civil War. Some of the curricular arrangements to which they lent their imaginations made good sense but were premature. One perhaps was essentially eccentric, even if it was the University of Virginia according to Thomas Jefferson. Most were modest accommodations, respectable subversions of the classical course of study. One—Union College under Eliphalet Nott—was a brilliant success.

The inspiration for reform at Harvard in the 1820s was the arrival on the faculty of four young instructors, fresh from study at German universities, among the first Americans to be exposed to the German university experience. The occasion for reform was the aftermath of a student riot in 1823 that resulted in over half the senior class being expelled almost on the eve of commencement and that stirred an already hostile state legislature. Of the four—George Ticknor, George Bancroft, Edward Everett, and Joseph Cogswell— Ticknor was the most persevering and the most effective. Bancroft, on the other hand, gave an inspired demonstration of how not to reform a college; he spent the year 1822–23 covering as much ground in his Greek classes as was normally covered in three years, thereby earning the disfavor of students and faculty alike.[77]

Ticknor, who in 1819 had taken up the professorship of modern languages after his studies in Germany, was appalled at the contrast between the prevailing absence of standards and intellectual vitality at Harvard and the energetic pursuit of learning characteristic of the German universities. Under President John T. Kirkland, 1810–1828, Harvard had met the problem presented by the old prescribed curriculum and the challenge of new learning and new interests by adding new professorships and grafting a series of required nonexamined lectures on the new subjects onto the old course. This was a formula for making the curriculum increasingly superficial, a policy deliberately rejected by Yale. Ticknor's solution was to urge the adoption of the principle of voluntary or elective studies, as he had experienced it in Germany, where university students took only those courses they wanted to. His scheme for reorganizing instruction at Harvard called for elective courses beyond the prescribed curriculum, adding tutorials and a syllabus to lecture courses, grouping students by ability, the creation of departments, the development of a graduate school for advanced work, a policy of more searching questioning by instructors, and the admission of students as nondegree candidates.

Adopted in 1825 by the corporation, these proposals represented an imaginative effort to confront the paralysis that had overtaken the college curriculum, a paralysis for which the only remedy had seemed to be the endless addition of new courses, new lectures, new materials to the old course, a remedy that weakened the curriculum as it tried to strengthen it. The Harvard reforms of 1825 failed because the faculty, except for Ticknor, had no intention of moving in the directions in which Ticknor and the corporation had pointed them. Ticknor was delighted at the results when 227 of a possible 240 students elected instruction in modern languages, were divided by proficiency into sections, and then moved through a sequence of lectures, conference sections, and readings. When the year ended, Ticknor's fastest freshman was 500 pages ahead of his slowest. But most of the faculty sabotaged the reforms as best they could and found a model in their colleague who made a great display of dividing the class and then assigning identical lessons.[78] President Kirkland himself was less than sanguine about the reforms; to one of the professors he remarked, "They want to legislate that professors shall be amiable, tutors popular, and students loving."[79]

All the reforms of 1825 cast a long shadow across the future, but none of them was as crucial as the adoption of the recommendation of an overseers' committee that "separate departments . . . arranged as to embrace . . . studies of an analogous and connected nature" be created, with the professors in charge of each department possessed with authority to nominate appointees and to supervise and control instruction.[80] The overseers' action of 1825 created the first departments of instruction in an American college and placed the faculty in a position of effective control over the curriculum. The Harvard professors did not yet have control over appointments; control over both the curriculum and appointments would place the faculty in the position of being an ultimate determinant of what a college education was. In time, at Harvard and elsewhere, they would achieve such power.

Ticknor gave support to the reforms and argued for their extension in a pamphlet published in 1825; it cannot be said that his *Remarks on Changes Lately Proposed or Adopted in Harvard University* carried the day in Cambridge, but it hit the mark in New Haven, where Professor Kingsley in the Yale Report quoted from it in his effort to refute the especially grating question: "Who, in this country, by means here offered him, has been enabled to make himself a good Greek scholar?"[81]

When Josiah Quincy was elected president of Harvard in 1829, he visited New Haven, where he was convinced of the soundness of the Yale position. One early result was a more demanding classical curriculum at a time when Harvard was being pressed to be more utilitarian and more democratic. Quincy's efforts to make Harvard, like Yale, a model classical college so adversely affected enrollments that by 1835 a solution to the problem of numbers had to be found in the recruiting of special students, probationary admissions, and remedial sections.[82] Refusing to put Harvard on the road to utter utilitarianism as a means of overcoming the unpopularity of its classical course, Quincy turned toward the concept of Harvard as a college from which a university might one day emerge and away from the implications of Professor Jacob Bigelow's dictum: "Whatever the majority of the people desire to know, seminaries must sooner or later teach."[83]

For five or six years after 1835, at the instigation of German-trained professors who did not want to teach lazy or uninterested students, mathematics, Latin, Greek, and English were made optional after the freshman year. The impulse for this attack on the prescribed curriculum came from elitist, professionally oriented professors who shared Quincy's unwillingness to shift Harvard College from a classical to a utilitarian model. Benjamin Pierce's proposals for a two-year trial of an elective program in mathematics, adopted by the corporation in 1838, were an admission, however, that the college curriculum, even Harvard's, must accommodate itself to a variety of demands—the utilitarian, the democratic, and the professional. Pierce's elective program offered Harvard students a choice among a one-year practical course in mathematics, a one-year theoretical course for potential teachers in the schools, and a three-year course for prospective mathematicians.[84]

This clear offering of electives as well as the beginning of a serious sense of professional self-consciousness on the part of the professors were signs that Harvard was being moved toward the preparation of specialists and that students were beginning to be left to organize their own course of study, at the cost of the values that Jeremiah Day had celebrated in 1828. By 1843 virtually all courses beyond the freshman year were offered on an elective basis, but the university builders had pushed their colleagues too far. A reaction against the elective principle set in that year and was not reversed until the presidency of Charles William Eliot, who needed until 1883 to get Harvard to where it had been in 1843.

In the meantime individual members of the faculty shoved the college forward to a university style. In 1842 Asa Gray accepted a professorship in botany with limited classroom obligations. His colleague in American history, Jared Sparks, had insisted as conditions of his accepting his professorship that he be free from teaching eight months a year and that he be allowed to do away with recitations altogether. Ticknor's successor in modern languages, Henry Wadsworth Longfellow, registered in his journal in 1838 a point of view that would increasingly represent the attitude of Harvard professors toward Harvard students: "This having your mind constantly a playmate for boys—constantly adapting itself to them; instead of stretching out, and grappling with men's minds."[85]

In environments as different as Nashville in Tennessee, Burlington in Vermont, and the city of New York, three efforts to come to grips with the apparent lack of harmony between the curriculum and society were attempted and failed. Philip Lindsley, the brilliant and dynamic president of the University of Nashville between 1824 and 1850, turned down a dozen college presidencies, including Princeton, in order to create on the Tennessee frontier a model American university—nondenominational, both utilitarian and scholarly, and gargantuan in its appetite for growth and meeting new needs, "growing, advancing, enlarging, accumulating till the end of time." His dream was not faulty; the neighborhood was. When Lindsley went to Nashville in 1824 there was no college within 200 miles; by 1848, there were thirty, nine of them within 50 miles.[86]

Between 1826 and 1833 James Marsh, something of a curiosity by virtue of being a transcendentalist college president, undertook to reinvigorate the ailing University of Vermont with a thorough overhauling: He introduced the partial course plan and electives to supplement the prescribed course; he reduced the reliance of the college on textbooks and petty discipline, substituting a Socratic method in teaching and an appeal to moral principle in discipline; he divided the faculty into four departments and allowed students to take courses in one or more departments as they chose; students were sectioned by ability and progress, the division of the college into four classes was abolished; and term examinations and an annual comprehensive examination were developed as an incitement to scholarship and as a replacement for the regimen of recitation from texts. Marsh made a respectable knowledge of one modern language a requirement for all degree candidates, and, although his aim was to make the college useful to poor Vermont farm boys with such arrangements as the partial course and the sectioning of courses by progress, he did not allow the substitution of modern for ancient languages in degree requirements.[87] He was adamant in his support of the classics: "A degree would soon mean nothing at all. . . . If degrees are to be given as sureties of scholarship of a determinate kind, it is all-important that they mean alike."[88] Vermont was not ready for a college, let alone a university, that could depart from the ancient model and succeed. It sometimes seemed in the 1820s and 1830s that failure was a certain prospect for any curriculum that held to the past and for any curriculum that dared to move off dead center.

A similar fate was in store for the University of the City of New York, which opened in 1832 and which would eventually become New York University. Perhaps the most notable aspect of the beginnings of the new institution in New York was the opportunity it gave the new republic to demonstrate that it possessed a distinguished intellectual community.[89] The gathering in New York in 1830 of an eminent group of intellectuals was in part a reaction to the Yale Report: The men assembled there were not willing to acquiesce in Jeremiah Day's postponement of the American university, and the University of the City of New York was to some extent a demonstration of will on their part. The discussions that October in the Common Council Chamber of the City of New York brought together such notables as Albert Gallatin, Benjamin Silliman, Theodore Dwight Woolsey, Frances Leiber, James Marsh, Henry Vethake, Henry Dwight, and Jared Sparks. They did not get the university they thought was germinating in New York that week, although for a while it looked as if they might. The university introduced a program of graduate instruction leading to an earned M.A. degree in 1835. A beautiful gesture, really, but in 1835 an earned M.A. had no more value than the routine unearned M.A. awarded to holders of the B.A.

who applied for it three years after their graduation.[90] There was not a position in the United States that had any use for the M.A. Before long the University of the City of New York was indistinguishable from other classical colleges of Presbyterian inclination.

The University of Virginia at least had on its side perhaps the first, and perhaps the last, Renaissance American. The role of Thomas Jefferson in founding the university tipped the weight of history in its favor, but it did not make its curriculum a model that was widely copied. From Benjamin Franklin through Thomas Jefferson to Abraham Lincoln, and then on to Harry Truman, is one route to an understanding of the Americans. Jefferson created a university; the others lent themselves to a folklore that did not require one. While the curriculum and style with which Jefferson launched his university were eccentric enough to assure them of importance as historical curiosities, they were not the stuff of which a curricular movement could be made. A university that opened with a staff of eight professors but no professor of divinity was clearly an extension of the Jeffersonian philosophy, but it did not fulfill any generally accepted expectation of what a college was. The division of the curriculum into eight schools, each headed by a professor and designed to expand indefinitely as funds allowed and to differentiate itself into departments as staffing permitted, was an imaginative blueprint for accommodating university expansion.[91] The time and the place were wrong; the university was put together at a cost greater than all the funds raised by Yale in its entire history, but a university could not be made to grow in indifferent soil.[92] Jefferson's eight schools—ancient languages, modern languages, mathematics, natural philosophy, natural history, anatomy and medicine, moral philosophy, and law —plus the three schools of commerce, manufacture, and diplomacy, which were missing only because of lack of funds—constituted a design for a university at a time when the country had not yet come to grips with what a college was. His rationale clearly revealed that he understood the difference between an American college as then constituted and a continental university; his plans for the University of Virginia were a curious blending of both, the paternalism of the former combining with the freedom of the latter to place the best sons of Virginia in small apartments in watchful proximity to their professors' residences, while each student was "free to attend the schools of his choice, and no other than he chooses."[93]

Jefferson's imaginative use of architecture as an expression of curricular purpose—each school in a pavilion of its own, each pavilion a cluster of lecture rooms and professors' residences, each pavilion inspired architecturally by a different classical order; the freedom of every student to take as little or as much as he wished; the abolition of such designations as freshmen and sophomores; the awarding of diplomas by the individual schools—a student might manage eight diplomas from the University of Virginia—but a refusal to award degrees: Here was a design as fascinating as Monticello, but it was light-years beyond the imagination of most of Jefferson's contemporaries.

The great virtue of the University of Virginia system was its outright attack on both superficiality and compulsion; Jeremiah Day defended Yale from superficiality by holding to compulsion; Josiah Quincy and his colleagues at Harvard defended themselves from the charge of excessive superficiality, for a while, by reducing the element of compulsion in the course of study. Virginia confronted the dilemma head on and rid itself of both. A combination of election and prescription within each of the schools assured a decent level of intellectual performance: A student was free to pick any school, but within the school there were course requirements for the diploma.

The University of Virginia was so far out of step with existing practices and needs that by 1831 it had capitulated to tradition and was offering a degree for successful completion of work in the schools of ancient languages, mathematics, natural philosophy, chemistry, and moral philosophy—the subjects covered in the normal course of study elsewhere. But even in retreating the university asserted its individuality: It thought well enough of itself to award the M.A. degree instead of the traditional B.A.[94]

In the years before the Civil War the University of Virginia fascinated reformers—Ticknor, Lindsley, and Francis Wayland at Brown among them—but even the elective freedom that it espoused spread in the colleges for reasons other than influence emanating from Charlottesville.[95] The fundamental law that established the University of Missouri in 1839 was a pretentious elaboration of Jefferson's design for Virginia, but it was soon recognized as unworkable and was off the statute books by 1843. Virginia was rediscovered after the Civil War as a model for rebuilding higher education in the South and as an aspect of university development in the North, but by then many other forces were at work in reshaping the American college curriculum.[96] The trouble with Virginia was that it was a place that abolished Christmas recess, but where the students absented themselves anyway and where the professors announced in retaliation that in any case their lectures would be considered as having been delivered and the students would be so examined.[97] No place so oriented could extend its influence far. Oberlin in Ohio provided another demonstration of the limits of innovative eccentricity; coeducation, the admission of blacks, a professorship of music as early as 1835, and an emphasis on Hebrew at the expense of pagan Greek and Latin were some of Oberlin's peculiarities; they were not contagious.[98]

Most colleges in the decades before the Civil War found themselves drifting into certain practices intended to hold themselves and the curriculum together—electives, options, partial courses, parallel courses. Since survival was always on their minds, college authorities were not purists about the course of study. Ticknor, Marsh, Lindsley, Jefferson, and a few others were allowed a stage on which to dramatize some of the needs and opportunities with which higher education was confronted. At Amherst Jacob Abbott and his faculty colleagues in 1827 were likewise encouraged by the trustees to develop a parallel course of study that would have excluded Latin and Greek and substituted French, Spanish, German, and Italian; English literature, agricultural chemistry, engineering, architecture, and pure and applied physics; American political and religious history and the American Constitution.

The proposed parallel course retained such traditional subjects as moral and intellectual philosophy, oratory, and rhetoric. The trustees were unable to find the funds with which to support the entire program, but they did publish the faculty report in which it was proposed: a curious pamphlet, an 1827 description of what many a student's course of study would look like a hundred years later. The Amherst experience was instructive: The faculty possessed the imagination to design a coherent curriculum without Latin or Greek for which it proposed to give the B.A. degree, but the institution lacked the will and the means to give it a respectable try. Like more substantial efforts elsewhere, the Amherst plan demonstrated that in most places reform before the Civil War was going to be incremental but not revolutionary.[99]

Since keeping knowledge out of the course of study was a sure way of keeping students out of the colleges, the simplest method, and the one most widely practiced, for accommodating new subjects was to welcome them, tuck them into the required course here and there, make them optional when they piled up embarrassingly, and package them as electives, sometimes as pairs, sometimes as alternatives to Latin or Greek. Places such as Williams experienced a gradual whittling away of the old curriculum. French, which in 1828 was lumped with Hebrew and fluxions (differential calculus) as a one-term option in junior year, was on its way to becoming a requirement; German appeared as an option in 1846; in 1843 a term in junior year was devoted to American history.[100]

The practice of including peripheral lectures on the new subjects was another way of keeping abreast while falling behind, for falling behind clearly could not be avoided if the colleges insisted on holding on to the old course while adding on to it. At a time when depth in study and understanding was a common concern of the reformers, the vast majority of the colleges were edging toward greater superficiality and toward a confrontation that they were trying desperately to avoid: a confrontation with a whole set of inherited truths —a college course can contain everything a student needs to know, college authorities know best what that is, a student's special aptitudes and interests are a poor guide to what he should study, the mind is a set of muscles with inherent faculties that can be trained only by a demanding course in ancient languages and mathematics. Electives conceived of as freedom for students to choose what they would overwhelmed the curriculum only after such a confrontation, after the curriculum collapsed of its own superficiality and inability to sustain the interest of students.

The partial course policy introduced by James Marsh at the University of Vermont was a device for being democratic and for balancing the treasurer's books. It allowed students to take what they wanted, and it allowed the colleges to collect their fees without requiring them to compromise their philosophy. Ohio University's "general course" provided no degree but it did supply Ohio with teachers for the common schools. Horace Holley, president of Transylvania in Kentucky, remarked of its partial course students: "Sometimes our irregulars, as we term them . . . are our best scholars in the branches which they select."[101]

But both the partial course policy and the parallel course program endangered the integrity of the traditional curriculum and were thus entered upon warily. Columbia, Hobart, Wesleyan, Miami in Ohio, and Hampden-Sidney in Virginia were among the institutions that gave life to the parallel course idea, which had been aborted at Amherst and given an early death at the University of the City of New York.[102] Sometimes known as the English or literary-scientific course, the parallel course was generally a three-year program, essentially the prescribed course without Latin and Greek, with some measure of the modern languages. Under conditions of near panic in the colleges, it caught on in the 1850s, but until then it suffered a number of embarrassments—its brevity in contrast to the regular course, the refusal of authorities to recognize it with a degree, an inhospitable environment.

The happiest curricular arrangements of the first half of the nineteenth century were made under Eliphalet Nott at Union College, and the wonder of it is why Union was so unique in arriving early and successfully at a workable course of study, one that neither damaged the intentions of the old curriculum nor denigrated the legitimacy of the new subjects. Union was the best of all possible worlds: It believed in the classics and it believed in the new subjects; it believed in a sound moral education and it believed in the application of science to the conquest of the American continent. It believed in young men: It welcomed the Greek-letter fraternity movement to its campus and it had no qualms about welcoming as transfer students young men who had experienced disciplinary collisions at their colleges of origin.[103] Union believed in itself, and perhaps that is all that was necessary to make a vital difference—that, and the driving presence of Eliphalet Nott, who presided over the destiny of the college in Schenectady for an unparalleled sixty-two years, 1804–1866.

As early as 1802 Union's first laws permitted students to take a partial course; in 1815 a parallel course of study, the first of those designed to meet the interests of students for whom the ancient lan-

guages were a discouragement, offered a four-year curriculum in
which the senior year was devoted exclusively to science.[104] In 1828,
the year of the Yale Report, Union College took the step that Codman
Hislop, Nott's biographer, soundly describes as "breaching the great
wall of the then traditional American college curriculum . . . and . . .
forcing an entrance at last into campus sanctuaries for students who
would prepare themselves for life in the Nineteenth Century."[105] The
reforms of 1828 were in response to a faculty resolution of 1827:
"Resolved . . . to arrange the studies in this . . . institution . . . as to
afford a choice between the ancient and modern languages and also
between the branches abstract and scientific and branches practical
and particular."[106]

Union College was ready for the reform. Over the years Nott had
assigned significant portions of the college's income to the purchase
of scientific apparatus; he had been careful in his appointment of professors; and he himself fully embraced the optimistic materialism of
the age. In an 1824 address at the college Nott invited his audience to
join in a great Christian-scientific assault on nature, an assertion of
man's dominion over nature through science in order to achieve
moral and material perfection. It was an intoxicating invitation, and
Union College proceeded to revise its curriculum in order to make it
even more attractive.[107]

Union's 1828 parallel scientific course provided freshmen with
a greater concentration in Latin and Greek than was customary in the
traditional program, but omitted them altogether after that. The
remaining three years were divided equally among science, mathematics, and a group of studies that included modern languages, social
studies, law, English composition, and oratory. An ornament of the
Union experience since 1804 had been senior year in moral philosophy with Eliphalet Nott; it would continue to be, in both the traditional course and in the new scientific course. The most symbolic evidence of Union's belief in what it was doing was its decision to award
the B.A. degree to graduates of both programs. Nothing here about
the integrity of the B.A. degree, no assertion of second-rateness, no
apologies. Union's two programs were equal in every way.[108]

Where others failed, Union flourished. Columbia's comparable
program reached an enrollment of zero in 1843 and was abolished. In
its first seventeen years two thirds of the students at the University of

Virginia stayed no more than a year. Union apparently benefited from what is alleged to be one of the unwritten laws of American advertising and public relations: There is no such thing as bad publicity. The opposition to Union's four-year scientific course and the college's insistence on not differentiating it from its classical course in the awarding of degrees blew up a storm that drew attention to Union as a place where a sound practical college education was available. The enrollment went merrily up. In 1830 Union graduated 96 seniors to Yale's 71, Harvard's 48, and Princeton's 20. Ten years later Union held its own: 105 to Yale's 107, Harvard's 45, and Princeton's 80. As late as 1861 its graduating class was the third largest in the country. About a third of each class was enrolled in the scientific course, young men on their way to careers in engineering, railroading, medicine, law, and mining.[109] Union under Nott had designed a course of study that was sensitive to the shift that had been taking place in the way young men looked at themselves: Once they had asked, "How can I be saved?" Now they asked, "How can I be successful?"[110] By 1845 thirty of Nott's students had become college presidents, spreading the good news from Schenectady, battling in their own way to achieve some rational system of higher education.[111]

The most outspoken of these was Francis Wayland, who for twenty-eight years used the presidency of Brown as a command post in his ceaseless war with the old course of study and all its props.[112] His tone was suggestive of the peevishness that Thorstein Veblen would turn to great critical consequence on the late nineteenth-century university. With no want of accuracy he looked out on the academic landscape in 1842 and concluded, "The College or University forms no integral and necessary part of the social system. It plods on its weary way solitary and in darkness."[113] In what now looks like an endless quarrel with the Brown corporation, Wayland recorded their differences in a series of public documents.

His *Thoughts on the Present Collegiate System in the United States*, published in 1842, revealed him as something of a visionary. His position on the role of the colleges in using stiffer entrance requirements to upgrade the schools was meaningless without a College Entrance Examination Board. His sensitivity to the effectiveness of the Lowell Institute in meeting community needs and his dismay at the isolation of the traditional colleges from the American people did not find an effective expression in his own time: The extension movement of the universities of the Midwest in the late nineteenth century, the community college movement since World War II, fulfilled his vision. He was flexible in meeting the problem of superficiality: His solutions—reduction of the number of subjects required for the degree, an extension of the number of years to complete a course, a multiplication of the kinds of degrees—defined him as foolish in his own generation and prophetic a hundred years later. He seems not to have been understood when he wondered out loud how a college could economically employ twelve professors using the same amount of student time as four once had.[114] Perhaps only educational foundations were meant to solve this puzzle.

Wayland was suspicious of faculty psychology as early as 1830.[115] He thought that the whole *in loco parentis* tradition, including residential dormitories, placed an inappropriate burden on the colleges. The Brown corporation apparently had no serious objections to having him around, but he had to resign in 1849 in order to move them from the refuge that they found in the Yale Report of 1828. His reforms of the 1850s, after they persuaded him to reconsider, and his valedictory of 1854 were not quite as premature as they would have been at an earlier Brown, nor were they exactly voices crying in the wilderness. His troubles, nonetheless, demonstrated that what Eliphalet Nott could achieve in Schenectady was not yet possible at Brown—nor at any of the other old colonial colleges, each an extension of some local elite, each a remnant of a now-vanished colonial connection, a fading ecclesiastical interest. It was a strange role in which Wayland found himself. He was not an enemy of the already powerful; he wanted a curriculum that would make an effective connection with the potentially powerful. He did not choose to resist democracy; his style was to embrace it. He wanted a course of study, an admissions policy, a system of supporting schools that could ameliorate the conditions of which he complained to the corporation in 1841: "Students frequently enter college almost wholly unacquainted with English grammar and unable to write a tolerably legible hand." He had not even read the letter a student at Miami University sent home in 1837: "I have just light my lamp, and drawed my table up near the fire, and locked the door, and commenced to wright."[116]

Everyone seemed to be agreed that college teaching was

wretched and even had to be, but there was wide disagreement as to why.[117] Was it that college students were so young? In 1819 the average age of a Harvard freshman was sixteen or younger.[118] Was it the recitation method of teaching? Think of the education that did not happen in 1819 when Ralph Waldo Emerson, as he described it to his father during his sophomore year, was "getting and intending to get my 'lessons verbatim and the rest word for word' "![119] One student's memory was graphic: "We were expected to wade through Homer as though the Iliad were a bog."[120] Yale in 1825 congratulated itself on improving the manner in which it conducted recitations. Until then tutors sat on the same level with students, called on them alphabetically as a combination of attendance check and learning prod, but they kept no record of the performance. In 1825 the system was improved: The tutor sat at an elevated desk and drew out of a box the names of students as he called on them; a while later he added a little black book for recording the quality of the performance.[121] The landscape was not everywhere so bleak. Francis Wayland arrived at Brown in 1827, after having participated in the reformation of Union, and a student in Providence recorded the difference: "Francis Wayland has taken the presidential chair. . . . He has made great alterations in the manner of reciteing—He carries no book into the recitation room nor suffers any of the students to do it."[122]

Lectures by inspired teachers and textbooks on subjects that were still in the process of definition introduced an element of intellectual excitement into the classroom. William Smyth at Bowdoin called on a blackboard to assist him in the 1820s; Mark Hopkins at Williams was making use of a manikin and a skeleton in his teaching of ethics in the 1840s. The classroom was not everywhere a wasteland.[123] Under the presidency of Nathan Lord, Dartmouth tried to create an academic environment, derisively known as the "nonambitious system," in which college honors, distinctions, ambition, and emulation were curtailed in the interest of virtue and wisdom. So un-American a philosophy would in time of course have the Dartmouth alumni in alarm, but Dartmouth must have been, at least on this score, a pleasanter place for a young man to be than many other American colleges in the 1840s and 1850s.[124] At Princeton in 1846 Professor Evert M. Topping made the mistake of discovering that if he interspersed commentary on Greek literature with the study of the

Greek language he could elicit a gratifying improvement in student interest. For this heresy he was called before the president, and a few days later his resignation was accepted.[125] He was a sacrifice offered on the altar of a dying curriculum and a dying psychology of learning.

Students everywhere soon learned what to do about the curriculum. As for its formal parts, most of them recognized the senior course in moral philosophy as a compensatory experience. As for what was not there, they developed an extracurriculum of significant dimensions. The senior course in moral philosophy justified the curriculum, it rationalized it. It asserted the unity of knowledge, sent the young graduates out into the world with a reassuring sense of their own fitness to play a role in upholding the moral order; it treated them like men, they who had thus far been treated like boys. By the nineteenth century the moral philosophy course, Aristotelian in origin and English and Scottish in modification, had become a remarkable excursion into social and individual ethics. Politics, economics, sociology, law, government, history, esthetics, international law, and fine arts were territories into which the moral philosophers, usually the presidents, roamed.[126]

The course was eminently utilitarian, and the students knew it. As a guide to ethical conduct, it served the happy purpose of bringing into harmony reason, intuition, and Christian orthodoxy. The moral philosophers were not social critics: They came down on the side of God, the United States, and the governing class. Each new generation was equipped in the senior course in ethics to join the governing class in serving the larger community. Moral philosophy encouraged the choice of Hercules; it lacked democratic pretensions; it located virtue and wisdom not in the people but in an educated few fit to be their leaders. And it carried the reassuring message that knowledge could be ordered, unified, and contained.

Indeed, the senior course in moral philosophy was the last moment when the idea of a liberal education as an expression of the unity of knowledge could be honestly held. Once a dozen discrete subjects began spilling out of the course, as they did late in the nineteenth century, the idea of general education was required to subsist on a synthetic faith. The course in moral philosophy held out the false promise to college seniors everywhere of "checking, ordering, and directing an otherwise mounting intellectual chaos."[127] Perhaps the only college student in the United States before the Civil War who was ready to accept the chaos that really was there was Henry Adams, and for this readiness he could not thank Harvard College but had to acknowledge that he was an Adams.

Did the students of Timothy Dwight's senior course in moral philosophy at Yale delight in the president's "relevance"? They should have. They probably did, or why else was it noticed "that those who had expressed least regard for the preceding studies, were among the most regular and attentive at the recitations of their senior year"?[128] Between November 2, 1813, and April 26, 1814, Dwight's moral philosophy course was enlivened by forty-one ethical debates that fell among recitations on Blair's *Lectures*, Duncan's *Logic*, Locke's *Essay*, Paley's *Philosophy*, and Vincent's *Catechism*.[129] In 1833 someone had the happy thought of publishing a student's class notes.[130]

The debates in which he engaged his students began with questions of immediate social concern—capital punishment, immigration, freedom of the press—and ended with the big questions: "Is man advancing to a state of Perfectability? Are Wars beneficial? Can the Immortality of the Soul be proved from the Light of Nature?"[131] His prefatory remarks to the decisions that followed every debate were an occasion for the president of Yale to say whatever to him seemed appropriate at the time. Senior year with Timothy Dwight, as revealed in his student's notebooks, was a more forceful argument for the Yale course of study than the combined forces of president, faculty, and corporation were able to put together in the famous report of fifteen years later.

On November 24, 1813, in remarking on a debate about whether a "Lie is ever Justifiable," Dwight interrupted his remarks on William Paley's consideration of "white lies" ("You will find them as black as any other," he insisted), in order to discourse on complaints from tutors of noisy behavior of students in the college buildings, on the obligation of students to behave in a way that was responsible to the community, their fellow students, and their parents. "These arguments, young gentlemen," he concluded, "I should think sufficient to convince an opponent: but I hope I have no opponents here. I hope I speak to friends."[132]

And of course he did. They knew where he stood. Against territorial expansion, for an established church, and against the break-up of the Union. "I do not believe the Reformation would ever have taken place but for the Crusades. . . . I will leave it to you to determine whether the good or evil effects are greatest." On common ancestry of all the races of man: affirmative. On emulation as an incitement to learning in the schools: negative. "He who sends a child to the theatre risks his soul. . . . Actors and actresses are beings as polluted as it is possible for the mind to conceive of."[133]

In passing: "I never saw a Frenchman who could not speak fast enough. . . . Whatever other acquisitions have been made, the youth who has not acquired the art of eloquence will, for many occasions, have thrown away his talent. . . . Never borrow money unless you can pay it at the time appointed. The person who practices borrowing on any other plan, will be a beggar, and probably end in a jail. . . . It may be set down as a strong probability, that many more women than men will go to heaven."[134]

At Union College later in the first half of the nineteenth century Eliphalet Nott used the course in moral philosophy as a running commentary and attack on the commonsense philosophy of Henry Home, Lord Kames, whose *Elements of Criticism,* published first in Edinburgh in 1762 and in at least thirty-one subsequent American editions, was standard fare in many of the moral philosophy courses. Nott's course was designed for men of action rather than men of thought; his seniors were assured that they were not simply creatures of reason but of passion and emotion as well.[135] Nott's students learned that Methodist ministers did not live as long as others because they did not laugh enough; that the population of New England was growing because of the attachment of New England to singing schools, which led to early marriage; and that actors did not develop their own character because they were so busy assuming the character of so many others.[136] Discoursing on love, he gave counsel on how to win a woman's affections and also quoted approvingly the verses: "Be an angel, my dear, in the morning, / But oh, be a woman at night!"[137]

The reputation of Mark Hopkins at Williams College rested on the senior course in moral philosophy.[138] As a college president he was a failure: The enrollment at Williams in the year of his inauguration, 1836, was exactly the same as in the year of his retirement, 1872. He was openly antiintellectual, and he was insensitive to the aspirations and needs of his faculty. But he was a magnificent teacher, and from 1830 until his retirement from teaching in 1887 the senior course in moral philosophy was reason enough to go to Williams College. "The coming year," a Williams senior wrote, "is fraught with responsibility and yet pleasure. It must tell heavily on our after lives. . . . We are treated, like, and feel like men now and must quit ourselves like men. Soon the greatest mind in New England will take and train us." Another said of the moral philosophy course with Hopkins: "It embraces man in his unity, and God in his sovereignty."

At the semicentennial celebration of the college in 1843 Hopkins took time to tell the alumni what he was doing. "We take up first the physical man, and endeavor to give . . . an idea of every organ and tissue of the body," he explained, and went on to describe the systematic route that led Williams seniors through the byways of mental faculties, grounds of belief, logic, and emotion, to the ultimate destination—the moral government of God. Into the warp and woof of this complex fabric known as philosophy were woven esthetics, ethics, economics, politics, and theology.

Probably as important as any one element in contributing to Hopkins's fame as a teacher was his ability to make his classes something more than exercises in memory, recitation, and verbal regurgitation. He took seriously his own definition of a good teacher as conveyed at his inauguration to the presidency of Williams in 1836:

> It is easy to see what it is that constitutes the first excellence
> of an instructor. It is not his amount of knowledge, nor yet
> his facility of communication, important as these may be;
> but it is his power to give an impulse to the minds of his
> pupils, and to induce them to labor. For this purpose,
> nothing is so necessary as a disinterested devotion to the
> work, and a certain enthusiasm which may act by sympathy on the minds of the young.

Hopkins succeeded in meeting his own requirements, as generations of students attested. William Dwight Whitney had hardly begun his instruction under Hopkins when he wrote to a cousin: "The Prex. is the greatest teacher entirely that was ever suffered to appear on this earth." James A. Garfield wrote into his journal: "Today and yester-

day I have done what I ought to do in four days. . . . But this mighty
Dr. Hopkins is so infinitely suggestive." Samuel Chapman
Armstrong wrote to his family, "Prex makes a man *think,* and think
quickly too." In the Socratic tendencies of his own teaching, in the
persistent "What do you think?" with which he conducted his classes,
he found a method of inspiring students to be individuals, to think as
men, to try their mental powers. Although he taught the course in
moral philosophy in a way that inspired individual effort and permitted independent thought, like his fellow moral philosophers elsewhere, he considered the big questions beyond dispute and to their
settlement he contributed the serenity of a settled mind. No one can
miss the tribute to Hopkins the advocate in these nostalgic memories
of a former student: "After you had . . . given us somewhat in detail
the great principles that underlie all reasoning . . . you laid aside your
glasses, passed your hand slowly over your forehead, bowed your head
amid the reigning silence for a few seconds, then slowly uttered the
words 'But—Nature . . . [is] moral' and the class dismissed."

On the other hand, it was possible to make of the course in
moral philosophy an experience as lacking in inspiration as a recitation in Latin. For every Dwight or Nott or Hopkins there must have
been a score on the model of Horace Webster, who, at what was to
become the City College of New York, for twenty years was neither
stimulating nor clear nor succinct nor inspiring. There was no dis-
sension, no discussion, only the endless recitation of passages memorized from the assigned reading.[139]

In an apt phrase Jonathon Messerli has described the extracurriculum of the early nineteenth-century college as the source of a
"bootlegged" education.[140] The implication for the formal curriculum is readily apparent: It was dry, sober, unexciting, and unfulfill-
ing, or—if not always, most of the time; and it refused to keep up with
American life or the needs and imaginations of generations of lively
young men. Beyond the classroom undergraduate life was shaped by
many influences—typically in the first half of the century by the requirements of a residential college and by an all-pervading religious
atmosphere, but more important than these was the extracurriculum, that complex of organizations and activities with which students filled that apparently vast vacuum left in their lives by the for-

mal curriculum and the official arrangements and expectations of the
authorities.

The extracurriculum was sometimes an invention of necessity.
At Kenyon in the 1830s the students were their own undertakers, laying out the bodies of deceased classmates, preparing the coffins, conducting the interments. In the 1820s and 1830s an interest in natural
history that could not find adequate expression in the formal course
of study led to an outbreak of undergraduate lyceums and "colleges"
of natural history.[141] By 1834 students at Harvard had created for
their own edification and amusement organizations built around
such diverse interests as military drill, public speaking, drinking,
chemistry, geography, poetry and essay writing, orchestra, debating,
and singing.[142] Greek letter fraternities were in the ascendancy by mid
century as centers of social diversion and pretension, but they had not
yet succeeded in defining or redefining undergraduate life. The athletic hero was still in the offing; organized athletics had produced little more than an occasional Harvard-Yale boat race. The central institution of extracurricular life was the literary society; the debater, the
orator, the essayist were the heroes of the extracurriculum.[143]

The first effective agency of intellect to make itself felt in the
American college was the literary society. Making a temporary early
appearance at Harvard in 1728 and a more lasting appearance at
Yale in 1753, the literary society movement soon created a pair of
rival societies at almost every American college. In their debates, orations, libraries, and literary exercises, they imparted a tremendous
vitality to the intellectual life of the colleges. Lacking the restraints
imposed on the classical curriculum by tradition and a narrow social
purpose, they were in a position to welcome new subjects and interests into their libraries and their exercises.[144] James McLachlan's
analysis of the literary society movement has led him to a bold but
convincing conclusion:

> From the last third of the eighteenth century through the
> middle of the nineteenth . . . the student literary societies
> engrossed more of the interests and activities of the stu-
> dents than any other aspect of college life. . . . Student liter-
> ary societies were, in effect, colleges within colleges. They
> enrolled most of the students, constituted—and taught—

their own curricula, granted their own diplomas, selected
and bought their own books, operated their own libraries,
developed and enforced elaborate codes of conduct among
their members, and set the personal goals and ideological
tone for a majority of the student body.[145]

The proof is overwhelming. At Princeton the Whig Society
extended the study of Greek from the Cicero of the formal curriculum
to Ovid, Tacitus, Terence, and Herodotus, often in translation.
Seniors of the society corrected the compositions of members for
grammar and spelling. The compositions themselves were designed
as explorations of self, excursions of a contemplative nature. The
debates were intended as preparation for the world's stage, for public
life. In the colleges the literary societies, rather than the course of
study, invited heated discussion of the Alien and Sedition Acts, slavery, the idea of a national university, the Louisiana Purchase.[146]

The literary societies revealed in their libraries and literary exercises a receptivity to subjects that were knocking without avail on the
door of the prescribed curriculum—English literature, French literature, poetry, literary criticism, modern history, and creative writing.
The functional student-centered college library first entered the
American college as an extracurricular agency of the literary societies.
In the 1830s students at Columbia were on the average drawing two
books a year from the college library and more than twenty from their
society libraries. Literary society libraries almost everywhere were
larger, more accessible, and broader in range of interest than the college libraries. At Yale the Society of Brothers in Unity created a library
that justified their appointment of fellow members to professorships
in history, composition, oratory, natural philosophy, mathematics,
and geography.[147]

The literary society libraries could reveal a sectional caste: At
South Carolina, Cooper, Scott, Dickens, and Irving were welcome;
Emerson, Hawthorne, and Thoreau were not. At Miami University
the rivalry between the two literary societies gave to the sculptor
Hiram Powers, as yet unknown, his first commission for a bust.
Ralph Waldo Emerson traveled the country as the guest of college lit-
erary societies, preaching the message of self-reliance and individual-
ism that the students were documenting in the extracurriculum.[148]

The societies existed with the approval of college authorities, who generally provided the space necessary for society activities and even arranged the hours of the regular course of study to accommodate those activities. At Indiana University a student wrote his mother in 1844: "The President . . . told me . . . it was equal to one professor, and strongly recommended me to become a member." In the documentary remains of early nineteenth-century student life, only the senior course in moral philosophy approaches the literary societies in evoking enthusiasm and a sense of individual identity and growth. Horace Mann's three years at Brown led him to the position of valedictorian of the class of 1819; his biographer, noting that Mann borrowed only eighteen books from the Brown library in those years, attributes to literary society activities and libraries a greater importance in Mann's eduction than the formal course of study. F. A. P. Barnard, who sat on the Yale corporation when the report of 1828 was approved, said of his Yale undergraduate experience: "No part of my training at Yale College seems to me to have been more beneficial than that which I derived from the practice of speaking and debating in the literary society to which I belonged." A Princeton alumnus reminisced of his literary society: "It was worth more as a part of education than the college itself, not only in a literary point of view, but in manners and morals." The judgment of a Yale undergraduate in 1854 was overwhelming: "[Literary societies] have done more toward making men than all the rest of college training put together. . . . They are the schools which train . . . best for the practicalities of . . . [the] world."[149]

There is no single explanation for the appearance of literary societies nor for the ease with which they became an integral element in the education of American college students for more than half a century. Their early years coincided with the development of an interest in belles lettres in the colleges, an interest that was accorded only modest curricular recognition, apparently insufficient to support the kind of aspirations that the Whig literary society at Princeton symbolized in its use of Hercules on its diploma. The literary societies were testing grounds for those purposes of the colleges that could not be examined in the regular course of study—character, leadership, imagination, self-reliance—and therefore were surely construed by college authorities as fulfilling in action what the senior course in moral philosophy could provide only in theory and guidance. The literary societies were also advance agents of secularization, children of the Enlightenment, institutions that welcomed the world and all its challenges.

The literary societies were extensions of undergraduate imagination and aspiration. In some ways they leaped beyond the traditional course of study; in other ways they complemented it. They gave a sense of completeness to the college experience that would have been largely absent without them. They made a vital connection with an uncertain future just as surely as the course of study was more effective in making an intentional connection with a revered past. Their importance to what by mid century had developed into the American system of education makes the term *extracurricular* a misnomer. The literary societies were as curricular as the chapel, and the American college curriculum in the first half of the nineteenth century could not have dispensed with either of them. By mid century the American system of higher education consisted of the college chapel and all the attendance rules and occasions that sent students there, the dying but still socially respectable and useful classical course of study, the capstone course in moral philosophy that was its great glory, and the extracurriculum with which the students took charge of their own education. At mid century these four components were in as happy balance as they ever would be again. Henceforth all four would be on collision course.

4

Crisis and Redefinitions

Seniors gathering around the "Old Pine" at Dartmouth for class day exercises, students at Amherst celebrating Pocahontas's birthday with two barrels of cider, imaginative young men at the University of Georgia—forbidden to go to circuses—disguising themselves as blacks and sitting among the slaves, raccoon fights in the dormitories at Miami in Ohio, a three-day suspension of classes at the University of North Carolina because of an eighteen-inch snowfall. College life in the United States in the 1850s. And so few takers.[1]

The colleges were plagued by unpopularity and uncertainty of purpose into the 1870s and beyond. A developing rationale, even as the colleges headed unwittingly toward curricular chaos, made its appearance, however, not by some magic wand's stroke but because it could no longer be delayed. Ezra Cornell, Andrew Dixon White, Daniel Coit Gilman, and Charles William Eliot were not magicians, but they were magnificent organizers, men for whom the word *large* connoted an expansiveness, a sense of the whole, an imagination capable of encompassing the entire educational landscape. In the nineteenth century they were the sort their contemporaries referred to as "men of large vision." They confronted the nervousness, the uncertainties, the disjunction between higher education and society in the way that great surgeons meet all but insurmountable medical challenges in movie and television drama, the way we have been taught that the West was won, the Indian eliminated, the valleys and prairies, the rivers and forests bent to man's will.

Until the colleges succeeded in making curricular arrangements that supported *that* vision of America, they could not be popular or, although unpopular, very effective. The trouble with the colleges was not so much their religiosity and sectarianism: Most of them learned how to be Christian and blandly cheerful without being denominational, responsive to a small class in a limited neighborhood; when the focus of the extracurriculum shifted from the literary society to the playing field, an early casualty was evening prayers. The cost of going to college was no hindrance for those who could afford it, and those who could not do not appear to have been held off: College records in the nineteenth century abound with unpaid tuition bills ("remitted" was the polite term of cancellation used in the trustees' minutes at Williams), and the annals are heavy with true stories of young men who worked their way through college by teaching in district schools, running boardinghouses, and entering at an advanced age after saving earnings enough to make college possible.[2]

The colleges enrolled all for whom the curriculum was designed and for whom, given the nature of American society, the curriculum made sense. The colleges were not essential to careers in medicine, law, and the ministry, only to those young men who intended to outdistance their peers and be the leaders of those professions. As late as 1870 a college degree was not at all necessary for admission to Harvard Law School; in fact, there were no admissions requirements at all, and a degree was the automatic reward for the payment of three term bills (the equivalent of eighteen months of study).[3] The high percentage of college men in the gatherings at Philadelphia in 1776 and 1787 that created the United States must have helped to support what college enrollment there was in the early decades of the nineteenth century. A career of public service by virtuous college graduates was an ideal held out to young men by the curriculum as well as the extracurriculum, by the college authorities as well as the undergraduate literary societies. No one knew at the time that a whole generation of young men who would take that ideal seriously would be politically stranded after the Civil War, frustrated reformers and idealists, bypassed by a rougher and more effective politics than they had been schooled to anticipate or understand.[4]

The liberal Republican leaders of 1872 who could not accept U. S. Grant, the Mugwumps of 1884 who bolted the ticket headed by James G. Blaine were overwhelmingly graduates of eastern classical colleges. The notable politician of their generation who went to

Harvard and was also successful was Theodore Roosevelt: He supported Blaine in 1884 and relearned the guides to public service in the school of machine politics. In the meantime, while 38 percent of U.S. congressmen were college graduates in 1875, ten years later fewer than one out of every four were college men.[5]

The colleges did not need gatherers of gloomy statistics to tell them that they were in trouble, but they may have needed them to demonstrate that their problem was not a purely local one. At Columbia, President F. A. P. Barnard in 1870 showed his board of trustees statistics that demonstrated that the enrollment capacities of a still-growing number of colleges were increasing at a greater rate than the college-going student population; he thought that Columbia's difficulties had to do with its being in a city, lacking dormitories, and facing too much local competition, and he said that the University of Pennsylvania shared Columbia's problems. Whatever the statistics showed, however much New York may have overextended its capacity, Barnard had the wit to recognize the real difficulty: the classical course, the yawning distance between the Columbia curriculum and the world's work; he thought that an elective course, one more responsive to student interests, would help.[6]

Another set of statistics, put together by Professor Edward Hitchcock of Amherst in 1877, helped to explain why, even as college enrollments were going up—from 52,286, or 1.7 percent of the eighteen to twenty-one age group, in 1870 to 115,817, or 2.7 percent of the eighteen to twenty-one age group, in 1880—the colleges experienced a sense of swimming against the tide. Professor Hitchcock's statistics demonstrated that the country's population had been increasing at twice the rate of college going. The college man, and now also the college woman, were being spread more thinly through the population, and until some dramatic development brought college going into some relationship to college classroom and dormitory capacity, that thinning percentage of college men and women was being spread just as thinly in their undergraduate years in more and more colleges for which there was no apparent justification other than that someone had wanted to found them.[7]

Every village and small town in the country had room for a class of college-educated elders—the leading doctor, the minister of the best church, the judge, a few wealthy landowners, perhaps the edi-

tor of the weekly country paper, the master of the local academy, but
after that roll was called, life in small-town America had used up its
opportunities. The city and urban economic enterprise were alternatives to rural stagnation and farm life for hundreds of thousands of
young Americans who made leaving the farm for the city a migration
of important dimensions.[8] The city and urban economic enterprise,
in addition, however, were also alternatives to going to school and
college; they provided environments in which life was recast and new
opportunities seized. The transformation that took place in
nineteenth-century America was celebrated in the great fairs in
Philadelphia in 1876 and Chicago in 1893. This same transformation
found expression in the colleges as they stumbled toward clarifying
how they were going to fit into the world of new technology, vast
material gains, and broadened opportunities. Colleges geared to the
need of village elites to flaunt their Latin and Greek required either a
new rationale for the old curriculum or an altogether new curriculum. One or the other or some packaging of both would be necessary
if the colleges were to be vital instruments of a democratic society.

An 1850 committee of the Massachusetts General Court
expressed one way in which a democratic society might expect
Harvard to behave; it proposed that Harvard adopt a wholly elective
curriculum and that the professors be paid by the size of their classes:
"Those only would succeed who taught . . . in a manner acceptable to
the public. That which was desired would be purchased, and that
which was not, would be neglected." This was neither the first nor the
last occasion when the dogmas of classical economics were applied to
an evaluation of the course of study. In 1860 an Iowa school journal,
contemplating curricular matters at the state university, observed: "If
a majority of the intelligent youth who will assemble in the halls of
the university shall determine to devote themselves to scientific and
practical studies, the very fact will be evidence that the interests of the
community call for scientific and practical men."[9] In Massachusetts
and Iowa the message to the colleges was the same: Be practical or
perish.

To move the colleges from the training of a professional elite
and a virtuous governing class to the preparation of "better farmers,
mechanics, or merchants"—which essentially was the message being
sent to Harvard from the General Court—was not merely a matter of

developing the appropriate curriculum and finding the funds necessary to support an expansion of collegiate purpose. The shift in purpose proposed in both Massachusetts and Iowa required an embrace of utilitarian and materialistic values that it had been the function of the colleges since the beginning to combat. The founding of Harvard College was an act of faith, but Harvard was also born in fear—in fear of an unlettered ministry and an illiterate people.[10] The founding of little colleges in endless progression as the country moved West, often with the support of a concerned eastern missionary impulse, was also a movement founded in fear as well as faith.

Almost every new college in the developing West—beginning in upstate New York in the early nineteenth century—expressed the concern of its eastern-educated founders for the future of a society that allowed itself to be taken over by barbarians. Those who would change the course of study would somehow have to prevail over the old and deeply ingrained mistrust of the people, they would have to make utilitarianism and materialism as respectable in the colleges as in the markets and mines or in some way temper that utilitarianism and materialism or masquerade it with piety. Those who would hold to both the old curriculum and the elitist values and fears on which it rested would not, on the other hand, find themselves without supporters, even as the barbarians took over.

Was there any way to keep them out? Should there have been? Were the colleges ready? Did they recognize the enemy? The evidence would suggest that when a generation of self-made manufacturers, engineers, and merchants were ready to attach their names and their fortunes to the development of schools of applied science, the classical colleges were standing in line with their hands out. Some of those colleges did what they could to avoid contamination—they affiliated, but they did not integrate. Others were barefoot as they stood in line and were not disposed to quarrel.[11]

The first of the scientific schools were developed from within the faculties of Yale and Harvard. At Yale in 1847 Benjamin Silliman, Jr., and John P. Norton created a school of applied chemistry as a section of a newly authorized department of philosophy and the arts. At Harvard the same year plans for a graduate program in arts and sciences were corrupted into an undergraduate program in science. Engineering was added to the Yale program in 1852 and kept out of the Harvard program through the determination of Louis Agassiz, the zoologist in charge. The Yale and Harvard schools grew in strength and stature. The Harvard school started with a slight advantage, a $50,000 benefaction of Abbott Lawrence, the Boston merchant-manufacturer, whose name was bestowed on the school at its founding. Yale's school made up for an early lack of sponsorship and changed its name to Sheffield Scientific School in 1860, in exchange for a $100,000 gift from Joseph Sheffield, a New Haven merchant-financier. The existence of these schools, demonstrably popular and overwhelmingly committed to the uses of science, within the walls of New England's oldest colleges soon confronted them with a major question of institutional integrity. Harvard solved the problem by giving the graduates of its scientific school a bachelor of science degree, beginning in 1851; the next year Yale created for the graduates of its scientific school the degree of bachelor of philosophy.[12]

The B.A. was thus protected from violation. Students at the scientific schools, for whom admissions standards were low and whose course of study was of three years' duration, were made aware of their second-class citizenship in the citadel of the arts. At Yale the students at Sheffield, whose presence was an enormous boost to subjects—including English literature and Sanskrit—that had had great difficulty in making headway in the standard curriculum, could not really be treated like barbarians, but on the other hand neither were they allowed to sit in chapel with the students of Yale College.[13]

The scientific schools did not open up the way for science in the classical colleges. Newtonian physics, the mathematics necessary to comprehend it, and the sciences appropriate to understanding the natural world had been enlarging their domain in the curriculum since early in the eighteenth century. In 1800 almost every college boasted a science professor; by 1830 a respectable teaching staff included two professors of science and, by 1860, four. The science that was making headway at the Lawrence and Sheffield schools of Harvard and Yale, and all the comparable programs and schools that soon became a necessity at once self-respecting colleges of liberal learning, was science with a difference. The science that Benjamin Silliman the elder had made respectable in Yale College was science as an instrument of human understanding and contemplation of the divine; the science that his son was making respectable in the new scientific school was science as an instrument of human arrogance and the exploitation of nature.[14]

The younger Silliman made the difference quite obvious, without any apparent embarrassment, in a commencement address at the College of California in 1867: "If we cannot excuse the self-conceit of the so-called practical man who conceals his ignorance beneath his empiricism, neither can we pardon the college which has turned out its graduate in arts so artless that his learning fails him when brought face to face with nature and experience."[15] For the colleges, their graduates failed in the presence of nature and experience only if they were found wanting in responsibility, integrity, and humility—in other words, character. The making of bridges, the harnessing of rivers, the flooding of valleys, and a thousand other conquests of nature, both large and small, were not the business of the colleges until the younger Silliman and his successors and his colleagues made them so, except at Union College, where Eliphalet Nott combined the traditional college with the applied subjects in a course of study that put some restraints on human arrogance. The Harvard and Yale arrangements that set the pattern for the science schools that multiplied in the 1850s and 1860s placed applied science outside the circle of respectability and in doing so must have introduced a certain edge to the attitude of the budding technicians and engineers toward the arts. Perhaps there was no real alternative. If no other institution followed Union's lead, there must have been good reasons. Union had the field to itself at a time when it and the existing centers of applied science—West Point and R.P.I.—could meet the demand, and there is no evidence that a Union-educated railroad builder was of more tender and loving disposition and less rapacious toward nature than the others.

When the time came to make peace with applied science, however, the tactics of the friends of liberal learning were self-defeating. The affiliated scientific school was meant to be and succeeded in being insulting, and the colleges themselves were financially in no position to refuse the first great wave of industrial philanthropy that was of such dimensions as to dictate its own terms. In 1865 Asa Packer, who had never been inside a college, created an entirely new institution at Bethlehem, in the rapidly industrializing Lehigh Valley of eastern Pennsylvania; from its first day Lehigh University was a scientific and technical college; second-class citizenship there was reserved for the classicists. At nearby Lafayette College in Easton a dying classical college was transformed in 1866 by the benefactions of Ario Pardee, a self-made natural resource millionaire, who gave the college $100,000 with which to develop a parallel scientific course leading to the B.S. degree. In 1865 the total enrollment at Lafayette was in the neighborhood of 115; by 1872 its freshman class was that large, surpassed only by those of Cornell, Harvard, and Yale.[16]

What Packer and Pardee accomplished in eastern Pennsylvania other self-made millionaires achieved elsewhere, creating centers and monuments of applied science, temples of materialism and utilitarianism, schools that rested on the assumption that they were training young men in the tools that would make them rich—and, also, too often, disdainful of the humanizing, liberal, intellectual purposes that were associated with the old colleges and the old learning.[17]

John Harvard, William and Mary, Elihu Yale spoke a different language and argued an educational philosophy different from that symbolized by Alexander Hamilton, John Dickinson, George Washington, and Thomas Jefferson. The difference was understood when a postrevolutionary wave of colleges appeared and bore the names of the Founding Fathers. Was the Republic being refounded, remade, when another wave of institutions of higher learning appeared bearing such names as Stevens, Case, Rose, Pratt, Drexel, Armour, and Carnegie?[18] The new scientific schools did not really remake the Republic; they confirmed the results.

In the 1850s the technical institute in Troy stopped being a high school and began performing like a scientific college. Engineering made its way into the undergraduate course at Dartmouth, the University of Michigan, and Brown before 1855. The University of Rochester, founded in 1850, offered a choice of the B.A. or the B.S. degree from the beginning. Illinois College, Denison, the University of North Carolina, New York University, and Wesleyan reorganized their values and their courses of study in the 1850s to offer a course without classics leading to the B.S. degree. In 1858 the first degree awarded by the State University of Iowa was a B.S. degree.[19] In the 1860s at least twenty-five institutions adopted the three-year parallel B.S. scientific department as a device for expressing their willingness to do what was expected of them. Somewhat later, 1873, Princeton introduced a three-year scientific course, requiring Latin for admission, and the next year a wealthy alumnus, John C. Green, paid Princeton's way into an undergraduate offering in engineering. By then, engineering was not even simply engineering any more. In 1870 at the Sheffield School at Yale a department of mechanical engineering was established; in 1881 Cornell offered the first course in electrical engineering. At Williams, on the other hand, the first endowment funds available for science were assigned in 1865 to the professorship of astronomy, then being filled by an elderly professor who saw God when he looked at the stars.[20]

Professor John William Draper of New York University looked in other directions when he beseeched "friends of American Colleges . . . to abandon the existing system . . . [and not] swamp Science by crowding into the boat with her the skeletons of thirty centuries." Draper's position was based on his conviction that "the practical branches must take the lead and bear the weight, and the ornamental must follow. . . . Mere literary acumen," he warned, "is becoming utterly powerless against profound scientific attainment." Friend though he was of applied science, even an extremist of sorts, Draper deserved a more respectful attention than he received from many friends of the colleges as then constituted. Draper diagnosed the colleges' difficulties as being ecclesiastical in origin: a course of study unable to embrace science with the passion necessary to understand it, an embrace that was denied because of religious opposition. Clergymen made a mistake, he cautioned, by thinking they could check materialism by checking science; they would do better to understand it.[21]

He had a point. Among the old colleges only Union had had confidence enough about its own values to embrace and understand science as the nineteenth century intended to apply it. The others were indulging in protective quarantine by isolating applied science in discrete schools, hedging their bets by bending somewhat slightly in the direction of utility, or behaving foolishly. At Denison laboratory work managed to be construed as teaching ethics (truth, self-control, industry). When geology students at Amherst asked their German-trained professor, Benjamin K. Emerson, to give an extracurricular course on evolution, at the next faculty meeting President Julius Seelye spoke for himself and Amherst: "Gentlemen—to speak

of Evolution—the Department of Psychology and Philosophy . . .
feels perfectly competent to handle this subject—and will thank all
other Departments to keep hands off." As late as 1868 at Princeton a
faculty of ten included seven Presbyterian ministers. Efforts to create a
scientific university in Albany in the 1850s failed, and certainly one of
the reasons was confusion over what science was all about; one of the
would-be friends of the university, Bishop Alonzo Potter, held that
"there were physical and physiological phenomena which it was a
sin to investigate."[22]

At Emory, however, every effort was made to reconcile science
and religion. In 1856 Professor Alexander Means conducted electrical
experiments with which he hoped to corroborate the first chapter of
Genesis. In 1858 the Reverend Samuel Ware Fisher, at his inauguration as president of Hamilton College, urged the adoption of the
Bible as the central text in the course of study. "The Bible is worth
more than all philosophy, all natural science, all other forms of
thought," he said. "We pride God's word above all earthly science. . . .
It is in the light of the celestial we shall see more justly the terrestial."
In 1872 the opposition of many Methodist churchmen and laymen to
a proposed new Methodist university in Tennessee was well expressed
by Bishop George F. Pierce, who was hostile to the idea of theological
training for ministers, which was to be a major role of the proposed
university: "Give me the evangelist and the revivalist rather than the
erudite brother who goes into the pulpit to interpret modern science
instead of preaching repentance and faith, or going so deep into
geology as to show that Adam was not the first man and that the
Deluge was a little local affair." The defiant catalogue at Marietta
College had insisted in 1856 that "the great principle of thorough
classical study will not be relinquished," but with such friends as
these, how could the old course of study long withstand the utilitarian and materialistic expectations of the age?[23]

The sixty or so Catholic colleges of 1866—many of which were
colleges in name only—tried valiantly to hold to a curriculum that
was a version of the Jesuit *ratio studiorum*, a program of three years of
preparatory work and three years of traditional humanities courses.
But what was Holy Cross to say to the mother of one student, who
sent him back to college with a letter to the president: "It is my wish
that he should be confined to the English branches. . . . I think it will

be quite useless for him to recommence Greek or Latin. . . . Let him apply himself to English grammar, geography, and arithmetic . . . for they will be more useful to him than any others."[24] By 1866 two thirds of the Catholic colleges were offering commercial courses of study designed to prepare young Catholics for the world's work.[25] In the old colleges of Protestant orientation control was shifting from the clergy to lay alumni. Students were openly wondering about a curriculum and a psychology of education that were hostile to intellectual growth: "You are told," one student complained, "that any undue development of a special faculty is nature's abhorrence, and you observe how the whole college machinery is seduously employed to nip in the bud the promise of any particular talent."[26] Even the reaction against electives at Harvard in the two decades after 1843 was evidence less of warm endorsement of the old course than it was evidence of the absence of sufficient scholarly purpose in the faculty and adequate funds in the treasury.[27] In the South the rebuilding of a land and people wasted by slavery and war called forth courses of study more practical than Latin and Greek.[28]

And at mid century, still playing the critic's role, Francis Wayland was given the opportunity to try out at Brown some of his prescriptions for what ailed the American college.[29] Wayland's inspiration was Nott's parallel scientific course at Union, with the significant difference that Brown gave an M.A. degree for the traditional course of study, a B.A. for a three-year version of it, and the bachelor of philosophy degree (Ph.B.) for a three-year program in practical subjects. The elective system, the infusion of a larger amount of scientific and practical studies into the course of study, did not require what amounted to Brown's policy of devaluating the M.A. and B.A. degrees. What did? Apparently Brown's degree policy was dictated by Wayland's views of political economy as much as by his educational philosophy. He aimed at a curriculum that would be popular enough to pay for itself, that would be democratic in its diffusion of learning and economical in its effect on enrollments and the college's budget.[30]

His analysis of the political economy of higher education was a key element in his 1850 report to the Brown corporation: "We have produced an article for which the demand is diminishing. We sell it at less than cost, and the deficiency is made up by charity. We give it away, and still the demand diminishes. Is it not time to inquire whether we cannot furnish an article for which the demand will be, at least somewhat more remunerative?"[31] Instead of subsidizing students to attend colleges, he proposed that the colleges offer a course of study for which students would be willing to pay. By his own calculations every Harvard undergraduate was subsidized to the extent of $491 for tuition (provided for in the form of scholarships, professorial endowments, uncollected tuitions) and over $500 in interest income lost from investment in buildings, libraries, and so forth. Wayland's outrage at the colleges' mismanagement of their resources was equaled by his contempt for the old course of study. "What," he asked, "could Virgil and Horace and Homer and Demosthenes, with a little mathematics and natural philosophy, do toward developing the untold resources of this continent?"[32] In Wayland a rising middle class of businessmen, merchants, and industrialists had found an advocate, and the reformed curriculum that went into effect in 1850 included new subjects, such as agricultural chemistry and civil engineering, as well as structural arrangements that encouraged students to take only what they wanted, when they wanted it, no more, no less.

The new course, the new structural flexibility, the new degree policy met with an immediate favorable response; enrollment moved from 174 in 1850–51 to 225 the next year and 283 in 1853–54, but these figures were not sufficient to support the many departments of instruction that Wayland envisaged as essential to his views of a proper political economy for American higher education. Nor did he have the resources adequate to establish departments in depth. Without greater resources he could not offer prospective students an opportunity to specialize in an area of vocational interest. Wayland was learning something about the economy of the modern department store: An investment in inventory is necessary to attract customers. The $125,000 made available for Wayland's reforms were inadequate to his purposes. There were other problems too, but in the end the Brown reforms failed because of insufficient financing. In 1855 Wayland was replaced, the curriculum was curtailed, and the new president intoned: "We are in danger of becoming an institution rather for conferring degrees upon the unfortunate than for educating a sterling class of men."[33]

Like so many others, Wayland joined the roster of failed reformers. None, however, better understood the conditions that defined and limited what the undergraduate course of study in the United States was becoming and had to be. The fiftieth anniversary of the presidency of his old mentor, Eliphalet Nott, gave him an opportunity in 1854 to deliver a summation of his educational philosophy in an address dramatically entitled "The Education Demanded by the People of the United States." The great natural abundance of the North American continent and its enticements to individual effort and social mobility constituted, for Wayland, the fundamental social environment in which the curriculum operated. The readily apparent transformation of society from an agricultural to an industrial order, with its accompanying dependency on mechanical rather than physical power, meant that Americans would be in a position to prolong their years of formal training. They rightfully would expect that training to be of help to them in translating natural abundance and mechanical power into social mobility and material progress. In Wayland's view, an educational tradition reaching back to the Puritans' attachment to learning, but also including the common school movement and the federal policy that endowed the state universities with grants of federal lands, acknowledged the responsibility of the formal institutions of education to assist the American people in their individual efforts to achieve success. Knowledge is as elementary to success, he noted, as success is elementary to the philosophical and psychological outlook of the American people. The responsibility of the colleges was implicit in these conditions: They must become instruments of an aspiring middle class, the centers of learning for new vocations.[34]

"Shall we say that the lawyer, and physician, and clergyman, need a knowledge of principles in order to pursue their callings with success," Wayland asked, "while the farmer, the mechanic, the manufacturer, and the merchant require no knowledge of the laws upon which the success of every operation which they perform depends? . . . Shall we say that intellect is to be cultivated and talent developed in one direction alone, or developed in every possible direction?"[35] As Wayland understood them, the American people expected the colleges to educate a democracy of talents and a democracy of vocations. The colleges owed themselves and the country a course of study that would cater to such expectations and that would bring the rising middle class under the influence of institutions that also catered to the needs of the soul and the moral order. Without using language that said so, Wayland proposed that the middle class be provided with the means of its own ascendancy by colleges that at the same time would save them from barbarism.

The difference between Wayland's view of the role of the course of study in such an undertaking and Jeremiah Day's was dramatic, and Wayland's view was subtly different from that of the separate scientific school. In 1828 Day had recognized the threat to the moral and social order in a class of vulgar and extravagant millionaires, but he was not prepared to help them to become men of property. He insisted that Yale's role was to provide men of all employments with the "high intellectual culture . . . large and liberal views . . . solid and elegant attainments" associated with the classical curriculum. Yale's role was to make sure that the rising middle class achieved "a higher distinction, than the mere possession of property," but it had no intention to help it in its rise.[36] By the time that Yale, in the Sheffield Scientific School, was ready to teach young men how to become men of property, it had so divided itself that the college's refining and moral intentions were attached to the B.A. program, while the Ph.B. program was allowed to be defined as a school for producing barbarians. All this was not broadly advertised, but if there was one place where Yale might have acknowledged a democracy of talents and vocations and aspirations and its own obligations in the moral training of all employments, that place surely was before God in the Yale chapel. Yet the message there delivered to the segregated students of the Sheffield Scientific School was subtle but unmistakable: We are the Greeks, you are the barbarians.

If the barbarians were to be civilized, they had to be brought within some effective influence of the humanist tradition. Jeremiah Day's curricular philosophy kept them on the outside; the philosophy of the separate scientific school put them on the outside. The position pioneered by Nott at Union and expressed by Wayland in 1854 at least kept open the possibility that for ambitious young men the environment of a sympathetic classical college might restrain their more barbaric tendencies. There at least belief in the moral order transcended any commitment to the governing classes, the elite professions, and the traditional course of study.

But Union and Brown did not point the way. The adoption of B.S. and Ph.B. degrees by Harvard and Yale turned out to be the device the colleges were looking for: an instrument for meeting a clear demand for a more practical course of study, for increasing enrollments and avoiding bankruptcy, and for maintaining the integrity of the B.A. degree. The partial course program—student selected and degreeless—continued to grow in popularity, and here and there it began to teach college authorities how to move away from the psychology of mental faculties to a psychology of individual interests. In 1872 the catalogue of Miami in Ohio, noting that students with strong career motivations had demonstrated their competence to choose courses intelligently, rationalized its partial course option with the observation: "It is found that wherever the principle of option has been introduced greater diligence and contentment on the part of the students have been secured."[37] These two alternatives to the B.A. program—the parallel course and the partial course—became standard practice as the colleges, one by one, confronted the conditions that Francis Wayland had described for them in 1854.

The crisis in which the colleges were engaged had been building since the dawn of the republic. An acceleration of frustration and divisiveness in the 1850s suggested that in the not too distant future some decisive impending change would rationalize the curriculum, but every major effort to hasten that day in the years before the Civil War came to grief. There was as yet in the United States no university in fact, although there were many in name, just as there were many colleges in name that were in fact high-grade academies. Wayland's reforms at Brown intentionally carried the seeds of a university, but they did not germinate. The faculties at Harvard and Yale were edging toward the idea of graduate programs in arts and sciences when they found themselves, instead, developing separate undergraduate science schools.

But the example of the German university, which had become a presence in American higher education with the return of George Ticknor and his friends to Harvard in the 1820s, would not go away. Just how the concept of a higher faculty of scholars who created new knowledge and trained their successors could find a place in the American college was a baffling problem. The German university with its graduate faculty of arts and sciences and professional faculties in theology, medicine, and law rested on the firm foundation of a system of rigorous academic high schools known as *Gymnasien,* whereas the American college did not yet have the support of a rational system of secondary schooling. In addition, the German university played a central role in the life of the state, certifying new recruits to the civil service as well as controlling entry into the elite professions. Neither the legal nor medical profession in the United States had yet established standards that required a college education. Theology was at the mercy of dozens of denominations and sects, some of them openly hostile to learning. College teaching was not yet a profession, and just as there was no university producing young scholars with their Ph.D.s, neither were there any universities to hire them.

Among those who tried to hasten the arrival of the university in the United States was Henry Tappan, like Wayland a graduate of Nott's Union College.[38] From 1852 to 1863 he attempted to tug the University of Michigan into an approximation of a German university. That is not what the regents had had in mind when they took him away from New York University, after having failed to entice Mark Hopkins from Williams.[39] Tappan succeeded in getting the regents to offer earned M.A. and M.S. degrees in 1858, but his emphasis on advanced scholarship and his unwillingness to move as rapidly and thoroughly into undergraduate programs of a vocational nature cost him his position in 1863. He did succeed in teaching the university that its future depended on making it an instrument for developing and rationalizing the entire system of public education in the state, but even in that enterprise he was too early for Michigan.

In New York, Columbia once more looked into the mirror and again decided that it saw a university. Beginning in 1857 it offered an M.A. program, but the menu was sparse and the response was appropriate.[40] Between 1855 and 1857, once more in New York, the idea of placing a great modern university in the city exercised the imaginations of an intellectual elite reminiscent of the gathering of 1830 in the chambers of the city council. Then the result was what became New York University, by 1850 so typical a classical college that it too asked Mark Hopkins to be its presiding officer. This time the benefactors necessary to support an ambitious university undertaking could not be persuaded that the United States needed a university: William Astor decided that an endowed library should come first, and Peter Cooper favored an institute for the dissemination of the immediately useful.[41] Yale in 1860 concluded that its faculty was equipped in some fields of inquiry to train graduate scholars; in 1861 it awarded three degrees of doctor of philosophy, the country's first Ph.D.s.[42]

The meaning for the undergraduate curriculum of these university stirrings was still hidden. Thus far in the nineteenth century the course of study had withstood any major assaults on its shape and tone. Partial courses, parallel courses, and the introduction of some options and electives may have pointed in new directions, but they were adopted as props for the classical course. Significant curricular departures, such as those at Virginia, had failed or, as at Union, been isolated. Change had been contained. The conjuncture of forces, conditions, and men necessary to precipitate a curricular revolution had been avoided.

Whether the founding and successful launching of Cornell University at Ithaca, New York, was a consequence of historical inevitability or of human impatience is a philosophical question not necessarily beyond the concern of a history of the curriculum. The question is raised here, however, for purposes of speculation rather than resolution, although a letter survives in which one founder of Cornell wrote to the other, "The physicians have ordered me to stop work. I shall not. It is not *work* that wears me out—it is waiting."[43] Cornell was revolutionary in design and influence at a time when being revolutionary was no longer stylish in the United States. It burst into the consciousness of the American academic community, such as it was, in 1866 as a blueprint; two years later it opened, enjoying the almost unique experience of being selective in its admissions. After two years in operation, Cornell enrolled more than 250 freshmen, the largest first-year class thus far in American college history. Its total enrollment at the beginning of its third year was greater than that of any other three colleges in the state of New York.[44]

All this a few short years after Francis Wayland, Henry Tappan, and the others were ushered into the museum of historical failures. What had happened in so short a time to bring into creative harmony the resources, the needs, the demands, the human energy and imagination to blow apart—literally—the American college curriculum? If the two men who shaped the course of study at Cornell had been less impatient, the revolution that Cornell found itself leading would have found other sponsors not much later. Cornell brought together in creative combination a number of dynamic ideas under circumstances that turned out to be incredibly productive. There was no way to stop the arrival of the American university. Andrew D. White, its first president, and Ezra Cornell, who gave it his name, turned out to be the developers of the first American university and therefore the agents of revolutionary curricular reform. But, if they had not, others would have. Indeed, the United States has been so coastal in its definition of what has happened that even now in Cambridge and Baltimore, New York and Philadelphia, the suggestion that Ithaca, New York, is where the American university was first successfully defined still comes as news. It could not have happened just anywhere; on the other hand, it could have happened in many places where it did not.

Ezra Cornell, whose wealth and imagination allowed him to be Western Union's largest stockholder, turned these same assets into a few words that transformed the American college curriculum: "I would found an institution where any person can find instruction in any study."[45] Andrew D. White, the university's first president, translated a classical education at Yale, scholarly training in European universities, and experience on Henry Tappan's faculty at the University of Michigan into a resolution to create a great American university.[46] The Morrill Federal Land-Grant Act of 1862, disposing of 17,430,000 acres of federal lands to support agricultural and mechanical colleges, provided them with an opportunity fashioned to their aspirations.[47]

The university that Cornell and White put together at Ithaca represented the tapping of two great sources of financial support that in their own way would reshape the curriculum: private philanthropy, which in the years after the Civil War created entire colleges and universities, and federal and state legislatures, which, in the Morrill Act, for example, created in every state a college that became a model challenge to the old colleges and the old course of study. By mid twentieth century one of every five students enrolled in degree-granting colleges and universities in the United States was attending an institution supported by the Act of 1862 and subsequent related legislation.[48]

The Act of 1862 charged each state with using proceeds from the sale of the federal lands for the support of colleges of which "the leading object shall be, without excluding other scientific or classical studies, to teach such branches of learning as are related to agriculture and the mechanic arts."[49] In the absence of a science of agriculture geared to American needs and the American landscape, agricultural education was a concept in search of some concrete validation. A few false starts preceded the colleges spawned by the Morrill Act, as well as somewhat more promising beginnings in agricultural education in Pennsylvania and Michigan.[50] The land-grant colleges took up the challenge presented to them by Congress and in the process confronted the necessity of redefining the American college curriculum. Each state ventured into essentially unchartered territory, making arrangements as seemed most appropriate to its own peculiar educational, social, and political environment.

Massachusetts founded an agricultural college and turned over some of its funds and its responsibility toward "the mechanic arts" to a new engineering college, the Massachusetts Institute of Technology. Other states, such as Wisconsin and Minnesota, turned over the land-grant endowments to existing state universities. Many states set up entirely new colleges. Two states combined the chartering of a new college with a private benefaction: Indiana created an agricultural and mechanical college by adding its endowment to a $100,000 gift of John Purdue. New York's endowment was added to Ezra Cornell's $500,000 to create the new university in Ithaca.

Not quite four decades after Jeremiah Day and his colleagues at Yale issued the definitive statement on the classical college, Andrew D. White prepared a report that was in many ways both a blueprint and a forecast of the curricular arrangements that would henceforth describe the college experience of most American undergraduates. In his *Report of the Committee on Organization, Presented to the Trustees of the Cornell University October 21st, 1866*, White confronted all the choices that had been troubling college authorities: practical or classical studies, old professions or new vocations, pure or applied science, training for culture and character or for jobs.[51]

In walking away from choice and embracing all alternatives, White made an American decision consistent with Ezra Cornell's democratic intentions and the imprecise but clear obligations of the Act of 1862 to "the liberal and practical education of the industrial classes in the several pursuits and professions of life."[52] Practical vocationalism, scientific research, applied technology, classical learning, and university scholarship all found a welcome in the Cornell Report of 1866. Ezra Cornell had thought of his university as a trade school; the curricular expectations of the U.S. Congress were not spelled out; White *knew* what he wanted: The result was the first American university and a radical transformation in the undergraduate course of study.

White spelled out his conviction that undergraduate education should be both special and general and that special—or professional—education not be "subordinated to any other."[53] He committed the university to generous access to fully developed programs of a vocational nature in a wide range of professions in which none was to be considered superior to any other.[54] He elaborated his belief in a general and less vocational education for those who desired it, but he deplored the reliance of the existing "system of collegiate instruction" on a *"single combination of studies,* into which comparatively few enter heartily." As for "where more latitude in study has been provided for, all courses outside the single traditional course have been considered to imply a lower caste in those taking them."[55] This, too, he deplored.

In White's scheme for Cornell, therefore, a readiness to extend formal training and professional recognition to such old occupations as farming, engineering, and business was accompanied by a desire to remedy the failure of the colleges to provide a general education of a nature that the public would support. Nine departments of instruction constituted a division of special sciences and arts: agriculture, mechanic arts, civil engineering, commerce and trade, mining, medicine and surgery, law, education, and a department of public service subsuming jurisprudence, political science, and history. This division of the university, which was patterned on the group option system of the Sheffield Scientific School at Yale, combined the old professions of law and medicine with seven occupations in process of professionalization and left out theology altogether.[56] For students with a specific vocational orientation, the nine departments of the division of special sciences and arts expressed a welcome hitherto denied them in any comparable way in the American college. The department of commerce and trade was intended to bring under university auspices and guidance the kind of practical business training available in so-called urban commercial colleges. The department of jurisprudence, political science, and history reflected White's sense of the importance of European universities in the development of a competent civil service.

A second division, a division of science, literature, and the arts in general, gave to students without any particular vocational preference five routes to a general course of study.[57] In a magnificent gesture toward human beings, White said that Cornell was ready to allow its young men another five ways of finding out who they were. Although the variety was unprecedented, the five Cornell general programs were not, individually, remarkable: a classical course, as always; a classical course substituting German for Greek; a classical course substituting German and French for Greek and Latin; a scientific course for specialists in the natural sciences; and an "optional course" imported from the University of Michigan, in which the choices were up to the student. Cornell University offered nine ways to move toward specific professional careers and five ways to explore: For less, F. W. Woolworth would be remembered as a pioneer in merchandising. The Cornell curriculum brought into imaginative balance the openness of American society, the temporary nature of its directions and opportunities; it multiplied truth into truths, a limited few professions into an endless number of new self-respecting ways of moving into the middle class.

In an 1862 letter to Gerrit Smith, a wealthy philanthropist whose interest he hoped to engage in his dream of a great university in the interior of New York, White wrote: "To admit women and colored persons into a *petty* college would do good to the individuals concerned; but to admit them to a great university would be a blessing to the whole colored race and the whole female sex—for the weaker colleges would be finally compelled to adopt the system."[58] Gerrit Smith was tired, and he declined the opportunity to be an instrument of White's imagination. At Cornell the admission of women was postponed four years while a benefactor provided the funds for a woman's dormitory. As for "the whole colored race," White's concern in 1862 was directed toward the particular philanthropic purposes of Gerrit Smith. Nothing special was done at Cornell for "colored persons" for another hundred years, and although White's letter said much more than it was allowed to accomplish, it was evidence of his consuming desire to overthrow the old course of study and its particular social and economic, racial and sexual orientation. With Gerrit Smith, an appropriately named Smith University would have especially advanced the education of women and blacks. With Ezra Cornell, the agricultural and mechanic classes were served. In either case, Andrew D. White was building a university.

Had White read Jeremiah Day's report of 1828 in preparation for this reasoned, even-tempered, understated assault on the old colleges? Even though he asked that it be put into italics, his rejection of the psychology of mental faculties was not so much an act of boldness as it was an expression of common sense: *"The attempt to give mental discipline by studies which the mind does not desire, is as unwise as to attempt to give physical nourishment by food which the body does not desire."*[59] In this spirit, White described the fixed prescribed curriculum as "fatal to any true university spirit" and as responsible for "bringing about that relaxation of the hold which the colleges once had upon the nation."[60] Admitting that "most students need advice," he nonetheless turned his own European university experiences and a profound skepticism toward the old psychology into a wise and liberating educational philosophy: "An overwhelming majority of students are competent to choose between different courses of study, carefully balanced and arranged by men who have brought thought and experience to the work."[61]

White's "belief in the great value of classical studies" and his readiness to recommend them to "those who have time and taste for them" did not, in his view, license Cornell to "fetter all students to them."[62] His rejection of the disciplinary faculty psychology as he had known it as a student, first at Hobart and then at Yale, was sweeping: "Discipline comes by studies which are loved, not by studies which are loathed. There is no discipline to be obtained in *droning over* studies. Vigorous, energetic study, prompted by enthusiasm or a high sense of the value of the subject, is the only kind of study not positively hurtful to mental power."[63]

In a report that attempted to establish some of the fundamental dimensions of a university—its obligations to research, yet its commitment to teaching; its recognition of the nation's need for scholars, yet its sense of a need for leaders of quality and style—one of the most jarring emphases was its promise that Cornell University would do something about the miserable relationship between faculty and students in the existing colleges. Jeremiah Day had thought of his faculty as elements of an intricate internal police force. Andrew D. White proposed in his Cornell Report of 1866 that professional salaries be supplemented so that students might be invited to tea.[64] So misleading has been the mythology of the old colleges that White's recognition of faculty-student relations as a curricular function seems misplaced. Yet the truth is that history and myth have exaggerated the Mark Hopkinses, ignored the suppressed combat in which conflicting values separated student from professor, and presented a picture of institutional harmony that was altogether false. "One of the saddest deficiencies in existing colleges," White wrote, "is want of free intercourse, and even of acquaintance, between professors and students." Cornell University proposed to make it "worth our trouble to try some experiments at least in bringing students within range of the general culture of professors, and keeping them within it."[65]

White was defining a university, an intellectual community, an environment such as Woodrow Wilson would attempt at Princeton fifty years later and that Thomas Jefferson had tried to create from inspired architecture forty years earlier. Was the shared sympathy of professor and student for one another and the academic culture that bound them together a curricular discovery and consequence of the university movement? To believe Andrew D. White in the Cornell Report of 1866 is to have to think so.

Cornell was not a complete university at birth, nor was it intended to be, but it soon established an identity and style of its own, as it went about defining an American university. The absence of a department of theology and White's determined stance of nonsectarianism for the university allowed its enemies among the threatened small colleges to charge it with being godless. An appropriate balance between pure science and training in applied science was difficult to achieve. Students attracted to Cornell were so vocationally oriented that their pattern of course selections shoved Cornell more in the direction of an expanding technical curriculum than in the direction of a broadened range of opportunities in the liberal arts and sciences. At Harvard a different clientele used the elective system to shove Harvard in the opposite direction.[66] In both cases, however, the

lesson was clear: The shape of the curriculum, the growth of departments, the peculiar instructional mix of any particular institution
was a measure of the degree of choice allowed to students and the
responsiveness of the institution to those choices.

White played a creative role in establishing military training
and physical education as elements of the undergraduate course of
study. His enthusiasm for both these diversions from the serious business of the university may have been a reflection of the point of view
expressed to the students in his inaugural address:

> You are not here to be made; you are here to make your-
> selves. You are not here to hang upon an university; you
> are here to help build an university. This is no place for
> children's tricks and toys, for exploits which only excite
> the wonderment of boarding school misses.[67]

Physical culture and military drill presumably provided boarding
school misses with more worthy sources of wonderment than more
traditional expenditures of excess student energy.

Although the Morrill Act, as any educational bill drafted during
the Civil War might have been expected to do, required the land-grant
colleges to establish student military companies, it did not make military training compulsory.[68] Military training in the colleges, land-
grant or otherwise, has been generally a postwar phenomenon, a
passing enthusiasm. The land-grant colleges founded immediately
after the Civil War were particularly vulnerable to the military training movement, and, as strikes, riots, and social unrest increasingly
defined late nineteenth-century America, another support for military training appeared. In 1874 White, who had made military training compulsory for all general course students, explained his position: "Of all fatal things for a republic, the most fatal is to have its
educated men in various professions so educated that, in any civil
commotion, they must cower in corners, and relinquish the control of
armed force to communists and demagogues."[69] For various reasons
and at various times and places, military training was taken seriously,
as seriously indeed as it was taken at Cornell under Andrew D. White,
but the characteristic experience for this detour from collegiate pur-

pose was that at Indiana, where compulsory drill was adopted in 1868 and discontinued in 1874.[70]

Physical education was quite another matter. The Cornell Report of 1866 wondered whether it would not be a good idea to experiment with a rule "to the effect that deterioration in physical culture will be held in the same category with want of progress in mental culture, and that either will subject the delinquent to deprivation of university privileges."[71] From the beginning Cornell required physical education and hygiene in all programs and courses except the optional course. By the end of the century, when the elective movement was at high tide, at Harvard the only surviving course requirement was English composition in freshman year; at Cornell it was physical education.[72] The image of the college student as "narrow-chested, round-shouldered, stooped . . . and in an exceedingly imperfect condition physically" is of ancient and reputable lineage.[73] Cornell's readiness to change that image coincided with an enthusiastic extracurricular interest in gymnastics and organized athletics and with the beginnings of formal instruction in physical education elsewhere, especially among such old New England colleges as Amherst, which was first in 1860, and Williams, which followed in 1866.[74]

The physical education movement had everything going for it and nothing going against it. Like military training, it was a diversion from the serious business of the colleges and universities, only it was more fun. It could be—and was—exaggerated into overriding importance by university administrators, including Andrew D. White, who surely knew better than to say, as he did in his inaugural address, that "today in the United States physical education and development is a more pressing necessity even than mental development."[75] It lent itself to the old promise that the colleges were committed to turning out "manly men"; it was responsive to a developing knowledge of human health and physiology; and it charged the sons and daughters of a rising middle class with putting themselves into the kind of physical shape necessary to fulfill their appropriate social roles. "As long as highly educated men are dyspeptics," White warned, "so long will they be deprived of their supremacy in society by uneducated *eupeptics.*"[76] The stress on physical education was not intended to lead to the great explosion of extracurricular athletic rivalries later in the century and the building of arenas for gladiatorial football contests in the twentieth century, but some curricular enthusiasms get out of control and lose their way. Physical education was one of these: A serious effort to develop a sound body as the receptacle of a sound mind in the end was overwhelmed by all those developments that diverted effort and attention from the gymnasium to the football stadium. What began as a venture in body building gave way to college and university athletics as a spectator sport.

The revolutionary reputation of Cornell was greatly advanced by the university's inevitable but delayed adherence to a policy of coeducation in 1872, a delay that had been prompted by the absence of a suitable dormitory.[77] Coeducation at Cornell—the first in the East—was an immediate success, sending new waves of uncertainty and nervousness through the old colleges. In the early 1870s, Amherst, Williams, and Wesleyan gave official consideration to adopting Cornell's policy; Wesleyan went coeducational in 1872.[78] The announcement of the founding of Vassar in 1860 and the opening of both Smith and Wellesley in 1875 as separate women's colleges advanced in the East, as did Cornell's policy of coeducation, the cause of higher education for women, a cause that had been making isolated advances before the Civil War, especially in western state institutions and small special institutions for women.[79]

Women's colleges and coeducation contributed a new set of influences on the American college curriculum, turning the course of study in a number of directions that were both innovative and troublesome. By adopting courses of study essentially the same as those in the men's colleges, the new eastern women's colleges burdened the curriculum with proving the mental, psychological, and physical fitness of women for higher learning. Early coeducational institutions developed courses of study that supported the concept of woman's compensatory role in performing tasks not appropriated by men—home management, such refinements as music and art, child care, and elementary schooling. Early Oberlin paid more attention to woman's domestic role than to her mind.[80]

Domesticity made less headway as a curricular value in the new women's colleges, where the creation of courses and programs of study that opened up new careers for women—in social work, public health, and education—widened woman's social role without raising her consciousness unduly or threatening men. To these new influences on the curriculum was added, especially in coeducational environments, the notion of masculine courses and feminine courses, the definition of particular subjects as feminine as a function of their popularity with women, the marking off of some domains of the curriculum, such as engineering, as territory forbidden to women. The curriculum was neither more nor less outrageous than the general society on the subject of the sexes. It neither led nor followed—it reflected. Cornell's role was to dramatize the legitimacy of coeducational arrangements in an at first skeptical East. In this it succeeded.[81]

Clearly the tone of Cornell was practical. The wonder of its style was the discovery that the most abstruse knowledge could be turned to social and political utility. Suddenly, it seemed, history could talk, was allowed to speak, because authority sent out the message: Listen! White, who projected a professional career in public service as a creation of Cornell's department of jurisprudence, political science, and history, wrote a functional definition of historical study in 1878:

> We ought to teach history in such a way that it can be applied to the immediate needs of our time. The period has hardly arrived for elegant and learned investigation on points of mere scholarly interest. Our knowledge of history must be brought to bear on our time to prevent, if possible, some few of the mistakes in the future from which mankind has suffered in the past.[82]

White cast Cornell University in a direction calculated to demonstrate that study paid off. History and social science appeared first at Cornell in functional guise and thus achieved popularity; "elegant and learned investigation" had first to be underwritten by popular acceptance.[83]

There is nothing really surprising to a student of the undergraduate curriculum in the discovery that in 1881 Cornell established "the first department of American history in any college in the land."[84] Where else? Five years later at Princeton, where there was but one professor of history, the president of the college there offered a defense: "I think the numerous narrative histories of epochs is just a let-off to easy-going students from the studies which require thought."[85] Matthew Arnold, better poet and essayist than educational critic, but nonetheless a persuasive voice in Victorian England, said: "Cornell University rests upon a provincial misconception of what culture is, and is calculated to produce miners, engineers, or architects, not sweetness and light."[86] Cornell University knew what it was doing; it could afford the disapproval of the president of Princeton and the son of the headmaster of Rugby.

It also weathered simultaneous attacks for debasing classical studies and for neglecting agricultural and mechanical studies. It deflected the criticism by religious journals of the university's policy of substituting a series of visiting clergymen for a resident university preacher. By 1873 it could afford to be amused by a Hamilton College literary journal that heaped scorn on a Cornell graduate because the Cornell degree might represent competence in "anything from a mongrel classical course to a course which treats of the ablest manner of utilizing manures."[87]

It won the support of farmers not initially but as soon as it was able to prove that it had hold of something from which farmers could benefit; every land-grant institution in the end had counterparts to Cornell's Professor Liberty Hyde Bailey, who became a consulting diagnostician and therapist for the ills of New York agriculture.[88] In January, 1870, the *Northern Christian Advocate* charged that "at Cornell . . . even atheists may be professors; President White is not a church member; the atmosphere is Broad Churchish; Christian ideas are ignored; the leaders, who call themselves 'liberal Christians,' are in fact polished skeptics . . . and attendance at chapel is not compulsory."[89] All this was true, and it did not matter.

The evidence that the Cornell curriculum was taking the country in the direction in which it wanted to go was overwhelming. The 1866 report met a favorable response in the *North American Review*. The editors of the *Independent* welcomed the promise of "a great advance movement in the high education of the country," noting that "Cornell University strikes down at a single blow that tyranny of 'classical studies,' which American colleges inherited from the old English universities, and which they inherited from an age of monks, priests, and bigots—an age scornful of science."[90]

Some of the early enthusiasm for Cornell was predictable. Daniel Coit Gilman, not yet the president of the University of California or the first president of Johns Hopkins, wrote from his position on the faculty of the Sheffield Scientific School at Yale: "The shade of Homer may hover with indignation over the modern Ithaca —but it will be in vain."[91] Francis Wayland asked in the *Nation:* "Are we not most truly pupils of Aristotle and Plato and Socrates when we practice original enquiry and abandon obsolete traditions?"[92] The *New York Evening Post* expressed a widely shared hostility to the ancient languages in an approving editorial when the university opened: "A thoroughly well-educated young man is quite as well entitled to be called a bachelor of arts as a student who has droned over Greek and Latin at the cost of nearly all his knowledge."[93] *Harper's Magazine* recognized in White's inaugural address a man "who plainly saw the demand of the country and of the time in education, and who with sincere reverence for the fathers was still wise enough to know that wisdom did not die with them."[94]

So quickly did Cornell establish itself that an attack on Ezra Cornell's handling of the university's endowment resulted in an outpouring of gifts; its openness to all religions and its commitment to none was a source of endowment, including a professorship of Hebrew, oriental literature, and history, to which Felix Adler was appointed, leading the *New York Times* to conclude that "we are approaching the day when the advanced education of the country will be given not in sectarian colleges but in universities where no test is imposed save fitness for the position conferred."[95] Twenty years after it opened, *Harper's Weekly* said of the university in Ithaca: "With a grip upon the best methods of education which is almost beyond the reach of an institution weighted down by traditions . . . Cornell University stands in the vantage-ground, if not at the head, of American educational institutions."[96]

Cornell University was the first new institution of higher education in America since the founding of Harvard College to succeed in becoming a model for other institutions and a far-reaching influence on the curriculum. White's success at Cornell initially moved the definition of the American university away from the dominant research interest that characterized the universities of Germany toward an emphasis on service to the material and moral aspirations of the mid-

dle class. This was an emphasis that the situation of higher education
in the United States required and that also explained Cornell's great
popularity. Before identifying Cornell with research and scholarship,
White identified it with an educational philosophy that helped poor
but energetic young men and women to get rich.

So persuasive to others was Cornell's success that the service
function of the curriculum became a guiding motive in the development of the course of study in the great state universities and land-
grant colleges that began to shape themselves in the image of Cornell.
Cornell's curriculum, with its emphasis on an equality of studies and
its welcome to occupations on their way to becoming professions, was
also instrumental in blurring the traditional distinction between the
professions and the vocations.[97] For as long as anyone could remember there had really been only three professions, the only three occupations requiring formal study and instruction—divinity, law, and
medicine. A case can perhaps be made for a fourth, the military, but
only the other three found support in the universities of Great Britain
and continental Europe. All other occupations could be entered without academic training, through apprenticeships and training on the
job. College professors might have studied for the ministry, but they
need not have; and not yet were they required to establish credentials
to teach their academic specialties.

These neat distinctions, however, were in the process of breaking down. New knowledge, new technology were creating both new
occupations and the necessity for formal training where apprenticeship had once sufficed. A recognition of the role of research and scholarship as a university function was creating a profession of college
and university professors. In placing the emerging professions on a
par with the old ones and then organizing a cluster of undergraduate
programs designed as preparation for a wide variety of careers,
Cornell put vocational education on a solid curricular base. These
developments, while blurring the old distinction between the professions and vocations, also blurred the distinction between what went
on in a college and what went on in a university. Once a place like
Cornell had demonstrated the existence of great popular approval for
making career preparation a guiding purpose of its undergraduate
curriculum, not only was the educational philosophy of the Morrill
Act of 1862 fully vindicated, but the college course of study itself was

now fully wrested from the control of the classicists and henceforth at the mercy of the vocationalists. To a considerable extent, the history of the curriculum since the opening of Cornell has been a continuing struggle between the humanists for whom Cornell's great success was a clear defeat and the vocationalists for whom Ithaca might properly be considered a shrine. In 1875 and 1876, in an era that was drunk with competitiveness and subject to centennial fevers, the eastern colleges indulged in more intercollegiate competition than had been their custom: In both the regattas and the academic contests Cornell students came in first.

Cornell's one great weakness allowed a new institution in Baltimore, Johns Hopkins University, to undertake an experiment that advertised Cornell's failing but that did not replace it as an ideal, except for three institutions that for a while were allowed to think that Johns Hopkins was a viable model. Colleges on their way to becoming universities could learn from the university in Baltimore that a stronger commitment to research and scholarship was needed than Cornell found possible in its early years, but to do so they did not have to adopt the hostility to undergraduates or the extravagant and worshipful regard for the Ph.D. that was nurtured at Johns Hopkins. New institutions that thought that they, like Johns Hopkins, could become instant copies of a continental university, with some necessary omissions and additions appropriate to the American scene— Clark University in Worcester, Catholic University in Washington, and Bryn Mawr in suburban Philadelphia—would not have developed as they did had it not been for Johns Hopkins. But Johns Hopkins, while its influence was widespread and its role in demonstrating the nation's need for and capacity for producing scholars was essential, was in its own way as out of touch with the basic directions of American society as were the classical colleges beyond which Cornell had quickly moved.[98]

Cornell had not yet picked up with enthusiasm or commitment or imagination the torch of pure scientific scholarship that was the great glory of the nineteenth-century German university. The torch was aglow in Ithaca, all right, but White knew his country and the university's principal benefactor well: He would drag both Ezra Cornell and Cornell University almost unsuspectingly into the realms of pure and esoteric scholarship while focusing on the application of learning to the material wants of a rising people. Johns Hopkins, under the leadership of Daniel Coit Gilman, one of White's Yale contemporaries, became an expression of a different emphasis and a different impatience. It chose to be the first great American university dedicated to advanced learning and the production of scholars, and its success, like Cornell's, sent a creative impulse through institutions struggling to get out from under the grasp of collegiate traditions.[99]

The benefactor who gave the university his name was a Baltimore railroad investor, but the real founders of Johns Hopkins were the trustees who set themselves the task of creating a university instead of a college. How to do so was not immediately apparent. Harvard and Yale were moving toward university dimensions by entirely different routes, Harvard by blurring undergraduate and graduate instruction, Yale by keeping them separate. Cornell and Michigan were bringing the theoretical and practical together in an effort to entice students into their classrooms and scholars onto their faculties. The Johns Hopkins trustees decided to try something new —a university that, while including an undergraduate college, considered productive scholarship and scientific research its central purpose.[100]

The impact of their decision was immediate and widespread. Offered an opportunity to leave Williams for a professorship at the new university, Ira Remsen leaped at the opportunity to escape from an environment in which his request for modest laboratory space was met with a stern rebuke from the president of the college: "You will please keep in mind that this is a college and not a technical school." At Harvard, Francis J. Child, a Chaucerian scholar drowning in a sea of freshman themes, translated an offer from Johns Hopkins into release from the duties that had frustrated his scholarly aspirations.[101] The new Johns Hopkins was dedicated to the search for truths as yet unknown; the slumbering colleges where its impact would soon be felt in the presence of young men with the Hopkins Ph.D. had in a sense possessed all the truth that they needed in revealed religion and the humanist tradition.[102] Johns Hopkins advanced a philosophy of research and inquiry that would force major readjustments on a curriculum already learning how to respond to the developments in Ithaca.

As a model of the research university, Johns Hopkins had much to convey—a spirit that could be carried anywhere and supported by vast philanthropies or by lonely scholars in their libraries; the concept of a *major* concentration in a cluster of related subjects constituting specialization, to which a broadening experience was added in a lesser cluster called a *minor;* the young men with their Ph.D.'s and their enthusiasm for study and learning.[103] The importance of what was going on in Baltimore was not lost on the outnumbered scholars in the laboratories and libraries in Cambridge, Providence, New Haven, New York, Princeton, and Philadelphia. The presidents of state universities, gathering new support from state legislatures for having discovered how to be popular, knew that they could not be universities in reality until the spirit of Johns Hopkins had become as pervasive as the spirit of Cornell. In an environment competitive, materialistic, and rich with new money, the imagination soared. College presidents went to bed and entertained themselves with dreams of universities.

The decline of Johns Hopkins both as a center of production of scholars and as an influence after the 1890s and the failure of its closest imitator, Clark University, were instructive evidence that scholarship and research could not easily be made the dominant purpose of an American university.[104] Johns Hopkins, however, had paved the way for a successful assault on the undergraduate course of study; advanced work leading to the Ph.D. degree became one earmark of an American university; the degree itself became a necessary credential in the emerging profession of college and university teaching; the teachers proceeded to redesign the course of study according to educational philosophy as practiced in Baltimore.

The opening of Cornell in 1868 and its immediate success required of the old prestigious eastern institutions soul-searching of an intensity that they had avoided since the reassuring era of the Yale Report. Both Harvard and Yale responded in character: Harvard elected a new president and moved ahead, Yale elected a new president hoping more or less to stand still. The instrument of Harvard's future was Charles William Eliot, a chemist at the Lawrence Scientific School passed over for promotion in 1863, called back to Harvard from M.I.T. to become its president in 1869. The instrument of Yale's hopes was Noah Porter, a graduate of Jeremiah Day's Yale, professor of moral philosophy at the college since 1846, an eloquent spokesman for the old course of study, and an obvious selection for the presidency of Yale in 1871.[105]

In two extensive statements of his educational philosophy, one an analysis of the relationships between the colleges and society published in 1870 and the other his inaugural address of 1871, Porter gave no indication that he was aware of the conditions that would allow a Yale historian a century later to write: "Though the old college course . . . had changed somewhat and had been made more difficult, it was near death."[106] Just as Day's Report of 1828 had to some extent been triggered by George Ticknor's curricular stirrings in Cambridge, Porter's 1870 treatise on the course of study was a defense of the traditional curriculum from the perversions that had occurred at Cornell. In a way, Porter's book was Jeremiah Day brought up to date. The ancient languages were described as essential, central, and crowning elements of the course of study; the modern languages were held to be less valuable in imparting mental discipline and less valuable as guides to the wisdom of the past and to "the intellectual and esthetic culture of the student." As for English composition and literature, Porter considered such studies important but of even less value than modern languages.[107]

What to do about science gave him no problem, since Yale had developed the separate but not equal Sheffield Scientific School as a response to the demand for what Yale would give only reluctantly.[108] His Yale colleague, Timothy Dwight the younger, thought that the matter of whether a classical or scientific course was better could be solved only by keeping them in separate institutions, such as Yale's, and then comparing the students:

> If the man who is classically educated feels and knows within himself, that he stands on a higher level of intellectual cultivation than his associate who has followed the new education, and if this associate knows and feels that he is himself on a lower grade —if this is true of every fair-

minded student in either line, or of the great majority of such students, the determination will, ere long, be reached by the public mind, that the old is better than the new.[109]

There is no reason to believe that either Dwight or Porter had any doubts as to what the results of such a test would be.

Porter's analysis narrowed his appeal to a much smaller audience than that which Andrew D. White addressed. His message to young men contemplating careers in business was: A liberal education rather than a practical education will serve you better. His message to young men from the lower and middle classes was downright discouraging: One aim of the college curriculum is to impart a "higher polish" to a "receptive and refined nature," such as found in "youths whose general as well as special training has been liberal and refined both at school and at home." Yale's intention to set its goal on what it considered the needs of a leisured upper class was clarified in Porter's inaugural address: "We prefer the theory of liberal culture which assumes that an increasing rather than diminishing number of our choicest youth of leisure will continue their literary and scientific studies, and thus be able to dignify and adorn their life by habits of systematic research and of earnest literary activity." If Cornell chose to place itself on the side of the aspiring middle classes, Yale just as clearly placed itself among gentlemen of culture.[110]

Porter used his 1870 book to attack both the theory and the practices that defined Cornell. He rejected such arrangements as White's use of visiting lecturers, electives, and parallel courses, the relative freedom of Cornell students from discipline, and the absence of "a vigorous religious influence" supported by a strong denominational tie.[111] He held to the emphasis of the Yale Report on the disciplining of the mind, but he had some trouble with the old furniture concept. With other critics of Cornell, all he could really do was object to Cornell's furniture, which moved him dangerously close to rejecting furniture altogether: "The college course is preeminently designed to give power to acquire and to think, rather than to impart special knowledge or special discipline."[112]

Lest anyone take seriously Cornell's claim to be a university, Porter defined one and then proceeded to disqualify the institution in Ithaca:

[Universities are characterized by] the presence of a considerable body of students of liberal culture who are prepared by that culture to select some higher department of knowledge and to pursue it under the teachers of their choice, by free and independent methods of study.[113]

Cornell's standards of admission and its commitment to Ezra Cornell's intention to teach "all comers . . . anything or everything which they need or desire to study" placed it "near the chaotic or amorphic condition; or rather is like one of those reptiles which were supposed to be produced from the slime of the Nile—the foreparts organized, and the remainder . . . 'plain mud'."[114] A university? Hardly! Porter may have been right in suggesting that Cornell was an invitation to chaos, but it was also a remedy to the imbalance between the moribund Yale curriculum and the excitement of the extracurriculum as revealed in Lyman Bagg's *Four Years at Yale* in 1869, a challenge to the invidious distinction between students in Yale College and students in Sheffield Scientific School, and a response to the needs of emerging professions and a dynamic middle class.[115]

At Yale all the vitality was on the wrong side of the campus. At a time when Yale College seniors were reciting from textbooks in political economy, moral philosophy, and theology written by self-taught members of the Williams College faculty, students in their final year at the Sheffield Scientific School were studying the history of language, French, botany, zoology, agricultural chemistry, geology, anatomy, and astronomy, and were attending lectures in military science, history, political philosophy, and international law. Sheffield's new premed option was the first of its kind in the United States.[116] In 1870, the year in which Noah Porter placed English below the modern languages in his scale of importance, Thomas R. Lounsbury joined the faculty of the scientific school and proceeded to work "a revolution in the teaching of English in America" by moving beyond rhetoric to English literature: Suddenly, Chaucer, Shakespeare, and Milton were not exercises in grammar but explorations in literature.[117]

The Yale College curriculum had not been unchanging. By 1870, in contrast to 1845, Latin had been considerably reduced in time required, and, while rhetoric, logic, and moral philosophy held their own, the so-called new subjects had made significant headway: There was twice as much history, modern languages had been elevated from optional to required, juniors could drop a term of Latin or Greek in favor of differential calculus, and the time devoted to science had doubled. Yet the general tone of the Yale curriculum was elementary, superficial, and unimaginative. It failed to encourage inquiry. Any esthetic concern was conspicuously absent. It was dying.[118]

The situation at Harvard was less discouraging. One happy sign, in fact, had been the appointment of the German-trained chemist, Wolcott Gibbs, to the Rumford professorship in 1863 and the bypassing of the local candidate, Charles W. Eliot, a young man with all the right connections but without German training or an established research reputation.[119] Like Porter, whose 1870 book was surely an advertisement of himself, Eliot put himself and his educational philosophy on display in two articles in the *Atlantic Monthly*.[120] "The New Education," as his essays were called, appeared while the Harvard fellows and overseers were in the process of electing a new president. They so clearly put him on the side of reform that at first the two Harvard governing bodies were divided on the choice of Eliot.[121] The reform-minded fellows won, and Eliot in 1869 launched himself and Harvard on a forty-year transformation of a provincial college into a national university.

At the time of his inauguration the freshman year at Harvard was wholly prescribed. The other three years, within certain limits, were approximately half elective.[122] Harvard had been creeping toward where Eliot intended to pull it, and that comfortable pace must have been what the president of the board of overseers had in mind when, as a speaker at Eliot's inauguration ceremonies, he referred to "the long procession of those who are to enter these halls, to pass through the prescribed curriculum of study."[123]

One of the reforms, however, with which Eliot was already clearly associated was electives, and he did not, either in the *Atlantic* articles or in his inaugural remarks, shy away from how he intended to use student freedom of course selection as an instrument for redefining Harvard. He did, however, fill his public statements with reassurances. The separation of the collegiate from the scientific was sound: He would not contaminate the classical with the technical or the technical with the classical. "It will be generations," he said, "before the best of American institutions of education will get growth enough to bear pruning," thus calming the fears of friends of the classics who saw Harvard headed for a program of curricular subtraction rather than addition.[124] Eliot's soaring imagination allowed only for growth. Harvard would have everything: "This university recognizes no real antagonism between literature and science, and consents to no such narrow alternatives as mathematics or classics, science or metaphysics. We would have them all, and at their best."[125]

Just as Noah Porter made clear that he intended to hold Yale to the best of the past, Eliot wanted no one to misunderstand where Harvard was heading. In his inaugural address he issued the college, on its way to becoming a university, a license as instrumental of change as was Ezra Cornell's similar simple statement of intention: "The college therefore proposes to persevere in its efforts to establish, improve, and extend the elective system."[126] It was now but a year after the opening of the university at Ithaca, and with Eliot's guidance Harvard was being pointed in university directions along lines consistent with its history and purposes, just as Andrew D. White and Ezra Cornell with great sensitivity defined a university that could grow in upstate New York.

Eliot's sense of the appropriateness of the elective system for his purposes was unerring. It allowed Harvard to respect the individual talents, interests, and worth of every young man. It encouraged him to become almost romantic in his expression of what was a forthright rejection of the faculty psychology to which Yale still adhered: "When the revelation of his own peculiar taste and capacity comes to a young man, let him reverently give it welcome, thank God, and take courage."[127] Andrew D. White had meant to say the same thing and indeed acted according to the very same philosophy, but there was a difference that mattered when the president of Harvard, sounding just a bit like Ralph Waldo Emerson, could be quoted as having said that "the natural bent and peculiar quality of every boy's mind should be sacredly regarded in his education."[128]

Eliot wanted a university in Cambridge quite as much as White wanted one in Ithaca and, as a matter of fact, as much as Porter wanted one in New Haven or as James B. Angell wanted one in Ann Arbor. The particular strength and peculiarity of Eliot's position was his recognition that the elective system would allow him to use the curriculum to fulfill that purpose as well as bring to the support of Harvard the resources necessary to carry it out. For a broadening of the elective system was an encouragement to students and professors to design a curriculum according to their interests, and there was no question in Eliot's mind, as there should not have been, what those interests would lead to. More applied science, more economic progress, more support from the manufacturing class. Enthusiastic students, enthusiastic professors, lively instruction all moving toward a higher level of scholarship.

There was something uncanny about how White at Cornell and Eliot at Harvard could be so thoroughly different and yet so thoroughly American and so headed in the same direction. The professionalization of the Harvard faculty was already well under way before Eliot assumed the presidency, but Eliot saw how to use the elective system to assist that process, and then to spend money (higher salaries, sabbaticals, tenure, pensions) to buy a faculty that would shape Harvard into a university at the expense of whatever had once been Harvard College.[129]

Eliot's design was not cynical. If it called for conquering Harvard College, it also called for raising the standards of admission at the professional schools to a level that required a B.A. for admission. The result was a strengthening of the college by giving it solid purpose and a new source of enrollment. Eliot was a man of his time. There was nothing particularly original in his curricular philosophy: It is recoverable from the writings of Ticknor, Wayland, and Tappan. His recognition of the importance to his era of individual self-reliance, choice, and self-determination was an echo of Emerson and Thoreau and a shared conviction of the new rich and the immigrant poor.[130]

He had the wit to keep himself from being identified with a losing cause: The classics had served whatever purpose they were going to, and no one could stem the tide against them, neither the president of Harvard nor the president of Yale. Something quite fundamental was happening to the curriculum and the students. At Henry Dunster's Harvard there had been no question about whether the curriculum had been designed for society. At Charles W. Eliot's Harvard the course of study was to some extent up for grabs. Students and faculty both now asserted curricular authority that had once been firmly lodged in institutional tradition. To a degree that would become clearer as the years passed students and professors possessed authority that had once been lodged in the course of study. Eliot at Harvard and White at Cornell, before the nation had reached its centenary, and Gilman at Johns Hopkins in the centennial year itself, all joined in striking down the curriculum as it had been received from the past. They spoke different languages, but in translation their message was the same.

The proliferation of undergraduate academic degrees was one measure of the flexibility that was on its way. To preserve the integrity of the B.A. degree required alternative degrees for all those variations of the course of study that did not meet general expectations of what a sound classical education was supposed to be. The bachelor of philosophy (B.Phil.) degree was introduced by Brown in 1850 and first awarded in 1851; Yale chose it in 1852 as the degree to be conferred by the Sheffield Scientific School. Wesleyan in Connecticut began awarding the bachelor of science (B.S.) degree for its scientific course in 1838; Harvard chose it in 1851 as the degree to be conferred by the Lawrence Scientific School. These two degrees, along with the bachelor of literature (B.Litt.), became the most widely used alternative designations for the various general courses in which science, modern languages, and English were substituted for Latin and Greek.[131]
The movement of a great number of vocational programs into the undergraduate curriculum created a wave of alphabet combinations that would not be equaled until the era of New Deal government agencies. The B.Sci.Ag. was first awarded by the Farmer's High School of Pennsylvania in 1861. In the 1870s the B.Home Ec. was awarded to women graduates of the land-grant institutions in Iowa, Illinois, and Kansas, where departments of cookery and household art, sewing, and home economics were established as counterparts to the vocational programs considered appropriate for men. Adrian College in Michigan awarded the first B.Mus. in 1873. Programs preparatory to teaching led to the B. of Didactics at Iowa in 1877 and the B. of Pedagogics at Missouri the same year.[132] Engineering required a set of its own—C.E., M.E., and E.E. In a period of curricular breakdown, however, the invention of degrees would accelerate. Not until a

later period of standardization and rationalization would some order
be forced upon the degree-awarding process.[133]

In the meantime, what to do about women? Bachelors of arts?
Oberlin had thought so when it awarded the B.A. to its first women
graduates in 1841. But the designation jarred in the late nineteenth
century. Wheaton awarded the degree of "sister of arts" in 1873;
Waco, the degree of "maid of arts," in 1879.[134]

New degree programs were symbolic of the rearrangements in
the curriculum that necessarily accompanied the movements that
White, Eliot, and Gilman were in a sense directing from their academic command posts in Ithaca, Cambridge, and Baltimore. The old
moral philosophy course became something of an anachronism in an
environment that no longer addressed itself to the unity of knowledge
but was so busy piling it up that to many observers only anarchy and
disunity could be at the end of the road. As Wilson Smith has said, as a
result of "the vast revolution and expansion of knowledge resulting
from the Enlightenment and the industrial revolution . . . there was
more new learning of an empirical and speculative nature than the
moral philosopher could handle technically in his course and con-
ceptually in his theological system of ethics."[135]

All the unity that had made the moral philosophy course the
capstone delight of the curriculum was in the process of collapse. At
Harvard the job of pulling psychology out from moral philosophy
and informing it with the insights and methods of physiology was
performed by William James. His freshman course on physiological
psychology in 1876 was innovative. Departments of social science—at
Cornell, Harvard, Johns Hopkins, and Columbia—took charge of
traditional political economy, added political and constitutional history, and assumed the responsibility for defining the parameters of
social responsibility and the principles of political and social organization. By the 1890s a profession of economists with theories and a jar-
gon of its own was laying claim to territory that had once been confi-
dently traversed by the moral philosophers.[136]

Imaginatively trained scholars appeared on campuses that
could no longer resist the invasion of the course of study by new subjects and a new style. Arthur W. Wright, one of the three young men
awarded the first American Ph.D. degrees at Yale in 1861, arrived at

Williams in 1868 to teach physics and chemistry, even though in his letter of recommendation President Theodore Dwight Woolsey described him as "probably a Christian in difficulty." Wright won the appointment regardless of his reputed skepticism because Woolsey's letter also said, "I have no doubt he would teach chemistry better than it is taught here." In 1870 John W. Burgess arrived on the Amherst campus and promptly enthralled his seniors with a demonstration of what German historical scholarship was all about.[137]

Eliot in his inaugural address complained of the neglect of the "systematic study of the English language," a neglect that would be so remedied during the next thirty years that by 1900, even at Yale, English language and literature had replaced the classics as the backbone of the humanities. One of the most remarkable curricular abnormalities of the century, one to which colleges and universities in search of English turned after the Civil War, began in 1857 at Lafayette College, where Francis A. March was appointed Professor of English Language and Comparative Philology. March taught *Paradise Lost* and *Julius Caesar* before 1860 as if they were classics; his combination of literary analysis and comparative philology had no counterpart elsewhere in the United States.[138] March wrested English literature away from the old rhetoric tradition, with its stultifying emphasis on form and rules, and took to it some of the concern with thought, criticism, and esthetics that had characterized the uses of literature in the literary societies.[139]

"We cannot afford to neglect the fine arts," President Eliot warned the audience at his inauguration, speaking against a long tradition of neglect that only recently had given way to the beginnings of some serious esthetic concern in the curriculum. In the 1770s the trustees of Princeton refused to reimburse President Witherspoon for a book of prints he had paid for, thus clarifying their own attitude toward the study of art. At Amherst a hundred years later, "the study of music was missing but not missed, the study of the other fine arts was an adjunct of ancient language, and the study of literature was a vehicle for imparting moral precept." Eliot himself as late as 1915 was lamenting that although "the training of the senses should always have been a prime object in human education . . . that prime object it has never been, and is not today. . . . As a rule, the young men admitted to American colleges can neither draw nor sing; and they possess no other skill of eye, ear, or hand."[140]

Under these circumstances, the career of the fine arts in the course of study would be slow, halting, and ambiguous. The earliest manifestation of a recognition of the arts in a college was likely to be the hanging of some pictures. When James Bowdoin died in 1811, he bequeathed a considerable collection of paintings and drawings to the college bearing his name. By 1850 the most serious esthetic problem at Bowdoin was not whether to teach art or where to hang James Bowdoin's collection but what to do with a copy of Titian's "Danae and the Golden Shower" as well as someone's "Nymphs Bathing." The Bowdoin board of trustees in 1850 approved the sale of both pictures in order to protect students from "contamination from spectacles thought among us to be in bad taste." The "Nymphs" went in 1852, the "Danae" in 1860.[141]

When John Trumbull in 1831 offered to Yale College his series of paintings of the American Revolution in consideration of a life annuity and a suitable building to house them, Yale, with the help of the Connecticut legislature, proceeded to build the first college art museum in the United States. College art galleries were more likely to be repositories of fig-leafed plaster casts of examples of Greek and Roman sculpture, portraits of the alumni, and water color or photographic reproductions of famous paintings. In the competitive and financially expansive decades of the late nineteenth century, however, a $50,000 art collection and $25,000 to house it were given to the University of California by a benefactor who hoped thereby to recapture in Berkeley something of the artistic grandeur that was Rome. In 1882 the offer of a collection of porcelain and pottery, followed by a gift of $60,000 for a building to house it, corrected at Princeton the narrow vision of a century earlier.[142]

Instruction in art and art history did not flow automatically from the existence of a gallery of pictures and other artifacts. And, of course, the extracurriculum played a compensatory role. In 1858 a group of Williams students, taking taste and refinement and "food for thought" as their purpose, organized an art association that succeeded in assembling a collection of engravings and laying the foundations of a modest art library. The student who asked in 1870,

"When is Williams College to have a professorship of the fine arts?'',
received his answer when Richard Austin Rice was appointed to a
professorship of art and civilization in 1903.[143]

Instruction in art and art history confronted formidable barriers. Esthetic considerations were not likely to be primary in the
minds of a people laying claim to an undeveloped continent, even if
Puritan values had not been dominant in matters of taste. As institutions exclusively for men, the old colleges assigned esthetics to
women and covered what little was thought necessary in an instructional nature in a passing way in the course in moral philosophy. The
movement of art into programs for women in the developing coeducational colleges of the Midwest and West may have given "taste" a
new hold in the curriculum but it also gave it a new handicap. The
appointment of Alvah Bradish to a professorship of the theory and
practice of the fine arts at the University of Michigan in 1852 was premature; he apparently gave occasional short courses of lectures without compensation. Since his appointment preceded the adoption of a
policy of coeducation at Michigan by over a decade, it was not a gesture toward female clients. Was it an effort to show the East that,
benighted though it was, the West was trying?[144]

The first art courses and programs of more than an ephemeral
nature required a determined benefactor, a determined professor, a
determined president, or a combination of the three. Yale, with its
Trumbull gallery, provided a sympathetic environment for a school
of fine art, made possible by the benefactions of a Yale alumnus who
was pained by the coarseness of contemporary American taste and
manners and wanted art to become a part of the legitimate instruction
at Yale. In July 1869, John F. Weir was appointed professor of painting in the Yale School of Fine Arts, offering the first university program in the fine arts; he was joined two years later by John H.
Niemeyer, the first professor of drawing. Yale experienced predictable
difficulty in incorporating its fine arts school into an organic relationship with the rest of the university. Yale was not coeducational, but
the school of fine arts enrolled women. Yale College and Sheffield students were allowed to take drawing for credit, although students fully
enrolled in the three-year course of the art school were not awarded a
Yale degree until the first B.F.A. was given in 1891.[145]

At Syracuse George Fisk Comfort, professor of modern languages and esthetics, intruded courses in drawing and the history of art into the course of study in 1872 and the next year was made dean of a new school of fine arts, which offered four-year programs leading to bachelor's degrees in architecture and painting. At Harvard President Eliot in 1874 created a department of fine arts and arranged for the appointment of his cousin Charles Eliot Norton as "Lecturer on the History of the Fine Arts as Connected with Literature." The University of Illinois, Michigan, and Cornell offered respectable art courses before the turn of the century. By then, too, programs in architecture had been developed at M.I.T., Cornell, Illinois, Syracuse, Columbia, Pennsylvania, George Washington, Harvard, and the Illinois Institute of Technology.[146]

In 1876 John Knowles Paine, who introduced the music of Bach to America, was appointed to a newly created professorship of music at Harvard, a development that moved music at Harvard from being a single elective in 1871 to an offering of five courses by 1886. At the University of Pennsylvania in 1875 the trustees revealed a cautiousness characteristic of governing bodies when they agreed to the appointment of a professor of music with the stipulation that he "shall hold his office for the term of three years if he shall so long behave himself well."[147] Before they could make much headway in the curriculum, painting, drawing, and music would have to overcome not just suspicion toward those who taught such subjects but of those who would take them. In the United States, as it was then psychologically and intellectually oriented, such subjects might be appropriate for young women if their talents suggested that careers in teaching lay ahead, but the great American public did not find the appreciation of art and music pertinent to the national design.

Because these were subjects that required instruction of a technical nature they were sometimes also looked on as being insufficiently intellectual in nature. A prevailing attitude was expressed by the Bowdoin student newspaper toward the college's art collection in 1883: "If these pictures are worth as much as claimed, they ought to be exchanged for a decent telescope and observatory."[148] Yet, where the environment was receptive and where able and ambitious teachers seized the opportunity, especially in coeducational institutions, impressive gains were established for creative and esthetic courses, as was attested by the early accomplishments of the schools of music and art and design at Pomona.[149]

New degrees, new subjects, old courses redesigned—all proceeding from the movements that were receiving dramatic expression in Ithaca, Cambridge, and Baltimore. To these manifestations of change in the course of study itself were added an accelerating change in the style of instruction and examining. The difference between the old and new spirit of instruction was wonderfully contrasted by the plight of Arthur Twining Hadley, a young Yale tutor, and by statistics that revealed a significant trend in appointments to the Harvard faculty. Hadley, who had been graduated from Yale in 1876, was tutor in Greek in 1879–80, in Latin in 1880–81, and in German in 1881–83, all the time also teaching some Roman law and logic; Hadley's special competence, however, happened to be political economy. At Harvard by 1872, on the other hand, the development of departments and instruction in depth had proceeded so far that the "traditional numerical preponderance of professors over nonprofessors" had ended. The professors found themselves surrounded by young professionals instead of supported somewhat ingloriously by untrained tutors.[150]

Eliot in his inaugural address sounded like Jeremiah Day on the subject of lectures: "The lecturer pumps laboriously into sieves. The water may be wholesome, but it runs through. A mind must work to grow." Both Porter at Yale and Angell at Michigan were also suspicious of lectures, and properly so, for while White at Cornell was almost uncritical in his embrace of lectures as a major improvement on recitations, lectures did not guarantee that students would enter into their academic responsibilities either enthusiastically or effectively.

The lecture, however, became a characteristic substitute for the waning recitation method of instruction. Noah Porter still believed in recitations in 1870, but by 1880 Eliot could refer to the passing of recitation and the ascendancy of what he called "conversational instruction." The discussion-group approach to teaching moved into undergraduate instruction under the auspices of teachers trained in the tradition of the German university seminar in which the professor and a few students exercised themselves with critical textual study and interpretation. The seminar approach appeared in the American college first in the classrooms of Charles Kendall Adams at Michigan, Henry Adams at Harvard, and Moses Coit Tyler at Cornell. Henry Adams's report on his experience was exultant: "As pedagogy nothing could be more triumphant." But seminar instruction was expensive, difficult, and so contrary to tradition that its future to some extent depended on allowing the lecture system to get out of hand and bringing section discussion into the scheme of instruction as a remedy.[151]

In the sciences, laboratory instruction became evidence of a forward-looking institution. An 1858 junior elective in chemistry with required laboratory work was probably the first Harvard course where students worked in a laboratory rather than observing a scientific demonstration in a lecture hall. At the University of Iowa in 1870 Gustavus Hinrichs, professor of chemistry, required laboratory work of his students and made his department a source of influence in the West. At Emory in Georgia laboratory instruction was introduced in 1875.[152]

There was nothing mysterious about these developments. Professors and students alike were making use of new forms and practices that allowed them to express their interests with greater ease and effectiveness. For professors interested in their subjects and for students interested essentially in themselves and their own growth, a whole range of devices encouraged the shaping of an environment that honored the meaning of the word education in a way that recitations never did. Laboratories, field trips, seminars, small group discussions, research libraries and related library developments, and lectures at their best were instruments of liberation. As for the curriculum, what was taught or could be taught, what was learned or could be learned depended in part on the conditions under which it was taught or learned. The new methods were salutary.

Two other areas of academic practice yielded to the pressure of change. The colonial college student was essentially ungraded and unexamined. At the high-water mark of the classical college, grading and examining were poisoned by the recitation system and made somewhat ridiculous by the extent to which public oral examinations were gestures in public relations and therefore not designed to show up student deficiencies. Indeed, often enough it was the examiners who were shown to be deficient. "I remember to have heard when a boy," Francis Wayland reminisced, "of a Trustee of a College who attended an examination in Greek, and for two hours used his book upside down."[153]

The traditional examining procedure—aside from the daily recitations—was to set apart several days at the end of the year when a trustee committee observed the professors while they asked their students questions that were drawn from the year's recitations. Trustees could also ask questions but, again, only on the set reading of the course in which the student was being examined. Not only were there no surprises in these performances, but there were also no searching questions, no stimulation to the imagination, and no real testing of the student or of the teacher's effectiveness.[154] For the curriculum, such a system acted as a wall of protection. In a sense, it confirmed the whole educational philosophy on which the curriculum was based—faculty psychology, rote memorization, a prescribed course for all.

Oral examinations were of no use in encouraging students to intellectual exertion; they added nothing to the academic experience but a confirmation of the centrality of rote memorization. For this reason, in the 1830s, first at Yale and Harvard and then increasingly elsewhere, written biennial examinations, at the end of the sophomore and senior years, were introduced in the hope that they would be taken more seriously than the oral course examinations.[155] In retrospect, the differences may appear to be slight, but they were significant. Written examinations were a more serious test of a student's literary skill than were the few words uttered in answer to a few random oral questions. Written examinations asked the same questions of an entire class and therefore provided a basis of comparative judgment and a measure of standards as was not possible when a class was taken, man by man, through a series of routine questions. And printed examination questions had a way of being a more revealing test of the quality of the course and of the instructor than were the fleeting questions of the oral tradition.

In 1857 at Harvard the faculty and overseers decided that oral examinations had outlived their usefulness. In their decision substituting, for the traditional overseers' oral examinations, written course examinations to be graded by the instructors, they introduced the blue book to American academic practice. The significance of this departure for the course of study was far-reaching. The oral examinations had been a prop of the recitation system, which had been defended as the only way to prepare students for them; the argument was circular, but when one went, the other was bound to go also. Written course examinations freed instructors from an overemphasis on daily graded recitations and memorization; they changed what went on in class and what could go on in class; they helped to transform instructors from policemen to teachers. The practice of written course examinations was adopted at Yale in 1865. The rest of the colleges fell in line.[156]

As for grading, while some system of grading was implied in the ranking of seniors for commencement parts in the colonial colleges, "the initiative in attempting to formulate a scale for grading students" was not taken until 1813 at Yale, which adopted a numerical scale of four for evaluating course work. The numerical scale took the place of the four terms that had been used as early as 1783 as a means of differentiating the quality of student performance: *optimi, second optimi, inferiores (boni),* and *pejores.*[157] By mid century intricate marking systems supported both curricular and disciplinary policy in the classical college. Every class recitation was graded; every violation of the college laws caused a loss of points earned in the classroom. At the end of the year every student was represented by a number that was meant to be a measure of his academic worth and character.[158]

Harvard removed a student's disciplinary record from the calculation of grades in 1869, and eight years later adopted a scale of 100, replacing it in 1883 with five letter grades—A through E. In 1895 letter grades were replaced by a new scale of rank by merit: "passed with distinction," "passed," and "failed." All this thrashing around in search of the perfect grading system was a response to a changing curriculum and a changing climate of academic life. Examining and grading systems were barometers of curricular health and style and purpose. In adopting the numerical scale, Harvard stressed competition as an inducement to student effort. Letter grades reduced competitive pressures and deemphasized class rank, which now could not be calculated. Ranking by merit shifted the focus from grades to the community of shared scholarly endeavor. Colleges and universities have been subjected to many cross purposes, and the curriculum itself has carried so many diverse burdens—stimulation of students, satisfaction of professors, encouragement of scholarship, discouragement of loafing, creation of credentials—that no grading system has succeeded in satisfying very long. One answer to what system to use was adopted in 1896 by Mount Holyoke, which dropped the scale of four, substituted rank by letter, and gave each letter a descriptive adjective of merit and a numerical equivalent.[159] It was an all-purpose system, certainly, but whatever advantage one system had over another was canceled out by a system that tried to be everything. All it needed in order to work and make sense was for each student to be allowed a choice of whether she would be graded by letter, adjective, or number.

In a country where race and caste regulated human relationships even while the national creed asserted human equality, the abolition of slavery and the obligation of society to the freedmen created an educational network, including colleges, intended to meet the needs of black Americans as defined by white Americans. The same missionary impulse that had created classical colleges in the West moved out of New England to the South after the Civil War and there designed institutions that had the double purpose of training the former slaves away from forms of behavior believed to have been encouraged by the slave experience—"licentiousness, dishonesty, cunning, theft, and moral irresponsibility"—and training them for occupations of service to whites or appropriate to a segregated community of free blacks.[160]

Few of the institutions then founded deserved to be thought of as colleges and universities until well into the twentieth century. One that did, Howard University in Washington, with a more comprehensive curriculum than any of the others and with intentions appropriate to a liberal arts college, graduated relatively few young men and women from its collegiate course in the nineteenth century. Two northern institutions, Ashmun at Lincoln, Pennsylvania, and Wilberforce, near Xenia, Ohio, had been founded as schools for free "men of color" before the Civil War; designating them universities after the war did not keep them from being essentially academies, as was true of many so-called colleges of longer history.[161]

Developing institutions for free blacks after the war placed unique demands on the curriculum and on the standards and purposes that defined it. Less than a dozen free blacks had been graduated from the classical colleges before the war; belief in black mental inferiority was deeply imbedded in the society's racist convictions; funds necessary to support the institutions were as inadequate as was the secondary school preparation of prospective students.[162] A struggle between advocates of an industrial or a manual training education, centered at Hampton and Tuskegee, and a liberal arts education, centered at Howard and Atlanta, did nothing to help existing institutions to find their way in a largely unsympathetic environment. The so-called Negro colleges were founded by an occupying force of evangelical New Englanders bent on reproducing northern institutions in the vanquished South, but a shift from the humanist traditions of the classical colleges became a necessity if the new institutions were to accommodate themselves to the racial mores and expectations of the South.[163] Land-grant colleges supported by federal funds and the intentionally traditional colleges soon found themselves transformed into institutions for the training of elementary and secondary school teachers.[164]

As one historian of black education has summarized the early history of the new institutions: "[They] were the product of philanthropic generosity and inevitably became captives of the South's program to educate Negroes for their caste assignments. . . . Organized originally for liberal arts purposes, the Negro college slowly instituted industrial education as one of its basic functions."[165] When industrial education declined in favor toward the end of the century, the colleges originally of liberal purpose returned to "orthodox curricula in liberal arts and teacher training."[166] These so-called missionary colleges, moreover, with their commitment to the education of a class of black leaders were responsible, as Carter Woodson said, for imposing "a New England curriculum and white middle-class values upon the black elite, and . . . thereby alienated black leaders from the indigenous culture of their people."[167] At a time when the curriculum of higher education in the North was responding to the aspirations of new professions and of a success-oriented middle class, higher education for blacks in the South was being designed to keep blacks in their place.

All the significant elements of major curricular change were now engaged in redefining American higher education. Clarity of

purpose was still elusive. The old and new existed in uncertain balance, the old receding and the new advancing at different speeds and
with different consequences, depending on a given institution's particular history and its social and political environment. Poverty,
which had had much to do with stabilizing the classical course of
study, was no longer a hindrance to reform. Government and new private wealth were available to underwrite in the colleges and universities courses of study that were responsive to a dynamic industrial society and to an expansive democracy.[168] It was no longer possible to
define the curriculum restrictively. The idea of a general education as
it had survived even into Noah Porter's Yale was on the edge of death;
clearly, general education was now required "to include a study of
knowledge useful for understanding the contemporary world."[169] A
vocational focus and a recognition of "the expansion of the boundaries of man's basic knowledge" were in the process of both reforming
the curriculum and making it and the colleges popular.[170]

In the East literary societies were in decline, their place being
taken by an invigorated curriculum and by extracurricular activities
that would be less complementary to curricular purpose than they
had been.[171] Cornell and the developing state institutions were altogether free of the old religious commitment. The old moral philosophy course was passing away, and there was no capstone, no integrating experience, taking its place.

5

Disarray

Getting ahead in the United States and being ahead are two different experiences and always have been. By 1900 higher education in the United States was serving the purposes of both the arrived and the aspiring. In contrast to a century earlier, the aspiring young men (and now women) who enrolled in the colleges (and now universities) greatly outnumbered those for whom the curriculum was a confirmation of social and economic status. The contrast between a course of study for those whose social position was ascribed and those whose social position was achieved was the difference between Jeremiah Day's Yale and Andrew D. White's Cornell. A young woman student at the Harvard Annex (Radcliffe) recorded in her diary what could happen at Harvard to the university's most popular teacher: "November 24, 1894. A handful of men to hear Professor Norton on monasteries, the rest being gone childishly to Springfield (for a football game)."[1] "I am a farmer's boy," a young man wrote to the land-grant college at East Lansing, Michigan. "As soon as the wheat is sown, I am at liberty to go to school."[2] There it was: higher education in the United States, confused, in disarray.

Disarray came in many shapes and forms, from many sources. When Charles Francis Adams, Jr., Harvard class of 1856, complained that he had never known or met a successful political or financial figure of the second half of the nineteenth century he would "care to meet again in this world or the next," he was registering a loss of economic and political power by his own college-educated class and its transfer to a generation of noncollege-educated achievers. Lacking in "humor, thought, or refinement," those achievers were "a set of mere

money getters and traders . . . essentially unattractive and uninterest-
ing.''³ Adams was one of the leading scolds of his time, but, like his
brothers Henry and Brooks, he was perceptive and knew that their
world was in disorder, that a very particular ethical concern and style
to which they and others of their generation had been exposed in the
classical colleges was no longer effective. Men, machines, values were
on the march, and sons of the old colleges discovered that they were ill
equipped to take the trip.

A somewhat disillusioned alumni element among the older colleges, therefore, sensing its own displacement by a bolder, more
aggressive, race of men, became an unexpected source of influence for
curricular change. So did the sons and daughters of Adams's "money
getters and traders," young men and women whose status was assured
by their fathers' wealth but whose style might benefit from the veneer
of a collegiate experience, a veneer that derived less from the course of
study than from an array of extracurricular activities that were important in defining and nurturing personality, character, and values.
Young men and women of this sort searched out the collegiate and
university environments appropriate to their purposes, as did the
likes of the young man in Michigan who, now that the wheat was
sown, was "at liberty to go to school."

The college-going population increased not only in numbers
but also in diversity of social and economic background and of intention. The numbers and percentage of the eighteen to twenty-one age
group enrolled in colleges began to move up steadily: 1870, 52,286, or
1.7 percent; 1880, 115,817, or 2.7 percent; 1890, 156,756, or 3.0 percent;
1900, 237,592, or 4.0 percent.⁴ These figures were modest in contrast to
the 2,659,021, or 30.2 percent, of 1950, but they were achieved in a society that had not yet provided universal access to other than the most
elementary education. Accelerating enrollments in higher education,
moving 4.7 times as fast as population growth, represented a victory
for the forces of reform: Colleges and universities were making themselves felt in the lives of a wider clientele; they were translating the
curricular designs of White, Gilman, and Eliot into new paths to new
careers.⁵ In a world where everything was changing—the clientele,
the professors, the curriculum, career opportunities—even the out-
moded would in time gain a new lease on life for those who could
afford it.

Could young men and women go to Albion, Stanford, Wisconsin, Emory, Michigan State, Howard, Vassar, Amherst, Cornell, and Harvard for the same reasons? Individuals might and did, but in the aggregate they chose according to the expectations that were generated by each institution's style and reputation. Generous systems of state support and scholarships made state institutions the goal of the poor and the middle class. Small liberal arts colleges in the country held a certain attraction for wealthy young men and women from the cities, at the same time that they provided a relatively easier and cheaper access to higher education for young people in the neighborhood. Large urban institutions with curricular programs that opened the way to careers in the city beckoned young men and women from towns and villages, and later, to the delight of the new breed of professors, were discovered by the intellectually oriented sons and daughters of Jewish immigrants. Old institutions along the eastern seaboard, colleges that had never lost touch with the upper class for which they had been created in the colonial era, became environments for social education, whatever may have been happening to the course of study.

The colleges and universities of the late nineteenth century were undergoing the changes that support James McLachlan's conclusion that "aside from direct training in immediately utilitarian skills, and perhaps in science . . . football and other extracurricular activities have had more significance in shaping the mind of the undergraduate than the formal elements of the course of study."[6] Of earlier college generations this is a less certain generalization. There is a respectable curricular history before the 1870s, from Dunster's Harvard on through James McCosh's Princeton, when, by accident and design, the curricular and the extracurricular, the religious and the secular, fell into a certain harmonious unity, when, as McLachlan himself has said, "a style of thought, a mode of discourse, the emerging outlines of a particular social and intellectual world view" expressed that harmony.[7] Charles Eliot Norton looking into an empty lecture hall on the day of the football game at Springfield in 1894 and that young man on his way to East Lansing full of serious intent, maybe about curing the diseases of the cow, were undergoing experiences that the old colleges would neither have allowed nor understood. Diversity and democracy would exact a price in harmony, just as harmony had been bought at the cost of unpopularity, irrelevance, and a limited usefulness to an upper class.

One instrument of the new disharmony was a class of professionally trained academicians, professors with specialized training in a field of study that may not even have existed when they were born. The new breed of professors introduced into the classroom a seriousness, a respect for energetic inquiry, a concern for standards that were an inspiration to like-minded undergraduates, but the new academic style was so in awe of scholarly productivity that neglect of undergraduates became a corollary of professional purpose. Of course, the students knew how to turn the tables, as Professor Norton and his colleagues were learning. It may have been only a coincidence that the professionalization of the faculties and the rise of football were simultaneous developments, but clearly, while both the professors and students had found for themselves thoroughly engrossing activities, these were activities that lacked the common purpose that held together the old course of study and such elements of the collegiate experience as chapel and the student literary societies.

The manner in which faculties were professionalized was clarified at Harvard in the years after Charles William Eliot assumed the presidency. The Harvard faculty had been becoming increasingly professional even while Eliot, in his concern with electives and the professional schools and a hundred other matters, had been indifferent to the scholarly productivity of his faculty. The opening of Johns Hopkins, however, and the lure it represented to dedicated scholars in Cambridge transformed indifference to alarm. At the time of Eliot's election to the presidency a majority of the senior professors were men who had made an early professional commitment to an academic discipline; by 1880 the junior faculty was significantly more professional than the senior faculty.[8]

In 1880, in the first of a series of conscious efforts to meet the rise of Johns Hopkins, Eliot succeeded in recruiting Frederick DeForest Allen from the Yale faculty by assuring him that as professor of classical philology at Harvard he need not bother himself with undergraduates. On the other hand, although as a function of the new professionalism, Barrett Wendell was kept in the English Department, against Eliot's wishes, because departmental autonomy prevailed and

Wendell's colleagues wanted this outspoken defender of the college kept busy teaching the undergraduate courses they wanted nothing to do with.[9] Working his way through the comings and goings of the Harvard faculty in the second half of the nineteenth century, Robert McCaughey has concluded that "those candidates with specialized training, teaching experience, and established scholarly reputations regularly beat out those who lacked one or more of these qualifications."[10]

McCaughey's researches establish 1892 as the time by which "control of the Harvard faculty had shifted from the locally rooted, nonspecialized, institutionally loyal 'academic gentlemen' to the somewhat more socially heterogeneous, highly specialized, intensely competitive professional academics on the faculty."[11] By then, according to Samuel Eliot Morison, the practice had been established of having the president submit to the Harvard corporation only those appointments and promotions suggested or approved by the department involved.[12]

Boston money, Eliot's determination, the threat of Johns Hopkins, the historical burden of being the oldest, and the institutional conceit of thinking itself always the best made developments at Harvard of more than passing consequence in the interior and elsewhere in the East. Yale and Princeton had thus far set the curricular style in the United States, and even if Harvard was not now about to take their place, it having already been taken by Cornell, Harvard required attention. It took itself so seriously that others had to; under Eliot's urging it gave up Harvard College in the interest of Harvard University; it turned electives into a charter of student rights. And there on the banks of the Charles River in Cambridge it shaped itself into a university, unlike Cornell, unlike Johns Hopkins, but owing much to both.

For at least two generations the Harvard faculty had been on its way to where Ticknor and his colleagues had been urging it prematurely in the 1820s. Now in the 1880s it became a university, its professional schools assuming some clear identity and some definition of standards, its faculty "less and less preoccupied with educating young people, more and more preoccupied with educating one another by doing scholarly research."[13] Until about 1900 the professional training of American scholars in the humanities and social sciences, and to a significant degree in the natural and physical sciences, took place in the universities of Germany.[14] After 1900 the domestic demand for scholars and the facilities to support it created, in one of its functions, the American university.

The learned societies that blossomed in great profusion in the 1880s and after certified the existence of professional specialists in areas of learning that a half century before had lacked sufficient self-consciousness to take themselves seriously. It was necessary before the creation of such organizations as the Modern Language Association (1883), the American Historical Association (1884), the American Economics Association (1885), the American Philosophical Association (1901), the American Political Science Association (1904), and the American Sociological Society (1905) that places like Harvard and Johns Hopkins make adventuresome gestures toward the professional mystique.[15] But that was not enough. These professional organizations were really licensed by the splintering of the old course in moral philosophy, and the clear message for the curriculum was that even in colleges that chose to remain colleges, even in colleges that whatever they chose to be could be nothing more, professionals in the splintered subjects, with their particular styles and purposes and American doctorates, were being readied to pick up the pieces of the old course in moral philosophy.

For the curriculum these developments were far-reaching and beyond calculation. Whatever others said, even in New Haven, Harvard under Eliot possessed power and influence. Moreover, he, the professionals, those who equated their professional lives with the needs of society itself, found a sympathetic response beyond the campus: Now they mattered as those caricatured old professors never had. Yet a remarkable thing happened on the way to all this special competence, which arrived eventually on all the campuses more or less in the order of their assets and freedom from clerical influence.

In the nineteenth-century colleges the study of society belonged to the benign amateurs who were not intimidated by cosmic questions or their own ignorance.[16] The narrow competence and specialization of the economists, historians, political scientists, and others who took their places deflected the classroom from advocacy and conspicuous moral judgment to a style that bore the approved description—"scientific," a style that was objective, cautious, and wary of judgment. The new social science was more subtle than the old moral philosophy and its sense of moral engagement was less certain. At the same time that faculties were consolidating their right to select their colleagues, their control over the classroom, and their professional self-consciousness, they were developing an academic style that was indifferent to undergraduates, removed from moral judgment, and so unrelated to the traditional social purposes of higher education that even at Cornell visiting preachers were imported to bring the students in touch with some of the great questions that confronted them with their own humanity. The roster of learned societies that multiplied so freely as the century drew to a close was intended as a substitute for Timothy Dwight, but of course that was impossible.

Yet for the curriculum as experienced by students the professionalization of the professors also brought significant benefits. One of these certainly was the establishment of academic freedom and tenure as characteristic goals and expectations governing the college and university environment. These conditions, so supportive of the right of the professor to move into a world of ideas that might be contrary to the wishes of the governing authorities, were institutionalized in the formation of the Association of American University Professors in 1915, but before then the professors were demonstrating how academic freedom and security in their jobs could invigorate the course of study.

Celebrated cases involving academic freedom in the 1890s and early decades of the twentieth century revealed how religious unorthodoxy, pacifism, and a critical attitude toward American economic institutions and practices could embroil professors in controversies with boards of trustees and benefactors. In the end, however, the professors won a hearing for academic ideals, the classroom was opened to unpopular ideas, and the curriculum as an instrument of intellectual training was enhanced. Although academic freedom achieved only a precarious and incomplete hold on academic practice, it was often a source of curricular vigor. Let it be said too, however, that while tenure protected the professors in advancing new ideas and unpopular ideas, it also sometimes protected them when the time for both them and their ideas had come and gone.

New patterns of secondary schooling, admissions requirements, and enrollment exerted pressure on the curriculum and created complexities and problems for which there were no simple solutions. Selectivity in admissions, a concern for standards, and a desire to protect the integrity of its own course of study accounted in 1878 for Nicholas Murray Butler, on matriculating at Columbia, being conditioned in ancient geography, one of his admissions subjects, because he could not "recite in order, beginning with Greece and going eastward and northward all the way around to the Euxine, the names both in Latin and English, first of the capes and then of the rivers of Europe."[17] State universities, in designing and perfecting a system of admission by certificate from the public high schools, put themselves in position to shape the entire educational system of the state, but there was a hidden threat to the curriculum in the certification device and the problem of how to accomplish the transfer of students from the lower part of an educational system, "highly democratic, differentiated, and varying," to a higher part that was concerned with protecting and establishing standards.[18] In the absence of cooperation among schools and colleges as to what constituted a secondary school education, the headmaster of an old New England boarding school complained in exasperation in 1885 that "out of over forty boys preparing for college next year we have more than twenty senior classes."[19] When Columbia changed its course of study and admissions requirements in 1897, the results were a larger student body and a markedly different ethnic composition.[20]

In a way that was not readily apparent, the colleges and universities were losing control over the course of study, not just to professors with new authority and students with elective freedom but to a burgeoning system of public high schools. The first public high school was opened in Boston in 1821; by 1860 several hundred public high schools operated in the largest population centers of the Northeast and the Midwest, but public high schools did not fully displace the academies until after the Civil War. In 1870 approximately 500 high schools were providing both terminal secondary schooling and college preparation. In 1895 the students admitted to colleges and universities were drawn 41 percent from public high schools, 40 percent from the college preparatory departments of the colleges and universities themselves, and 17 percent from private preparatory schools.[21]

Each of these three forms of college preparation influenced the college curriculum, but the high school was the institution with the greatest potential authority. Nothing could have been more forthright and explicit in its meaning for college and university standards and curricular offerings than the statement of the superintendent of the Chicago high schools in 1896:

> Every young man or woman who has successfully devoted at least four years to earnest study in a well-equipped secondary school should be admitted to any college in the country . . . [on the basis of any] combination of studies which has developed his power and been in harmony with his intellectual aptitudes.[22]

In an earlier day college presidents and college professors told the world just how much Latin and just how much Greek, and later just how much mathematics, a young man (and, later, a young woman) needed for admission to college. Now high schools, with a democratic willingness to encourage modern languages, applied science, agriculture, domestic science, and manual training, were giving high school diplomas for programs that did not look remotely like what tradition would describe as college preparatory.[23] How would the universities and colleges respond? It is clear that the western state universities "were ready to credit the modern subjects when they began to admit students on certificate." The eastern colleges and universities and church-supported institutions elsewhere were put on the defensive by the degree to which the public university and the public high school were redefining secondary education, subjects appropriate for admission, and, as well, subjects appropriate for the undergraduate curriculum.[24]

The experience of Wabash College, an old, small college of New England derivation in Indiana, was instructive. Should it follow the example of the state university and the state land-grant college and accept poorly prepared students and give them college credit for subjects pursued in college that in the past Wabash would have required for admission? Or should it try to hold to its standards in an effort to raise the standards of the high schools? Wabash opted for virtue and almost collapsed; in the interest of survival it adopted the lower standards of its competitors.[25]

The dilemma faced by Wabash was intricately related not simply to the high school movement and admission by certificate but also to the role of college and university preparatory departments in defining the nature of the college course. The upward movement in enrollment statistics satisfied a hunger for students, but it also confronted the colleges and universities with the necessity of defining exactly what a college course consisted of. Jeremiah Day had known this was happening, but the forces let loose since 1828 also gave every evidence in the 1880s and 1890s of being beyond control. Exasperation went beyond the offices of New England headmasters; confusion was not limited to the well-meaning authorities at Wabash College.

If the curriculum was once more to be standardized or, if not that, at least provided with some values by which to measure it, the practice of colleges operating their own preparatory departments would have to go. The practice has been something of a secret from history, but the colleges and universities knew what they were doing. They were laying their hands on every young man and woman they possibly could before their competitors did. Of course there were exceptions, especially in the East, where students well prepared by private tutors or the better academies had been admitted into advanced standing. In 1870, however, only twenty-six colleges in the country, twenty-three of them in the Northeast, were not operating preparatory departments. State universities everywhere had learned the uses of the device, as had their competitors, and the eastern preponderance of institutions without preparatory departments was less evidence of virtue than it was evidence of the existence of a strong network of academies and clergymen-tutors and the absence of state universities with preparatory departments and low standards.[26]

The rationalization of state systems of education, with the state university as ultimate arbiter, multiplied the number of high schools and required the abandonment of the integral preparatory departments in the universities. The abandonment of the preparatory departments by universities and their competitors, however, also meant capitulation to the high schools. The certification system, which replaced the preparatory departments as the basic instrument of transfer from school to college, was the creation of the University of Michigan, which found itself in 1870 without any simple avenue to admission, neither a preparatory department nor a system of examinations such as used in the Northeast. Michigan hoped to help itself to students and raise its own standards and at the same time lead the high schools to higher levels of preparation. In the 1870s, under Michigan's leadership, the growing state universities of the Midwest worked out and adopted systems of accreditation whereby schools were certified as doing creditable college preparatory work or where their examinations were accepted as an adequate basis for admission.[27]

The damage to the curriculum of all this maneuvering was in one sense only temporary. In abandoning their own preparatory departments as a gesture of support to the high schools that they were trying to encourage, state universities and their collegiate competitors lost some ground, but only for a while. The curriculum of the freshman year in many institutions declined in quality. Before they could set standards, institutions that cast themselves in roles of leadership—Iowa, Vanderbilt, South Carolina, Ohio University, among many others—were required to lower their own standards in order to articulate with the high schools.[28] Once both the schools and universities arrived at a reasonably comfortable relationship, however, standards were moved ahead. The lasting damage to the traditional college and university curriculum occurred in the definition of subjects that were acceptable for college admission and that could be continued as course programs leading to college and university degrees. Here a battle shaped up between the private universities of the East and the old classical colleges on one side and the state universities and land-grant colleges on the other.

Admission by certificate or some other form of accrediting had been adopted by 42 state institutions and 150 others by 1897. In the meantime, preparatory departments, already missing at Michigan and Iowa, were abolished in the 1880s and 1890s at Wisconsin, Minnesota, Indiana, Missouri, and Ohio State. In 1884 the University of California adopted a system of accrediting secondary schools, and, while as late as 1895 few high school students were enrolled at the University of Virginia, it was clear even at Virginia that the domination of the academy and the classical-oriented headmaster was at an end.[29] Although the chairman of the faculty at Jefferson's university could say of the state's high schools that "their highest students must stand on tiptoe to reach up to the bottom line of the State University's demands," sooner or later the University of Virginia would come to terms with the American high school.

Where democratic commitment was high and concern for standards low, especially among the land-grant colleges and state universities of the plains and mountain states, preparatory departments lingered longer. As late as 1900 nearly half of the students enrolled in land-grant colleges were in what amounted to the colleges' integral high schools. Without a preparatory department of its own, the University of South Carolina in 1904 could put together a freshman class by drawing on South Carolina's few high schools and the preparatory departments of a dozen or so South Carolina colleges, but such a dependency was unreliable. South Carolina found itself accepting an increasing number of students with conditions and sometimes ignoring entrance requirements altogether.[30]

Scrambling for students as they were, being incited to university dimensions and pretensions by the displays of purpose and wealth under development in the East, taking hold of new subjects while not yet quite sure what was happening to the old ones, colleges and universities everywhere were being brought to a consideration of what constituted a college course. When Wabash abolished its preparatory department in 1900 but continued the courses as college courses, thus bringing itself down to the level of Purdue and Indiana University, it followed where the high school movement had led the state's public institutions of higher education. In doing so, it dramatized the extent to which curricular disarray was one consequence of institutional loss of control.[31]

In the East a network of boys' boarding schools in alliance with the old seaboard institutions and the country colleges also altered the conditions that defined the curriculum. Here the impulse was not rampant democracy but often a combination of needs as expressed by a displaced elite and by those who aspired to their places. The boys' boarding schools and the old institutions found themselves becoming outposts of an upper class and of those who intended to break into it. Wealth had much to do with their style.

The American boys' boarding school, an institution designed for the sons of rich urbanites, took St. Paul's School at Concord, New Hampshire, as its model. Between 1883 and 1906 St. Paul's experienced the tribute of imitation as the demand for schools dedicated to the education of bourgeois gentlemen called into existence Groton, Woodberry Forest, Taft, Hotchkiss, Choate, St. George's, Middlesex, and Kent. New life was breathed into Deerfield and Lawrenceville.

Older schools, such as the Phillips Academies at Andover and Exeter, and newer schools, such as St. Marks, Milton, and Hill, joined them in shoring up a sense of responsibility and purpose in the sons of the rich and sending them for final consolidation and certification on to a cluster of eastern colleges and universities picked out for the purpose. Harvard, Yale, Princeton, Dartmouth, Williams, Amherst, the University of Pennsylvania, Brown, and Columbia were to some extent appropriated by a class of predestined adolescents on their way to social power and control, less through the traditional professions and more through business and management as time went on.[32]

Wealthy young men using the colleges and universities as instruments for consolidating and certifying their status did not have to be in the majority to bend an institution to their will, although by 1907 almost 40 percent of Yale's freshman class was drawn from a handful of eastern boarding schools, only 20 percent from public high schools, the remaining 40 percent largely from private day schools.[33] Wealth, self-confidence, the mix of family, school, and summer resort relationships licensed them to establish the tone and the style of an institution, using their clubs and fraternities, athletic teams, and clothes as professors might use libraries, laboratories, and seminars to make their contribution to institutional flavor. The curriculum appropriate for certifying an elite of bourgeois gentlemen—the new rich—was the extracurriculum, which was also a marvelous testing ground for aspiring outsiders. Old money and old family had no choice but to play the game as it was being defined by the boarding school-eastern college axis, unless they wanted to join the misguided youth, often on scholarship, of minority ethnic background, or ungainly in manner, for whom intellectual and curricular matters were most important.

Colleges and universities in search of a curriculum had problems enough—a self-conscious, professionalizing faculty, an expanding public high school movement, a retreating classical course, old occupations expressing themselves as undergraduate concentrations in vocational preparation, a new preoccupation with inquiry and a scientific posture. To these was added the burden of being relevant to the needs of ambitious but poor young men and women inspired by a Jewish tradition of respect for the intellectual life, the sons and daughters of an aspiring middle class, and the sons (and some daughters) of a wealthy elite for whom position and power waited outside the university doors.

One test of how the colleges and universities chose to define themselves and the curriculum was how far they went in prescribing the subject preparation they expected of an entering freshman. Before 1800 only Latin, Greek, and arithmetic (and the latter, not at Harvard), plus some character assurances probably from the village clergyman, made a teenage boy a candidate for a college degree. By 1825 both Princeton and Yale tested English grammar as an indication of suitability for admission, although the requirement should not be taken too seriously.[34] Surely Princeton and Yale did not so take it.

A willingness to accept or require for admission certain subjects beyond Latin, Greek, and mathematics (1745, arithmetic; 1820, algebra; 1844, geometry) did not carry the colleges very far before the Civil War. Geography, between 1807 and 1822, appeared in the admissions requirements for Harvard, Princeton, Columbia, and Yale. Because a generation of college students was about to exploit interior North America or some other remote district? Hardly. Geography was the classics on maps. Ancient history for admissions, oriented to the classics, was a way that both Michigan and Harvard found for being radical as early as 1847; but not until after the Civil War, when the sciences particularly had established their legitimacy, did admissions requirements become an effective device for saying what should go on in the secondary school and for declaring the lower limits of what could go on in a college course of study. Even so, universities and colleges were in no position to hold themselves to their own requirements and therefore in no position to hold themselves to their own curriculum.[35]

In 1870 three subjects appeared for the first time as admission requirements: U.S. history at the University of Michigan, physical geography at Michigan and Harvard, and English composition and grammar at Princeton. During the next thirty years the modern languages, English literature, and natural science were added to the admissions requirements of a number of colleges. When Harvard in 1887 required a laboratory course in physics for admission it lent its prestige to science in a most effective way.[36] Yet, since each college and university set its own admission requirements, the responsiveness of the high schools and the private secondary schools depended on their commitment to college preparation and their function in feeding students to particular colleges. By 1897, for instance, eighty colleges giving the B.A. degree required a combination of English literature, composition, and grammar for admission. On the other hand, thirty of them required for admission neither Latin nor Greek.[37] While studies showed a general pattern of requirements in mathematics and history in institutions as diverse as Harvard, Yale, Princeton, Columbia, Michigan, Cornell, Brown, Williams, Oberlin, and California, the evidence was unmistakable that the breakdown of the classical curriculum, the rise of the high school, and the emergence of new subjects had overwhelmed both the schools and colleges and left them uncertain as to their respective curricular responsibilities.[38] If the founding of colleges in the United States had followed rather than anticipated the development of a system of sound secondary schools, this particular prescription for academic disarray might have been avoided, but of course that is not the way it happened. By 1900 the lack of articulation between a late-blooming high school system and an ancient but collapsing college course of study was so great that only arrogance or innocence would have permitted discussion of *the* college curriculum. Since then such discussion has required a playful imagination and a respect for qualified generalization.

Measures to bring order out of confusion began as early as 1879 at a conference of New England colleges seeking agreement on uniform admissions requirements in English. Similar meetings in 1881 and 1882 on the classics and mathematics led to the beginnings of uniformity among the colleges and universities of New England and the formation of the New England Association of Colleges and Secondary Schools in 1885, the first of a number of similar regional organizations that developed out of school and college curricular disarray.[39]

At the 1892 meeting of the National Education Association the appointment of a Committee on Secondary School Studies, known as the Committee of Ten, was in some ways an act of inspired exasperation: It put President Eliot of Harvard in charge of a committee of university, college, and school people who were expected to call a series of subject matter conferences and then prepare a report recommending an approved secondary school curriculum. The committee's report put the weight of an influential body of opinion behind a course of study that was essentially already being offered as a college preparatory course in the boarding schools and in the large urban school systems; it shortchanged the vast majority of noncollege-going high school students for whom it recommended the same courses as for those who were preparing for college; but it put the modern languages, science, and history on equal footing with the classics and mathematics and for a while it placed in the hands of colleges and universities some authority over school studies and their own curriculum.[40] One strange consequence of the adoption of the recommended school curriculum was an increase in high school students taking Latin at a time when colleges were expanding their own programs without Latin.[41]

The report's recommendation of a widely adopted college preparatory curriculum skirted the obligations of the high schools to their noncollege-going clients for whom vocationally oriented courses were of more immediate value, and it did not automatically solve the problems of college admissions requirements. The Committee of Ten succeeded in defining a college preparatory course, but it did not define an American high school, and it did not tell college and university authorities on what grounds to admit students, although urging admission of any student completing any variant of its suggested program. A consequence of continuing curricular uncertainty was the organization in 1900 of the College Entrance Examination Board, offspring of a dozen leading eastern universities and colleges that in 1901 began to offer under the board's auspices a common examination in a number of subjects approved for admission.[42]

Although by 1910 twenty-five eastern colleges and universities were supporting the College Entrance Examination Board (CEEB) and thereby creating a climate of curricular stability among themselves, the CEEB was a regional effort. It made no headway against the widely used certificate system in the Midwest and West, and even among its own members it shared admission procedures with an informal system of certification of leading private schools and a continued reliance on examinations prepared by the colleges and universities themselves.

Too many conflicting purposes were enmeshed in the admissions problem to allow for any clear solution. Each college and university chose the method or methods that it thought best served its purposes and allowed it to enroll a class. Eliot's purposes at Harvard

—to use higher standards of admission as a means of achieving university status—were of no use to colleges lacking university ambitions. Harvard's later adoption of options and groups of subjects appropriate for admission was a function of the university's commitment to the concept of student freedom in course election, a concept that was in no sense universally admired. When Stanford University in 1902 accepted woodworking, forge work, and machine shop work in partial fulfillment of admission to candidacy for the B.A. degree, it made a conscious decision to be responsive to the interests of western democracy. When small New England colleges chose to hold to a Latin requirement longer than their public rivals, they also chose to select their students from a narrower clientele.[43]

The idea of a uniform universally recognized undergraduate course of study was dying along with the old curriculum. School and college associations of subject matter teachers, even the creation in 1908 of the Carnegie Unit (one of four courses carried five days a week during the secondary school year), could temper but could not stem the disarray that had overtaken the college curriculum.[44]

Special-purpose colleges and universities for blacks, women, and Roman Catholics made their own contributions to the confusion of purpose and style that characterized the curriculum. While from one coast to the other there were institutions of higher learning where blacks, women, and Roman Catholics were welcome along with everyone else, particular needs and purposes found curricular expression in racially, sexually, and religiously differentiated institutions. The first American college was founded for white, Anglo-Saxon, Protestant males; the traditions that shaped the course of study for the next two centuries and longer acknowledged such beginnings.

The so-called Negro college, established "as an emergency measure" after the Civil War, continued into the twentieth century to be "guided by the missionary motive arising from a sense of the duty of a stronger social group to a weaker." W. E. B. DuBois, the black leader who took issue with the emphasis on manual skills and elementary school teaching in these institutions toward the end of the nineteenth century, thought of the missionary-developed colleges as "social settlements; homes where the best of the sons of the freedmen came in close and sympathetic touch with the best traditions of New

England."[45] By then, unfortunately, the "best traditions of New England" were out of touch with the main thrust of the age. In combining classical learning and manual training in the same institutions, some of these colleges were guilty of offering their students a choice between an education appropriate to a cultured gentleman or an education in manual skills that were being displaced by industrial technology. To the extent that they were properly funded and equipped, the land-grant colleges created by a separate-but-equal extension of the Morrill Act in 1890 were useful instruments of the education of a shunned and exploited people. Yet none of these so-called colleges gave work of collegiate grade until 1916.[46]

By 1900, however, the curricular directions of colleges and universities for blacks had been established basically in imitation of the institutions that served the dominant caste. Acceptance of segregation as the defining practice in the relations between the races required of the southern colleges for blacks the education of trained, vocationally prepared graduates in many diverse fields. The curriculum of the black colleges was shaped by a policy of apartheid in a society sufficiently democratic in the abstract to encourage the development of a class of responsible professional leaders; the intentions of Atlanta, Fisk, and Howard were directed toward the shaping of a curriculum appropriate to a black professional elite. But the models for these institutions were those of the dominant caste: Fisk University's music department concentrated on classical European music to the exclusion of the music that expressed the black experience in America, and black history and sociology courses were rare and exceptional until after World War I.[47]

In tying the education of the freedmen to industrial and manual training, Samuel Chapman Armstrong and Hampton Institute placed before black students an image of themselves derived from an unacknowledged, perhaps even unconscious, racial bias. Booker T. Washington's curriculum at Tuskegee, like Armstrong's at Hampton, expressed a belief in the symbiotic relationship between the races. And, while the aspirations of such spokesmen as DuBois and such institutions as Fisk and Atlanta evoked an image of self-respecting, accomplished black professionals leading their people, like Hampton and Tuskegee they acknowledged and served a caste society. As late as 1909 nearly ten million American blacks depended for leadership on no more than 3,500 college graduates, most of whom were school teachers and ministers.[48]

Colleges for women were not founded as an emergency but as an experiment in applied psychology, philosophy, and physiology. Vassar, Smith, and Wellesley, in quick succession, using the classical liberal arts curriculum that was on the brink of collapse in the old men's colleges, proved that women were mentally and physically equal to a demanding collegiate course of study and, in doing so, vindicated the philosophy of equal rights for women. By 1890 the roster of full-fledged liberal arts colleges for women also included Bryn Mawr, Wells, Mount Holyoke, and the Society for the Collegiate Education of Women in Cambridge, Harvard's clumsy way of acknowledging what it would have preferred to ignore. As was true of the colleges for blacks, colleges for women were often colleges in name only; those that deserved the name, having survived the opposition of critics who sought to discredit them with accusations of having failed to live up to the curricular standards of men's colleges, soon found themselves criticized for imitating the men's colleges too well and for not providing a course of study appropriate to women's work.[49]

So intent were they on fulfilling traditional collegiate goals that the women's colleges eschewed the subjects that the old female seminaries had regarded as necessary for the cultivation of the graces and preparation for the duties of the home. Early Vassar provided some of the so-called female subjects as electives, and it developed strong programs in the fine arts and music, thus encouraging among the witless the repute of such subjects as being feminine in character. Responding to an altogether different clientele, the land-grant colleges developed home economics as a curricular program that focused new knowledge, new technology, and new concepts of management and organization on the functions of the home. Departments of domestic economy at Iowa, Kansas, Oregon, and South Dakota in 1890 defined woman's role as compensatory to man's, in the sense that woman's work was whatever men would not do, but the courses themselves imparted dignity to that role by according the status of profession to homemaking.[50]

Complementary equality was the determined goal of the eastern women's colleges, whose upper- and middle-class students learned that, just as there were male characteristics and male professions, so there were female characteristics and appropriate female professions. Bryn Mawr's course on "charities and corrections" could not have been an invention of a late nineteenth-century men's college. Social work, widely defined, was the preferred instrument of complementary equality, but for those young women who would not accept the male/female division of professions Bryn Mawr was something of a shrine. At Bryn Mawr, M. Carey Thomas encouraged young women to become scholars and college professors. It may have been at Bryn Mawr, on the edge of the unknown, that faculty and students ignored their sex and for the first time in an institution of higher education in the United States allowed human beings to be human first, men or women second. M. Carey Thomas was a lesbian and surely not the first person to head an American college or university whose sexual life was an influence on the college course of study. Under her tutelage several generations at Bryn Mawr learned not to be taken in by men. That was progress.[51]

Students at Roman Catholic colleges in the United States, as they worked their way through one period after another of convent burning and political ostracism in the early nineteenth century, did not have to go to college, especially a college of their own persuasion, in order to grab the promise of this most open and inviting of countries. But for the Catholic Church in America the colleges and the students were as essential to the creation of an American priesthood as had been the colleges of the eighteenth century to the needs of society for a learned ministry. Yet the Church's problems were unique. English-speaking Irish had come to the United States in such numbers that they had all but defined the Church in America; on the other hand, no other church was confronted with the diversity of ethnic origins and the challenge of illiteracy that confronted the Catholic authorities in the United States as the century progressed.[52] Their colleges were mostly Irish colleges, along with some German colleges, before they were American colleges. Torn between the needs of the Church and the ethnic sensibilities of its diverse membership on the one hand and the pressure to fit into the American mold on the other, Catholic colleges and universities did not become essentially indistinguishable from other colleges and universities until the country as a whole was really going to school with the "Today" show, *Reader's Digest,* and Henry Luce. The styles of the country and of Catholic colleges were such that the first Roman Catholic president of the United States moved into his office by way of Choate School and Harvard University.

Catholic colleges had their challenges clearly set before them in large part because urban political life and large-scale construction in the United States provided ambitious Irishmen career opportunities that, to put it softly, were more American than the priesthood. In 1887 St. Louis University adopted the standard organization and curriculum of the other colleges, in other words an organization and curriculum open to almost any aspiration and definition, and other Catholic colleges followed the lead. Five years earlier Father Thomas Walsh, the president of Notre Dame, had perhaps issued the license on which St. Louis University's audacity was based: "Until the conductors of colleges . . . concede that students and their parents possess a certain right in . . . determining the course of studies . . . they will be looked upon . . . as men who have no sympathy with the world of beneficent actualities."[53]

By 1890 Fordham in New York, still offering the B.A. course based on the *ratio studiorum,* was also holding the aspiring faithful to a safe religious environment by offering a commercial course (English and business forms), the vocational possibilities of its scientific department (surveying, electrical engineering, photography, and analytical chemistry), and instruction in what, in a comfortable euphemism, were called "special studies"—music, drawing, painting, and modern languages. Somewhat earlier Fordham had moved out from control by a school of old French priests into a new era of liberal, young, imaginative Jesuits.[54]

Curricular peculiarities were just as possible at Catholic institutions as elsewhere. Land-grant colleges and black colleges expended great resources in developing programs in teacher training. Catholic colleges did not. Not believing in public education (which was anything but Catholic education), they blessed a liberal arts education as being an altogether suitable passport to elementary and secondary school teaching.[55] Catholic colleges held on to their original commitments and style as long as they could, but when it became apparent that a growing Catholic population needed more than a trained

priesthood conversant with Latin and Greek, the curriculum in
Catholic colleges responded to the young men and women who were
drifting away to godless state institutions or careless private colleges
and universities. Reluctantly the Catholic colleges abandoned a curricular system that was "religious, literary, and humanistic in spirit,
synthetic in vision, rigid in approach, liberal in aim, and elitist in
social orientation," and followed the drift of the age toward a curriculum that was "secular, scientific, and technical in spirit, particular-
ized in vision, flexible in approach, vocational in aim, and democratic
in social orientation."[56]

Other religious and ethnic groups made peace with themselves
and higher education according to their own needs. Mormons turned
the state of Utah and the universities there into beehives of middle-
class ambition. The relatively few Jews in the United States, cherish-
ing an intellectual tradition that was altogether foreign to the style of
the raw materialistic country to which they emigrated, placed
demands on Columbia, New York University, the City College of
New York, and other urban colleges and universities that reinforced
every native effort to move intellectual purpose into the center of the
academic enterprise.

Critical but acquiescing Protestants had no particular problems. They gave up protesting, they identified themselves with the
materialistic and exploitive growth of the country. Many colleges and
universities openly stopped being Congregational, Presbyterian,
Methodist, and whatever, and if they did not send out pictures of
themselves making money and sinning like barbarians it was because
they did not need to. By 1900 colleges and universities were wealthy
and clumsy with uncertainty, and a great number of Americans
accepted these qualities as signs of strength and special grace.

The funeral was widely reported, but the patient refused to die.
Colleges held on to life even as their friends mourned and their enemies dismissed them. Bewilderment overtook institutions that in less
than two decades were displaced as standard-bearers of higher education by universities that were brazen in their self-confidence and
embarrassingly young in years. In 1881 enrollments at Amherst, the
University of Wisconsin, and the University of Virginia were
approximately the same; Williams was larger than Indiana Univer-

sity; Bowdoin was comparable in size to Johns Hopkins and the University of Minnesota.[57] So rapid, however, was the overtaking of the old colleges by the new universities that at the turn of the century the colleges were indeed being publicly interred. The president of the University of Chicago in 1900 expected 25 percent of existing small colleges to survive and the same percentage to collapse into academies; the rest he expected to transform themselves into combination preparatory schools and two-year colleges. The president of Columbia University in 1902 concluded that the colleges could be saved only by reducing their course of study to two or, at the most, three years. The next year the president of Stanford University gave the colleges a collective death sentence and two methods of reincarnation: "The best will become universities, the others will return to their place as academies."[58]

Self-serving though these pronouncements were, they rested on observable conditions that the colleges themselves could not deny. Their students were restless, bored, complaining.[59] None of the formulas for meeting the disturbing challenges to the old course of study seemed to work, neither a combination of intransigence and weakness as practiced by Porter at Yale nor intransigence and temper as exhibited by McCosh at Princeton. Julius Seelye's flexibility and accommodation at Amherst were no more successful in maintaining the disciplinary and pietistic strengths of the old curriculum than was the sheer negative rigidity practiced elsewhere.[60] For good news it was necessary to look to certain starving outposts of a vanished era, lingering on in the South and West, untouched by recent history or intimations of the future.

A weakening of reliable standards, a loss of integrity gave rise to a declining self-confidence in the colleges. By 1886 it was possible to earn a Harvard B.A. by passing the admissions requirements for Harvard College and then proceeding to take a full program of engineering courses offered by Lawrence Scientific School. While the partial course option, which allowed a student to take a program of his own choice but which promised him no degree, was a boon to enrollments, it was also a dangerously demoralizing device. For in addition to raising questions about why so many young men and women would want to be in college and still find a degree of no value, the partial course students must have caused some degree candidates to wonder themselves what *they* were doing. In 1893 at Yale, which for so long had seemed to be such a symbol of stability—for the first time since the college began in 1701—physics could be avoided. Moral philosophy dropped out of the senior year. Columbia in the 1880s moved toward university status because the trustees decided that as a small college Columbia had failed and would never prosper. And it certainly did not help to have that preeminent hero of the age, Andrew Carnegie, quoted as saying that "while the college student has been learning . . . such knowledge as seems adapted for life upon another planet . . . the future captain of industry is hotly engaged in the school of experience. . . . College education as it exists is fatal to success in that domain."[61]

For the colleges more was at stake than curricular strategies. In settling on the concept of "the whole man" as an expression of their curricular purpose, the colleges late in the nineteenth century selected a symbol around which they could rally their forces, a symbol that represented values that were conservative, antiprogressive, elitist, and nonmaterialistic. In rejecting the values of the new universities—specialization, power, materialism—"the whole man" was in direct descent from Hercules. The colleges did not yet know how to move their whole man toward greater intellectual purpose, but they did know that the tradition of liberal learning was a safe repository of the whole man style in its organic view of society and its respect for class responsibility, religion, property, and unhurried change.[62] All this may have, as one historian has put it, "placed them out of harmony with the democratic imperatives of the age," even as it also made them true to their past.[63] If in retrospect the whole man was what the nineteenth-century college was all about, the question with which it confronted the twentieth century was whether both the college and the whole man possessed any survival value in a world that appeared to have settled on the great state and urban universities as the ultimate expression of the culture's intentions.

One pillar of strength was missing as the century turned. With the retirement of Charles Eliot Norton at Harvard in 1898, an era ended. Norton had been hired to teach the history of art in 1874, and he used his professorship as a means of teaching "youths whom I can try to inspire with love of things that make life beautiful and generous." In 1875 Norton's classes enrolled 34 students; twenty years later they enrolled 446 students. By then Norton was famous, he was not demanding, and students delighted in him as a relic from an earlier era and as a critic of the age. His field was art history, not moral philosophy, but in a university that was learning how to adopt the suspended judgment appropriate to a scientific posture, Norton's opinionated lectures must have been a refreshing evidence of vibrant human energy and thought. His purpose and style took him close to the now vanished course in moral philosophy; he discussed everything—manners, morals, politics—and dispensed judgment rather than sterile objectivity quite as freely as had Timothy Dwight early in the century.[64]

Norton's whole man was threatened by barbarism, but he used his Harvard lecture hall to lead those who would follow to some level of refinement. "Professor Norton lectured in Italian 4 this afternoon," a Radcliffe student recorded in 1895. "The dear old man looks so mildly happy and benignant while he regrets everything in the age and the country—so contented, while he gently tells us it were better for us had we never been born in this degenerate and unlovely age."[65] Norton's Harvard lectures were not the last stand of genteel culture, but their tone and popularity gave encouragement to those who would protect the humanist tradition from the barbarians.

About 1880 Harvard undergraduates began using the library in significant numbers in order to prepare research papers for their seminars. At more or less the same time Josiah Willard Gibbs, maybe the first significant theoretical scientist since Newton, received a paycheck from Yale; until then Yale had not objected to his presence, nor had it paid him; he hardly ever had a student who understood him. In 1890 Harvard reorganized its faculty in a way that obliterated any distinction between professors engaged in graduate teaching and those for whom undergraduates still mattered; the scales were now clearly tipped in favor of the new values.[66] "Scepticism [sic] is the beginning of science" was the message of Thorstein Veblen to his academic contemporaries; translated into action, his message, among other things, was an invitation to the assault on the New Testament, already an aspect of the German and English universities. Somewhere out there in an American university after everyone else had gone to bed there was a professor at work on "new breeds of potatoes."[67]

Social reform required a statistical justification: Courses in statistics were promoted as agencies of reform. Strikes were a threat to the social order: Schools of applied science that dignified, perhaps even overdignified, new technologies and skills were "the safest remedy." Study and intellectual activity must not get out of hand: An 1894 bequest of $400,000 to the University of California provided for the founding of a school "to teach boys trades; fitting them to make a living with their hands, with little study and plenty of work."[68] Any questions? The universities had an answer, or were at work on one, or would be.

The universities were so effective in demonstrating their indispensability and the colleges were so nervous about their curricular relevance that no one really needed Josiah Royce's 1891 essay in which his characteristic idealism came to the support of the university style. Royce, professor of philosophy at Harvard, confronted the materialistic, practical, progressive, popular tendencies of the course of study and somehow managed to see them as making the university "more ideal in its undertakings, more genuinely spiritual in its enthusiasm and its scholarship, and . . . far less philistine in its concerns." He recalled his own days as one of the first students at the marvelous new university in Baltimore: "One longed to be a doer of the word, and not a hearer only, a creator of his own infinitesimal fraction of a product, bound in God's name to produce it when the time came." In the spirit of those experiences, both Harvard and Columbia, he rejoiced to say, were in the process of reorganizations that would free the graduate department "from its old bondage to the ideals and the paramount influence of the collegiate course" and make it "the most important department in the University."[69]

Was Royce ashamed of himself? Who knows? He rattled on. Political science was a useful study in preparing the public "for that serious time of grave social dangers which seems to be not far off." Natural science was "opening new fields to the industrial arts." And philosophy itself was "preparing the way for a needed spiritual guidance in the religious crisis which is rapidly becoming so serious."[70] If all this was true, any honest college president, any candid college professor also knew that the resources at the command of his own institution had thus far hardly allowed for the purchase of a typewriter. Royce was writing about whole departments!

Royce asked what was, and should have been, the ultimate question: "What . . . is to become of the undergraduate?" His answer, while not so intended, should have reassured the colleges: "In the true university the undergraduate ought to feel himself a novice in an order of learned servants of the ideal."[71] Under the circumstances, is there any wonder that instead the undergraduate played football?

One problem confronting the colleges was an old problem made more insistent: how to accommodate and afford all the new knowledge that was spilling out of the universities and taking shape as new academic subjects. It had been easy enough to manage the breaking away of political economy from moral philosophy during the first half of the nineteenth century. No significant change in direction or emphasis or purpose was involved, simply the transfer and elaboration of one aspect of moral philosophy of pressing public interest— practical political and economic policy—into a separate subject. The professors of political economy were indistinguishable from the professors of moral philosophy (Francis Wayland wrote textbooks in both subjects). Political economy was simply applied moral philosophy, serving the interests of the same merchant and banking interests that the moral philosophy course served in its consideration of the rights of property.[72]

Out of the universities and out of the collapsing fabric of moral philosophy, with some lingering ethical concern regardless of their scientific posture, now came social science, sociology, and economics. In combining the study of society and the pressing "social question" of the 1880s and 1890s with a traditional concern for right action, the emerging social sciences were popular with students. And because they were popular, in the free market of university curriculum making, departments, professors, and courses multiplied to meet student demand.[73] On the other hand, the colleges—with limited funds, staff, and enrollment—were necessarily selective. By 1900, however, this selectivity was not only in need of a convincing educational philosophy, it was also widely recognized as evidence that the colleges were out of sympathy with the times.

What was true of the social sciences was true of all the other subjects. In 1880 there were only eleven professors of history in the United States, each of them a recognition that there was some history other than the ancient history that was implicit in study of the classics. Between the appointment in 1883 of Albert Bushnell Hart as instructor to teach U.S. history and his retirement from Harvard in 1926, a profession of historians and a discipline of history had been created.[74] *The American Nation,* a collective history of the American people in twenty-eight volumes, edited by Hart and written by professional historians, appeared between 1904 and 1918, a magnificent assertion that American history was a subject fit for the course of study. European history, English constitutional history, the history of periods and of nations—history literally had no limits, and every university history department was prepared to prove it. History was not alone. Between 1887 and 1889 professors of psychology appeared in quick succession at the University of Pennsylvania, the University of Wisconsin, and Harvard.[75]

Universities used the elective system to develop advanced courses and clusters of courses where once there had been but one course. At Brown between 1889 and 1896 the number of hours of subject matter taught increased from 135 to 348: English jumped from nine and a half to forty-eight, history from three to twenty, social science from zero to seven, and Romance languages from nine to thirty-six.[76] The curricular growth implicit in these figures, which were paralleled in universities across the country, was costly and painful. Many a university campus resembled a battlefield.

At Chicago chemists fought zoologists over disputed scientific territory, and economists fought sociologists as both laid claim to statistics. History and classics fought for control of ancient history at Harvard, and within the new academic disciplines themselves battles raged—between literary culture and research and utility in history. Philosophy was a free-for-all: physiological psychology versus idealism versus pragmatism.[77] Colleges could not afford these curricular battles. In 1900 they could only wait for the results and pray.

Efforts of professional organizations and the universities to upgrade standards for entry into the professions had not yet given to colleges the function of passing prospective lawyers, doctors, and clergymen on to graduate schools. The median level of education required for admission to an American law school in 1900 was the equivalent of eighth grade. Of 86 law schools, only 3 required four years of high school, and only 2 required any college preparation at all—Harvard (three years) and Columbia (four years after 1903).[78] The median level of education required for admission to an American medical school in 1900 was one year of high school. Of 157 medical schools, only 12 required four years of high school, only 2 required a college course—Johns Hopkins and Harvard (in 1901).[79]

Theological schools were more demanding than law and medical schools, the median level for the 165 existing theological schools in 1900 being one year of college. Seventy-one theological schools required a college degree for admission.[80] Over two thirds of the existing law, medical, and theological schools in 1900 had been founded since 1850, responding to the dynamics of an expanding society and the decline of apprenticeship as a reliable agency of instruction.[81] In 1900, except for a considerable number of theological schools, institutions for instruction in the traditional elite professions were in competition with the colleges, and there was small comfort in the standards required for admission to the theological schools: Prospective ministers could not fill a college.

Developments in the training of teachers left the colleges stranded, separated from a function that they had informally filled since the founding of Harvard College and more formally attended to since the Civil War, particularly in small colleges competing with state colleges and universities. At the turn of the century, when the training of a large number of teachers became a necessity as a result of increased compulsory school attendance, the colleges were faced with a choice of shifting their curriculum from the old humanistic focus to an emphasis on teacher training or of declining the opportunity in favor of the normal schools and teacher's colleges and departments of education in the universities. Inasmuch as the colleges' historical role in teacher training was incidental and informal, a consequence of a liberal arts education being accepted as a suitable preparation for elementary or secondary school teaching, the colleges' decision to back away from involvement in the development of a profession of schoolteachers was consistent with their sense of their own history. Besides, college faculties, being invaded and transformed by young instructors with the Ph.D. degree, had their sights on higher goals and higher studies. The normal schools, on the other hand, finding themselves both outflanked by high schools capable of turning out perfectly adequate teachers and given a blank check for teacher training by the colleges, moved easily, with the cooperation of state legislatures and accrediting agencies, toward becoming teacher's colleges and purveyors of a variety of appropriate bachelor's degrees.[82]

Crafts on their way to becoming professions, skills once learned on the job or in the field—mechanical engineering, journalism, architecture, business—used the university schools and departments as environments in which was determined who the professionals would be and how they would be trained.[83] Increasingly victory went not to the shop but to the standardizing bureaucrats of university professional schools and programs. In this vast work of defining and certifying new professions the old colleges had no part to play. Were they to be left with no purpose other than the nurture of a heritage the world was abandoning in indecent haste, destined to be the home of dead languages and books no one cared to read?

An event took place in the East in the 1880s and 1890s. In college and university histories it was often referred to as the "Battle of the Classics." The idea was that something could be done to keep alive two languages that were already dead. Greek and Latin may be immortal, but long before the end of the nineteenth century their place in an American college curriculum was not really a matter of debate. But a debate, a very intense debate, was held anyway, for the stakes were high, powerful social classes were engaged, and in some ways a definition of American culture—what it had been, was, and would be—was being written.

A Darwinian biology professor at the normal school in Greeley, Colorado, was fond of telling his students that in Colorado "the beet root took precedence over the Greek root as a subject for study," and the editor of the *New York Evening Post* wondered, without leaving any doubt about the answer, whether it was better "to know the Greek word for liver than it is to know the position and function of that organ." Undaunted, the president of the University of Rochester announced in 1869 that "the raid now made upon the old Greek and Latin classics will not be of long duration." Under attack for being exactly the kind of college the farmers of Kansas did not need, three years later Kansas State Agricultural College gave up instruction in Greek.[84]

On the other hand, when Indiana University dropped Greek as an admission requirement in 1873, enrollment in the university's classical course, with four years of Greek, increased. The next year, at the behest of upper-class friends, the City College of New York strengthened its course requirements in both Latin and Greek.[85] Most madness, including these examples, can be explained, at least tentatively. In Indiana a volunteer for the university's classical course may only have been announcing candidacy for a place in the forthcoming leisure class. In New York, was it possible that the idea was to keep the college as unpopular as Columbia and New York University and preserve even City College of New York (CCNY) for the privileged?

It did not really matter, for in 1886 Harvard took the significant step: President Eliot figured out how to let someone into Harvard College without Greek and still keep the hurdles equally high. Sensing that he could not hurry Harvard along toward university status only with enrollments drawn from the boarding schools of New England and the high schools of Boston, Eliot persuaded the faculty to provide an admissions route that did not require Greek. His was a gesture toward the high schools, although a rather demanding one: Harvard would accept advanced mathematics and physics as substitutes for Greek as an admission requirement. Eliot's message to the high schools was clear: Do right by science, and Harvard will forget that you have already forgotten Greek. His message to the colleges, whatever it may have been intended to be, was taken as a declaration of war. As a reform, the Harvard admission alternative of 1886 did not work: The American high school had just about as much difficulty gearing up for physics and mathematics as it did for Greek. But as a bomb dropped into all the places that were identified with the stability of society and the serenity of the upper class, it was a magnificent, if accidental, success. In no time at all the presidents of Yale, Brown, Dartmouth, Wesleyan, Williams, Trinity, Amherst, and Boston University addressed themselves to the Harvard Board of Overseers, imploring them "not to destroy the meaning of the B.A. degree by allowing students to graduate without taking Latin and Greek."[86]

Harvard gave up what was already gone, but it was the symbolism and the firmness of its apostasy that were most troublesome. An earlier generation had been able to rally the forces of evangelical religion to hold back the Unitarian heresies emanating from Cambridge, and, besides, Unitarianism was both so intellectual and mild in manner that it was almost beyond the understanding of all but some rather special people in the vicinity of Boston. This time Harvard was on the popular side, and every faculty that supported the threatened New England college presidents knew it. One college faculty, at Miami in Ohio, forced out of office a reforming president and found themselves teaching, and some of them not teaching very much, in a college where a majority of students as the joyous price of avoiding Greek were not even candidates for a degree.[87]

An old college custom carried to Indiana was the burning of Horace at the end of each academic year. In 1894 at Indiana University the burning of Horace was given up, probably because by then there were not enough students around to understand what the burning was all about. The same year, perhaps as some measure of the distance between Cambridge and Williamstown and between Williamstown and Bloomington, Williams College abandoned Greek as an entrance requirement. The next year at a Bowdoin commencement dinner a graduate of the college, himself a teacher of Greek, spoke up in defense of Bowdoin's decision to follow the Williams example: He knew of no reason for requiring Greek rather than Sanskrit for candidacy for the B.A. degree, and the truth of the matter was that students could get art and culture, if that were the purpose, the same place they had been getting their Greek—out of "ponies" and "trots."[88]

In 1903 no one had to take Greek at Yale any more. By 1905 all of the state universities in the Midwest and West had long since dropped Greek and were about to eliminate Latin. There were regrets. President Hadley of Yale surrendered, but Jeremiah Day would have been proud of the style: "Greek is an intellectual game where the umpires know the rules better than they know the rules in the game of French, for instance, or history or botany. . . . But colleges cannot teach a thing to a public which does not want to study it."[89] In this environment the colleges reached out for some slender thread. It was not Greek. Was it Latin?

William Torrey Harris, in 1880 superintendent of schools in St. Louis, already recognized as an educational philosopher of some importance, later to be U.S. Commissioner of Education, was not willing to give up Latin *or* Greek. As staunch an enemy of the old faculty psychology of learning as there was, he nonetheless took the opportunity of an address before the National Education Association to argue that Latin and Greek were essential to a modern liberal education. He shifted the argument from old to new psychological grounds; it was not for mental training that Latin and Greek were necessary; the necessity was a function of the Greek and Latin cultures as the ancestors of modern civilization and therefore "the absolute necessity of mastering our history, in order to know ourselvs [sic]."[90] Although this friend of the ancient languages was also an imaginative practitioner of spelling reform, his argument was clear:

> In lerning to think in their idioms, and to giv our thoughts their forms and words, we lern to see how the world lookt to them, and can redily seiz and appreciate the exigencies which gave rise to their forms and usages, for language is the clothing of the inmost self of a people.[91]

Harris's position rested on a complex philosophical argument that he stated as an aphoristic paradox: "Self-alienation is essential to self-knowledge." This paradox was soon challenged in *Popular Science Monthly* by Paul R. Shipman, who was capable of his own aphorisms but offered them without paradox: "Self-alienation is self-repression. . . . The true condition of culture is self-activity. . . . Our mother tongue alone, as the instrument of our thinking, is the instrument of our culture. It is hence the thing of all things that we should master first and master thoroughly. In this philosophy and common sense are at one."[92] Whatever else he may have accomplished, Harris elevated the level of debate from whether cows could be milked by Latin and Greek to whether modern man could know himself without knowing the languages in which the history of his own culture was imbedded.

Perhaps the most publicized of the assaults on the domination of the curriculum by the ancient languages was the bitter Phi Beta Kappa address delivered at Harvard in 1883 by Charles Francis Adams, Jr. Fastening the term "college fetich" [sic] on the role of Greek as a passport to learning, his remarks were something of a confession of worldly impotency for a whole class for which he was the spokesman.[93] He elaborated his position in a letter to Charles Eliot Norton: "I think we've had all we want of 'elegant scholars' and 'gen-

tlemen of refined classical taste,' and now I want to see more university men trained to take a hand in the rather rough game of American
nineteenth-century life. To do that effectively, they must . . . be
brought up in communication with that life. At least they should
comprehend the tongues in which it talks.''[94]

By *tongues* Adams meant more than just English, French,
German, and Spanish. He meant "the ordinary tools which an educated man must have to enable him to work to advantage on the developing problems of modern, scientific life." Harvard, he complained,
"in these days of repeating-rifles . . . sent me and my classmates out
into the strife equipped with shields and swords and javelins. . . . Rep-
resenting American educated men in the world's industrial gatherings, I have occupied a position of confessed inferiority. I have not
been the equal of my peers."[95] If Adams's argument suggested that
Harvard's overemphasis on Greek assigned its graduates to the drawing room rather than the board room, it also accused the college, by
virtue of the superficiality of its instruction in Greek, of having
assured that when they moved into the drawing room Harvard graduates would at best be dilettantes:

> You cannot haul manure up and down and across a field,
> cutting the ground into deep ruts with the wheels of your
> cart, while the soil just gets a smell of what is in the cart,
> and then expect to get a crop. Yet even that is more than we
> did, and are doing, with Greek.[96]

What Adams wanted was an emphasis on the ability "to follow
out a line of exact, sustained thought to a given result," an intellectual upgrading of the course of study that made thought rather than
memorization and the worship of dead languages its essential style.
In the immediate aftermath of his address, what Adams got was a
vigorous dissent from the chapter of Phi Beta Kappa at Amherst, public support from William Graham Sumner at Yale, and a chorus of
attacks from an alarmed academy.[97]

There were, by now, no new thoughts on either side, but the
intensity of the battle engaged many talents that were able to bring
new combinations of argument and special interests to focus on the
problem. Every journal opened its pages to the controversy—*Atlantic*

Monthly, Century, Princeton Review, North American Review, Bibliotheca Sacra. Special bulletins came from Noah Porter and from Daniel H. Chamberlain, both in 1884. The same year at a meeting of the National Education Association, John Bascom, then president of the University of Wisconsin, concluded that Greek and Latin were antidotes to the materialism of the age.[98]

Sarcasm was heaped on both positions. Andrew Preston Peabody, retired professor of moral philosophy at Harvard and hymnologist, directed his at Charles Francis Adams, Jr.: "When a member in the fourth generation of the most successful family in America ascribes to Greek all of the misfortunes and failings of his ancestors and kindred, we might almost suspect him of antirepublican aspirations; for the only misfortune that can be conceived of in the history of that family is their failure to become a race of hereditary monarchs." Clarence King, geologist and a product of Sheffield Scientific School, used the *North American Review* to recall with bitter sarcasm his days in New Haven: "Because four hundred years ago an Italian youth, having nothing else to study, opened his heart and head to the splendid illumination of classical learning and was conscious of his superiority over the ignorant dolt of the day . . . an American professor of a classical subject felt entitled twenty-five years ago to look down upon a teacher of natural science, and by the same quaint sort of logic the Yale academic students excluded 'scientifics' from boat and fence." In King's view the academic alumni were destined "to sink below the surface of mediocrity and achieve positively nothing," comforting themselves with the notion that they were "of the company of the illumined," possessing a degree to be valued "even more as time rolls on and . . . [they] forget how to translate it."[99]

As practical as its defenders tried to make Greek seem, there was something ridiculous in the justification offered by Professor William G. Frost of Oberlin—"the enjoyment of quotations." Opponents of Greek were not necessarily friendly to an uncoordinated elective system; both Sumner in the *Princeton Review* and Albert S. Bolles in the *Atlantic Monthly* chose to regard the development of the system of electives less as a solution to the problems confronting the curriculum than as evidence that the course of study needed an overhauling. Defenders of Greek were generous toward their opponents,

including Adams, on one ground only: They accepted the charge that
Greek had been poorly taught.[100] They proposed a number of remedies, all of which they would soon have an opportunity to try out in
the unprotected free market into which Greek fell in the years after
1886, when eastern colleges followed Harvard in removing Greek
from its privileged position as an entrance and degree requirement
for the B.A. degree.

Noah Porter's 1884 defense of Greek was a remarkable attack on
Eliot and Harvard in which he used every resource of debate, argument, and sarcasm that he could summon. "The old Athens on the
Aegean Sea is still superior to the new Athens on Boston Harbor" was
the reassuring news from New Haven, but both Porter and Eliot knew
that the new subjects could not be denied entry to the curriculum.[101]
Eliot had concluded that since everything could not be studied ade-
quately the idea of curricular unity and symmetry would have to give
way to studying certain subjects in depth. Porter refused to give up:
He intended to hold on to the old subjects more or less at the level they
had by then reached, admitting the new subjects on an elementary
level only.

His was a losing position. Greek's best hope was that someone
somewhere would find a way of making it interesting. That discovery
was in fact made at Harvard in 1881, when for the first time a Greek
play was presented in America, the *Oedipus Tyrannus* of Sophocles.
The production so overwhelmed Cambridge that scalpers raised the
two-dollar tickets as high as fifteen dollars. Notre Dame, the University of Pennsylvania, Beloit, Albion, Olivet, and Ripon joined in the
modest Greek revival that accompanied its loss of advantaged position in the curriculum.[102]

At the same time that the curriculum was being subjected to a
battle over Greek in the East, the West was having a battle over vocational subjects. If the focus of concern differed, the intention was the
same: to find some balance, some rationale, in a curriculum that had
been wounded and demoralized.

The only purely classical college founded in Colorado,
Longmont, lasted exactly four years—1885 to 1889. With an enrollment of approximately ten in its liberal arts college, the University of
Denver in the early 1880s offered four parallel courses—classical, literary, scientific, and mining engineering. The classical course

included chemistry and assaying. Those who defended the classical curriculum in Colorado in the 1890s stressed its practicality, but in the open, aspiring environment of Colorado a simple classical liberal arts college was an anachronism, too intellectual, insufficiently democratic.[103] In Colorado, and surely in other western states, the culture was so aggressively democratic and materialistic that the concept of education as a commodity imperiled any curriculum that was not gloriously popular. Michael McGiffert's assessment of conditions in Colorado is unquestionably applicable to its neighboring states: "The problem was not to fight free of classicism but rather to defend the values of liberal learning against the advocates of a radical vocationalism."[104]

James H. Canfield, who presided over both Nebraska and Ohio State in the 1890s, urged students to put vocational training first in their selection of courses. At Wisconsin an engineering dean in 1899 dispensed with the liberal arts as instruments of idealism and located in "scientific agriculture, mining, manufacturing, and commerce . . . the material foundation of all high and noble living." The dependency of state universities and land-grant colleges on legislatures moved their courses of study easily in the direction of "job-related education," but even the private colleges, as a necessity of survival, readily acquiesced in the development of undergraduate programs in education, chemistry, business, nursing, and other occupations.[105]

In displacing the academy as the characteristic institution of secondary schooling in the nation, the high school likewise shifted the focus of secondary education from liberal learning to job training, and thereby presented the colleges with a challenging group of choices: either to acquiesce in the values of the high school and become advanced extensions of their vocational emphasis, balk and define themselves as narrowly elitist, or try to do and be everything.[106]

Russell Thomas's study of the career of general education in the nineteenth-century college and university reached the conclusion that "by the end of the century . . . the required element in a student's course of study was more likely to consist of vocational specifications than of courses serving a common cultural need. Thus in a century the principles by which specific degree requirements were determined had been reversed."[107] In the 1890s Yale College widened the door by which vocationalism was permitted to move in on the ancient preserve of Greek and Latin: a course in law for seniors, admission to the second year of the Yale medical and law schools for holders of the Yale B.A., the opening of divinity school courses to undergraduates. These developments in no way refuted Noah Porter's definition of liberal education as "the kind of culture which tends to perfect the man in the variety and symmetry and effectiveness of his powers, by reflection and self-knowledge, by self-control and self-expression, as contrasted with that which brings wealth or skill or fame or power."[108]

Liberal learning, however, was not dead. Threatened perhaps, but only temporarily, and probably no more so than any body of values so oriented always is. In its focus on the ideal, on human worth, on the intangibles of reflection and taste, it of course would have rough going in an age that was being defined by a raw materialism and widespread exploitation of both men and nature. In the colleges and universities, however, an aggressive vocationalism and a humorless pursuit of the higher learning were not alone in giving new definition to the curriculum. Friends of the humanist tradition were not immobilized by the termination of Greek's long stranglehold on the course of study; to some extent they were liberated by it.

They discovered that the old values, the enduring questions, the challenges to judgment and morality, inhered in the new subjects quite as readily as they had in the old ones and that, relieved of the burden of the pietistic focus of an earlier day, they could move toward some accommodation with the intellectual focus of the new breed of professors without compromising their own values. Liberal education was a matter of style more than it was a matter of subjects, and although it was appropriately uncomfortable with the new orientation it had no difficulty in expressing itself through the modern languages, English literature, the fine arts, and philosophy. There utility, research, power, and service established no exclusive claims. Freed from the remnants of Puritan piety, the humanists edged toward an openness about taste, asserted a legitimacy for esthetics.[109] In the belles lettres tradition that had worked its way into the curriculum on the eve of the American Revolution and that had been nurtured and sustained by the undergraduate literary societies, they embraced learning as something to enjoy, as an instrument of self-definition and refinement.

"Culture" became their special territory. Culture, not as anthropologists were coming to define it, but as "the higher and better things," the enjoyments and understandings and appreciations that distinguished the liberally educated from the barbaric. Esthetic, social, and moral considerations entered into culture as it was perceived and practiced in the universities and colleges.[110] Quite simply, culture was manifested in the better selves of the best people doing better things. Art galleries, afternoon tea, and a self-proclaimed superiority to the masses and the bourgeoisie were components of culture's style, a style that, in some of its practitioners, came dangerously close to being effete. It did not intend to be democratic, for it clearly was an open and honest assertion of superiority.[111]

As an expression of educational philosophy and institutional purpose, liberal culture found advocacy among the professors of the new subjects. At Harvard, Barrett Wendell and Charles T. Copeland cultivated soil that had been prepared for them by James Russell Lowell and Charles Eliot Norton. William Lyon Phelps at Yale, George E. Woodberry at Columbia, Hiram Corson at Cornell, and Charles Edward Garman at Amherst, in contrast to the utilitarians or the researchers or the surviving pietists among their colleagues, were the successful classroom teachers of their time, reveling in opinion, seeking to ignite among their students not just an enthusiasm for their specialties but for the whole world of liberal culture. The advocates and practitioners of liberal culture were as friendly to breadth of education as had been Jeremiah Day and the Yale faculty, but, instead of locating breadth in a course of study that was designed to train all the mental and moral faculties, they sought it in a knowledge of art, literature, history, and philosophy.[112]

Liberal culture was unwilling to bring science within its understanding or under its influence. A professor at the University of Michigan in 1907 struck the liberal pose: "Choked in erudition or experimental deftness, the spirit of man withers." At a time when the vocationalists and the scholars were making significant connections between the curriculum and the world, the humanists were giving the concept of the ivory tower new currency. William Lyon Phelps described life in the tower in a very few words: "One is removed from the sordid and material side of the struggle. . . . One does not dwell in a daily atmosphere of cloth and pork."[113]

"Liberal culture," Laurence Veysey has written, "could flourish only on those campuses which possessed the traditions (or lack of resources) that enabled them to resist the clamor for the useful and the scientific."[114] Poverty, indeed, was one of the great supports of liberal learning but it was also a condition that weakened the resistance of authorities to vocational studies. Liberal culture required more than a lack of resources and, in fact, could flourish in newly affluent environments. What could have been more encouraging to the intentions of liberal culture than to have been a member of St. Anthony Hall at Williams College, living in a fraternity house designed by Stanford White and embellished with the art of John LaFarge and Augustus St. Gaudens?

Liberal culture established itself at those colleges and universities where the Yale Report of 1828 had served for three quarters of a century as fundamental educational philosophy, even as that philosophy made necessary adjustments to a changing society. Yale and Princeton and the colleges that had fashioned themselves according to the curricular wisdom of Jeremiah Day and that were likewise old enough to know themselves and their particular strengths and weaknesses were in the best position to give new definition and focus to liberal study. A fading but in no sense abandoned Puritan tradition strengthened the resolve of some institutions to protect the curriculum from the coarse materialism and grasping utilitarianism of the age. Yale, Princeton, Williams, Amherst, Bowdoin, Hamilton, and others had resisted the clamoring democracy of the Jacksonian period; they shared a history that allowed them to hold to a humanistic course of study and an emphasis on liberal learning in a new age of democratic expansiveness. Their clientele was receptive, recognizing in "culture" an approved system of studies, values, and behavior that separated educated men and women from their contemporaries by distinctions more noble than money and power, less demanding than piety and intellectual rigor. Liberal culture did not capture the professor or student for whom the mind was everything. Its bias toward appreciation, expression, and contemplation made the curriculum of liberal culture perhaps less exacting than the more readily measurable scientific curriculum. Its respect for self-education as the enduring purpose of the curriculum was subject to abuse and misunderstanding. In any case, an epithet—"culture course"—was a product of this particular moment in the history of humane letters.[115]

At its best, liberal culture insisted on more than the celebration of civilized man; it encouraged thought, judgment, criticism, but none in excess; self-realization, rather than power or service or utility, was its purpose. To the deadly seriousness of the scholars on campus and the hurrying ambition of materialists in the career programs, it opposed a style that promoted leisure as a virtue and a way of life.

Some colleges and universities, wealthy enough or uncertain enough or simply philosophically eclectic enough, managed to embrace utility, research, and culture and not to give themselves over in any really definitive way to any one of the curricular styles that were available. No academic tool was more helpful in allowing an institution to do almost everything and anything than was the elective system with which Eliot of Harvard in 1869 had announced his intention to transform Harvard. At the time of his retirement in 1909 no one denied his success in making a university out of a college nor the extent to which he had employed the elective principle as the instrument of reform. Not everyone was happy with the results. Still complaining, Charles Francis Adams, Jr., in another Phi Beta Kappa address in 1906, described "the elective system in its present form of development as an educational fad, and a very mischievous one."[116] Only Harvard, the state universities, and such wealthy new private universities as Chicago and Stanford indulged in electives with complete and enthusiastic abandon.[117] Others resisted or edged toward some restricted definition, either from poverty or from philosophical considerations. Like the battle over Greek, from which it was sometimes indistinguishable, the battle over electives was intense, bitter, and prolonged, and it was essentially an eastern affair. "The elective system became the issue" over which faculties fell into hostile camps, because, as George Wilson Pierson wrote, "it was the instrument of transition" and "as such it became both a weapon and a symbol."[118]

For higher education in the United States in the decades between the Civil War and World War I, the elective system was something of a safety valve. No comparable device could have contained the energies that were seeking expression in the undergraduate curriculum: the advance in average age and seriousness of the entering classes immediately after the war, the technological forces unleashed by the war, a democratic high school movement, old occupations in the process of being professionalized, a self-conscious breed of professors devoted to scholarship and scientific research.

The victory of electives was facilitated by an era of government and private philanthropy that was ready to underwrite the growth that was an unavoidable result of student choice and professional self-interest, as well as being a necessity of institutional reputation. In one sense, then, the elective principle allowed an institution to do things to its curriculum, the consequences of which were good for its competitive image. In addition, for over a century and a half experimental science and an empirical approach to truth had so enlarged their domain, both inside and outside the colleges, that both revealed religion and the old faculty psychology had lost ground to an ascendant pragmatism and to the beginnings of experimental psychology.[119]

In an age and in a country less awed by individual triumphs of will and mastery of men, nature, and events, the elective system might have met greater resistance and even been recognized as anything but a system. The old course of study, however, required greater authority than it could summon and greater strength than it possessed if it was to withstand the forces that Eliot and others were able to harness.

For undergraduates the elective system was an invitation to both wider and more specialized learning opportunities, responsive to individual interests and skills. It made a connection between the world of study and the world of work that appealed to hopeful and aspiring young idealists who wanted to be participants, not observers, in a time of great material advance. In moving students out from under the inherited curricular debris and fetishes of several centuries and allowing them, in varying degrees, to design their own courses of study, the elective system recognized human individuality and the conditions necessary to maturation and self-possession.[120]

An emerging profession of scholars used the elective system to free itself from a tradition of academic bookkeeping, class attendance, and examination by rote and to license the new professors as investigators, innovators, the advance agents of next year's truth. The consequence was new: new subjects, new depth, new skills, new truth. Morale skyrocketed, and the professors of the new persuasion found themselves creating graduate schools of arts and sciences, factories of learning, even as they were pulling old institutions away from their aristocratic bias and their almost unbelievably leisurely pace.[121] (William Dwight Whitney, who was very bright and energetic, but nonetheless a Williams College student who did not yet know that he would become a great Sanskrit scholar, wrote in 1842: "I never study more than an hour and a half a day, and plenty of time is left for reading, writing, hunting, and skinning and stuffing." At the time, Whitney in his spare hours was "doing" a series of forty birds "after Audubon." The cousin to whom he was writing, a recent graduate of the college, became a missionary and sent some of the ruins of ancient Nineveh to Williams in 1851, making the student scientific society the only exhibitor of Assyrian bas-reliefs until other missionary-blessed colleges were equally recognized by alumni in foreign parts. These were the terms on which leisure was defined in the old colleges. They were the terms of liberal culture.)[122]

For these advantages, for both student and professor, the elective system exacted a price. It did not destroy the unity of knowledge, but it made that ancient fiction more difficult to believe: It frightened the thoughtful into recognizing that elective variety was a philosophical statement quite as much as was prescribed uniformity. To the extent that election roamed beyond the borders of the old curriculum, it expressed a loss of spiritual character, it became a measure of secular power. In the interest of expansion, it lowered standards. It was expensive. In shifting the authority for defining a college education from society to the individual student, it allowed students to regard the college or university as an environment for establishing "prestige or connections," rather than as an environment fundamentally designed by the course of study. As they never could with the old curriculum, colleges and universities used the elective system to attract students on other than educational grounds. Election spread the Cornell style, its buoyant optimism and its well-meaning vocationalism, from one coast to the other.[123]

Now, all these developments were happening or would have happened without the elective system. Whether the elective system was the cause or the consequence of "the speed and magnitude of social change" is a question that is beyond answer.[124] Of course it had to be both: "In a single generation the world of knowledge exploded. The hierarchy of values was upset. . . . Orderliness disappeared."[125]

On the eve of his retirement from the presidency of Harvard, Eliot took the position that "the largest effect of the elective system is that it makes scholarship possible, not only among undergraduates, but among graduate students and college teachers."[126] From the perspective of 1869, this 1908 justification of his own career as a curriculum reformer was sound. While it did not cause the fragmentation of the curriculum, however, the elective system may have been more important for having provided the structure that facilitated that fragmentation. The elective system was an admission that the professors no longer possessed the authority to justify or insist on "any particular combination of courses while barring out others."[127] With freakish exception, any subsequent efforts to recapture that authority in order to establish or enforce a course of general education would not be taken seriously for very long by students or professors. Vocationalism and the death of Greek turned liberal learning from subject matter to style. The elective system required that it give up curricular symmetry and unity while students and professors established these qualities on their own very individual terms. Strange as it may seem, the elective system threw undergraduates back where Mark Hopkins in his 1836 inaugural address had said they belonged: on their own.

James McCosh, the president of Princeton, sufficiently distrusted undergraduates that he found himself in 1885 Eliot's adversary in a widely publicized debate. The style of the world they inhabited was best expressed in the circumstances under which their disagreements about the course of study became public property. Under the auspices of the Nineteenth Century Club, at the Fifth Avenue residence of Courtlandt Palmer, a Princeton graduate, they agreed to a debate that was reported in the metropolitan press in a manner that would soon be appropriate for a Harvard-Princeton football game. The press, which spoke out of the experience of its editors and publishers with the old curriculum, in this instance reported Princeton as the winner. History reversed the score.[128]

At the time of the debate Eliot was well on his way to achieving total election at Harvard. All subject requirements for seniors were abolished in 1872, for juniors in 1879, and for sophomores in 1884. They were greatly reduced for freshmen in 1885 and eliminated altogether, except for English composition, in 1897. Harvard's elective system was the freest in the country; with it Eliot increased his faculty from 60 to 600 and Harvard's endowment from $2 million to $20 million. McCosh, in the Princeton environment, was also a reformer, as he had promised to be in his inaugural address, which favored the new subjects, electives, and respect for professional considerations in the selection of courses. Under McCosh, by 1885, Princeton had greatly opened up electives for both juniors and seniors, but, unlike Harvard, it was not on the eve of giving up Greek as a requirement for admission to candidacy for the B.A. degree.[129]

In his remarks in New York in February 1885, McCosh was in no way unbending, but the distance between his emphases and Eliot's was beyond closing. A belief in faculty psychology, Presbyterian mistrust of human beings, and piety were the sources of McCosh's attack. Sarcasm was sometimes its style. "What if a medical student should neglect physiology, anatomy, and materia medica, for music and drama and painting?" "Has there been of late any great poem, any great scientific discovery, any great history, any great philosophic work, by the young men of Cambridge? I observe that the literary journals . . . have now fixed their seat in New York rather than Boston." "They are to teach them music and art, and French plays and novels [at Harvard], but there is no course in the Scriptures."[130]

McCosh's position was an appealing one; it was not obstinate, but it was reassuring to men and women who had been taught to respect the concept of mental faculties, who believed that the unity of knowledge could still be conveyed in a college course, and who were suspicious of unbridled freedom and of an education wholly free from a religious orientation. As appealing and as reassuring as McCosh was, he was nonetheless really defining a fading college, whereas Eliot was demonstrating how to use individual freedom, a high regard for science, and an environment friendly to learning in the making of a great university.

Electives were unavoidable except in colleges with suicidal tendencies. At Yale between 1886 and 1901 the progress of the elective system resulted in reducing requirements in ancient languages by one third, mathematics by one half, and in increasing foreign languages and English by almost a half. Social sciences, which accounted for 3.5 percent of a student's classroom work in 1886, increased to 13.5 percent by 1901. An 1897 survey of college catalogues placed Harvard, Cornell, and Stanford at the head of the elective parade. Down at the end, with the most course requirements, especially among freshmen and sophomores, were Yale, Williams, Hamilton, Colgate, Rochester, Rutgers, Columbia, Union, and Brown. Institutions with a considerable commitment to the elective system by 1897 were New York University, the University of Pennsylvania, the University of California, Northwestern, the University of Michigan, the University of Chicago, the University of South Carolina, the University of Indiana, Illinois College, and Bryn Mawr.[131]

A 1911 study of the impact of the elective system on the curriculum at Bowdoin indicated that Harvard's reforms of the 1870s and 1880s took from fifteen to twenty-five years to cross over into Maine, but, however long it took, the elective system gained steadily in institutions of all kinds.[132] By 1901 Harvard, Cornell, and Stanford were no longer alone in being wholly or almost wholly elective; Columbia, Cincinnati, Missouri, William and Mary, and West Virginia had by then given up most course requirements. A survey of ninety-seven colleges that year found thirty-four with at least 70 percent election, twelve with from 50 to 70 percent, and fifty-one with less than 50 percent.[133] To a student leafing through college and university catalogues in 1901, the meaning of such statistics must have been profoundly clear. Only a Pollyanna would have described as diversity what was in fact curricular disarray. The classical course was dead, but who could say what had taken its place? A century of curricular movement, of reform and reaction, paralysis and growth had brought the course of study to a stage of development that, in Russell Thomas's words, "signified only that the majority of educators had agreed that certain subjects were *not* the *sine qua non* of a liberal education. They were not agreed about what *was* essential."[134]

Nor was it likely that they could ever again be agreed about essentials. Henceforth order, certainty, in an institution of higher education in the United States, would be less a function of the curriculum than of the bureaucracy that held it together.[135] Bureaucratic organization may not have been, for those who still adhered to a chimerical unity of knowledge, a satisfactory substitute for curricular certainty and uniformity, but it was the instrument that supported an illusion of structure in a course of study that was close to being an expression of chaos. The last great statement of curricular uniformity and symmetry was the Yale Report of 1828; the first great statement of bureaucratic organization and symmetry was the University of Chicago. It opened its doors in October 1892, a full-blown American university, a remarkable rationalization of the diverse purposes, styles, and values that had been seeking expression in the American university. In William Rainey Harper, its first president, it found a man who could do for the university what its chief benefactor, John D. Rockefeller, had done for oil and what J. P. Morgan would do for steel. Harper created an organization in which everything fell into place.

The university's *Official Bulletin No. 1,* first distributed almost two years before the university opened, projected an all-inclusive scheme of university organization that was reminiscent of Thomas Jefferson's plan for the University of Virginia in its boldness and imagination.[136] The most startling difference between the two plans, of course, was the speed with which Harper's was translated into reality. The University of Chicago was not complete when it opened in 1892 with an enrollment of 742, but within ten years it was operating an educational program that stretched from kindergarten through the Ph.D., into the mails by way of correspondence courses, and into the neighborhoods of Chicago by way of its evening classes and extension courses. Four undergraduate colleges—liberal arts, science, literature, and practical arts—were essentially a restatement of the parallel course system widely practiced elsewhere, but Chicago gave them a characteristic local definition by assigning the work of the first two years to junior colleges and the work of the second two years to senior colleges. This division was intended to differentiate the elementary and preparatory subjects from the advanced work of the last two years, and to provide an organization that clarified Chicago's commitment to university work in its graduate school of arts and sciences as well as in the divinity, law, medical, and engineering schools, and in the schools of pedagogy, fine arts, and music.[137]

An intricate administrative organization that moved from president through examiner, recorder, registrar, secretary, librarian, publisher, and steward to deans and heads of departments conveyed a masterful sense of the logic that was paradoxically implicit in the disorder that had befallen the course of study.[138] All that was needed to complete the design (other than the course of study itself and students) was a hierarchy of ranks that would facilitate the competitive movement of faculty, the measuring of departmental strength, and the clarification of academic procedure. Harper designed a twelve-rank classification that was quite as symmetrical in its way as had been the classical course of study: At the top was the head professor, and at the bottom was the scholar, and in between were the professor, nonresident professor, associate professor, assistant professor, instructor, tutor, docent, reader, lecturer, and fellow.[139]

Imbedded in this structure were curricular innovations as well —the division of the year into four quarters, and each quarter into two six-week terms; the classification of courses as majors (ten to twelve hours a week) and minors (four to six hours a week); the requirement that each student take one major and one minor a term, perhaps two minors under special circumstances.[140] Harper's intentions were complex. His design offered to students, as pedagogical wisdom, an opportunity to avoid superficial learning by concentrating on no more than two or three subjects at a time. The four-quarter system made plant utilization more economical, and it allowed students to use their summer months profitably and to accelerate their education by a year or to take more than four years if necessary.

The University of Chicago was an immediate and resounding success, not simply because students flocked to it nor because Harper was able to attract to Chicago, as a consequence of the greatest mass raid in American academic history, a faculty that included eight former college and seminary presidents, five Yale professors, and over half of the academic staff of dissension-torn Clark University.[141] Chicago worked because Harper—unburdened by the clutter of centuries with which Eliot had to contend and possessed of a mind that understood the organizing genius with which American industry had been rationalized in the years since the Civil War—provided a framework that allowed professors and students alike to go about their business with a maximum of individual freedom and a minimum of institutional coercion and discipline, as well as with a sense of certainty about how things were done and why. It may have helped to have been founded after the battles over Greek and electives, even in the East, had been decided, yet there was something close to genius and magic in the way in which Harper substituted bureaucratic organization for the course of study as the focus of institutional consensus.

The curriculum at the University of Chicago was quite as chaotic as elsewhere, but it did not seem so, and that was an achievement not just for public relations but also for institutional sanity.

The University of Chicago, of course, was greeted with skepticism in the East. One distinguished scholar scoffed at the idea of establishing a graduate university in Chicago as being "the next thing to putting it in the Fiji Islands." The *Nation* ventured the view that "these long courses in short terms, the attempt to keep the university under full steam through the moist heat of a Chicago summer, the encouragement given to the student to compress four years' work into three years—the whole scheme breathes that nervous, restless haste which is one of the most deplorable features of American life."[142] Chicago hurried on, however, and proved how far in advance it was of the cautious spirit with which Andrew D. White had launched Cornell in 1866. Then White had said, "In an institution of learning, facility and power in imparting truth are even more necessary than in discovering it." William Rainey Harper simply reversed the gerundive phrases: "It is proposed in this institution to make the work of giving instruction secondary," and set about establishing the conditions and the agencies of scholarly research and publication.[143]

Within three years of its opening the University of Chicago had enrolled more graduate students than any other American university. Its extension courses, which reached into neighborhoods that by tradition were hostile to higher education, became instruments of democratic encouragement and university recruitment. The four-quarter system was so uncongenial to the sybaritic practices and social style of the upper class that the city and its wealthy suburbs continued to send their sons and daughters East to college, allowing the university to become a magnet for the aspiring middle-class sons and daughters of a vast hinterland.[144]

In its first ten years graduates were divided approximately equally among those who went through the university at a normal pace, those who hurried, and those who took longer. Of the seniors graduating in 1902 almost three out of four had transferred to Chicago from some other institution. In 1899, as an encouragement to students who wanted only two years of college and as an encouragement to confident professional schools considering two college years for admission and to faltering colleges thinking about giving up the last two years, Chicago began to award an associate degree for two years of study. Lines of division among the components of the university were intentionally blurred: Students were allowed to enroll in courses in the junior colleges, senior colleges, and graduate schools even if not registered in those divisions; efforts were made to eliminate the distinction between professional and liberal studies "by making the professions truly liberal and the content of liberal education in part frankly professional."[145]

From the very beginning liberal culture, utility, and research—the contending styles that Laurence Veysey has identified as arguing over control of the old colleges and the emerging universities—were incorporated in the University of Chicago's sense of its own legitimacy. At Chicago culture and scholarship were regarded as "equipment for service," not as ends in themselves.[146] Perhaps this emphasis and the university's environment accounted for some of the arrogance with which the East watched as the University of Chicago turned itself into a statement of American purpose. The opening of the university coincided with the Columbian Exposition, the Chicago World's Fair of 1893. Both were celebrations of a national experience that was both idealistic and materialistic. The University of Chicago in that year was no more raw and no less idealistic than had been Henry Dunster's Harvard of 1642.

The eagerness with which members of Harper's faculty rushed into print with their own interpretations of the Chicago experience was evidence enough that something quite remarkable had happened. Robert Herrick's not always sympathetic novel, *Chimes;* Coach Alonzo Stagg's hymn to football, *Touchdown!,* in which the same chimes rang especially for the university's athletes; Robert Morss Lovett's autobiography, *All Our Years,* a monument of liberal culture; and Thorstein Veblen's scorching analysis of the values of *The Higher Learning in America* were all efforts to understand and explain the early years of the University of Chicago. Contradictory as they were, they supported the idea that, while the first university in the United States was Cornell, the first fully developed all-purpose American university was the University of Chicago.[147]

The University of Chicago was delivered in an almost finished state in a few short years, but it had been in process for a very long time. Its elective curriculum was receptive to almost anything as long as some Ph.D. trained professor wanted it there. Less than a year after it opened, its biology department was reorganized into five new departments.[148] Neither of these developments was peculiar to the University of Chicago or a matter of institutional choice. They were the consequence of the collapse of the old theological-philosophic framework and its inability to provide a hospitable environment for new knowledge. The University of Chicago confirmed a shift in purpose that had already been experienced elsewhere, from inoculating undergraduates with large doses of revealed religion and deductive truth to exposing them to methods and curricular experiences that forced on them some ultimate responsibility for the truths with which they had to live.

Those eager young men and women streaming into Chicago from Iowa, Wisconsin, and downstate Illinois—how well equipped were they to live with the uncertainty, the tentativeness toward truth, that was developing into an academic habit? The University of Chicago had style, and it was a model of bureaucratic organization. In the history of academic blueprints it was certain to be remembered. But it lacked authority. There were now too many authorities, all speaking from a platform of science and empiricism and fact, all stumbling toward generalizations that lacked the reassuring certainty of an earlier age. The university's curriculum was many things— courses, instruments for arriving at truth and for liberating young men and women, a running dialogue among scholars and teachers and students on questions once thought to have been forever answered. What had once been so clear was now open to reconsideration.

Yet, just as colleges were learning to live with the consequences of the university movement, universities were learning that they could not avoid or eliminate the necessity that men felt to make judgments, to choose, to act, to believe. For all the science that guided the new developments, for all the suspended judgment it encouraged, for all the excited attention to the best ways of making money and bridges and constitutions and other necessities, the universities, Chicago included, could not escape the humanist, liberal, ethical traditions that informed the behavior and values of Western society.

There were ways of pretending one could—by eliminating all

the substitute degrees and awarding a B.A. degree for almost any combination of courses, by stressing individual choice and freedom at the
expense of wisdom and experience. David Starr Jordan, the president
of Stanford University, in 1899 unquestionably thought that he was
expressing the essential spirit of the university in a free society, and
perhaps he was, although his remarks were also an announcement of
curricular bankruptcy: "It is not for the university to decide on the
relative values of knowledge. Each man makes his own market, controlled by his own standards."[149]

6

Remedies

The old moral philosophy course almost everywhere was extinct. Science was making tremendous headway even where religious orthodoxy was strong. But the curriculum was in disarray. Accommodation of the unaccommodating, reconciliation of the irreconcilable, became the order of the day. Dismay and nostalgia overtook even the masters of change. Students discovered "college life."

By 1914 moral philosophy at Columbia, the course once taught by John Daniel Gros from his own text, had become forty professorships. John Dewey was fond of telling a story that confirmed the skill with which orthodox denominational colleges arranged to teach science. One such college, he recalled, while as yet unable to reconcile Genesis and geology, was having no difficulty with anatomy "because there is biblical authority for the statement that the human body is fearfully and wonderfully made." The determination not to allow religion to stand in the way of science was so widespread, however, that a visitor once found posted on Noah Porter's office door the notice: "At 11:30 on Tuesday Professor Porter will reconcile science and religion."[1]

Colleges that had once been so much alike that their catalogues, courses of study, professors, students, and regimen were essentially interchangeable were no longer ideologically and stylistically on speaking terms. Mark Hopkins did not accept the various positions offered to him in the 1850s, including the chancellorship of New York University and the presidency of the University of Michigan, but if he had, the change from Williams would not have taxed him or altered his way of life in any serious way. All three were small colleges, two of them with big names. Fifty years later, however, they were so dissimilar in their undergraduate environments that every effort to bring order out of the disarray into which the curriculum had fallen necessarily confronted significant differences. Williams was still what it had been, a homogeneous eastern college, cohesive, isolated; Yale, Princeton, other New England colleges, and those that cast themselves in the New England image, such as Carleton and Pomona, shared its style. New York University had moved into possession of its name and was developing into a heterogeneous eastern university, with a mixed student population and a close relationship to the urban society in which it was located; similar developments had redefined the University of Pennsylvania and Harvard and were moving other once-small colleges into university status. The college at Ann Arbor had also become a heterogeneous university, less diverse than the eastern universities by reason of a less diverse surrounding society; in this sense, it resembled other western universities.[2] Demographic factors had taken similar institutions and differentiated them, imposing styles of undergraduate life and interest appropriate to each institution. Every institutional change, including these, was an influence on the curriculum.

There was no end of suggestions on how to put everything back together again or, if not that, how to put everything together. A professor at Brown in 1908 prescribed for "all the stronger institutions" a mingling "in due proportion . . . [of] the best from the old English-American college with the best from the modern German university." Just how that could be done was not clear, but four years earlier a meeting of the American Association of Universities had heard President Eliot argue that professional interest and purpose could not and should not be divorced from a student's undergraduate course. The tone of the conference suggested a desire to mesh the liberal arts tradition with German professionalism without damage to either, to establish some "fusion of research and teaching, of discipline and freedom, of vocational instruction and liberal education."[3]

Such a prospect frightened Abraham Flexner, educational critic and innovator who devoted a lifetime to raising the standards of American professional schools, especially the medical schools. Flexner wanted the college removed as far from the university as possible; he had no argument with combining appropriate preprofessional general work in law and medicine with a broad general education in the undergraduate college, but he feared for the integrity of the research function of the university if it was contaminated by the style and the spirit of undergraduate studies. He considered the undergraduate curriculum excessively trivial, elective, vocational, and disparate. Its quality was sacrificed to democracy, numbers, social mobility, and the denial of distinctions. Liberal culture and mental training were submerged in a process that owed too many other conflicting allegiances. He was outraged by the professorships that twentieth-century undergraduate education gave birth to—a professor of extracurricular activities at Columbia Teachers College, of books at Rollins, of police administration at Chicago and biography at Dartmouth.[4] His alarm was well-founded.

How could the university ideal of pure research and scholarship flourish in an environment such as that at Chapel Hill, where in 1905 undergraduates were taking courses in money and banking, transportation, labor, hydraulics, sanitary engineering, and electric wiring and distribution? At Yale the same year undergraduates could select from a curriculum of 554 semester courses—a demonstration of the inability of even a resisting institution to hold back the tides of specialization, new knowledge, election, and preprofessionalism.[5]

Uniformity had fallen not only out of the content of the course of study but also out of its duration and its quantitative demands. In 1900 a Yale B.A. degree represented sixty hours of courses to Harvard's forty-eight to fifty-one. For a while three years as the appropriate academic course possessed some authority. It did not collapse as an innovation simply because Franklin Delano Roosevelt, Harvard class of 1904, stayed around for a fourth unnecessary year in order to edit the *Crimson,* but the idea of curricular hurry at Harvard was not inspired by the clientele, as it may have been at Harper's Chicago. Groton graduates at Harvard wanted their four years' worth, although not necessarily of the course of study. As many as 36 percent of Harvard's class of 1906 finished in three years, and while the practice of making the fourth college year almost totally professional in character also lent itself to a reduction of the college course, by the time these administrative changes were attempted, students had grown accustomed to four college years. Eliot and Harper and Butler may have seen the college course as susceptible to contraction,

to the benefit of upgraded secondary education and upgraded professional education, but students almost everywhere selected their
undergraduate college as much for the institution's extracurricular
life as for its course of study and perhaps even more.[6]

College as fraternities, sororities, athletic teams, experience in a
refining and polishing social life, and as a pursuit of the "contacts"
that paid off in the real world did not lend itself to the same kind of
acceleration as did the course of study. Or at least students did not
think so. President Harry Pratt Judson at Chicago was certain that
the years necessary to prepare for and complete a college course could
be reduced from sixteen to twelve or thirteen.[7] Judson made efficiency
and productivity measures of human life. To their credit, students
everywhere, even at Chicago, refused to be hurried. Acceleration did
not take hold.

As useful as the elective system had been, even as necessary as it
had been, in breaking down the resistance of the old course of study to
full recognition of the sciences and other new subjects, the results
were dismaying for students. In 1870 at Harvard 32 professors taught
73 courses; by 1910 the professors numbered 169, the courses 401.[8]
Somewhere between those professors and the courses in 1910 were
twice as many instructors of less than professorial rank. The curriculum of 1910 in theory allowed a student to do what he wanted to, but
it did not show him how and it put great distances between him and
the senior professors.

In imposing the elective system on the American college, Eliot
and others accomplished by indirection what they could not accomplish by persuasion: They broke down the hold of the classics and
they created universities. In many ways, however, the traditions of liberal learning and the purposes of the German university were incom-
patible. The elective system in the European universities permitted
the rigorously and liberally educated graduates of the gymnasium
and lycée to design appropriate professional programs; the same system, as Willis Rudy has written, "produced only confusion and disorder, dilettantism and overspecialization, when applied in the United
States on a different intellectual level, and in a different academic and
social milieu."[9]

The elective system in the German university did not destroy the gymnasium, the institution to which was assigned the responsibility of providing students with a comprehensive introduction to the liberal arts and "a feeling of the basic unity of all knowledge"; instead, it built itself on the gymnasium. An altogether different result befell liberal learning as a consequence of mixing the elective system with the liberal arts college in the United States. Eliot and the Committee of Ten may have thought that they could reshape the American high school into a gymnasium or lycée and thus establish the liberal tradition as firmly in the secondary schools of the United States as in those of Germany and France, but they failed and at the same time left the college, the society's repository of liberal values and humane learning, crippled and confused.[10]

Early in the twentieth century a sense of dismay at the results of the elective system overtook even its friends. At Yale, which refused ever to be comfortable with it, Arthur Twining Hadley's complaint that electives removed from the curriculum its proper function as a competitive "race course" was predictable. But Nicholas Murray Butler's change of mood, from impatience in 1905 to nostalgia in 1909, was a sure sign of impending reform. As an advocate of acceleration, in 1905 Butler urged "an end [of] the idling and dawdling that now characterize so much of American higher education," but within four years he spoke wistfully of the training that the curriculum had once provided for "the simple profession of gentleman," for the "generous and reflective use of leisure." Clearly the elective system was in for trouble if the time had come for Nicholas Murray Butler to declare: "The cult of the will has gone far enough just now for the good of mankind."[11]

Others had come around to similar views. At the 1902 centennial celebrations at the U.S. Military Academy at West Point, William Rainey Harper praised the academy's course of study for the "concentration of effort . . . thoroughness . . . spirit of subordination, of obedience, engendered in the student," and he was almost openly envious of the administrative control asserted by academy authorities over a totally prescribed curriculum, taught though it was on an essentially secondary school level. And in 1909 Charles Francis Adams, Jr., expressed to Woodrow Wilson at Princeton a defensible judgment on Eliot's forty years as president of Harvard and educational leader: "I consider that Eliot has, by his course and influence, done as much harm to the American college as he has done good to the American university."[12]

Critics and friends of the elective system found themselves coming together in search of some way to live with all the academic purposes that had accumulated during the nineteenth century, some way to remedy the ills that the elective system had introduced into the curriculum. Was there some way to recover the coherence that characterized a specified combination of courses? Was there not some way to provide the kind of breadth that derived from a required range of courses? Could a curriculum be designed that would avoid the dissipation of student energies in a collection of elementary courses and that instead would provide depth of study in a graded series of courses in one academic discipline?[13]

Surely something needed to be done. A Harvard faculty survey came up with evidence that the average Harvard student studied thirteen hours a week, an average that was in a sense artificially high, for it included the study habits of a large number of naive freshmen who had not yet found their way. A "Gentleman's C" was not a term of opprobrium at Harvard, Yale, and Princeton, whatever it may have been elsewhere. Each June freshmen at Cornell threw their books into a fire. Michigan, Stanford, and Chicago were worried by serious undermajoring in the humanities by men students.[14]

In 1902 the Yale faculty reported cheating so widespread that leading students were involved and instructors did not report them. Freshmen described themselves as studying three hours a day, seniors an hour and a half. One member of the class of 1901 earned $1,100 between Easter and June from the sale of course abstracts and essays. One explanation, but not the only one, for what appeared to be a common academic malaise was offered by a professor at the University of Montana: "Young doctors of philosophy, fresh from the prolonged study of some remote nook of science or literature, have been turned loose on freshmen and sophomores and have bored them to desperation with minutiae." Harvard thought it had a solution to this problem in 1904, when every department was urged to offer a course for students not intending to specialize in it.[15]

Three new conditions placed limits on the extent to which the elective system could be brought under control: acceptance of the psychology of individual differences and interests, an accelerating increase in enrollment, and the expansion of the American high school as an instrument of social control and aspiration. All of these developments would have taken place, but not in the same way, without the elective system. Each of them strengthened its hold on the undergraduate curriculum because of the elective system.

Without experimental psychology to support them, Wayland and Eliot had used common sense to come to the conclusion that every human being was different and that differences of aptitude and interest should be paid attention to in educational theory and practice.[16] Nothing was more encouraging to individual choice than was the elective system. Escalating undergraduate enrollments were both a response to electives and their guarantee: Electives drew to the course of study young men and women for whom the classical curriculum held no attraction, but they also made possible a growing number of marginally motivated students who majored in the extracurriculum while attending or not attending, as it might be, courses sufficiently undemanding not to interfere with their priorities. Here was a situation that pleased almost everyone, even though it also used the elective system as an instrument for demeaning the course of study. Failure of the Committee of Ten, the College Entrance Examination Board, and any of the regional school-and-college associations to bring the American high school under control meant, in the end, that the colleges and universities would have to offer, among other things, courses of study that were extensions of whatever was offered in an American high school. Electives were the language that allowed conversation between the secondary school and higher education.

Sir Francis Galton in England and James McKeen Cattell in the United States were pioneers in the psychology of human differences.[17] Their early work in experimental psychology and individual testing confirmed what everyone knew and intruded both new knowledge and the mark of science into a redefinition of educational psychology. The old psychology of mental faculties was an assertion of faith; the new psychology was a matter of scientific observation and demonstration. For all of its authority in the colleges, faculty psychology had never convinced the vast majority on the outside that without Greek their minds were but half developed. That it prevailed so long was a tribute to the tenacity of superstition and the power of a class reared in the faith. For the colleges and universities the new psychology was a reinforcing license to do what they had to.

President John E. Bradley of Illinois College was probably unaware of both Galton and Cattell when, early in the 1890s, he observed: "To my mind the object of elective studies is not so much to permit a student to choose those branches which bear upon his future work as to enable him to select such as will interest him and thus lead his mind to act with greatest vigor."[18] Neither the old school nor the new school had the final answers on how the human mind worked; the new school may have helped to kill off some of the silly pretensions that had been advanced in the name of Greek, but it did not eliminate the idea of mental discipline and training, of habit and routine and work as sources of intellectual vigor. Edwin E. Slosson's verdict on the elective system was also a pronouncement on the new and old schools of psychology: "That many students abuse the elective system is obvious, but the prescribed system abuses many students, and this is worse."[19]

Enrollments marched steadily upward, and all the statistics pointed in the direction of accelerating growth. Babies born between 1855 and 1859 had 1.1 chance in 100 of finishing four years of college; between 1875 and 1879, 1.7; 1895 and 1899, 2.7; 1915 and 1919, 8.1. In 1900, 4 percent of the eighteen to twenty-one age group was enrolled in college; in 1910, 4.8 percent; 1920, 8.1 percent; and 1930, 12.2 percent. In 1914 the number of baccalaureate degrees awarded in the United States was 26,533, approximately 55 percent B.A.s, 23 percent B.S.s, 4 percent Ph.B.s, and 2.1 percent Litt.B.s. Of the approximately 150,000 students enrolled as undergraduates in institutions of higher education in the United States in 1910, fewer than a third were enrolled in what the U.S. Bureau of Education loosely defined as the classical course, a course that could lack ancient languages but was neither so oriented to a profession or to science that it had lost the flavor of liberal learning. The vast majority of American college and university undergraduates by 1910 were enrolled in courses of study shaped by utilitarian and vocational values.[20]

These statistics were a tribute to the accommodating nature of the American college and university, to their readiness to respond to the aspirations and needs that Andrew D. White and Ezra Cornell had so forcefully dramatized in Ithaca in the 1860s and after. The elective system not only underwrote enrollment growth; it underwrote social mobility and emerging new professions. Anyone who intended to tamper with the elective system would have to be careful. Just as the power and place of a governing elite once rode on the authority of the classical course, the aspirations of a growing middle class now rode on the course of study transformed by the elective system.

Public school authorities probably never would have allowed the American high school to be defined only by the ideals of liberal culture or subjected to university control, but any effort to impose a university-defined course of study on the high schools was destined to failure once the colleges and universities embraced the elective system. President Eliot proselytized so ably for electives that the effort of his Committee of Ten to impose a curriculum of exclusively liberal studies, including the new subjects, on the high schools was a demonstration in futility. The elective system robbed the colleges and universities of effective authority to describe any secondary school course as essential and any subjects as the only ones leading to a college course. The eastern colleges and universities used the College Entrance Examination Board to give a semblance of authority and uniformity to their definition of an appropriate secondary school course; the western state universities, however, preferred another definition; and the land-grant colleges were almost willing that there be no definition at all.

Because it possessed the authority of numbers and the powerful support of democratic mythology, the high school was able to use the principle of student electives and the psychology of individual differences to create high school programs that were in no way beholden to college and university authorities. By 1918 when its commission on school and college studies brought in a report on *Cardinal Principles of Secondary Education,* the powerful National Education Association placed itself on the side of a movement that succeeded in defining the American high school, not as a repository of liberal values, but as a school in citizenship, job skills, and homemaking.[21] From schools so oriented American colleges and universities would in the decades ahead develop their accelerating enrollments, with clear implications for the curriculum. As a source of students, the compulsory, unselective, democratic American high school was a vast reservoir, but as a support for any precise definition of a college course of study it was as reliable as Ezra Cornell's famous invitation to everyone and everything.

High schools and high school students multiplied astonishingly and with predictable consequences for the colleges. In 1870, 72,156 students were enrolled in 1,026 high schools; in 1900, 519,251 students were enrolled in 6,005 high schools. In the twentieth century high school enrollments doubled decade by decade. It had taken the century between 1815 and 1915 for the secondary school population to move from 10 percent of the fifteen to eighteen age group to 20 percent; by 1928 it had reached 50 percent.[22] Expanding colleges and universities could not ignore these figures and hold to standards that could be met only by private preparatory schools; they needed students, they did not want to be undemocratic (if they did, they found ways of defining themselves as democratic), and they bent accordingly.

Not all the land-grant colleges subscribed to the utter absence of standards explicit in the heading under which Kansas State Agricultural and Mechanical College defended itself in 1909: "Take them as they come and set them going." Generally, however, the private colleges were better in maintaining admission standards than were the state universities, and the state universities were better than the land-grant colleges, many of which were so close to being high schools themselves that in 1908 the Carnegie Foundation would not even consider them for affiliation in its various early efforts to define and standardize higher education in the United States.[23] But they all had their problems.

At a time when the University of North Dakota was raising its own standards, it was also losing control over the high schools that it had helped to develop. In 1914, having asserted their independence and defined their own purposes, which were not purely of a college preparatory character, the high schools of North Dakota forced on the university a reduction in entrance requirements. Special drill classes in mathematics and English entered the course of study at the University of North Dakota as a consequence. A different problem confronted colleges and universities in states where the high school movement was retarded. In 1908 the colleges of South Carolina admitted from high schools 200 ninth-graders and 40 eighth-graders;

half of the state's colleges placed tenth-graders in the sophomore class. In 1909 when one town added an eleventh grade to its high school, it discovered that 22 of the prospective class were already college freshmen. Since the University of South Carolina could not enforce standards that the state's public schools did not prepare for, it adopted the early nineteenth-century practice of the New England colleges of admitting well-prepared students to advanced standing.[24] But the university nonetheless was a captive of the state's public school system; it could not hold itself to a more rigorous and demanding curriculum until the high schools of the state allowed it to.

As a function of President Eliot's success in eliminating Greek as an admissions requirement, by 1908 fewer than half of the Harvard student body were graduates of private schools. Yale and Princeton were still essentially dependent on the private schools; at Yale the same year 68 percent of the students were private school graduates; at Princeton 78 percent. Holding to standards, all three, however, found themselves unable to enroll freshman classes without making a considerable allowance for inadequacies in secondary school preparation. Between 57 and 58 percent of the freshmen at all three institutions in 1909 were admitted with conditions or as special students.[25]

For undergraduate education the rise of the high school, with its commitment to the majority for whom high school was a terminal experience (even as the high school became the source of an accelerating college and university enrollment), defined only one side of the problem created by the career of the elective idea in school and college. If the colleges were dependent for students on schools that were indifferent to liberal learning and to curricular order, they were likewise dependent for professors on universities that were increasingly oriented to scholarly specialization and at the same time indifferent to liberal culture and a balanced course of study.[26]

There was no chance of recovery for the classics. The new psychology, the new enrollment figures, the new high school movement: They all said no. Greek was gone, and Latin was on its way. Columbia, having abandoned Greek in 1897, both as an entrance and a graduation requirement, in 1900 gave up Latin as an entrance requirement but exacted three years of college Latin from those who entered without it. Eastern institutions that had held out for Greek surrendered: Dartmouth and New York University in 1902; Yale in 1904. In 1912 Owen Johnson's popular college novel, *Stover at Yale*, made the classical curriculum a major villain and despoiler of youth, but indignant novels were not necessary to bring American colleges and universities, even Yale, to a recognition that the dead languages were dead.[27]

By 1915 fewer than fifteen major colleges still required four years of Latin for the B.A. degree. In 1919 Yale accepted students without admission Latin and enrolled them as candidates for the Ph.B. degree. Four years later the faculty voted to abolish Latin as a requirement for admission or for the B.A. degree, but they were overruled by the Yale corporation, one member of which, William Howard Taft, exclaimed: "Over my dead body!" Taft died in 1930. Latin went in 1931.[28]

Although the struggle over Latin, like that over Greek, was an eastern phenomenon, its significance for the curriculum was national. The eastern colleges and universities—in other words, the old colonial establishments and the newer colleges of New England, wealthy and prestigious—commanded authority. They set standards. Their graduates possessed power in the society out of proportion to their numbers. When these institutions gave up Latin, as they did with less public acrimony than in the struggle over Greek, the medieval curriculum quietly passed into history.

In 1923 a survey of leading colleges and universities identified only two institutions not offering some degree without Latin and Greek. Both Amherst and Williams, awarding only the B.A. degree, still required Latin. Brown and Yale used the Ph.B. degree to avoid Latin; Dartmouth, Harvard, and Princeton, the B.S. degree. Cornell, Columbia, Minnesota, Wisconsin, and Swarthmore gave the B.A. without Latin. If they had not done so before, most American colleges and universities joined Yale in the 1930s in eliminating Latin from requirements for the B.A. degree: Princeton, in 1930; Bryn Mawr, 1931; Amherst, 1932; Williams, 1934.[29] As George Wilson Pierson explained, Latin had arrived in the curriculum and held on as "the grammar of scholarship, the tool of the learned professions, the language of diplomacy, and the song of the Church."[30] The practices and institutions to which Latin lent itself collided with a society hostile to inherited standards and fixed values. In the classroom Latin fell under the blight of pedantry and an absence of imagination. Its vocational utility evaporated. Fewer students were preparing for the ministry. In a competitive grab for students and dollars, each institution went its own way, certain that its prospects for both would be improved by abandoning its Latin requirements. They were right. President Eliot had told them in 1917 that "the highest human interests are concerned with religion, government, and the means of supporting and improving a family," and that none of these interests required a knowledge of Latin.[31]

Colleges and universities closely allied to private schools, especially the eastern boarding schools, held out the longest, and in doing so used Latin to maintain essentially homogeneous communities of middle- and upper-class young men and women. Latin, whether intended or not, was an instrument for enforcing religious and racial prejudice, ignoring the American high school, and limiting an institution's clientele essentially to the sons and daughters of *Social Register* families and their neighbors. The abandonment of Latin must to some extent have been an admission that even the privileged no longer had need for it.

The classics were gone, but vocationalism enlarged its domain. After 1900, responding to the needs of the high schools, most colleges and universities that had not already done so created education departments with a major commitment to the training of secondary school teachers. In 1905 Michigan listed among its liberal arts departments metallurgy, drawing, industry, and commerce.[32] By 1917 the University of North Dakota offered B.A. programs in art and design, commerce, manual training, and mechanical drawing. Union College offered courses in engineering English, engineering mathematics, and engineering economics.[33] Haverford held to a Latin requirement longer than most, while offering in its catalogue sample clusters of courses appropriate as preparation for engineering, medicine, law, and business administration. In 1925 William and Mary offered undergraduate programs preparatory to careers in dentistry, medicine, forestry, and public health.[34] The University of Missouri offered the first undergraduate degree program in journalism in 1910, and business departments and schools of business and commerce proliferated as the years passed.[35]

These latter developments were responsible for the exasperated and characteristic remarks of Robert Maynard Hutchins in 1936: "If the public becomes interested in the metropolitan newspaper, schools of journalism instantly arise. If it is awed by the development of big business, business schools full of the same reverence appear."[36] Indeed, a wider public was shaping the curriculum, and, while Hutchins's remarks may have seemed inappropriate for a chancellor at William Rainey Harper's university, they were accurate. By 1871 over twenty colleges and universities, mostly in the Midwest, were meeting the competition of so-called business colleges, with commercial courses of their own, but the establishment of an undergraduate school of commerce at the University of Pennsylvania in 1881 became a model for universities and colleges elsewhere. The Wharton School at Pennsylvania proposed to combine liberal studies with practical business training, and it was this quality of the Pennsylvania program that the American Bankers Association stressed when in 1889 it took the initiative in a movement to found business schools in connection with universities and colleges. In 1898 the University of California's business course included philosophy and geography; Chicago's included the economic history of the United States.[37]

Enrollments in these departments were initially relatively slight, but they skyrocketed after the first decade of the twentieth century. New York University's undergraduate School of Commerce, Accounts, and Finance, offering a degree of bachelor of commercial science, moved from an enrollment of 67 in 1900 to 969 in 1909.[38] The programs that were developed in the schools of business and commerce departed from their original liberal orientation when a body of applied learning was developed appropriate to careers in accounting, banking, business, industry, and farming. Business and commercial courses and programs did not replace Latin and Greek in the curriculum. They came; the others went; it was not a clear case of substitution. But if the course of study is viewed as a commentary on the values and aspirations of the society, then the decline of the classics and the rise of commercial subjects did indeed mirror the culture. The displacement of clergymen as trustees by prominent alumni in business and finance was a comparable development of equal significance for the curriculum. The clergymen went before Latin and Greek; commercial and business subjects came after the industrialists and financiers.

More than one way was found for compromising the B.A. degree with the intrusion of vocational values. Outright occupational programs leading to degrees and careers was one method. Another was the professional option or combined program, which brought together the hurry of Eliot's three-year accelerated degree with a year of study, more or less, in a university's professional schools. Columbia may have been the first to devise a method of reducing the collegiate course to three years or less and raising professional school admissions requirements (for some students) to three years of college. Such, in effect, was the thrust of Columbia's combined program, which encouraged students to enter the professional schools after three years or less in Columbia College. Completion of the appropriate professional program qualified students for the B.A. degree as well as a professional degree. Between 1892 and 1902 approximately 25 percent of Columbia's undergraduates enrolled in the combined program, which commended itself to a large number of universities that understood its meaning for enrollments and its appeal to particularly ambitious and impatient young men and women. By 1905 Michigan, Wisconsin, and most other state universities and large private universities had adopted the professional option plan.[39] In 1900 the Amos Tuck School of Administration and Finance at Dartmouth combined the Dartmouth senior year with the first year of its two-year graduate program. Dartmouth's announcement of the opening of the Tuck School was an expression of the impulses that made the professional option device a characteristic expression of the age: "This school is established in the interests of college graduates who desire to engage in affairs rather than enter the professions."[40]

Yale had developed a peculiar capacity for not letting its principles interfere with what it or some influential segment of its faculty wanted to do. Yale exalted the classical course in the Report of 1828 and then proceeded to advance science and other new subjects in the Sheffield Scientific School. It was slow and clumsy about coming to terms with the university idea, but it awarded the first American Ph.D. degrees before it was a university. It believed in its course of study, but not blindly: One of Noah Porter's defenses of the old curriculum was his argument that the classroom was not everything, that a serious and well-motivated student would supplement his college course with "self-imposed and self-inspired studies" that were responsive to his interests and his needs.[41] One consequence of the environment thus created was an aura of official sanction for that vast and worldly testing ground, the extracurriculum of secret societies, athletic teams, newspapers, and journals. In 1910 a distinguished Harvard alumnus, asked why he had sent his son to Yale, replied: "I used to think that Harvard gave the better training, but at my time of life I find that all the Harvard men are working for Yale men."[42] His answer may be taken as a tribute to Yale, but not to its course of study.

On the other hand, while Yale would have preferred to have its undergraduates perfect the skills of social poise, human manipulation, and the management of affairs in their daily lives on and off campus, its style suggested that it would not be left tongue-tied or unresponsive to the appearance of the combined program elsewhere. Beginning in 1899 Yale students could include a year of medical training or five hours of law in their B.A. programs. In 1903 a year of law could be credited toward the B.A. degree. Comparable programs were worked out with Yale's divinity, art, and music schools.[43]

Combined programs and professional options were a passing phenomenon, an acute case of curricular vocationalism made possible by the elective system and encouraged by the notion that the traditional college course was ripe for abbreviation. They were an expression of the same kind of impatience and university headiness that had Harper, Jordan, and Butler turning colleges into *Gymnasien* at the turn of the century. They also were a simple statement of economic fact. It was a time of growth: Little colleges were nervous, but the scene as a whole was buoyant. And because the colleges were unsure of themselves and uncertain as to how they were to be defined, and none more unsure or uncertain than Yale, these programs with their professional bias met with little resistance. In time they became victims of upgraded professional school standards and a widespread undergraduate attachment to four "bright college years."

If the curriculum moved steadily away from the old subjects toward an explicit and sometimes strident vocationalism, it also succeeded in transferring some of the old moral purpose and service ideal into new courses and new programs. Harvard created a department of social ethics in 1906 in response to undergraduate interest in courses relevant to the problems of urban poverty. During the next ten years it offered courses on immigration, housing, social insurance, criminology, the alcohol problem, and radical social theories. University-sponsored settlement houses added a practical dimension to such courses, in effect creating social laboratories for the study of sociology, economics, and political science in action. At Marietta, in Ohio, a new president, a former newspaper editor, created between 1913 and 1917 a four-year program in political institutions, beginning with "Liberty and Democracy in Greece" and capped by his own course for seniors called "Applied Publicism," a consideration of the major questions of the day. To some extent it was an imaginative translation of the old course of study, an application of ancient history and moral philosophy to the public problems of the Progressive era.[44]

Colleges and universities developed a service rationale for social studies and social sciences, and altogether new programs with a service orientation entered the course of study, such as those early nursing programs leading to a bachelor of nursing degree or the Training School in Public Service founded in 1911 and becoming eventually Syracuse University's School of Citizenship and Public Affairs, offering a B.A. in public administration.[45] When President Hadley of Yale in 1915 defined a liberal arts subject as one in which "a public motive rather than a private one must constitute the dominant note in its appeal," he was not disparaging the self-centeredness of humanistic learning nor was he discovering a new purpose for Yale College.[46] Service had always been a function of the colleges. After all, the wrangle over the curriculum in the nineteenth century had been over how the colleges might best fulfill their traditional role of public service. Then the colleges had argued that their purpose was best attended to in the training they gave in the mental and moral development of the nation's leaders. They had refused to accept the arguments, advanced by their critics, that service could inhere in a subject and that they were teaching all the wrong subjects.

Hadley gave himself over to the service ethos of the American university movement in embracing the idea that service inhered in a subject, but he proved himself true to the old morality in his insistence on public rather than private motive as "the dominant note in its appeal." Hadley was not rejecting the discovery of self as a purpose of liberal learning; he was asserting the old ideal of an elite of virtuous leaders against the coarse materialism of the day. He hoped to establish at Yale a school in colonial administration to provide the United States with trained public servants; he refused to establish a business school "to serve money-making or private ends."[47] In such ways a determined university could keep alive the choice of Hercules in an age given over to self-seeking vocationalism and stripped of its classical heritage. Yet, if the elective system, the American high school, the ambitions of the middle class, and college and university competition for students were not to be the undoing of the curriculum, something would have to be done more effective than simply keeping a business school out of New Haven.

Remedies for curricular disorders defined the career of the course of study in the twentieth century. Dismay, nostalgia, even success—a whole bundle of sensations and experiences—led deeply concerned people to begin once more to see if any order, any coherence, any integrity could again be associated with the undergraduate curriculum.

In the absence of any tradition of government licensing, supervision, and control, the first expressions of concern over the absence of common standards and practices came from the institutions themselves in their regional and national associations. Out of the entrance requirements chaos that led to the formation of regional associations of colleges and secondary schools as well as the College Entrance Examination Board, there developed associations of like institutions —the National Association of State Universities (1896), the Association of Catholic Colleges (1899), the Association of American Universities (1900), the Association of Land-Grant Colleges (1900), and the Association of American Colleges (1914).[48] Recognizing the existence of common problems, they could not avoid the question of standards.

For years the only role of the U.S. Bureau of Education in defining what constituted a college was, beginning in 1870, its annual listing of institutions that awarded degrees. By 1911 the meaninglessness of its annual lists was apparent even to the bureau, which agreed to a request from the Association of American Universities that it attempt a classification of American colleges and universities. Using as a basis the existing policies of the major graduate and professional schools toward graduates of the colleges, the bureau classified 344 institutions into four groups: colleges whose graduates could earn the

M.A. degree in one year, in somewhat more than a year, and in two years, and colleges whose B.A. program was two years short of the standard B.A. course. Premature partial publication unleashed a storm of protest from injured institutions, and official publication was prohibited by President Taft. Classification, standards, the whole implication of grades of excellence and inferiority proved to be so politically explosive and so contrary to democratic dogma that the 1911 abortive classification was the government's last effort to measure the quality of undergraduate education. Using the same standards as the bureau, the Association of American Universities in 1913 reluctantly took on the responsibility of accrediting American colleges and universities when it found no one else willing to.[49]

In these efforts the association was assisted by the network of state and regional accrediting agencies that developed out of a 1906 meeting of representatives of the various associations and by the predicament that confronted the new philanthropic foundations when they began to give money away to the colleges and universities in the early years of the twentieth century.[50] The foundations discovered what others already knew: The definition of an American college was elusive, the curriculum was in disarray, and in fact, if a list of colleges and universities was to be drawn up, the foundations themselves would have to decide what a college was. To this task the foundations lent themselves with varying degrees of enthusiasm. The General Education Board (1903), the Carnegie Foundation for the Advancement of Teaching (1906), the Carnegie Corporation (1911), and the Rockefeller Foundation (1913) were instrumental in defining an American college and in exacting standards from institutions as the price of benefactions.[51]

The Carnegie Foundation's ambitious decision to provide every American college professor with a pension was almost as good news as if someone had done something about faculty salaries, but aside from its actuarial difficulties, the foundation's good intentions ran immediately into the question of what constituted a college. Officers and trustees of the foundation reduced the size of their problem at the outset by eliminating state institutions as well as private institutions with denominational affiliation and technical institutes that were not of college grade. Given the sense that their resources were limited, even if they were Andrew Carnegie's, these exclusions were reasonable: Most of the technical institutes were not colleges, and it could be argued that the state governments and churches owed their faculties pensions. Taking care of all the rest, in fact, proved to be more than the Carnegie Foundation could manage; its good intentions in 1918 became the Teachers Insurance and Annuity Association, a pension system endowed by the foundation toward which institutions and teachers now made contributions.[52] But before then, the foundation decided what a college was.

It found forty-five and published its list in June 1906.[53] To make that magic list a college had to require fourteen units of high school credit for admission, each unit signifying five recitations a week throughout the year in one subject. The "Carnegie Unit" had been born, although its source was the Regents Board of the State of New York, whose standards for accreditation were borrowed by the foundation, including the requirement that "an institution to be ranked as a college, must have at least six . . . professors giving their entire time to college and university work . . . [and] a course of four full years in liberal arts and sciences."[54] To be ranked as a college an institution also was required to have "a productive endowment of not less than $200,000."[55]

Without so much as a word about the curriculum, the Carnegie Foundation nonetheless narrowed the definition of a college and established standards by which the college course of study could be distinguished from the secondary school. Its list of forty-five institutions—expanded to fifty-two by the end of the first year—was misleading in its omission of the strong state institutions and such strong private institutions with denominational affiliation as the University of Chicago, Vanderbilt, and Wesleyan in Connecticut. But implicit in its selection was encouragement to colleges and universities that had been courageous in establishing admission standards, more faithful than many of their contemporaries to the traditions of liberal learning, and most responsive to a heightened sense of importance for intellectual values. Curricular disarray was not eliminated by the Carnegie Foundation's first gesture of educational philanthropy, but the foundation's list did single out where the leadership for reorganization and reform would have to come from and where standards, order, coherence would have a chance if they were going to have it anywhere.

Geographically the list was an expression of historical developments: Because it was limited to private institutions, it was heavily weighted among New England and mid-Atlantic institutions; because its standards were likely to be an achievement of age or wealth or both, only one institution was from the South (Tulane), only one from the West Coast (Stanford). The technical institutions included were those whose commitment to pure science supported their programs in applied science: Case, Clarkson, Lehigh, Massachusetts Institute of Technology, and Brooklyn Polytechnic Institute. Colleges outside the East were the old institutions of New England derivation where the sensibilities if not all the practices of the Yale Report lingered on: Beloit, Carleton, Colorado College, Knox, Iowa College at Grinnell, Lawrence University, Marietta, Oberlin, Ripon, Wabash, and Western Reserve. The women's colleges were those that had most succeeded in being like men's colleges: Mt. Holyoke, Radcliffe, Smith, Vassar, Wellesley, and Wells. Otherwise the roster consisted essentially of eastern men's colleges and universities: Amherst, Clark, Columbia, Dartmouth, George Washington, Hamilton, Harvard, Hobart, Johns Hopkins, Middlebury, New York University, Princeton, Trinity, Tufts, Union, Pennsylvania, Rochester, Washington and Jefferson, Williams, and Yale.

Among the more embarrassing consequences of the Carnegie list was the phenomenon of denominational colleges rushing out of their religious affiliations in order to get on it, but a more important result was the existence of an authoritative list of colleges considered worth emulating. In 1906 only 5 southern institutions required graduation from a four-year high school as a condition of admission; within five years of the posting of the Carnegie list, 160 southern colleges and universities "had announced a four-year high-school course as necessary for matriculation."[56] In cooperation with the institutional associations, state accrediting agencies, and the National Education Association, the foundations, in attempting to define a college, were describing the limits, the quality, and to some extent the aspirations of the undergraduate curriculum.

Between 1908 and 1912, responding to the requirement of the National Association of State Universities that "the standard American university . . . include, as an important part of its organization, a standard American college," the University of Virginia discarded the remnants of its Jeffersonian practices and became a four-year, fifteen-hours-a-week "standard American college." In 1915 the Catholic Education Association adopted a new set of standards for recognition, as a spur to the movement of Catholic colleges into the mainstream. Additional requirements were added to standards for accreditation: The Association of American Universities dictated minimum requirements for libraries and scientific laboratories; the American Council on Education, a sort of holding company of institutional associations, dictated the maximum number of teaching hours and the maximum class size. The American Association of University Women denied membership to graduates of the University of Buffalo because its faculty had an insufficient number of women professors. The Carnegie Foundation required that every department head be a holder of the Ph.D. degree.[57]

By 1914 the General Education Board, a Rockefeller philanthropy, was confident enough of its mission and of the need of higher education for its role as enforcer of standards that it all but licensed itself as an unofficial U.S. ministry of higher education. In a report reviewing its work since its founding in 1902, it observed:

> The states have not generally shown themselves competent to deal with higher education on a nonpartisan, impersonal, and comprehensive basis. . . . Rival religious bodies have invaded fields fully—or more than fully—occupied already; misguided individuals have founded a new college instead of strengthening an old one.[58]

In its work among the old Negro colleges, the General Education Board succeeded in using its benefactions to induce the merger of clusters of colleges in Atlanta and New Orleans.[59] In 1905 it supported in each southern state a university professor whose purpose was to organize, strengthen, and popularize the state's high school system.[60] In 1913 a Carnegie Foundation survey of public education in Vermont persuaded the state legislature to terminate state aid for its three private colleges and to expand its support of the University of Vermont. A 1914 General Education Board survey led to fundamental reform in Maryland.[61]

Sensitive as they were to public suspicion of their motives, foundation officials would have preferred that their role be understood as facilitating rather than standardizing. "It is . . . perhaps a natural inference," wrote Henry S. Pritchett of the Carnegie Foundation in 1911, "that we were in a measure seeking to standardize colleges, but our only effort has been to obtain some sort of agreement amongst the colleges and secondary schools as a first step toward unity and progress." In the foundation's fourth annual report he described the foundation's work as not having been "undertaken to furnish standards to the colleges—that would be standardizing. What it has done is to make clear the standards of the colleges themselves and to throw the light of publicity on the deviations from the standards they themselves have set up."[62]

Be that as it may, by 1919, as a result of more than two decades of effort to reach some acceptable understanding of the conditions necessary to support a respectable standard college course of study, the National Conference Committee and the American Council on Education gave firm content to a definition of an American college.[63] Not quite a hundred years earlier the Yale faculty had tried to define a college by specifying the nature of the training and subjects appropriate to a college education. Educational philosophy and psychology had put any similar purpose beyond the range of the authorities who put together a new definition in 1919. If they did not know what should be taught or how, they did know the conditions under which it could best be done, and they were therefore shaping the curriculum.

Their definition described a college as a place that required for admission the completion of a four-year secondary course approved by a recognized accrediting agency and correlated to the college course to which the student was admitted; that required for graduation the completion of at least 120 semester hours of credit; that supported a faculty of at least eight heads of departments for a student body of 100, with professors required to have completed at least two years of graduate school, expected to teach no more than sixteen hours a week in classes of no more than thirty students. The environment essential to such a college was further defined as requiring an annual operating income of $50,000 or more, half derived from permanent endowment; a library of at least 8,000 volumes exclusive of public documents; the absence of any connecting preparatory school operated by the college; and a record of achievement in preparing its students for graduate schools.

What did this definition, which confirmed existing practice at the leading institutions and which succeeded in hurrying the rest into emulation, mean for the undergraduate curriculum? It acknowledged the academic department as an organizing principle and therefore strengthened the role of subject matter specialists in defining the course of study. It accelerated the displacement of the self-taught amateur generalists on the faculties by technically prepared specialists with scholarly, if narrow, competence. It sharpened the distinction between school work and college work and thus greatly elevated curricular standards, most notably in the South. In its concern for libraries, laboratories, class size, and teaching loads, it recognized the scholarly commitment of the new professors and at least helped to provide the conditions under which some of that commitment might rub off on undergraduates. It stressed form over content.

Both the Carnegie Foundation and the General Education Board, in using philanthropy as a device for nudging the colleges and universities toward an acceptance of this definition, expected to succeed in weakening and killing off the weakest denominational colleges.[64] In this hope they failed. The weakest colleges retained a hold on their clientele; smallness and a reputation for a "safe" environment attracted some students, low standards attracted others. On the other hand, their standardizing efforts were greatly assisted by upgrading movements in the medical and legal professions and by the intellectual orientation of the new professors. Academic and institutional rivalry imparted a powerful motive to the expansion and growth and innovation in colleges and universities in the late nineteenth century, but it also led to the stocktaking, establishment of norms, and the standardization of the twentieth century.[65] The foundations were, therefore, not the only agents of standardization, nor did they intend their creative use of money to lead to curricular rigidity. And, when it did, they were quick to shift the focus of their gifts from the general strengthening of institutions to specific projects of an innovative nature.[66] If the nineteenth-century benefactors of the order of Abbott Lawrence and Joseph Sheffield appeared to have supported the colleges and universities in what the institutions wanted to do, the great foundations in the twentieth century, with their enormous resources and their standardizing intentions, supported colleges and universities in what the foundations thought they ought to do.[67]

Whether the most pressing problem confronting the colleges and universities was an absence of widely respected standards was arguable. Uniformity and coherence had fallen out of the course of study and somehow had to be brought back, but whether that could be done more through emphasis on form rather than content was about to become a permanent puzzle for college and university authorities and educational philosophers. Probably nothing could have been done, even in the slightest way, about content, until something had been done about form, but even before the great standardizing developments of the twentieth century, disillusionment with the elective system had set in motion efforts to use form in support of content.

Complaining of his college course, a recent graduate of the University of California said in 1903, "All these studies were simply separate tasks that bore no definite intrinsic relation to each other.... The right studies were there; what was lacking was the conscious organization of them for the student."[68] President Eliot's successor at Harvard, Abbott Lawrence Lowell, was a determined enemy of the elective system because of the evidence that, instead of encouraging specialization and a rational program, it too often led to a selection of easy elementary courses. In 1898, for instance, 55 percent of the students at Harvard "elected little or nothing but elementary courses" and almost 75 percent had programs without any major focus.[69] These conditions surely raised as many questions about the Harvard student body as they did about the elective system, but it was easier to do something about the elective system, since certain remedies were already available.

As early as 1885 David Starr Jordan, then president of Indiana University, had developed the idea of a major subject, an area of interest and concentration in which a student moved from elementary to advanced work during his or her four years.[70] Carried by Jordan to Stanford when he went there as president, the major subject system had to meet two hurdles before it could become a fixture of the undergraduate curriculum. Although the elective system was the device that encouraged the growth of departments and the proliferation of courses, the very materials out of which majors were made, initially the elective system was an expression of chaotic freedom, an invitation to student choice rather than a set of directed options. The spirit in which the elective system was developed served the purposes of expansion, the needs of new subjects scrambling into the curriculum, and the interests of the new breed of professors staking their claims on the course of study. These designs would have to be ratified and consolidated before the results could be rationalized; in other words, before there could be order, first there had to be chaos.

Before the major field or subject could take hold, enthusiasm for the elective system would have to run its course. In addition, majors could not be developed out of thin air. They would have been impossible in the old colleges, where knowledge was elementary and the professors were generalists. A sufficient number of subject matter specialists would have to flow out of the graduate schools of arts and sciences into the colleges, a sufficient demand for new subjects and for study in depth would have to be delivered by the elective system, before the course of study was ready to offer itself over to the major subject system. Unlike the nineteenth-century parallel course program or group system, which packaged elementary courses in related fields or designed a prescribed cluster of courses in ways that avoided the distasteful dead languages or emphasized the more lively modern ones, the major subject system required and respected the concept of concentrated study in depth. Here was an idea that George Ticknor and his fellow New Englanders had brought back to the United States from Germany in the 1820s; its flowering in the United States in the first decades of the twentieth century was not so much an expression of delayed culture transfer as it was a statement on the coming of age of a peculiarly American institution.

Other colleges and universities had recovered from their overzealous affair with the elective system before Lowell took hold of Harvard. Yet Harvard's dramatic reversal, after forty years of Eliot's prodding and masterful role as the country's most influential university spokesman, was the signal that was noticed. Yale had by 1901 begun moving to a system of concentration and distribution, a combination of a major field of study and courses chosen from certain groups defined by their intellectual style. In 1905 Cornell gave up its free elective system and required that approximately one fifth of a student's course work be distributed among four specified areas of knowledge. Wesleyan in Connecticut in 1908 adopted concentration and distribution requirements.[71]

President Lowell's 1909 inaugural address produced a classic example of academic double-talk. "We must go forward and develop the elective system," he said, "making it really systematic."[72] Actually, the City College of New York, never having embraced the elective principle, did adopt the concentration and distribution system and properly described it as progress and reform.[73] But in the Harvard context what Lowell proposed was reversal and moderation, even though concentration and distribution was indeed a device for bringing system out of disarray and for, at least, taming the elective system, if not developing it. Lowell's distribution groups divided the course of study into the arts of expression (language, literature, fine arts, and music), the natural or inductive sciences, the inductive social sciences (including history), and the abstract or deductive studies (mathematics, philosophy, and law).[74] As with similar groups developed elsewhere, students were required to take a specific number of courses in each group while at the same time concentrating in the subject matter of one department or in a major designed by putting together a group of related courses from several departments. Adopted in the fall of 1909, concentration and distribution went into effect in 1910 with the entering class of 1914. The significance for the course of study was large but hardly as momentous as claimed by Samuel Eliot Morison, who said of Lowell: "He proposed to put back into the academic basket some of the things that had fallen through the mesh during the process of expansion. Of these, the most important was education."[75]

Elsewhere the triumph of concentration and distribution over election was facilitated by the adoption in most colleges and universities, by 1910, of the subject major.[76] Major and minor areas of concentration were the first fruits of the elective system. Requiring a student to select one major, perhaps a minor, and to distribute some of his courses among four prescribed groups of courses after 1910 was essentially a matter of organizing an existing mass of courses into a systematic arrangement. The materials were already at hand. Concentration and distribution provided the curriculum with a rationale, which was something of an improvement on free election, which was only a license. It attempted to do for all students what a 1910 study suggested that the best students and most successful graduates of the free elective era had done for themselves—concentrated more than others, distributed less than others.[77] Once more in possession of a rationale, colleges and universities gave up their accelerated three-year programs as well as their combined programs with the professional schools, programs described by Dean William C. DeVane of Yale as having "threatened the colleges with inconsequence."[78] Among the many institutions that seized on concentration and distribution as a curricular lifeline was Hamilton College, which succinctly stated its intention to use it to achieve through the course of study "breadth without superficiality, and thoroughness without cramping rigidity."[79]

With similar purpose and with equally salutary effect on a curriculum that had lost focus, Swarthmore College, under the leadership of Frank Aydelotte, pioneered in using an honors program to fulfill its obligation to liberal learning. Before World War I a number of eastern institutions—Harvard, Yale, Princeton, and Columbia among them—explored the use of honors programs, of special opportunities and heightened expectations for especially able students, as a way of remedying a climate of undergraduate indifference to scholarship. These early programs were denied the necessary commitment and resources, and they provided a clear challenge to the idea of the undergraduate college as a democracy of equals. As a former Rhodes scholar, Aydelotte had observed at Oxford the intellectually stimulating practice of separating honors students from pass students. Not until he took charge of Swarthmore was there an effective demonstration that the American undergraduate curriculum could embrace the values implicit in the honors idea. The demonstration cost the General Education Board $4 million, but it also created another remedy for curricular disarray and undergraduate apathy and introduced an element of diversity into the course of study, at a time when standardization may have been fostering a stultifying rigidity.[80]

Aydelotte did not allow the Swarthmore honors program to depart from the spirit of liberal learning. "The central purpose of liberal education cannot be restricted to the study of any particular subject or combination of subjects," he wrote, as if to deny to concentration and distribution any exclusive or even necessary guardianship of the humane tradition. "Liberal knowledge is not a formula; it is a point of view," he continued. "The essence of liberal education is the development of mental power and moral responsibility in each individual. It is based upon the theory that each person is unique, that each deserves to have his own powers developed to the fullest possible extent."

His notion of the Swarthmore honors program required that it be part of an educational experience that focused on the development of "intellect . . . character, and . . . sensitiveness to beauty—as over against merely learning some useful technique."[81] Aydelotte did not intend to have the Swarthmore honors program confused with the purposes of graduate seminars in arts and sciences or contaminated by the narrow specialization appropriate to candidates for the degree of doctor of philosophy. On the other hand, the Swarthmore program, which was inaugurated in 1922, did set candidates for honors degrees apart from their classmates, allowed them to concentrate in a single field of study, exposed them to tutorial and seminar instruction, required them to write a thesis, and subjected them to a comprehensive written examination as well as an oral examination by outside examiners.[82]

Swarthmore set an example that created problems for institutions such as Yale, where the honors program concept developed into an issue over how best "to reconcile quantity with quality and, especially, how to cultivate intellectual distinction in a democracy."[83] Yale eventually required a thesis of all its seniors, thus generalizing and democratizing a practice that in its origins had been intended for the most able and most motivated. By 1930, however, at least ninety-three honors programs, few if any as elaborate or as institutionally central as its program became for Swarthmore, were functioning in places as diverse as Coe College, Wesleyan, Pomona, Dartmouth, and Indiana University.[84] Not every institution could make its honors program work: At Indiana an already overextended faculty balked. Others were delighted by the results: The historian of the Wesleyan curriculum described its honors program as one of the two "most significant improvements" in the curriculum between the two world wars (the other was comprehensive examinations).[85]

In combining some of the qualities of the old college—small classes, emphasis on written and oral communication, some recognition of the student as a person—with the scholarly and specialized focus of the new professors, the honors program established a certain sense of continuity and stability even as it expressed a special regard for the brilliant student and for the intellectual quality of the course of study. A 1924 comparison between the American and English systems of higher education gave the advantage to the English universities for their commitment to the most able students, their assumption that learning was less a function of attending classes than of study, their reliance on formal instruction as a correlating rather than primary learning experience for the student, and for their use of honors courses, tutorials, and outside examining boards as a spur to intellectual achievement.[86] Where the honors program pioneered by Swarthmore took hold, these English advantages were matched.

Twenty years earlier a Harvard faculty committee, on the basis of wide study, had come to the conclusion that there was too much teaching and not enough studying at Harvard: The average student each week spent twelve hours in class and thirteen hours at his desk.[87] And too many of those classroom hours, everywhere not just at Harvard, were a calculated insult to students. At Columbia, E. L. Thorndike, its famed psychologist, paused a moment, while in engrossed conversation with one of his colleagues, "glanced at the clock and remarked, 'I must give a lecture in five minutes. It would be 50 percent better if I spent this time in preparation. But let's compute another coefficient of correlation.' "[88] All over the country coefficients of correlation were computed at the expense of college teaching. And, while almost everyone everywhere nodded in approval when President Hadley remarked at his inauguration at Yale in 1899 that he had never "met a good teacher who really approved of the lecture system, or who did not prefer small classes to large ones," the lecture system, vastly preferable as it was to the recitation system, had fastened itself onto the curriculum.[89]

For the professors lectures possessed certain attractive advantages: Lectures kept students at a distance, they could be repeated with small cost in time and effort, they provided an opportunity for trying out new ideas and showing off the results of new research, they were books in progress. Lectures also stretched the distance between teacher and student by turning over to someone else the responsibility of reading tests and papers. For students the advantages of lectures over recitations were also attractive: They did not have to be prepared, they could sleep, they could skip class and borrow notes or even purchase course outlines. Yet lectures opened up such a great gulf between professor and student that each learned how to act as if the other did not really exist. What possibly could have been achieved with such enrollments as these at Harvard in 1903 that might not better have been accomplished by chaining students to their desks: Economics 1 (529), Government 1 (376), Geology 4 (439), and History 1 (408)?[90]

As early as 1901 thirty-nine Harvard courses enrolled over 100 students, fourteen over 200. A 1904 faculty report led to some modest remedies: In every large lecture course, a conference-quiz section, too often taught by an inexperienced assistant, was substituted for one lecture; sectioning by ability was rediscovered; and the awarding of the degree with distinction was adopted as an encouragement to students who might otherwise allow boredom to get in the way of achievement. By 1908 President Eliot could claim that a vast array of curricular devices had come to the aid of the lecture, not just conference-quiz sections: reserved reading shelves in the library, laboratory work in science, the problem approach to subject matter, field work, theses, reports, the case method, source books, and seminars.[91] Everywhere that they were tried—and they soon became standard practice—these new elements of the course of study encouraged students to take charge of their own education. To the extent that they were peripheral and the lecture central, however, they could not combat the injurious effect of the lecture system. Where the lecture dominated, the most successful curricular tactic was the humanistic virtuoso, the "great lecturer." In 1910 Edwin Slosson reported a prime example: "The teaching of Professor Phelps differs from what is commonly found in English classrooms in that many of his students like poetry even after they have studied it."[92]

Students did not have to be encouraged to embrace the values and agencies of the extracurriculum, but a curriculum in the grasp of remote professors, only occasionally enlivened by the charisma of the Billy Phelpses, certainly played a role in supporting an exaggerated attachment to the extracurriculum in the early decades of the twentieth century. Abraham Flexner told a committee of the Yale faculty in 1903 that if the exaltation of athletics, club life, and social activity continued, the undergraduate experience would become an important agent in the demoralization of the wealthy classes.[93] But this was a variety of demoralization of which the university thoroughly approved. President Hadley assured a visitor in 1910 that "if the chairman of the *Yale News* board is a man of the right type—and he almost always is—he is the most efficient disciplinary officer of the university."[94] Four years later Yale opened the Bowl, the largest athletic arena in the country, to a capacity attendance of 70,000.[95]

In redesigning the curriculum in ways intended to remedy the disarray delivered by the pressures that brought down the classical course of study, college and university authorities were burdened by a student body attracted to their campuses for reasons different from those that had motivated the small enrollments of the old colleges. Economic prosperity underwrote a degree of college attendance that, except for its fashionableness, was almost purposeless. The business ethos of a commercial society supported college going as an experience in social maturation and human relationships. The country lost its head over college athletics. In this environment, concentration and distribution, honors programs, and even the great humanist lecturers among the professors were rowing upstream.

In an effort to remedy old faults and to incorporate new values, Woodrow Wilson at Princeton in 1905 created a body of young instructors whom he called *preceptors*. Their appearance on the Princeton campus was a unique phenomenon; Harvard would have tutors, but the Princeton preceptorial system was innovative and expensive enough to become both the envy of many institutions and a historical eccentricity. Wilson hoped to use his young instructors—forty-five of them, most of them recruited from the faculties of twenty-five other colleges and universities—to counteract the depersonalization that university growth had imposed even on Princeton and to bring forceful teaching personalities to bear on students for whom intellectual purpose was peripheral. The design was imaginative: Each preceptor owed a responsibility to four or five students, who met in the preceptor's living room or perhaps over beer at an inn, discussing their reading, sharing their intellectual growth in an atmosphere of informal encouragement.[96]

As a device for weaning students from the extracurriculum, the preceptorial system was of no consequence: It may even have become confused with the extracurriculum. And, because the reading over which the students met was generally related to their reading requirements for other courses, the preceptors operated almost on a level that combined some of the functions of a scoutmaster with those of a proselytizer. Some subjects—mathematics, the sciences, economics, elementary Greek—did not lend themselves readily to the design. In these disciplines apparently there was nothing to discuss. The preceptorial system worked best where extensive reading was the central element of a student's courses, but the absence of any related general examinations, while supporting the student-faculty relationship, deprived the preceptorials of any value as curricular currency.

They were pleasant, they helped students to clarify their regular course work, they placed English university practice alongside Princeton's Gothic buildings, and they allowed one reporter to conclude that "here is a university that knows what it wants and is trying to get it. . . . It has an ideal of education and is working it out."[97] That ideal was an old one: Princeton, Wilson said, was "not a place of special but of general education, not a place where a lad finds his profession, but a place *where he finds himself.*"[98] In the environment of an expanding university, Wilson's commitment to liberal learning and his affinity for some of the spirit of the old small college were reassuring, as was his purpose of using preceptors to attract young men to a respect for intellectual rigor. On any large scale, Wilson's intentions would be served in the American undergraduate curriculum not by Princeton's preceptorials but by Swarthmore's honors program. More than the support of a $4 million grant from the General Education Board accounted for the greater acceptability of the honors program idea, and probably the most important factor in its favor was the degree to which its focus on research and scholarship coincided with the highest values of the new breed of professors.

An additional stimulus to curricular order and scholarly purpose was the appearance of a new examination rationale. Beginning in 1913 at Harvard the division of history, government, and economics adopted the practice of examining seniors in general or comprehensive examinations that covered material considered appropriate for the student's area of concentration but not necessarily presented in his courses. In 1919, on its way to becoming a requirement, Harvard's general examinations were made optional in all departments.[99] In the 1920s, partly as a result of the examining procedures associated with the Swarthmore honors program and partly as a function of Harvard's commanding presence as a promulgator of academic standards, the comprehensive examination as an instrument for bringing coherence and design and some semblance of unity to the academic course made considerable headway. One way of making students serious about the curriculum was to make clear to them that the colleges and universities took the curriculum seriously. Comprehensive examinations served that purpose. So did Yale's decision in 1911 to abolish the privilege of saving up sixty allowed class cuts and converting them into a course credit toward the degree.[100]

As effective as all these devices were for bringing some order to the course of study, they avoided the question of whether knowledge itself could be brought under control and given some semblance of symmetry and unity. Or perhaps they did not so much avoid the question as they acknowledged the impossibility of ever recovering that sense of certainty that had held the old curriculum together for so long. Moreover, to the extent that the scientific method had been substituted for other once reliable sources of truth, truth and knowledge had become process rather than packages of inherited wisdom. And process gave off every evidence of turning out knowledge at a rate beyond the capacity of any individual to encompass or comprehend. If man was to be master of his own destiny, in charge of knowledge rather than its victim, however, somehow subject matter would have to be mastered and brought under control quite as effectively as the elective system that had allowed the new knowledge entry to the curriculum. Could a new unity of knowledge, some definition of what an educated person should know, be synthesized? Could a curriculum be designed appropriate for all young men and women, even as the psychology of mental faculties was being overwhelmed by the psychology of individual differences? There were those who thought so.

The general education movement, as the effort to define and enforce a common curriculum has been called, began as a response to the sense of bewilderment with which many young students faced the freedom of the elective course of study. It received clarification during and after World War I, when a consciousness of Western values and national problems found expression in courses designed to orient students to their cultural inheritance and their responsibilities as citizens. And, like all impossible dreams, the general education idea was carried along from decade to decade, receiving new encouragement in one institution or another, the product of a quixotic conviction that the limits of essential knowledge could be defined.

In 1911 Reed College in Oregon designed a course for freshmen that provided students with an orientation to the college, its goals, the curriculum, methods of study, and other normal sources of freshman bewilderment. Obviously the course did not establish any design of general education, but it did bring students to some sense of the humanistic tradition which their college endeavors were expected to nurture. In a sense, the Reed course was guidance for credit. The same year at the University of Rochester an orientation course for freshmen stressed broad areas of thought and social problems and institutions of contemporary interest. Before World War I courses similar to the one developed at Reed appeared at Brown, Whitman, Willamette, DePauw, the California Institute of Technology, and the University of New Hampshire. In the spirit of the Rochester course President Alexander Meiklejohn introduced a course for Amherst freshmen in 1914 called "Social and Economic Institutions," intended to serve as an introduction to "humanistic sciences."[101]

Not until after the war, partly as a consequence of the Army-required "War Aims" courses taught in Students' Army Training Corps programs, did comprehensive survey courses take on the character of a movement. Columbia's required contemporary civilization course in 1919 was a product of the university's wartime Students' Army Training Corps course; Reed's humanities course of 1921 and Chicago's 1924 course on the nature of the world and man were not. But all three wrestled with the problem of how to sustain and nurture the values and content of Western learning in an age of fragmented and specialized knowledge. Columbia's course, as did the others, rested on the proposition "that there is a certain minimum of our intellectual and spiritual tradition which a man must experience and understand if he is to be called educated."[102] Columbia, Reed, and Chicago, as well as others that ventured into the curricular territory opened up by the general education idea, were trying to retrieve for the curriculum a function that it had sustained since the Middle Ages: the cultivation and transmission of the intellectual and philosophical inheritance of the Western world as an instrument of man's understanding of himself.

Acknowledging the responsibility of colleges and universities to that tradition required more than the demonstration that a few dedicated faculties could find ways to defy the whole drift of contemporary history—the high school movement, vocationalism, academic specialization, relativism, science. Courses that were at least symbolic gestures appeared at many institutions: Wisconsin, Princeton, Dartmouth, Indiana, Stanford, Missouri, Northwestern, and Williams.[103] By 1926 over 100 courses of a general orientation nature were identifiable—42 of the college adjustment and guidance nature, 16 providing an introduction to the methodology of learning, and 34 serving as introductions to aspects of contemporary civilization.[104] Because courses of a general nature required professors with synthesizing imaginations of a sort that was not encouraged by graduate training, the general education movement in its early years was incapable of launching a formidable assault on the course of study. College faculties were being recruited from young men and young women who were being trained to be loyal to their subject, its scientific methodology, and to their department. Professors of unconventional views and institutions of innovative persuasion would have to look out for everything else.

The problem was widely recognized. Andrew D. White lamented in 1908:

> We seem to have "swung around the circle," and to be back
> at the reverse of the old problem. . . . There is certainly a
> widespread fear among many thinking men that in our
> eagerness for these new things we have too much lost sight
> of certain valuable old things, the things . . . which used to
> be summed up under the word "culture."[105]

In recognizing the human and social consequences of a curriculum that was a surer instrument of service and power than of culture and character, White perhaps unconsciously provided a new rationale for small suburban and country colleges that lacked the resources necessary to support expensive science programs and a large array of electives. This was a rationale, as a matter of fact, that they were quite capable of asserting themselves. William Louis Poteat of Wake Forest College argued in 1905 that "the college is a body of associates in pursuit of the higher things of life, a brotherhood in which character takes form in the atmosphere of culture . . . a mutual benefit society yielding dividends in efficiency and character." The same year at Amherst President George Harris voiced a concise expression of the tradition of liberal culture, the very culture that the general education movement would later hope to make comprehensible to students divorced from their cultural inheritance. "The educated man is the all-round man, the symmetrical man," Harris said. "The aim of a college is not to make scholars. The aim is to make broad, cultivated men, physically sound, intellectually awake, socially refined and gentlemanly, with appreciation of art, music, literature, and with sane, simple religion, all in proportion . . . all-round men."[106]

If the small colleges were in a better position to resist an action-oriented curriculum and to protect such values as leisure, contemplation, self-discipline, wisdom, and character from the overwhelming materialism of the age, the universities also continued to support in professors of rare effectiveness advocates of liberal culture. At Yale their success required President Hadley to explain to the alumni in 1913 that indeed it was true that a successful club had been started where faculty and students drank tea in the afternoons and talked about books. Just what was the meaning, in the spring of 1923, of William Lyon Phelps leading a procession of 400 students to the Yale library, there presenting to the librarian a Browning first edition paid for by student subscription and then leading the students in a cheer that repeated "Browning" nine times?[107]

Liberal culture, however, was counterrevolutionary in purpose. It hoped to dislodge the emphasis on "training for service and training for power" from the curriculum. One of its most eloquent spokesmen at Harvard, Irving Babbitt, decried the tendency of a course of study defined by electives, the vocational interests of students, and the research interests of professors to educate students in "techniques which would give them control of their objective environment but not over their own subjective needs."[108] Babbitt early sensed a sickness in the course of study that would play a role in the revolt of a generation of students in the 1960s, but it was a sickness that defied control.

For students the courses in English, the modern languages, history, and philosophy, in which were imbedded cultural purpose and humanistic values, lacked the professional motivation that could be taken to the sciences and the avowedly vocational. Courses that were respectful of leisure and contemplation as human values of great worth made different demands on students, demands not readily testable, and with consequences not immediately measurable. A student of college and university life in 1907 expressed great uneasiness about "culture courses," those lacking in professional purpose but claiming some refining influence. To them he attributed "moral perversion" and a "false and pernicious atmosphere."[109] In coeducational colleges masculine ridicule was directed at men students who enrolled in the so-called literary departments.[110] To a degree that they were unaware of, the old eastern men's colleges and universities, in holding out against coeducation until after World War II, provided an environment in which men students could engage in liberal learning without fear of ridicule.

Liberal culture as an educational philosophy made its most significant impact in the eastern men's and women's institutions, where a long hostility to the commercial and industrial, even democratic, directions of American life supported a position that was fundamentally critical of middle-class values. Surely one purpose of liberal culture was to wean students away from the main chance, to make men students less manly and more human, women students less womanly and more worldly. These intentions were too civilized for the somewhat barbaric era in which liberal culture contended for influence. Moreover, it stressed enjoyment, understanding, appreciation, and taste at the expense of intellectual rigor and critical incisiveness. It backed away from any vigorous assertion of creative activity. It was associated with the rights, privileges, and responsibilities of a limited class, and, while its emphasis on the uses of leisure was for many a welcome relief from the glorification of the work ethic, liberal culture was too alienated from American society to take charge of the undergraduate curriculum.[111]

Between 1910 and 1930 three institutions—one new, one old and on the verge of collapse, and one stable and secure but taken over by an urbane reformer—turned themselves into laboratories of curricular innovation. Reed, Antioch, and Swarthmore in the first quarter of the twentieth century cast themselves into the tradition of Jefferson's

Virginia, White's Cornell, Gilman's Johns Hopkins, and Harper's Chicago. They had to be paid attention to.[112]

In 1911 Reed College opened in Portland, Oregon, as a protest against the trivialization of the academic experience by extracurricularly oriented students. In the words of its first president, Reed proposed to free itself from "harassing traditions" and proceeded to do so by adopting simplified spelling, eliminating the extracurriculum, requiring a combination of thesis and oral examination of its seniors and a qualifying comprehensive examination of its juniors, importing a faculty of young enthusiasts from the East, and holding to high admissions standards. This design, which would have been impossible to impose on an old institution, was possible in a new one because the bequest that supported it, the inclinations of the trustees, the encouragement of the General Education Board, and the imagination of the president all favored an experimental model.[113] In 1921, all of ten years old, Reed was ready for reform and adopted a program of two years of broad humanities courses with small discussion sections as a prelude to specialization in the junior and senior years. Reed's reform was not simply a version of concentration and distribution; it went beyond form to content and specified in the first two years a version of general education, a synthesis of the knowledge and understanding it considered appropriate for a liberally educated person.[114]

Antioch, an old college at Yellow Springs, Ohio, first presided over by Horace Mann, was so close to collapse in 1919 that when "the trustees tried to give it away to the YMCA, the YMCA returned it."[115] Arthur E. Morgan, a trustee, took over and turned the college into a strange new mixture of traditional respect for the liberal arts and a progressive philosophy that emphasized work experience, in combination with some of the social and group purposes of nineteenth-century American communal societies. Antioch proposed to do right by the humanities, careers, and the community. Antioch was a missionary movement that took as its challenge the development of the whole student, not simply the intellect.

Its five-year program, half spent on campus and the other half spent off campus in remunerative employment, centered on a work-study plan that had originated at the engineering school of the University of Cincinnati in 1906, but the curriculum itself mixed culture, career, and community in equal parts. Antioch's style emphasized

democratic campus relationships, basic requirements in liberal learning, and self-directed study. The extramural phase of the Antioch
experience, which had students working for 175 employers in twelve
states in 1930, may have been vocational and self-supporting in result,
but in purpose Morgan thought of the off-campus experiences as
bringing students face to face with "practical realities in all their
stubborn complexity" and as contributing to the education of the
whole man and whole woman. As difficult as it was for old colleges
and universities to support liberal culture and general education in
the course of study, Antioch presented them with a model that was
completely beyond emulation: It offered a curricular alternative that,
if adopted at all widely, would have required the dismantling of the
entire structure of American higher education. In combination, Reed
and Antioch proposed to repeal several hundred years of curricular
history.

Swarthmore, on the other hand, proposed a more modest and a
more easily adopted reform. Although the curricular transformation
of Swarthmore into an honors/pass college was accompanied by the
decline of the college's intercollegiate athletic program and an erosion of social life, the honors program idea did not have to be taken as
far as it was at Swarthmore in order to be an effective agency of order
and focus in the course of study. Swarthmore used honors to cultivate
a national constituency, to shift its financial base from the Quakers of
Philadelphia, and to define the college's uniqueness.[116] Other colleges and universities incorporated the honors idea and its purposes
without succumbing to them.

G. Stanley Hall, popularizer of the new psychology, first president of Clark University, the failed emulator of Johns Hopkins at
Worcester, Massachusetts, expressed in 1894 a sentiment that would
be many times repeated by others during the early decades of the twentieth century. He made a plea that room be found in the course of
study for "a little inebriation with ideals," for "something . . . which
cannot be marked or examined on."[117]

Hall's concern was in part inspired by a sense of the degree to
which the graduate school and the whole Germanic apparatus, of
which he was a prime exemplar, were moving the undergraduate liberal arts college from its liberating and humanistic role to a narrower

focus, whether or not that focus was a function of specialization, professionalism, or scientific scholarship. The broad synthesizing role of the curriculum, the regard for qualities of character and judgment and responsible social leadership, were being lost in the pursuit of often mundane realities of great importance for scholars and careers but of no more than marginal relevance to the history of Western ideals.

The various efforts to remedy the consequences of the elective system for the curriculum were intended to preserve a little bit of Hall's "inebriation," to keep it in some definitive way both human in scale and humanistic in tradition. For all of its weaknesses, the old classical course—in its own time—had succeeded in imparting knowledge in the major branches of learning, had provided instruction in the skills of oral and written communication, and had, in combination with the extracurriculum and other integral elements of the academic experience, helped to nurture young men and women along the way to maturity, integrity, and some small degree of wisdom. The Yale Report of 1828 accepted the concept of imparting a universal body of knowledge as one purpose of the curriculum, but it also stressed, in the words of Earl McGrath, training in "a common set of intellectual skills" and "a uniform concern with . . . persistent philosophic problems."[118]

In the twentieth century that old curriculum lingered only as an anachronism. In many places the purposes had fled with the curriculum. Even efforts to deal with curricular disorder could be self-defeating. Majors and minors, fields of concentration, specialization were antidotes to superficiality, dilettantism, and purposelessness, but they often allowed students to perfect particular intellectual skills and human qualities at the expense of others; they were unfriendly to wholeness. Distribution, liberal culture, and general education all were characterized by an embarrassing lack of authority and an absence of agreement on the knowledge that should define an educated person.

Yet those who bemoaned the shift from character, judgment, and wisdom to service, power, and vocation as the focus of the curriculum perhaps overstated the role of the colleges and universities in defining character and personality, as if family, church, and community had not already done that job quite indelibly. Was not the college doing all that it could when it reaffirmed, supported, tightened the restraints, and disciplined and ordered experience for adolescents on their way to maturity, and did so in accordance with whatever shifting styles, definitions, values, and purposes the society preferred? Colleges and universities in the course of study were, however, not simply transmitters of the culture; they were also creative influences on it. In this role, the curriculum moved beyond its task of delivering the past to young men and women; here it literally had possession of the future.

At the end of the first quarter of the twentieth century the evidence was overwhelming that the American college was not going to disappear and that the American university would not be either a transplanted English university or a transplanted German university. The curriculum was still a repository of conflicting purposes and contradictory educational philosophies, but a body of standard practices and expectations and a sophisticated bureaucracy imposed a semblance of rationality and sanity on a course of study that was sometimes beyond understanding. And in some measure the curriculum had been delivered from potential chaos.

7

The Last Fifty Years

In the twentieth century the curriculum fell apart more comfortably than it did in the nineteenth, when great battles were waged and great social and intellectual forces were engaged. The rise of science, the death of Greek, the emergence of professions, the ascendancy of an ambitious middle class, the resounding victory of intellect over piety —these were events that brought down into a thousand pieces the old college and all of the certainties and practices that had held it together. The death of the classical course of study opened the way to a curriculum burdened with such a diversity of purpose, style, and institutional form that the word *curriculum* became a concept of convenience rather than precision.

Continuous as it was, stretching back beyond the founding of Harvard into the Middle Ages and on to antiquity, the curriculum was fragile, yet flexible, and it was in constant motion. Old purposes seemed never to be cast aside, even as new ones were added. New knowledge entered the course of study even as old knowledge lost validity. A message of reassurance to the liberally educated student in 1976 was the estimate that his technically educated contemporary ten years hence would need to discard as outdated half that he had learned and would need to replace it with knowledge that no one yet possessed. On the basis of statistical studies of the catalogues of 110 four-year colleges for the years 1962 to 1967, JB Lon Hefferlin concluded that "theoretically . . . the content of the undergraduate curriculum is being reconstituted completely at least every twenty-two years."[1] He found old courses departing at the rate of 5 percent a year and new courses arriving at the rate of 9 percent a year. The curriculum had become a changing inventory. It continued to fall apart, but quietly.

Tradition held its ground, of course. In 1935 the catalogue of the University of the South at Sewanee sounded like a combination of the Yale Report of 1828 and a Mark Hopkins baccalaureate address; at Sewanee the curriculum was still a progression of experiences in Christian revelation.[2] Yet the liberal arts as a set of values and expectations, let alone subject matter, had lost much of their meaning. Commencement speakers spoke as if they knew what the liberal arts and sciences were all about, and the few resisting Catholic colleges, the ones that held on longer than others to the prescribed liberal curriculum, knew what they meant by an educated Catholic. But the concept had been robbed of meaning by its caretakers. They had allowed —if not encouraged—election and specialization to triumph.

Concentration and distribution and all the other controls imposed upon the elective system were subjected to sophisticated refinement, but electives continued to enlarge their domain. One study of fifty years of changing curricular styles and fashions looked at the degree requirements of 105 liberal arts colleges and found that between 1890 and 1940 required courses were replaced by elective courses at an accelerating rate. In 1890, on the average, a student's four-year program was more than 84 percent required; in 1940, no more than 40 percent. As late as 1890 a third of the colleges held to the old totally prescribed curriculum; fifty years later, of this group, 13 percent still prescribed mathematics, 50 percent prescribed foreign languages, and since 1930 none had required Greek.[3]

The B.A. degree, once the symbol of a simple set of standards and expectations and a statement of curricular integrity, became an umbrella: Harvard gave up its B.S. degree in 1946, as many colleges already had, as others had given up the Ph.B. and Litt.B. degrees for an earlier generation. Colleges and universities that considered themselves upholders of quality decided that whatever programs they offered all deserved the B.A. degree.[4] At Denison in the 1940s undergraduate majors in business, personnel administration, and citizenship joined the old standbys, English, history, and physics.[5] Pomona added preprofessional programs in forestry, agriculture, and landscape architecture.[6] By mid century at Whittier the B.A. course included programs in medicine, education, law, social work, nursing, Christian service, Y.M.C.A. work, and athletic coaching. And in

1954, at the University of North Dakota, a department of occupational therapy was added to the offerings of the liberal arts college.[7] While it could be argued, and often was, that any subject could be infused with the spirit and style of liberal learning, honesty also required the admission that some subjects lent themselves to such infusion more readily than others. It is doubtful if occupational therapy and athletic coaching, either as taught or taken, were among them.

So far had the curriculum gone in its merry chase after vocational knowledge, in fact, that the various career programs in the land-grant colleges, state universities, and their competitors would have no more to do with the B.A. degree than was necessary. Even by 1930 the state universities of the North Central Association, the powerful and prestigious association that spoke for the great state universities of the Midwest, were offering forty-six baccalaureate degrees. Those forty-five other degrees were not intended to protect the integrity of the forty-sixth: They were announcements of differentiation and distance; they were intentionally job descriptive. Just as the holder of the B.A. degree sensed that he or she possessed no clear road to a career, the holders of those other degrees knew that their degrees were passports to specific occupations, certifications of technical competence and professional training.[8]

At the same time professional anticipation and a preference for the specialized over the general were brought to bear on the curriculum by an increasing number of students on the way to education beyond the baccalaureate. By 1964 "for three quarters of the graduates of the best colleges in the East, the bachelor's degree . . . [had] ceased to be a terminal one."[9] Specialization and a professional orientation thus came full circle: They came to dominate the undergraduate experience at the very colleges and universities that had been the most trustworthy guardians of the humanist tradition. A Yale faculty committee warned in 1953 that "Yale is . . . not fulfilling the need for men with power to make judgments about complex subjects and to present those judgments coherently and precisely."[10]

If in the nineteenth century the curriculum defined the market for higher learning, in the twentieth the market defined the curriculum. The result was not only a reversal of a restricted course and of limited enrollments. Another consequence was to make the curriculum particularly mercurial, quickly responsive to changing student tastes, foundation fads, and the day's events. Under the impact of depression and New Deal, for example, Yale seniors between 1929 and 1937 registered a significant shift from English to economics and history in their choice of majors.[11] The University of Southern California greeted technological change with curricular relevance: cinema studies in the 1920s and automobile driver education in the 1930s.[12] Collapse of the job market in the 1930s directed students away from specialized education of limited use to courses of a more general nature.[13] At Ohio State University the Great Depression led in 1932 to the dropping of 337 courses, the bracketing of 69, the consolidation of 33, and a reduction in the frequency with which 30 others were offered. At the University of Michigan, reduced legislative appropriations led to a curricular reorganization in the 1930s that rationalized and put order into an overgrown course of study.[14] Economic retrenchment in the 1970s played a similar salutary role in trimming from the curriculum in many institutions frills and fads that had attached themselves to the course of study in the affluent 1960s, when a sensitivity to youth culture and world events had encouraged the development of courses in guitar and photography, Russian and Near Eastern history.[15] Vogues in student course selections pulled the curriculum by the 1970s toward "relevance" in economics and government and, in reaction, toward "irrelevance" in medieval history, classics, and art history.[16] Some institutions were more able than others to withstand the shifting moods and perceptions of the young —wealthy institutions more than financially weak ones, rural and suburban colleges more than urban institutions, universities more than colleges.[17] Relative curricular stability was a function of economics, geography, and history.

By 1976 concentration was in charge of the curriculum. A survey of curricular developments and course selections for the period from 1967 to 1974 confirmed persistent trends—increased specialization, choice of electives in the field of concentration, the increase of electives at the expense of general education but not at the expense of majors.[18] Senior interdisciplinary seminars at New College in Florida were abandoned in 1968 in the face of evidence that the seniors were too specialized for interdisciplinary work. Some devices for loosening the grip of specialization were more successful, however. Senior seminars on broad topics at Bowdoin College succeeded because they were designed to be of interest to and within the range of competence of students not majoring in the area of study with which the topics were associated.[19] Yale tried one solution to the problem of concentration by giving three definitions to the major program: "standard," which was concentrated; "intensive," which was more concentrated; and "divisional," which was broadened by putting together a cluster of courses from one of the divisions of the curriculum.[20] And in the absence of regulations to prohibit or discourage them, students who were so inclined found ways to broaden their course of study. At Harvard, where fields of concentration were "supposed to be chosen at the beginning of the sophomore year, a great many students switch[ed] majors in the course of that year, or even in some cases in the junior year, and still manage[d] to encompass enough courses [in the major] (usually six or eight) for a degree."[21] Ingenuity or eccentricity were available as means for deemphasizing the major. A tendency developed outside the sciences, moreover, to reduce the major requirements, both in the number of courses and in specifically required courses—offering students at least the options to roam more broadly in the curriculum or to double major as alternatives to concentration.

Interdepartmental majors or majors based on an interdisciplinary approach led troubled careers. The oldest and most successful of these, American Studies, in many places where it was longest established, was dependent for staffing on the not always reliable generosity of traditional departments. Interdepartmental majors and programs, although they ameliorated excessive concentration and supported breadth as a curricular purpose, struck at the specialization and departmentalization that were the repositories of bureaucratic power. American Studies, an inspiration of the cultural self-consciousness of the 1930s, was a good enough idea for both students and teachers that its organizing principles, especially the concept of culture, might have become a way of organizing majors and programs in French studies, English studies, Spanish studies, Russian studies, and so forth. But that is not the way that it happened. The area programs of the 1960s in Russian, African, Chinese, and Latin-American studies owed little or nothing to the curricular experience with American Studies. They were a product of foundation enthusiasm, government grants, and a certain nervousness about the future of American foreign policy and success in war and commerce. Because they were almost wholly synthetic and required almost everywhere the bringing together of a cluster of specialists who had not yet mastered the principle or the appropriateness of some integrating concept, these programs collapsed when financial support withered.

As for British studies and French studies and other interdisciplinary majors and programs that might have been developed from the existing materials of the curriculum, the barriers were overwhelming. In English departments the "New Criticism" no longer talked to history. In history departments specialization outran the ability to bring together the art, sociology, and literature of a people in a way that illuminated and expressed its political and economic history. Professors of French were virtuously suspicious of any movement that would make the declining modern languages, including French, more popular. History of art departments were enjoying all the growth that they could manage without entering freely into the wholesale development of various area programs.

Student-created majors promised imaginative alternatives to departmental programs of concentration, but faculties were cautious in releasing students from tradition and exposing themselves to new burdens. Students designed their majors in a significant and fulfilling adventure at Justin Morrill College, where, on reaching junior year, each student was required to create a major with the guidance of a faculty advisor. At a very few places—St. John's, Sarah Lawrence, and New College in Florida among them—the concentration problem was solved by having no major at all. The major, however, was in no danger.[22]

If alternatives to the traditional major were to make any serious headway, some powerful practices would have to go. Colleges and universities would have to organize their faculties on some bureaucratic principle other than the department or greatly reduce faculty control over the curriculum or persuade graduate schools of arts and sciences to relax their indirect but inhibiting influence on efforts to reform the undergraduate course of study. Departments had grown naturally as efficient groupings of discrete centers of knowledge and faculty specialization. They had provided logical organizational structure for passing out money and rationalizing the curriculum. But they also became imperial in their power and their grasp. Unless handsomely funded and courageously defended, efforts to launch courses and programs outside the departmental structure generally failed. Without anyone's quite intending it, the major became as restricting and narrowing as the old prescribed curriculum.

Concentration proved a suitable target for reform of a kind that did not rely simply on curricular regulations as a corrective: advising. Curricular guidance, aptitude testing, and career counseling had been unnecessary services in the era of the old college, but they were a natural outgrowth of concentration, the elective system, experimental psychology, and vocationalism. Any pretense that these services were peripheral to the educational experience rested on professorial ignorance or arrogance. Students needed such help in order to make the most of the course of study, even if the professors did not. The emergence of a profession of student personnel administrators was one aspect of the bureaucratic rationalization made necessary by institutional growth and the explosion of knowledge, but it was also a response to student bewilderment in an environment deprived of the certainty, paternalism, and limited horizons of the old college.

Guidance and testing services were strongest in the great state institutions, where vocationalism had received an open and sincere welcome and where middle-class aspirations perhaps most required the helpful assistance of knowledgeable professionals. Colleges and universities most friendly to liberal learning were least generous in their provision of guidance and testing. A number of conceits supported their niggardliness, among them the notion that all liberal arts major programs were equal in delivering the education appropriate to an educated person. Theoretically, this notion was indisputable, but it did not confront the appropriateness of a particular major for a particular student. A relative lack of support for organized guidance in the strong liberal arts institutions may have been nothing more than an unconscious admission that the curriculum was not really what it was all about. These colleges that were most successful in resisting the preprofessional and career orientation that called out for guidance had something to offer quite as important as career preparation. At these institutions, students had no special need for professional counseling. They had only to take a deep breath and plunge into an environment from which they would derive influence, image, label, association with the right people, invitation into or confirmation of membership in the "establishment," in the power centers of America. What could a student personnel administrator do that was not better accomplished by membership in Skull and Bones at Yale, St. Anthony at Penn or Virginia, or membership on the football team at Harvard? Who needed guidance who could say, "I went to Amherst" or "I went to Smith"? Elsewhere, though, counsel was imperative.

Every improvement in concentration, however, whether clarifying a student's individual program or strengthening that program's interdisciplinary scope, drew attention to the failure of the curriculum to support or define a general education. Curriculum planners, professors watching out for their own special interests, and students readying themselves for an uncertain job market designed programs for concentration more easily than they did for breadth. A 1944 Macalester College catalogue defined the goals of general education as "social competence, self-realization, cultivation of the arts of thinking and communication of ideas, acquaintance with the main fields of significant knowledge, and development of a 'Christian philosophy of life.'" These goals it distinguished from the goals of special education: "Knowledge of those areas of the organized work of the world to which the individual is adapted or adaptable" and "progressive adaptation of the student's education to his emerging aptitudes and probable career opportunities."[23]

The language was a bit pompous, but there could be little argument about whether these were the goals that had become attached to the undergraduate curriculum: self-realization, a sense of one's origins, jobs—the creation of human beings whose inner and outer lives were an integrated expression of self and society. Concentration and distribution provided the formula by which the special and the general were supposed to be achieved, and, while it seemed that special purpose was more successfully served than was general purpose, that advantage of the special over the general may only have been a matter of appearance. If the professors did not really know what courses could best fulfill the general goals, did they, on the other hand, really make much effort to determine the career aptitudes of their students, to explore their interests, or even to understand the manner in which the society made career opportunities available to young men and women?

The issue before the colleges and universities was stated over and over again by college and university presidents, by deans, by curriculum committees: "The central problem is . . . relevant breadth versus a limited and dangerously irresponsible competence."[24] With few exceptions, however, attention was regularly paid to improving the conditions under which the curriculum fulfilled its responsibilities to breadth, as if "limited and dangerously irresponsible competence" could be corrected by providing it with an appropriate environment of general courses. Breadth was supported by the general education movement; depth, specialization, concentration took care of themselves. Concentration was the bread and butter of the vast majority of the professors, the style they knew and approved, the measure of departmental strength and popularity. Breadth, distribution, and general education were the hobby horses of new presidents, ambitious deans, and well-meaning humanists of the sort who were elected to curriculum committees by colleagues as a gesture of token support for the idea of liberal learning. When that gesture collided with the interests of department and the major field, only occasionally did the general prevail over the special.

Dramatic experiments in general education, books and pamphlets explaining the need and extolling a plan, even a widespread wish that something might be done to compensate for the loss of unity and shared learning did not succeed in changing the focus of the curriculum from the special to the general. Where large universities created colleges of general studies, the new colleges did not lead to the transformation of the universities. Where highly publicized general education requirements reshaped the course of study in the 1940s and 1950s, less publicized erosion of those requirements took place in the 1960s and 1970s. When a faculty reached the agreement necessary to change the curriculum in any fundamental way, specialization was the most likely beneficiary. Senior projects, senior theses, reading courses, independent study, honors programs, and more demanding term papers, while narrowing the gap between the undergraduate course and the graduate school, threw further out of balance the special and general elements of the curriculum.[25]

If concentration imposed on the course of study its own unin-
tended consequences, distribution involved professors everywhere in
a sort of open academic dishonesty. In many places breaking the curriculum into three or four divisions and expecting every student to
partake of each was simply a device for requiring students to enroll in
science courses they would otherwise have preferred to avoid or, occasionally, in fields overstaffed with senior faculty.

Although there may not have been two colleges and universities
in the country with exactly the same distribution requirements and
opportunities, distribution generally applied to the first two years of
the undergraduate program and followed one of two patterns. Students were required either to take certain core general courses or else
to select unspecified courses in various subject areas brought together
in groups or divisions. Amherst, Columbia, the Residential College of
the University of Michigan, and Justin Morrill College of Michigan
State University became identified with the core approach. Most institutions, however, served distribution through groups and divisions,
and the tendency was for colleges that began with core courses to
move to groups and for those that began with many requirements to
move to fewer requirements. Eckerd College in Florida in eleven years
moved from eleven to four required courses, the decline being a measure of the difficulty of supporting distribution in an academic environment so much more hospitable to concentration.[26]

Even distribution through groups presented curriculum planners with formidable problems. No consensus existed on how to
divide subjects among groups or how to define groups. Some faculties
regarded history and philosophy as social sciences; others grouped
them with humanistic studies. Agreement was lacking on whether
subject matter or method was the significant differentiating factor in
the assignment of courses to groups. Whether the goals of distribution were more readily achieved through specially designed general
courses or generally oriented specialized courses or through regular
courses was a matter of endless debate. Not everyone accepted the
assumption that taking a course or two in any artificially designed
group was an adequate substitute for or introduction to the rest of the
group.[27]

In the face of clear evidence that they did not know how to
achieve distribution, faculties fell easily into the practice of support-

ing what they did know how to do, with the consequence that students were able to pursue a course of study at a sophisticated level of concentration and were also freer to learn what they were interested in. The price they paid for the failure of distribution to support any really meaningful general education was large. The burdens and expectations carried by the concept of distribution were unquestionably unreasonable, but its failure to deliver any magic unity of knowledge and coherent order to the curriculum certified a loss of the shared learning and common curricular experience that had once been a defining characteristic of an educated person and an instrument for transmitting the culture's intellectual and moral heritage.[28]

Its worst failure occurred in the sciences. Why professors of science developed few courses that were appropriate to the general education of nonscientists was a mystery, but the evidence would suggest that they did not care, that they had carved out prestigious territory of their own, and that, with the help of professional societies and graduate and professional schools, they had been able to use outside influence to support for themselves departures and exemptions from the course of study as generally stated. When Yale moved into groups and concentration and distribution, early in the twentieth century, the scientists were allowed to establish, as a distribution requirement, any two sciences, at least one with a laboratory. The Yale scientists cared not at all for distribution, nor for the scientific literacy of students majoring in subjects outside their division. When, in 1933, the distribution requirement in science was reduced to a year of science, with or without a laboratory, Yale was not registering a perverse hostility toward science, although there may have been those who thought so. Yale scientists simply could not and would not accommodate themselves to the intentions of distribution. Their success in making science altogether incomprehensible to all but those for whom it was a major field was a curious source of self-congratulation, but it was a success that academic scientists widely shared.[29]

Scientific illiteracy became a characteristic of college-educated Americans some time toward the middle of the twentieth century, if not before. The old course of study, in the eighteenth and nineteenth centuries, had managed to recognize science as of sufficient importance to give it room enough even to undermine revealed religion and to impart some understanding of natural and physical laws. By 1976 the course of study, in its failure to achieve even the minimum goals of distribution, required students to accept on faith concepts and ideas of no less importance than the now-discarded articles of faith that had supported both chapel and curriculum in the old college. Evangelical fervor had kept the nonprofessing out of chapel and prayer meeting. What style, what dimension of professional arrogance, encouraged the scientists to use the distribution requirements as a cover for their own indifference to general education? What were the conditions that allowed their intense professional commitment to obscure the damage they were doing to science as an element in the understanding of an educated man or woman?

Undaunted by the meager results of distribution and unwilling to accept defeat, the general education movement persisted in its intention to keep alive the romantic image of an educated person. It could not oppose specialization without condemning the course of study to irrelevancy and frivolousness, for without specialization, without the refined and deep study that specialization encouraged, modern society was impossible.[30] General education had to make peace with specialization if it was to succeed in compensating for the narrowness that made specialization so dehumanizing, divisive, and incapable of providing any common ground or bond among educated people. General education both in purpose and process sought to unite "a man with his fellow man" just as specialization divided "men according to their individual competences."[31]

Between 1920 and 1940 at least thirty colleges and universities adopted programs in general education, considerably influenced by the pioneering programs at Reed and Columbia.[32] At Reed general education benefited from organization of the faculty in divisions instead of departments. Two frameworks of freshman and sophomore courses, one embracing literature and social science and one mathematics and natural science, focused on man's social and biological heritage in the freshman year and on contemporary society in the sophomore year. Concentration was provided by majors in the junior and senior years.[33] Columbia's freshman course in contemporary civilization, essentially a survey of the rise of Europe, was widely copied. Its own program was perfected in the 1920s and 1930s, but, for all of its identification with the idea of core courses and a required basic general education, Columbia could not achieve in the natural sciences the kind of breadth and understanding that it accomplished with its core courses in the humanities and social studies. An excessive concern with prerequisites and preprofessional requirements, a shortage of scientists capable of seeing science as an aspect of culture, and a stubbornness and rigidity that seemed to apply everywhere except in the laboratory enabled Columbia's scientists to resist what may have been Columbia's most successful curricular innovation.[34]

Elsewhere the search for common ground created new programs and new courses. At the University of Oregon in 1928 an imaginative president, Arnold Bennett Hall, reorganized his faculty into four divisions—exact sciences, biological sciences, social sciences, and arts and letters—each with a required freshman year general course. At Oregon a freshman also took courses intended to assure a basic competence in the languages of modern learning—English, mathematics, and a modern language; sophomores moved into electives opened up by their freshman general courses.[35] At Denison in Ohio core courses, at first optional but later required, took the form of "Introduction to the Forms of the Fine Arts" in 1939 and "Problems of Peace and Postwar Reconstruction" in 1942. The final course of what would have been a trio of divisional offerings in general education never happened: Denison's scientists refused to cooperate.[36] In July 1943, a required humanities course for freshmen entered the curriculum at Wesleyan in Connecticut, the product of war, consideration for the psychological needs of the college's small wartime civilian enrollment, and the enthusiasm of a band of academic generalists on the faculty that included Victor Butterfield and Nathan Pusey. After the war Wesleyan created a cluster of freshman and upper-class general courses in humanities, social sciences, biological science, and physical sciences.[37]

Until President James B. Conant of Harvard appointed a faculty committee on "the objectives of a general education in a free society" in 1943, college and university faculties were able to avoid the general education movement and congratulate themselves on being beyond the influence of some of its more bizarre expressions.[38] Once the Harvard Committee had issued its report in 1945, however, the prestige of the country's oldest and most influential university was committed to the search for some way to provide a general education for the citizens of an atomistic, necessarily specialized, and unavoidably complex society. A landmark document in a way, the Harvard Report of 1945 was an effort to put back into the curriculum certain qualities and values that fell out of it when history repudiated the Yale Report of 1828. It represented an effort on the part of the nation's greatest university to confront the social and political forces of mid century America and to write a prescription for sustaining the liberal tradition with a curriculum that recognized the legitimacy of individual interests and talents while it at the same time established a common bond of general learning.

The Harvard Report was addressed to a society that was in the process of confirming its alienation from the tradition, heritage, and common belief with which education had once been associated. Confronted with evidence that the colleges and universities had lost control over their own course of study and over that of the American high school, the Harvard committee concerned itself with general education as a remedy to class divisiveness, as a thread throughout all the years of formal education, and as a common bonding device for high school students destined for different futures. In its recognition of the victory of the high school over university authorities and the consequent damage to liberal learning, it acknowledged the failure of President Eliot, the College Entrance Examination Board, and others to constrict the high school to a college preparatory focus. It pretended to put over two thousand years of intellectual history into fewer than a dozen words: "Science has implemented the humanism which classicism and Christianity have proclaimed."[39] And it accepted as its own the by then widely understood distinction between general and special education:

> *General education* . . . is used to indicate that part of a student's whole education which looks first of all to his life as a responsible human being and citizen; while the term *special education* indicates that part which looks to the student's competence in some occupation.[40]

Harvard's "Red Book," as it was called, was an act of public service, a statesmanlike warning that the decline of a privileged class of broadly trained leaders and their displacement by a democracy of equal citizens had placed in jeopardy the capacity of modern societies, especially the United States, "to make decisions . . . with perspective and a sense of standards."[41] In urging a revitalization of general education, Harvard proposed to democratize what had once been the education of a gentleman and an aristocrat and make it the education essential to the responsibilities of every citizen.

Harvard's 1945 warning that American democracy and social stability were threatened by a shift in political power from the educated few to the unenlightened many provided a new impetus for general education, and its own cafeterialike approach to the problem of how to serve up general education to the postwar generations was easier to imitate than the finely designed core courses developed by Columbia. In 1946, Yale, in a package of curricular reforms that was characterized by variety but not by focus, invited freshmen with scores of 750 in the Scholastic Aptitude Test to enter on a two-year program of required courses designed as a search for coherent learning and an experience in common intellectual endeavor.[42]

In 1947 Amherst, in a major curricular revision, introduced three two-year sequence courses in the natural sciences, social sciences, and the humanities. By 1955 Amherst's commitment to general education "had reached a point where the work of the first two . . . years was largely prescribed."[43] One of the adornments of the Amherst program was a calculus-physics course chaired by Arnold B. Arons and required of all freshmen; its success as a course that was both general and profitably preparatory for science students was a tribute to the imagination, genius, and dedicated enthusiasm of Arons himself.[44] Everywhere, however—even at Harvard—general education ran out of steam.

The Harvard committee had expected to follow its report with the development of three divisional core courses as requirements in general education. That aspiration fell victim to faculty power; no core courses were developed; in each of three divisions—humanities, social sciences, and natural sciences—a half dozen or so courses of uneven originality but of sufficient breadth to be considered general were offered under the rubric of general education. General education requirements at Harvard in 1955 were not exacting: three elementary courses, one selected from each of the three divisional clusters of courses designated as general education courses.[45] In 1975 David Riesman described Harvard's requirements in general education as "minimal, not much more than a mild expectation that a student will take several courses outside his own area of specialization."[46]

In 1955, in rejecting proposed requirements in general education recommended by a special committee headed by Yale's president, A. Whitney Griswold, the Yale course of study committee admitted defeat. It was unwilling to move into a broad scheme of general education in an environment defined by departmental autonomy and extracurricular life, both of which it considered hostile to the success of a program designed to restore the concept of an educated person. "How far," the committee asked, "can any manipulation of the curriculum make intellectual achievement more attractive than these outside activities in the context in which the educational process now operates? . . . How far does the faculty wish to go beyond the curriculum to explore the conditions that foster or impede the achievement of the educational goals which it sets?"[47]

Other faculties moved away from general education with less candor. A 1973 study of curricular reform reported that in the wake of an exceptionally high turnover rate in teaching staff Columbia reduced its core requirements from two years to one. Reed's core requirements were likewise reduced, and at Stevenson College at the University of California at Santa Cruz core course requirements, originally one third of a freshman's course of study, now covered only one ninth of the freshman year. And, while new colleges imparted new enthusiasm to the core course idea, at both Prescott College in Arizona and New College in Florida, which were launched with required core courses, "both programs utterly collapsed due to the difficulties in integrating disciplines and organizing the program, the increased faculty time consumed, and the lack of student interest."[48] At the University of California at Berkeley, after two two-year cycles between 1965 and 1969, Joseph Tussman's experimental college program of core courses for self-selected students was discontinued, the victim of disharmony and an absence of an essential integrating spirit.[49]

General education would never die. Perhaps, also, it could never be made popular. The idea managed to establish itself in a variety of designs in institutions that were new, eccentric, recently saved from extinction, or particularly responsive to the imagination of a leader who had no intention of being denied. In a very real sense, a whole range of institutions in the 1930s and 1940s infused new blood into the concept, but Sarah Lawrence, Bennington, Bard, Chicago under Hutchins, and St. John's under Stringfellow Barr, and the colleges of special design at Wisconsin and Minnesota were models without imitators. Their eccentricity denied them the influence that Cornell and Johns Hopkins had once exerted. The innovative colleges and universities of the 1930s and after ran against the tide, just as Cornell and Johns Hopkins became memorable because they caught up with it. The institutions with a commitment to general education were easy enough to poke fun at and terribly difficult to emulate, but they were also ornaments of liberal learning.

Outside of these institutions that chose to be primarily identified with general education, the idea that had exercised the imagination of the Harvard committee in 1945 made little headway. The generation that took over the executive branch of the United States government in the early 1970s danced around in the minds of the Harvard committee, but these were the people whom they had intended to prevent. It was too late. What was it about major statements from university faculties that made them curiosities before they became repositories of wisdom? Yale in 1828 and Harvard in 1945, both anticipated— and it was there for anyone to read—the administration of Richard Nixon. Yale had warned against powerful materialists; Harvard had hoped to deliver the nation from barbaric individualists. Yet the prescription for prevention—for Yale in 1828, the old course, faculty psychology, and elitist values; for Harvard in 1945, a submersion in tradition and heritage and some sense of common bond strong enough to bring unbridled ego and ambition under control—was more than their contemporaries, probably rightly, would accept.

Formula ran counter to the country's style. Theory outdistanced an earthbound imagination. Yale in 1828 and Harvard in 1945 did not speak the language of the country which they addressed. They may have been "right," but truth was beyond authority. It was a function of process, investigation, and experience. General education, on the other hand, was not an expression of the dominant culture. It spoke for a counterculture that acted as if it were *the* culture, it was an expression of the "establishment."

Even when college and university faculties found themselves accepting English, mathematics, a foreign language, history, some economics and government, natural science, and art and music appreciation as the appropriate intellectual baggage of a generally educated person, they were in no position to establish the level of attainment expected of all students.[50] These subjects smacked of tradition and reliability, and to call them *general education* was to draw attention to the course of study as a school of certification for a predestined white, Anglo-Saxon, Protestant elite.[51] Yet if general education was to serve the needs of newcomers in the struggle for economic and social power, it needed new labels, new arrangements, and new subjects, as well as the reassuring accommodation of specialized learning that possessed some measurable value. A question that escaped the attention of the Harvard committee in 1945 would forever plague those who embraced its arguments and its curricular designs: What evidence supported the notion that the world would be better off if everyone had been graduated from Harvard College shortly before the election of President Eliot?

The Harvard Report of 1945 knew what was best for everyone, quite as much as a similar self-assurance (or wisdom) had found its way into the Yale Report of 1828. Its failure to transform the undergraduate curriculum was no more an expression of institutional weakness than was Yale's failure to prevent curricular reform a century before. The course of study was beyond the control of the curriculum designers in New Haven or Cambridge. General education, whether defined by Jeremiah Day at Yale or James Bryant Conant at Harvard, expressed a belief in a relatively fixed moment of curricular truth. Both versions were subject to the same weaknesses. They invited superficiality, conformity, and sterility; they thwarted intellectual independence and differences of ability and interest; they risked undergraduate reaction against imposed learning. In addition, by 1945 Harvard proposed a formula that required a staff of instructors with an inhuman degree of cooperativeness and availability, as well as a willingness to venture out of established territories of special knowledge into the uncharted and the general.[52] Nothing in the Harvard Report of 1945 was going to keep language from being taught by linguists, science by scientists, and history by historians: They were all, by virtue of *their* educations and predispositions, poorly equipped to make their classrooms an experience in humanistic learning.[53]

Unquestionably someone somewhere said so, but even without the evidence, general education came under further suspicion as being un-American. Howard Mumford Jones, in a 1955 attack on core courses and general education, an attack that did not immediately carry the day among his Harvard colleagues, glorified the "free elective system" as "the untrammeled right of the undergraduate to make his own mistakes."[54] Jones's remarks were a particularly open license for learning and growth in an era dominated by the restrictions and limits imposed on intellectual inquiry by such barbarians as Joseph McCarthy, Eugene Jenner, and their distinguished apologists. By 1955 in the United States "mistakes" had become the subject of congressional loyalty investigations; Howard Mumford Jones suggested, instead, that they were an appropriate expression of learning. He saw general education as a barrier to the "expression of talent," and in a quiet sort of way he used the *Atlantic Monthly,* Harvard's and Boston's old means of keeping in touch with themselves, to relieve himself of a rage that would not be contained:

> The new required courses are . . . processing courses. . . . They are directed at the average, the medium, the median, or the mean, whatever one's statistical philosophy devises. The difficulty is that in these enormous surveys instruction, like the radius vector of the planets, sweeps over equal areas in equal times. Meanwhile those who are not average are bored.[55]

Jones did not like the democratic implications of general education. If the loss of quality and excellence was the price of making room at Harvard and elsewhere for the unenlightened, he preferred another course. He cast his vote for encouraging talent to find itself.

General education was not brought down only by those who shared the views of Howard Mumford Jones nor by the various inherent difficulties that made its 1945 Harvard version in some ways indistinguishable from the 1828 Yale version. General education required of its advocates a posture that approached the ridiculous. As Joseph Ben-David described them, they "claimed for themselves the monopolistic authority of experts in matters that were very often beyond the pale of any expertise."[56] At a moment in human history when igno-

rance was accepted as an appropriate point of departure in the search
for truth, they insisted on starting with truth. Whether they intended
it or not, they proposed to use general education as a device for hurrying the aspiring middle class into the enjoyment of wealth and leisure
that they did not yet possess. General education may even have been a
device for enslaving or perhaps simply emasculating the middle
class. Who knows? It certainly was not necessary for the young graduates of Groton at Harvard and their contemporaries from Thacher at
Stanford or St. Paul's at Yale. Their needs required attention, but
general education was not invented for them: It was what the old New
England boarding schools had been offering for the better part of a
century as college preparation.

As colleges and universities learned to live with the consequences of curricular breakdown and with the inadequacies of pre-
scriptive remedies, they were led through periods of at least small-
scale reassessing, perfecting, improving, sometimes prodded either by
foundation grants, models of innovation elsewhere, declining enrollments, or by the gnawing recognition that they simply could do
better.

In the early postwar years, for example, the American Council
on Education, the President's Commission on Higher Education, the
philanthropic foundations, and the Congress joined forces to counteract the almost exclusively Western orientation of the curriculum.
The emergence of the United States as a world power, the creation of
the United Nations, and the instability of peace in the atomic world
all argued against a return to the political and cultural isolationism
that had characterized the United States before the war. Develop-
mental economics appeared in economics programs; history departments added non-Western courses to their major requirements;
Russian joined the modern languages. Area studies programs proliferated; Agency for International Development (AID) contracts moved
professors on and off campus, invigorating instruction with new perspectives; government funding and foundation grants sent American
students abroad and brought foreign students to the United States.[57]
In these departures, the curriculum was both an expression of government policy and an expression of academic perception of the need for
making the course of study less parochial.

In the early 1950s the Mathematical Association of America, with encouragement from the Office of Naval Research and the National Research Council, began the series of institutes and other activities, later sponsored by the National Science Foundation, that undertook to redesign the undergraduate mathematics curriculum. Russia's successful launching of its Sputnik in 1957 not only accelerated interest in science and support for curricular reform in the high schools and colleges; it also led to the National Defense Education Act of 1958, which provided government funds for the support of foreign language study and of area studies as well. In the 1960s the National Science Foundation supported curricular reform in mathematics and physics and encouraged geology departments to enlarge their commitment to oceanography. Significant grants by the Ford Foundation in 1967 advanced ecology and courses with an environmental orientation as subjects of pressing relevance and of appropriate concern in a liberal curriculum.[58] Afro-American or Black Studies acknowledged in the 1960s not just the psychological needs of an accelerating enrollment of black students in what had been essentially white colleges and universities. Such programs, like the area studies programs and the broadening of major programs to include non-Western materials, were also an admission of the degree to which the curriculum had ignored or denied the cultural and historical meaning for blacks and Western culture of the legacy of racism, slavery, and colonialism, as well as the existence of vital traditions outside the Western framework. Women's Studies challenged one discipline after another—history, English, psychology—to welcome women into curricular equality with men: Women became a subject.

The most unobtrusive curricular development of the twentieth century, in contrast, was the recognition of esthetic values and creativity as legitimate components of the course of study. A combination of Puritan and frontier morality had placed restraints on the fine arts as appropriate sources of pleasure or expressions of talent. At Wesleyan in 1831 Wilbur Fisk had warned that cultivation of the arts led to "excessive refinement, luxury, and licentiousness," and he then gave a demonstration of how the classics were used to deny the arts entry to the curriculum. "I have no doubt," he said, that the high proportion of men who excelled in the fine arts in ancient Greece and Rome "hastened the corruption and final overthrow of these states."[59]

In 1915 Arthur Twining Hadley had had a different problem with the fine arts; he could not figure out how to use them in encouraging measurable competitive values. "How," he asked, "are we to test the appreciation of pictures?"[60] At Wesleyan music achieved departmental status in 1925, art history in 1926. Although a few courses in art and music supplemented courses in history and classical archaeology early in the century at Yale, the fine arts moved slowly into academic respectability. Yale offered its first major program in art history in 1938.[61]

Like so many other curricular developments, the ascendancy of the fine arts was a measure of the decline of the classics. Western institutions, the first to unburden themselves of Latin and Greek, were also friendlier, even in the nineteenth century, to creative work in art and music. Coeducation and the role of the colleges and universities in training teachers for the public schools underwrote some of the growth of the arts in western institutions. Was there also, in their greater commitment to course work in art and music, as well as in their enthusiasm for adding collections of pictures and plaster casts to institutional resources, a desire to prove that culture did not disappear as it moved West?

Before the fine arts could become standard elements of the curriculum, either as experiences in enjoyment and creativity or as subjects of serious intellectual inquiry, colleges and universities had to release themselves from the inherited suspicion of the arts that a clerical past had imposed upon them. Defining the arts as essentially the province of women was another barrier not easily overcome. The rise of the arts, however, benefited from philanthropy that was prepared to acknowledge a vacuum in the curricular offerings of most institutions, a vacuum that became embarrassing as the country itself moved beyond the conquest of the continent to a greater sophistication and maturity. Institutional rivalry also made new programs in the arts, quite as much as football, a measure of prestige and success.

In 1918 the University of Rochester arranged to have its charter changed so that it could accept from George F. Eastman his gift of an Institute of Musical Art. In 1919 at Miami University in Ohio the practice originated of having prominent artists take up temporary residence in academic communities as an encouragement to artistic creativity and appreciation. After World War I, with financial support from the Carnegie Corporation, the Association of American Colleges encouraged its members to develop programs in art history and art. By 1932 more than 200 art departments bore testimony to the victory of esthetic values and creative expression over the fears and prejudices with which Wilbur Fisk and Arthur Twining Hadley and others had narrowed the curricular definition of human life.[62]

Creativity presented the colleges and universities with problems different from those presented by programs in art history or the history of music, both of which, while clearly moving the curriculum into virtually unexplored esthetic territory, were nonetheless also bathed in the mystique of scientific research, specialization, and scholarship. Creativity called for different impulses, different environments, different measurements from those to which the colleges and universities on the whole were accustomed. Creative writing, drama, dance, and film made their way into the curriculum often obliquely and seldom without institutional condescension. Creative writing was supported by a tradition that included the old courses in rhetoric and the activities of the literary societies, but drama, in one historian's view, at least until after World War II, had to be bootlegged into the curriculum by language departments and departments of English, although there were exceptions.[63] Dance entered the curriculum of the University of Wisconsin in 1926 and was given for credit in 92 colleges by 1948, but the hold of dance was not yet secure: In 1969, of 110 institutions offering a dance major, 77 were under the auspices of physical education departments.[64] Film became an academic subject in the 1920s; the University of Southern California offered the first film major in 1932. As an interest of the youth culture of the 1960s, film underwent remarkable growth. In 1971 forty-seven colleges offered a bachelor's degree in film; 4,600 film majors took courses in film appeciation and history, film production, as well as theory and criticism.[65]

To the extent that these developments in the fine arts and the creative arts were not isolated into discrete schools and degree programs, to the extent that they began to achieve academic respectability in general B.A. programs and took their place as equals among the more traditional subjects, the curriculum was being subjected to new purpose. In these courses and programs the idea of an educated person was not being narrowed, as had been the case when vocationalism and specialization displaced the classical course, but expanded to include dimensions of human experience that had in the past been largely neglected or denied. Conceivably they portended, as Laurence Veysey has suggested, "a redefinition of the liberal arts curriculum away from the genteel tradition and toward identification with critical intellect and creativity."[66]

The United States was not about to become a nation of painters, writers, dancers, actors, musicians, potters, weavers, and filmmakers, nor could the appearance of the *New York Review of Books* be taken as evidence that everyone else was about to become an informed and brilliant critic of the creative work of others. As the country moved into its third century, however, perhaps less confident than it once was about either its ability or right to sway the destiny of mankind, and therefore, perhaps wiser, it also revealed a developing self-confidence about itself as a place where men and women might move beyond the world of work to new dimensions of experience and creativity. Here as elsewhere, the curriculum registered new directions and accommodated new purposes as it also shaped them.

Another unobtrusive revolution may be lurking in the competence-based education movement, a development of the 1970s that was responsive to demands for an education that was characterized by utility, institutional accountability, time-free patterns, and lack of prescription. Its focus was on the development and assessment of "specific human abilities rather than . . . [on] a set of studies with inhering liberal qualities."[67] Dean Bob Knott of Mars Hill College, one of the few institutions where the movement took hold, described a competence-based curriculum as "one where the competences expected of all graduates are agreed upon and defined, and courses or experiences are designed to assist the student in becoming competent . . . [and] sets of evaluative criteria for each competence . . . define the proficiency levels required for successful attainment."[68]

If in some ways the competence-based education movement seemed to be using new language to describe the traditional goals of liberal learning, the curriculum appropriate to those old goals, and the practices in support of that curriculum, were not traditional. At Sterling College in Kansas the curriculum was divided into nine competences that students might demonstrate in courses, by examination, or through experiences. At Mars Hill students were required to demonstrate their ability to "formulate and examine purposes . . . design and act upon means of executing those purposes, and . . . assess the consequences of such actions." Since students could not be expected to demonstrate such abilities unless they were skilled in communication, possessed an understanding of scientific method, and had developed critical esthetic perceptions, these competences had also to be achieved. A knowledge of self, a comprehension of ethics, and a synoptic outlook were also expected to assist students in demonstrating and assessing the process of their own maturation and in achieving some level of expertise.[69] In the 1970s competence-based education may have seemed as outrageous as George Ticknor's proposals of the 1820s were to most of his contemporaries, but the movement may have held the seeds of structural reform, synthesis, and sanity that the curriculum badly needed.

All the curricular experimentation, all the discussion of creativity and competence, however, could not affect instruction by reducing the centrality of the lecture.[70] Even as seminars and tutorials increased their role as alternatives to the lecture, especially in colleges and universities with highly selected student bodies, the lecture strengthened its position. Under the impact of new technology and numbers, closed-circuit television lifted the constraints that the size of lecture halls had placed on class size. Someone quipped: "The ideal college is Mark Hopkins on one end of a television tube and a student on the other." Economically, the lecture became recognized as the curricular device that paid for the seminars and small classes. Provosts, deans, and computers broadcast the message to the professors: Some must teach big if any are to teach small. The lecture was now grounded in the economic theory of educational management.

Doubtful as it was as an encouragement to the kind of research experience or to the humanistic and moralistic orientation possible in small classes, the lecture survived. Yet there was something contrary about these authoritative fifty-minute performances in a community of learning. In the English universities student and tutor sustained the learning process; the lecture was not taken seriously. In American colleges and universities, however, where professors tended to equate the lecture with learning, they seldom convinced the students and in the process (except where the "great lecturer" prevailed) encouraged contempt not only for the lecture but for learning itself.

Alternatives to lectures, particularly such variations as those developed in the 1960s and 1970s—freshman seminars, independent study, and pass-fail courses—were, in the view of David Riesman and Christopher Jencks, more readily sustained in institutions "composed almost entirely of competent, diligent students."[71] Such institutions were surely few enough to assure a long life to the lecture and all of its faults as an instrument of learning.

As unsettling as it was to the serenity of college and university campuses, the student movement of the 1960s wrought no great transformation either in the curriculum or in the lecture system. The movement, whatever its source, was not an attack on the curriculum or on instruction as such. For the student leaders it was often a search for political power within the university. If they lodged complaints against the curriculum as an expression of their discontent, it was no wonder. That was a student's ancient privilege, but their complaints —the impersonality of large courses, the neglect of students by faculty, the absence of a sufficiently overriding intellectual quality to the university environment—rested on conditions that were not new. What was new was an unpopular war that threatened their lives and their respect for institutions. What was new was the extent to which colleges and universities had become "detention centers" for hundreds of thousands of young men and women for whom society held out no meaningful employment as an alternative.[72] These were environmental hazards that the course of study had not previously encountered, but if it did not survive the encounter unscathed, neither did it, except in rare instances, succumb to student attack. Why?

Certainly the most important reason was the degree to which the curriculum was not what the college and university experience in the United States was all about. What young radical (conservative or liberal), confronted by a parent or lover could honestly say, "Oh—the reason I blew up the science lab? I hated the curriculum!" Colleges and universities, before the events that scarred Berkeley, Harvard, Columbia, Kent State, and Wisconsin, had already bent themselves toward the needs and aspirations of a new generation of able students. Perhaps too slowly and too haltingly, but just the same relentlessly, the curriculum was being readjusted, often against the wishes of reluctant professors, in order to accommodate a student body that for the first time was being subjected to standards of admissions sufficiently meaningful that some colleges and universities began to be known as selective.

In 1958, when Clark Kerr became president of the University of California, the university was composed of eight campuses or centers and some others on the way, but it was in no sense as responsive, imaginative, solicitous of every student's particular potentialities as it would be ten years later. By then the University of California included new campuses at San Diego, Santa Cruz, and Irvine, the latter being an answer to the provocative question: What should an agricultural and mechanical (A & M) college founded right now be doing? In the aftermath of the 1964 student rebellion at Berkeley curricular change was more easily facilitated. The four-quarter system encouraged a reorganization of courses, even required that some old lecture notes be thrown away. For a while, under the threat of crisis, professors, discovering a whole range of common interests—themselves, students, an overlapping of knowledge and unsolved mysteries—created new interdepartmental offerings. For four years Joseph Tussman was given his experimental college to work with. It failed.[73] One of the problems at Berkeley was the refusal of Clark Kerr's constituency, including a majority of the regents, to catch the message of his 1963 Harvard lectures on *The Uses of the University*.[74] On the eve of his confrontation with the unleashed irrationality of the student movement, Kerr clarified the context in which rebellion would take place, not only at Berkeley but wherever the traditional university had been dramatically transformed. His message was discomforting and challenging, and it could not have been clearer: We are no longer a university, we are a multiversity, a complex of competing purposes and expectations, with all of the threats to accustomed procedures and expectations that the coinage of a new concept suggested.

Students stirred to protest, sometimes out of conviction and sometimes out of expectation, did not have to designate the curriculum as the target of their unhappiness. Their elders had never heard of students who disrupted the campus for any reason other than unhappiness with dining-hall food. Protesting students were given the benefit of their parents' ignorance; their professors were happy to follow the tendencies of their own interests—more flexibility (fewer classes), fewer prerequisites (more students), the illusion of greater coherence (good catalogue material). And certainly on some campuses curricular reform was clearly a response to student pressure. Brown's promising but unfulfilled reforms of 1969 created a blueprint that was in some ways a perfect document of student perceptions everywhere: exciting freshman seminars, abolition of distribution requirements, elaborate counseling system, interdisciplinary focus, student-designed majors, substitution of evaluation for grades, courses for seniors given by senior professors free from departmental affiliation. In 1971 at Amherst student complaints played an essential role in the faculty's decision to wipe out all general education requirements.[75]

There were, too, clear and unmistakable intrusions on accepted academic practice by daring students who sensed the nervousness, even the weakness, of the colleges and universities in the presence of a movement that would destroy the notion that college and university authorities were ever really neutral—or should be. The student movement did not politicize the curriculum, as was sometimes alleged, but it did politicize the colleges and universities. And perhaps it also, unconsciously but dramatically, attested to the vitality of the values and concerns of humane learning. The authorities who spoke out against the war and against injustice were accused of being political by the conservative elements of their constituencies. By these definitions Kingman Brewster at Yale should have kept quiet and lost the university. He spoke, saved Yale, and only lost untabulated dollars, the price of withheld generosity and misguided alumni power. The students, at Yale and elsewhere, only demanded and received some evidence that their institutions were alive and liberal. The extracurriculum now included the presidents.

Some very strange events occurred. Harvard's chapter of Students for a Democratic Society gained approval in 1968 for a course taught by two young faculty radicals and staffed by graduate students, undergraduates, and off-campus romantics. In 1969 the Harvard faculty in an unprecedented gesture accorded to students a role in running the department of Afro-American Studies, designing its courses, and choosing its faculty.[76] Students elsewhere, on their insistence, began to appear at faculty meetings that professors had given up attending. Undergraduates, in their leap to power and community, found neither when they landed. Faculty power was secure; community was elusive; the curriculum was a demonstration in inertia.

Two young men, veterans of the era, 1970 graduates of Brandeis, subjected twenty-six colleges to inspection in the years soon after their graduation.[77] They checked the health of general education and of concentration. They inquired as to practices in advising, examining, and grading. They wanted to know what senior year was like and whether a student could put together for himself a course of study without being brought into harness by a department. Arthur Levine and John Weingart roamed broadly. Their study included the experimental, both old and new: Antioch, Eckerd at St. Petersburg, New College at Sarasota, Justin Morrill at Michigan State, Prescott College in Arizona, St. John's, Sarah Lawrence, the Residential College of the University of Michigan, and the University of Wisconsin at Green Bay. They visited established institutions from which the message had been broadcast that something significant was happening to the curriculum: Bowdoin, Brandeis, Brown, California Institute of Technology, Columbia, Harvard, Massachusetts Institute of Technology, Stanford, Trinity, Tufts, the University of California at Berkeley and at Santa Cruz, Wesleyan, and Yale. It was a sobering experience:

> We found that students do not participate in programs that permit them to plan their own education. Interdisciplinary and team-taught programs often fail because faculty do not want to teach them. When faculty do teach them, they are unable to integrate their disciplines or to work together. Written evaluations are also unsuccessful because faculty find them too burdensome, students are not interested in them, and graduate schools dislike them.[78]

Surely an element of their disappointment was a sense of disillusionment appropriate to their age, but the reporting was accurate. Their investigations might have been more far-reaching. They might have delved into reading periods, winter study programs, Hiram's intensive course system, the surviving versions of manual labor systems, the expensive and elegant efforts of Harvard's houses and Yale's colleges to walk the thin line between correcting their environments and subverting their universities. There were other institutions, including Hampshire in Massachusetts, New England College in New Hampshire, and the remaining campuses of the University of California, that waited in readiness to be studied and to instruct. Yet could the results have differed greatly? The curriculum could be nudged, it could be varied, it could read the daily newspaper, but in any fundamental way it could not be hurried. Every twenty-two years it might, it is true, be thoroughly reconstituted, but this was the kind of revolution Americans had learned to live with, the kind that no one noticed.

The nation, celebrating the two hundredth anniversary of its birth, thus entered its third century with an array of colleges and universities that defied classification and with a curriculum that had once certified an elite but was now being designed to make room, literally, for everyone. For how many years had American colleges been Harvard, Yale, Princeton, and honest if pale imitations that followed the flow of settlement and national purpose into the South and West? When state universities and land-grant colleges in the decades after the Civil War had added a significant new dimension to a tradition that had been nurtured by church and community, going to college had undergone redefinition, as it would again and again in the twentieth century. Junior colleges and community colleges would spell out new designs and place themselves between the high schools and the older institutions as bearers of new purpose, new values, and new courses of study. And innovative colleges and universities, in the tradition of Jefferson's Virginia, would draw attention to themselves as models, albeit without imitators.

Experimental institutions, newly constructed or else renovated in order to accommodate novel curricular styles and purpose, had something going for them that seldom attached to the older colleges and universities: They developed into causes. In defending their distinguishing qualities from the indifference and hostility of the great majority, they attracted to their campuses highly motivated likeminded students for whom community esprit did not depend on Saturday's football game. Those that left a mark on curricular history in the past fifty years were engaged in an effort to shift the focus of the course of study from vocations, service, and research to the enjoyment of learning.

Their success, with remarkably diverse curricular styles and emphases, suggested that there were students enough to populate even the most eccentric institutions. Failure of the older and larger colleges and universities to imitate their practices was no measure of their success in demonstrating that the curriculum could be vastly superior to the extracurriculum in enlisting the interests and energies of students.[79] St. John's neoclassical return to a concern with metaphysical first principles, Black Mountain's creation of a community of artists, the more recent development of a course of study with a focus on human encounter and sensibilities at Kresge College of the University of California at Santa Cruz—these were innovations, however admirable or successful, that could not really be incorporated into institutions that were required to remain loyal to the old purposes and that were dominated by professors with a traditional orientation.

Rollins, at Winter Park, Florida, was an old college on the verge of collapse when in 1926 it was turned around by Hamilton Holt, who used an eight-hour day (six hours of classes and two hours of tennis) as an expression of the classical definition of the right use of leisure.[80] St. Stephens College, an old church college, became affiliated with Columbia University, fell under the influence of Columbia Teachers College, and became Bard College in 1935.[81] Bard, as well as a renovated Goddard College in Vermont, and two new colleges for women—Sarah Lawrence in New York (1928) and Bennington in Vermont (1932)—were expressions of the educational philosophy of John Dewey.[82] At these and similarly oriented progressive colleges the course of study was designed around the particular interest of the student; initiative, self-expression, creativity, and independence were the controlling values; elevation of the theory and practice of fine arts to full curricular status, winter field work, a deemphasis on standard evaluating and grading practices, articulation of extracurriculum and curriculum, and a bias against holders of the Ph.D. degree in the recruitment of faculty provided an environment in which self-centered students learned to understand themselves and the society and world of which they were a part.[83]

Colleges with a progressive orientation used individual student interest and talent to achieve the goals of general education. A graduate of Bennington or Sarah Lawrence was expected to have a firmer grasp of herself and a more profound understanding of the context in which she existed than the ordinary college graduate who simply accumulated course credits. Colleges of progressive persuasion and the other innovative institutions did not deliver educations to their students. They required that education be a creative experience, and, with the guidance and limits appropriate to the particular institution, they put students in charge of their own course of study.

Bard, Rollins, and Black Mountain were coeducational. Sarah Lawrence and Bennington were women's colleges and they shared with Scripps and Mills in California and Stephens in Missouri a greater degree of enthusiasm for artistic expression than was even true of other women's colleges. Women students at experimental colleges often found themselves encouraged to develop creative talents that would have been stifled in more traditional institutions.[84] At Bennington and Sarah Lawrence, especially, daughters of the upper class experienced a kind of freedom denied their mothers. As for the young men who appeared at Bard and Rollins and Black Mountain, was not their enrollment a renunciation of society's expectations and an act of self-definition that the traditional institutions denied them?

At the University of Wisconsin and the University of Minnesota two experiments in general education demonstrated that large universities could be innovative, democratic without loss of distinction, and resourceful enough to create single-purpose colleges within the university framework.[85] Accustomed to living with contrary purposes, imaginative universities did not have to subject themselves to reform in order to alter the curriculum; they simply added a college. Alexander Meiklejohn, who had invigorated a surprised Amherst while president, was asked by the University of Wisconsin to give the people of Wisconsin an experiment in general education.[86] The university that had, during the Progressive era, made itself an extension of the state house needed no special license to be experimental. Wisconsin saw itself as an appropriate place to validate the broad faith that sustained the state colleges and state universities as an expression of American idealism. Meiklejohn was the right person to be allowed to try out some ideas that, if they succeeded, would create in Madison a community of learning. By 1927, when the college opened, a mythology had developed around the vanished small colleges of the nineteenth century, and Meiklejohn was willing to see himself as enlisted in an effort to bring back their vanished mystique of learning.

As hard as it was to believe, the curriculum at the Experimental College was utterly lacking in subjects and electives. There were no lectures, no classrooms, just young men and their instructors in conference, in discussion, working their way toward "a community of learning." The college took freshmen into the Athens of Pericles and Plato and took sophomores into contemporary America, not on their way to careers nor on their way to impressive depths of special knowledge. Every element of the program was designed to take young men on a trip of self-discovery. The mystery and delight of being human was its informing and organizing idea.

Meiklejohn's experiment lasted for five years. It was out of this world. Teachers' offices and students' bedrooms occupied the same buildings, and, therefore, because this was the 1930s, the experiment was for men students only. And while it was not possible to transform the dormitories into an environment reminiscent of ancient Athens, Meiklejohn tried valiantly to break through several centuries of curricular encrustations in order to invigorate the respect for learning that had fallen out of the American academic experience. But the environment was hostile. The Experimental College was "hounded to death" by "fraternities, local politicians, and unfriendly professors," by Wisconsin high schools, and by anti-Semitism and efforts to identify the college with communism.[87] Wisconsin's experience in breaking loose from the chains of convention was a disaster for the curriculum; Meiklejohn ventured too far beyond the imagination of his constituency.

At the General College of the University of Minnesota, established in 1932, a two-year program of general studies addressed itself to the challenging problem of what to do for and with young men and women whom the society with some degree of success had labeled as losers.[88] Minnesota's General College students tested poorly, lacked self-confidence, were badly prepared, or had failed elsewhere. Perhaps they were especially appropriate candidates for a curriculum that concerned itself with what it meant to be human. In 1939–40, an enrollment of 1,146 students took courses on such subjects as current reading, how to study, foods and nutrition, house furnishing, and earth and man. While Minnesota's General College could be interpreted as providing a graceful exit from the years of formal education for young men and women of no special talent, it was more than that. It was an assurance to the people of Minnesota that the university cared for everyone, and it was in its own way a magnificent undertaking in general education and an outright rejection of vocationalism. Its purposes and its style were more liberal and humanizing than many an undergraduate major program pursued by likely wearers of Phi Beta Kappa keys. Yet it probably did not deserve to be known as an intellectual community.

That goal was the ambition of Robert Maynard Hutchins in his stormy years as president of the University of Chicago.[89] His arrival at Chicago in 1929 coincided with the beginning of the Great Depression, an event that imposed on all colleges and universities the necessity of allocating resources, establishing priorities, and developing standards consistent with an evaporating financial support. Hutchins recognized in the questions inspired by that necessity the making of an intellectual community. In looking in on itself, the university was required to consider the principles that ordered its activities and informed its judgments. In an effort to break the curriculum loose from an excessive degree of specialization and emphasis on utility, he achieved a dramatic reorganization of the University of Chicago faculty and of the undergraduate college.

For the first time in an American university the responsibilities for undergraduate education were assigned to a faculty that had absolutely no responsibilities for graduate or professional education. The first two years at Chicago, the junior college years, were devoted to general education. Completion of the work of the college was measured by the passing of seven comprehensive examinations, of which five—English composition, humanities, social science, physical science, and biological science—were required. The other two comprehensive examinations were second examinations, calling for a greater depth and wider knowledge, in any two of the four general groups. While the curriculum included survey courses designed to help students to prepare for their comprehensive examinations, a student could take the examinations whenever prepared and without having had to take a corresponding course. Emphasis on the examinations made intellectual achievement rather than the accumulation of course credits the "criterion of academic progress."[90]

Hutchins's reforms at Chicago were imaginative and liberating. They created among the college faculty a vested interest in those two years that did not compete with the demands of departments and scholarship. They turned the focus of the first two years away from the special to the general, and the device of comprehensive examinations in broad general groups led students into a consideration of the principles that guided their experience as human beings. From 1942 to 1954 Chicago awarded an M.A. degree to students who passed the appropriate comprehensive examinations, confirming how far out of step with ordinary patterns Hutchins had been able to lead the university.[91] He even succeeded in abolishing football. One brave institution, however, could not alone create the lycée or gymnasium and give it currency in the United States; the American high school was spread across the land, and the multiversity was on its way. Hutchins nonetheless gave Chicago and all the critics and skeptics whom he failed to convince some lessons on how to encourage a community of learning in an environment unfriendly either to intellectual values or to the requirements of community.

Hutchins did not succeed in convincing either the college faculty or the university faculty that "the heart of any course of study designed for the whole people will be, if education is rightly understood, the same at any time, in any place, under any political, social, or economic conditions."[92] This message, imbedded in a series of lectures delivered at Yale in 1936, beclouded his intentions, for it made his neo-Thomistic metaphysics a target for critics who might otherwise have embraced his hope that Chicago could be transformed into an intellectual community. One of his own faculty, in a 1937 reply to the Yale lectures, characterized them as advocating "a monastic withdrawal to a community of scholars primarily concerned with the elaboration of a discarded metaphysics."[93] Hutchins was at war with the modern temper; his invitation to a return to first principles collided with the scientific style; in arguing that education should be an experience in ordering and understanding the principles of right action he ventured out of the twentieth century.

At St. John's College in Annapolis, Maryland, another nearly bankrupt college awaited the investment of intellectual venture capital.⁹⁴ Two University of Chicago professors who shared Hutchins's metaphysics as well as his dismay at the divorce between contemporary America and its intellectual heritage were given the opportunity to foster the ultimate design in general education. In 1937 Stringfellow Barr and Scott Buchanan moved from Chicago to Annapolis and accomplished a most remarkable feat: They imposed a four-year required curriculum, consisting of 120 so-called great books, on the ailing college in Annapolis and made a success of it. Their design was almost outrageous in its audacity: the elimination of electives; the embrace of classics of Western thought from the Greeks to Darwin and Freud, many of them relegated to a shelf of curiosities by modern scholarship; a faculty of generalists, all with tutorial rank and all required to teach all the great books. St. John's not only paid respect to the intellectual heritage of the modern world and built a community around a shared discussion of the problems and questions that confronted man because he was man; St. John's may also have been the first, and only, intellectual community in the history of American higher education.

To the extent that they were communities, American colleges from the founding of Harvard to the founding of Johns Hopkins were moral communities in which piety prevailed over intellect. So many contradictory purposes defined the American university—think of Herrick, Stagg, Veblen, and Lovett trying to make sense of Chicago from their narrow perspectives—that for all of its hospitality to intellect, it was in no sense defined as a community by that hospitality. Johns Hopkins in its early heady role as the advance agent of scholarship and research may have been an intellectual community, but the concept of community is overburdened when required to accommodate the single-minded specialization, the atomistic view of learning, and the competitive bureaucratic structure that Johns Hopkins fostered. On the other hand, with a common curriculum, a focus on Western man and his intellectual heritage, and a faculty that entered into shared inquiry as fellow men rather than authorities, St. John's created a community more thoroughly committed to intellectual purpose than any of its predecessors or contemporaries. St. John's did well enough to survive and to support a second campus at Santa Fe, New Mexico, but it was also a cultural anomaly, both more communal and more intellectual, less vocational and less serviceable, more general and less specialized than the style in which the American people wished to have the course of study served. It was also stubbornly reactionary.

Robert Hutchins told a story in 1976 about two Cornell professors who had recently challenged the university's president with the question: "If we prove to you that an arts and sciences student can now receive a B.A. degree at Cornell and thus be presumed to have acquired a liberal education, without having been required to read a line of Plato, the Bible, Shakespeare, Marx, or Einstein, would you consider this to be evidence that there is a crisis in education at Cornell?" The answer of the president of Cornell was not a part of the story, but Hutchins's was: "By this test there is a crisis in education almost everywhere except at St. John's College at Annapolis and Santa Fe."[95] The conditions described by the disturbed Cornell professors were in fact too ingrained, too established, to justify elevating them to the level of a crisis. Those who chose to might view them with alarm, but as with most other innovations and experimental colleges that entered into American academic experience between the two world wars, St. John's could sustain itself as a unique model of curricular reform but it was not persuasive as a viable alternative to the American college. Bennington, Black Mountain, Bard, St. John's, and all the others offered lively demonstrations of what might be done in new institutions or in old ones about to go under, but they offered little guidance to old, reasonably healthy institutions in which alumni, benefactors, state legislatures, faculty, and students had invested certain clear expectations.

Curricular reform after World War II failed to dislodge the professors, reduce vocationalism, substitute general for specialized education, or create new institutions that were convincing models for the restructuring and redesigning of old institutions. Indeed, the old institutions were by now in the grasp of their own histories. More than models were necessary to move a college in new curricular directions. Thus in the 1960s, in the selective colleges and universities of the East, the quality of faculties and courses of study sometimes failed to keep pace with the quality of the student bodies they attracted. But one institution's solution to that particular problem was not likely to be of much guidance in solving the problem elsewhere. For example, when a new president, John E. Sawyer, took over at Williams College in 1961, the prospects for intellectual revitalization and curricular reform depended on the abolition of fraternities. Until social life at Williams was freed from domination by fraternities, the faculty was not going to trust the student body sufficiently to reform the curriculum in ways appropriate to the quality of students then being enrolled. Fraternities were abolished, the curriculum was reformed, and the morale and quality of the institution shot upward; but the Williams experience was a product of its own history, it was unique. Its experience was not, as some expected it would be, a signal that the Greek-letter fraternity would collapse elsewhere.

Deeply rooted, fragile in some ways, but on the whole remarkably tough and flexible, most colleges and universities had learned how to be responsive to the demands of society and of their students without requiring dramatic and often traumatic transformations. Until the 1970s the innovations and changing emphases that have shaped the curriculum fit comfortably into the structure and style that had been hammered out earlier in the century.

By 1976, however, colleges and universities found themselves called on to fulfill yet another purpose—higher education for everyone. Once the instruments of the elite and then of the middle class, they were required to adapt their courses of study to all classes—to first-generation college students and minorities, especially blacks, for many of whom the college experience was in some ways a laboratory in culture shock.

No more burdensome and yet important purpose would appear in the twentieth century than this, which fell out of the program of benefits with which a grateful nation welcomed its veterans home from World War II. The G.I. Bill of Rights did not promote the idea of mass higher education nor underwrite collegiate education for everyone, but it pointed in that direction. The Serviceman's Readjustment Act of 1944, as the G.I. Bill was formally titled, sent "2.25 million veterans [to] . . . approximately 2,000 institutions of higher learning at a cost of about $5.5 billion."[96] While the veterans may have been the most respected generation of college students in the country's history, the presidents of Harvard and the University of Chicago, in opposing the G.I. Bill, had viewed the prospect with great foreboding. "We may find the least capable among the war generation . . .

flooding the facilities for advanced education" was the message from James B. Conant in Cambridge.[97] Robert Maynard Hutchins was equally apprehensive: "Colleges and universities will find themselves converted into educational hobo jungles."[98] Their hostility was based on fear of what numbers would do to the colleges and universities; a somewhat similar fear, inspired by concern over what would happen if a massive demobilization poured hundreds of thousands of veterans into a weak economy, motivated the bill's supporters. To some extent the university presidents resented having institutions of higher education turned into social safety valves.

As it turned out, the bill was not necessary, the economy was healthy. But the veteran response, influenced by the clear relationship between education and jobs during the Depression and between education and rank during the war, was unexpected and overwhelming. While it was believed that 20 percent of those who went to college would not have except for the financial support provided by the bill, who knows about the other 80 percent—for whom the G.I. Bill was essentially an all expense-paid invitation to social and economic mobility? The impact of the veterans on curricular structure and subject matter was relatively slight. Major requirements and divisional requirements were to some extent weakened, and electives were strengthened, but on the whole the colleges and universities converted themselves from wartime programs back to the prewar curriculum without a question being raised about the course of study.[99]

In a most subtle way, however, the veterans left their mark on the curriculum and on the colleges and universities, which underwent their first large-scale experience with numbers, crowded classrooms and lecture halls, and a lower grade and quality of instruction. Too often these conditions became the norm, rather than the exceptional results of a period of readjustment. In accommodating a dramatic increase in enrollments, the colleges and universities not only made room for new institutions but also demonstrated that, although not needed in this instance, they could perform as social safety valves in holding a significant portion of the college-age generation off the labor market.

The capacity of the structure of higher education to absorb numbers, in other words to move toward universal access, rested on a variety of developments. Municipal universities, although few in number but strategically located, expanded. The City College of New York and its affiliated campuses throughout the city were a startling demonstration of higher education as a function of urban purpose. On a smaller scale, similar universities, supported by municipalities and offering a wide variety of vocational and technical programs, absorbed increased enrollments in Louisville, Cincinnati, Toledo, Akron, Detroit, and Omaha.[100]

Normal schools upgraded to four-year degree-granting colleges played a role in equalizing educational opportunities beyond the high school, as did many old reorganized and revitalized Catholic colleges in the cities.[101] The old black colleges and universities wrestled not so much with the problem of numbers as with developing a curriculum that prepared for tomorrow's rather than yesterday's career opportunities and that was competitive in quality and offerings with standard colleges.[102] And almost everywhere state legislatures assisted in the development of new campuses of the state universities. Yet the institution most hospitable to numbers and most accessible was none of these: It was the comprehensive public community college, a two-year institution that was indeed a junior college but a junior college essentially of postwar vintage, broadly open in its admissions policies, and generous in the variety of its services and curricular offerings.

The two-year junior college, which provided both a terminal program of courses beyond the high school and preparation for transfer to a four-year institution, began as a modest experiment in Joliet, Illinois, in 1902. Four years later the state of California authorized cities to develop junior colleges as extensions of existing high schools. From these beginnings a movement developed that was of great potential for facilitating universal access to higher education. Before World War II ended, the New York state legislature approved a bill to establish twenty-two two-year technical institutes on the junior college level. The junior college as an institution of vocational training as well as general education received widespread legislative support after the war, when the G.I. Bill not only encouraged college going but helped to demonstrate a relationship between education and employment opportunities in the postwar job market.[103]

Laurence Veysey has suggested that the junior and community colleges that developed after World War II were "so closely related to the public school system that it may be questioned whether they are part of 'higher education' in more than a nominal sense."[104] More accurately, perhaps they deserved to be considered as a part of that fabric of postsecondary educational institutions that included nursing schools, business schools, technical institutes, and correspondence schools. For, while in their early days junior colleges functioned largely as institutions for preparing young men and women for transfer to four-year institutions, by 1976 for most of the students enrolled in them the community college was a terminal experience, more likely to be designed around some vocational program than a program of general studies.[105] As an institution of general education, the community college, even in its curriculum, was clearly an extension of the high school. As an institution providing two-year programs preparatory to technical employment, it was a technical school. As an institution providing opportunities in adult education and community cultural life, it was an institution of community service.

Only in its role of providing courses of study designed to facilitate transfer to a four-year institution did the community college function in ways that might fall under any traditional understanding of what was meant by "higher education" or by "college." By 1976 approximately 30 percent of young Americans enrolled in higher education were attending junior colleges, of whom no more than 14 to 17 percent would transfer and receive bachelor's degrees.[106] Many of these transfers would come from older private junior colleges, where a largely prescribed course of liberal studies provided a sound base for two specialized years elsewhere.

David Riesman and Christopher Jencks saw the community college as a bold and welcome departure from the traditional college and university, where values and standards nurtured in the graduate schools were dominant.[107] Yet in its rejection of national norms, cosmopolitan values, academic credentials, traditional standards, and professionalism, as well as in its embrace of the local, parochial, anti-intellectual, and familial, the community college, for all of its great service as an educational institution, may have placed itself beyond consideration, except in a limited sense, as a college. Its existence has encouraged young men and women to extend their education beyond high school. In the cities it has been responsive to the aspirations of deprived minorities. In a society increasingly in need of technicians and decreasingly dependent on unskilled labor, it has functioned as a training center and as a social safety valve. Perhaps more than any other element in the structure of formal education it has operated, in Clifton Fadiman's terms, as a "detention center."

But it has been more than that. It has both generalized opportunity and cushioned failure. It has held out the promise of economic and social mobility and also verified low intellectual, social, and economic status. Like the comprehensive American high school that it so closely resembles, it has been an instrument of individual liberation and of social control. It has been the lowest point of access to universal education beyond the high school, and it has been an invitation to the American Dream. It is Abraham Lincoln's snow-drifted cabin. It will produce a president of the United States.

Americans long ago were led to believe that they could probably learn more from high school drum majorettes than from wise old college professors. It is doubtful, therefore, that anyone paid much attention to the self-serving advice contained in a straightforward sentence of the Allegheny College catalogue of 1944: "The economic organization of our country is being transformed at such a rapid rate that it is no longer wise for students to elect a course that is too narrowly vocational."[108] Of course, Allegheny was defending its liberal, humanistic orientation; it was promising young men and women style and intellectual rigor instead of negotiable, but potentially worthless, technical competence. The alternative to Allegheny's concern with liberal learning was a lifetime of frantic running in and out of educational programs designed to help technicians catch up with the machines and organizations that controlled them. Allegheny did not argue against the inevitable and the necessary. Machines and organization were the order of the day, but the frantic style was not, and *that* liberal learning might bring under control.

It was too late to bring under control the atomic scientist who had worked on the Manhattan Project and who had said that "he felt as little responsibility for the bomb as a maker of cans should feel when a can is thrown through a window."[109] What of his successors? "The image of the technocrat appears to be emerging as the academic ideal," JB Lon Hefferlin concluded in 1967.[110] And while atomic scientists were not necessarily to be confused with technocrats, the all-purpose American university may have lost control of the distinctions. It avoided questions big enough to tarry over, it was comfortable with questions small enough to expend a lifetime on.

By 1976 the curriculum had made room for the laboratory as an experience, a conductor of truth, and even as a stumbling way for encouraging young men and women to establish some identity with the human race. For many students only the scientific laboratory acknowledged their hands and cultivated their senses, so far had the triumph of science and the persistence of old hostilities carried the course of study into a curious rejection of "the domain of feelings."[111] To a degree that bordered on scandal the curriculum supported neither mind nor feeling with any real dedication; sometimes it seemed only to be a friend of energy or lethargy.

At its most imaginative and sensitive the curriculum sometimes seemed to be more attuned to the market than it was to the heartbeat of students. Think of the magnificent perceptions that discarded the old subjects and majors in the 1960s, consider the abandonment of courses and programs that had done their job as mechanisms of social mobility: home economics, dairy farming, rural sociology, secretarial science, interior decorating, and advertising design. These and other reminders of a vanished age passed into history; instruction in new skills took their place: agricultural climatology, computer science, scientific writing, and wildlife management.[112]

For several hundred years the American college and university had survived both unpopularity and popularity, and which had damaged it more was an interesting question. If the curriculum had managed to transmit to students some sense of their origins and to ignite in them some sense of their humanity, surely the effort had become more difficult as time passed. Even as the community college, open admissions, and every proclaimed regulation against discrimination ushered in a new era of justice, a heightened expectation and a more demanding responsibility were thrust upon those who wore the mantle of educated men and women.

Yet recent events so pushed and pulled the American student toward a vocational bias that we now witness the accelerating downgrading of those aspects of an undergraduate education that encourage imagination, judgment, decision, values. If the Great Depression taught students to be skeptical of specialized learning, that has not been the case in the 1970s. Aware that national economies all over the world are in a mess, students flock into economics courses to find out how it is done. Enrollments in humanities courses drop, and enrollments in business administration, engineering, and metallurgy skyrocket, as students abandon a search for the knowledge that might make them interesting, even to themselves, and seek to achieve some kind of technical insurance against the future.

With the blessings of the U.S. Office of Education, the American high school is encouraged to embrace something called "career edution"—a movement that promises its victims technical skills and "positive" attitudes toward work, but neglects those educational experiences that might help to make them good, interesting, and wise men and women. Should we not register some sense of uneasiness when the government that gave us Cambodia, Watergate, and other assorted crimes supports an educational program that has as its goal the production of contented technicians rather than perceptive social critics?

The challenge to the curriculum today is to create an environment that is friendly to the production of social critics and that is responsive to a concern with values and the human experience. General education courses have sought to keep alive such a concern in the specializing, vocationalizing university, but the general education movement is hopelessly engaged in the artificial respiration of a lifeless ideal. Recent efforts to develop specific courses in values have a synthetic quality about them: Unless the entire institutional environment is recognized as making conscious and unconscious statements of value, value courses as such run the risk of being quaint and strangely and unintentionally irrelevant.

College and university faculties, strongly oriented toward their academic disciplines and wedded to the mystique of scientific investigation and suspended judgment, are not a likely source of encouragement for any renewal of concern with values and character. Even the coaches have let us down. The lore of college and university athletics would have us locate in athletic teams and coaching staffs the ultimate locus of value training. Yet four of the five last presidents of the United States were college football players, and any survey of the wreckage of these years would have to ask whether peace, justice, and liberty would not have been better served if our presidents had instead been ballet dancers. Colleges and universities, of course, can be counted on to continue to teach and support values haphazardly. Can there be any question about the values a college or university teaches when it says: "We don't care what courses you take; you can have a B.A., and not know how to write, how to understand nuclear fission, look at a painting, or listen to music"?

There may be one hopeful sign. We have all been frequently assured that we are moving into an era of a permanent unfavorable job market for college graduates. This message is generally delivered as bad news. It just may be good news. If there are not sufficient jobs available to justify an endless production of proficient technicians and if, as is quite apparent, we know not what else to do with the age group other than send it to college, perhaps we can stop making technicians and get back to the business of making human beings. The time may be at hand when a reevaluation of academic purpose and philosophy will encourage the curricular developments that will focus on the lives we lead, their quality, the enjoyment they give us, and the wisdom with which we lead them. If such a development does take place, human beings, as distinct from trained technicians, will not be at a disadvantage in the job market. And perhaps, once more, the idea of an educated person will have become a usable ideal.

Notes

Chapter 1

1. Educational Policies Commission, *Higher Education in a Decade of Decision* (Washington, D.C.: National Education Association, 1957), p. 22; Ezra Cornell's intention is emblazoned on the seven *Cornell University Announcements* that describe the offerings of the undergraduate schools and colleges for 1975-76.

2. George W. Pierson, *Yale: The University College, 1921-1937* (New Haven, Conn.: Yale University Press, 1955), p. 329.

3. Nevitt Sanford (Ed.), *The American College: A Psychological and Social Interpretation of the Higher Learning* (New York: Wiley, 1962), p. 432; Laurence Veysey, "Stability and Experiment in the American Undergraduate Curriculum," in Carl Kaysen (Ed.), *Content and Context: Essays on College Education* (New York: McGraw-Hill, 1973), pp. 22-62.

4. JB Lon Hefferlin, *Dynamics of Academic Reform* (San Francisco: Jossey-Bass, 1969), p. xx.

5. Louis Franklin Snow, *The College Curriculum in the United States* (New York: Teachers College, Columbia University, 1907), p. 78.

6. Henry Wilkinson Bragdon, *Woodrow Wilson: The Academic Years* (Cambridge, Mass.: Harvard University Press, 1967), p. 293.

7. Hefferlin, *Dynamics of Academic Reform*, pp. 10-16.

8. Veysey, "Stability and Experiment," pp. 5-7.

9. Hefferlin, *Dynamics of Academic Reform*, p. xx.

10. LeRoy J. Halsey (Ed.), *The Works of Philip Lindsley, D.D.*, Vol. 1 (Philadelphia: Lippincott, 1866), pp. 572-573.

11. John C. Schwab, "The Yale College Curriculum, 1701-1901," *Educational Review*, 1901, 22 (June), 2.

12. Pierson, *Yale: The University College, 1921-1937*, p. 330.

13. *Addresses at the Inauguration of Charles William Eliot as President of Harvard College, Tuesday, October 19, 1869* (Cambridge, Mass.: Sever and Francis, 1869), p. 62; Snow, *The College Curriculum*, p. 14; Hefferlin,

Dynamics of Academic Reform, pp. 34-35; Burton J. Bledstein, *The Culture of Professionalism: The Middle Class and the Development of Higher Education in America* (New York: Norton, 1976), pp. 289-327.

14. Waitman Barbe, *Going to College: With the Opinions of Fifty Leading College Presidents and Educators* (Cincinnati: Earhart and Richardson, 1899), p. 8.

15. William C. DeVane, *Higher Education in Twentieth-Century America* (Cambridge, Mass.: Harvard University Press, 1965), p. 123.

16. Robert L. Duffus, *Democracy Enters College: A Study of the Rise and Decline of the Academic Lockstep* (New York: Scribner's, 1936), p. 66.

17. Martin Trow, *Problems in the Transition from Elite to Mass Higher Education* (Berkeley, Calif.: Carnegie Commission on Higher Education, 1973), passim; David Riesman, "Educational Reform at Harvard College: Meritocracy and Its Adversaries," in Seymour Martin Lipset and David Riesman, *Education and Politics at Harvard* (New York: McGraw-Hill, 1975), p. 323.

18. George Wilson Pierson, "The Elective System and the Difficulties of College Planning, 1870-1940," *Journal of General Education*, 1950, *4* (April), 171.

19. Walter Crosby Eells, *Academic Degrees: Earned and Honorary Degrees Conferred by Institutions of Higher Education in the United States*, U.S. Office of Education, Bulletin No. 28 (Washington, D.C.: U.S. Government Printing Office, 1960), p. 16, passim.

20. Earl J. McGrath, *The Graduate School and the Decline of Liberal Education* (New York: Teachers College, Columbia University, for the Institute of Higher Education, 1959), p. 12.

21. Hefferlin, *Dynamics of Academic Reform*, p. 31; Brooks Mather Kelley, *Yale: A History* (New Haven, Conn.: Yale University Press, 1974), p. 167.

22. Parke R. Kolbe, *Urban Influences on Higher Education in England and the United States* (New York: Macmillan, 1928), p. 229.

23. James McLachlan, "The *Choice of Hercules:* American Student Societies in the Early 19th Century," in Lawrence Stone (Ed.), *The University in Society*, Vol. 2 (Princeton, N.J.: Princeton University Press, 1974), pp. 462-464.

24. Seymour Martin Lipset, "Political Controversies at Harvard, 1636 to 1974," in Seymour Martin Lipset and David Riesman, *Education and Politics at Harvard* (New York: McGraw-Hill, 1975), p. 247.

25. Edwin E. Slosson, *Great American Universities* (New York: Macmillan, 1910), p. 77.

26. James Albert Woodburn, *History of Indiana University, 1820-1902* (Bloomington: Indiana University, 1940), p. 151.

27. Louis C. Hatch, *The History of Bowdoin College* (Portland, Maine: Loring, Short, & Harmon, 1927), p. 20; Walter P. Rogers, *Andrew D. White and the Modern University* (Ithaca, N.Y.: Cornell University Press, 1942), p.

108; Malcolm Carron, *The Contract Colleges of Cornell University: A Co-Operative Educational Enterprise* (Ithaca, N.Y.: Cornell University Press, 1958), p. 76.

28. Earl J. McGrath, *The Predominantly Negro Colleges and Universities in Transition* (New York: Teachers College, Columbia University, 1965), p. 66.

29. Henry Adams, *The Education of Henry Adams: An Autobiography* (Boston: Houghton Mifflin, 1918), pp. 305-306.

30. Christopher Jencks and David Riesman, *The Academic Revolution* (New York: Doubleday, 1968), p. 199.

31. Sanford, *The American College*, p. 425.

32. Ralph H. Gabriel, "The Cold War and Changes in American Thought," *Virginia Quarterly Review*, 1959, *35* (Winter), 61-62.

33. Charles Henry Rammelkamp, *Illinois College: A Centennial History, 1829-1929* (New Haven, Conn.: Yale University Press, 1928), p. 140; Woodburn, *History of Indiana University*, p. 201.

34. *Addresses at the Inauguration of Charles William Eliot as President of Harvard College, Tuesday, October 19, 1869*, pp. 64, 47; Willis Rudy, "Eliot and Gilman: The History of an Academic Friendship," *Teachers College Record*, 1953, *54* (March), 317.

35. Mary Lovett Smallwood, *An Historical Study of Examinations and Grading Systems in Early American Universities* (Cambridge, Mass.: Harvard University Press, 1935), p. 83.

36. Daniel Walker Hollis, *University of South Carolina*, Vol. 2 (Columbia: University of South Carolina Press, 1956), p. iv; R. Freeman Butts, *The College Charts Its Course: Historical Conceptions and Current Proposals* (New York: McGraw-Hill, 1939), pp. 350-351.

37. William Murray Hepburn and Louis Martin Sears, *Purdue University: Fifty Years of Progress* (Indianapolis: Hollenbeck Press, 1925), pp. 41-42; George Matthew Dutcher, *An Historical and Critical Survey of the Curriculum of Wesleyan University and Related Subjects* (Middletown, Conn.: Wesleyan University Press, 1948), p. 70; Willis Rudy, *The Evolving Liberal Arts Curriculum: A Historical Review of Basic Themes* (New York: Teachers College, Columbia University, 1960), p. 116.

38. Thomas LeDuc, *Piety and Intellect at Amherst College, 1865-1912* (New York: Columbia University Press, 1946), p. 78; Rogers, *Andrew D. White and the Modern University*, p. 23.

39. Richard Warch, *School of the Prophets: Yale College, 1701-1740* (New Haven, Conn.: Yale University Press, 1973), p. 191.

40. Laurence R. Veysey, *The Emergence of the American University* (Chicago: University of Chicago Press, 1965), p. 336.

41. Lipset, "Political Controversies at Harvard," pp. 202-204.

42. William T. Foster, *Administration of the College Curriculum* (Boston: Houghton Mifflin, 1911), p. 131.

43. Hefferlin, *Dynamics of Academic Reform*, pp. 22, 45; Andrew M. Greeley, *From Backwater to Mainstream: A Profile of Catholic Higher Education* (New York: McGraw-Hill, 1969), p. 22.

44. Hugh Hawkins, *Between Harvard and America: The Educational Leadership of Charles W. Eliot* (New York: Oxford University Press, 1972), p. 95.

45. Charles Burt Sumner, *The Story of Pomona College* (Boston: Pilgrim Press, 1914), pp. 4, 52-71; Orrin Leslie Elliott, *Stanford University: The First Twenty-Five Years* (Stanford, Calif.: Stanford University Press, 1937), p. 199; Allen E. Ragan, *A History of Tusculum College, 1794-1944* (Bristol, Tenn.: Tusculum College, 1945), p. 174.

46. Esther Raushenbush, *The Student and His Studies* (Middletown, Conn.: Wesleyan University Press, 1964), p. 152.

47. Hefferlin, *Dynamics of Academic Reform*, pp. 20-24.

48. Lipset, "Political Controversies at Harvard," pp. 51, 122, 242. The quotation is from Richard Hofstadter.

49. Robert L. Church, in Paul Buck (Ed.), *Social Sciences at Harvard, 1860-1920: From Inculcation to the Open Mind* (Cambridge, Mass.: Harvard University Press, 1965), pp. 9, 24; Rudy, *The Evolving Liberal Arts Curriculum*, p. 7.

50. Veysey, *The Emergence of the American University*, pp. 324-325.

51. Kelley, *Yale*, p. 416.

52. Allan Nevins, *Illinois* (New York: Oxford University Press, 1917), p. 227.

53. Pierson, "The Elective System," p. 169; Jencks and Riesman, *The Academic Revolution*, pp. xi-xii.

54. Edmund S. Morgan, *The Gentle Puritan: A Life of Ezra Stiles, 1727-1795* (Chapel Hill: University of North Carolina Press, for the Institute of Early American History and Culture, 1962), p. 56; Kelley, *Yale*, pp. 78 ff.; Hefferlin, *Dynamics of Academic Reform*, pp. 24-25. See also LeDuc, *Piety and Intellect at Amherst College*, p. 78, and Riesman, "Educational Reform at Harvard College," p. 284.

55. Slosson, *Great American Universities*, p. 90.

56. *Addresses at the Inauguration of Charles William Eliot*, p. 31; Pierson, *Yale: The University College, 1921-1937*, p. 164; Leon B. Richardson, *A Study of the Liberal College: A Report to the President of Dartmouth College* (Hanover, N.H.: Dartmouth College, 1924), p. 20; Dutcher, *An Historical and Critical Survey of the Curriculum of Wesleyan University*, p. 64; Frederick Rudolph, *Mark Hopkins and the Log: Williams College, 1836-1872* (New Haven, Conn.: Yale University Press, 1956), pp. 255 ff.; Veysey, "Stability and Experiment," p. 62.

57. J. Whitney Bunting, "The College Graduate in Industry," *Educational Record*, 1957, *38* (April), 141-145; Riesman, "Educational Reform at Harvard College," p. 390.

58. Slosson, *Great American Universities*, p. 76.

59. Verne A. Stadtman, *The University of California, 1868–1968* (New York: McGraw-Hill, 1970), passim.

60. Veysey, "Stability and Experiment," p. 61.

61. Michael McGiffert, *The Higher Learning in Colorado: An Historical Study, 1860–1940* (Denver: Swallow, 1964), pp. 21-22.

62. Samuel Eliot Morison, *Three Centuries of Harvard, 1636–1936* (Cambridge, Mass.: Harvard University Press, 1936), pp. 389-390.

63. Earl Latham (Ed.), *John D. Rockefeller: Robber Baron or Industrial Statesman?* (Boston: Heath, 1949).

64. Hefferlin, *Dynamics of Academic Reform*, p. 146; David D. Henry, *Challenges Past, Challenges Present: An Analysis of American Higher Education Since 1930* (San Francisco: Jossey-Bass, 1975), pp. 100-101.

65. Jencks and Riesman, *Academic Revolution*, p. 61.

66. Clark Kerr, in introduction to Abraham Flexner, *Universities: American, English, German* (New York: Oxford University Press, 1968), pp. xiv-xv. (Originally published 1930.)

Chapter 2

1. Leon Burr Richardson, *History of Dartmouth College*, Vol. 1 (Hanover, N.H.: Dartmouth College, 1932), p. 251.

2. John C. Schwab, "The Yale College Curriculum, 1701–1901," *Educational Review*, 1901, *22* (June), 12.

3. Walter Crosby Eells, *Academic Degrees: Earned and Honorary Degrees Conferred by Institutions of Higher Education in the United States*, U.S. Office of Education Bulletin No. 28 (Washington, D.C.: U.S. Government Printing Office, 1960), p. 23; Walter Schultz Stover, *Alumni Stimulation by the American College President* (New York: Teachers College, Columbia University, 1930), p. 10.

4. Charles G. Osgood, *Lights in Nassau Hall: A Book of the Bicentennial: Princeton, 1746–1946* (Princeton, N.J.: Princeton University Press, 1951), p. 7; Henry Lyttleton Savage (Ed.), *Nassau Hall, 1756–1956* (Princeton, N.J.: Princeton University Press, 1956), p. 108.

5. Richard Warch, *School of the Prophets: Yale College, 1701–1740* (New Haven, Conn.: Yale University Press, 1973), p. 34.

6. Lawrence A. Cremin, *American Education: The Colonial Experience, 1607–1783* (New York: Harper & Row, 1970), pp. 324-328; Douglas Sloan, *The Scottish Enlightenment and the American College Ideal* (New York: Teachers College Press, 1971), pp. 225 ff.; David C. Humphrey, "Colonial Colleges and English Dissenting Academies: A Study of Transatlantic Culture," *History of Education Quarterly*, 1972, *12* (Summer), passim.

7. Brooks Mather Kelley, *Yale: A History* (New Haven, Conn.: Yale University Press, 1974), pp. 7, 70.

8. Warch, *School of the Prophets*, p. 18.

9. Warch, *School of the Prophets*, pp. 187, 277.

10. David C. Humphrey, *From King's College to Columbia, 1746-1800* (New York: Columbia University Press, 1976), p. 175.

11. Cremin, *American Education*, p. 208; Humphrey, *From King's College to Columbia*, pp. 109-110.

12. Kelley, *Yale*, p. 29; Humphrey, *From King's College to Columbia*, pp. 194-195, 81; Christopher Jencks and David Riesman, *The Academic Revolution* (New York: Doubleday, 1968), p. 91.

13. Samuel Eliot Morison, *The Founding of Harvard College* (Cambridge, Mass.: Harvard University Press, 1935), pp. 50-58.

14. Morison, *The Founding of Harvard College*, p. 26.

15. Morison, *The Founding of Harvard College*, pp. 12-17; Louis L. Tucker, *Puritan Protagonist: President Thomas Clap of Yale College* (Chapel Hill: University of North Carolina Press, 1962), p. 77; Willis Rudy, "The 'Revolution' in American Higher Education, 1865-1900," *Harvard Educational Review*, 1951, *21*, 157.

16. Cremin, *American Education*, p. 207.

17. Samuel Eliot Morison, *Harvard College in the Seventeenth Century*, Vol. 1 (Cambridge, Mass.: Harvard University Press, 1936), pp. 66-69, 147; Louis Franklin Snow, *The College Curriculum in the United States* (New York: Teachers College, Columbia University, 1907), pp. 22-32; Cremin, *American Education*, pp. 214-215.

18. Warch, *School of the Prophets*, pp. 193-194; William Lathrop Kingsley (Ed.), *Yale College: A Sketch of its History*, Vol. 2 (New York: Holt, 1879), p. 496; Kelley, *Yale*, pp. 41-42, 70, 80.

19. Morison, *Harvard College*, Vol. 1, pp. 208 ff.; Edwin Oviatt, *The Beginnings of Yale, 1701-1726* (New Haven, Conn.: Yale University Press, 1916), pp. 396-399; Theodore Hornberger, *Scientific Thought in the American Colleges 1638-1800* (Austin: University of Texas Press, 1945), p. 43; Warch, *School of the Prophets*, pp. 195, 218-223; Tucker, *Puritan Protagonist*, p. 83.

20. Warch, *School of the Prophets*, p. 221.

21. Hornberger, *Scientific Thought in the American Colleges*, pp. 49-52; Samuel Eliot Morison, *Three Centuries of Harvard, 1636-1936* (Cambridge, Mass.: Harvard University Press, 1936), pp. 92-93; Kelley, *Yale*, p. 70; Kingsley, *Yale College*, Vol. 1, pp. 66-67.

22. Warch, *School of the Prophets*, p. 209.

23. Morison, *Harvard College*, Vol. 1, pp. 236 ff.; Hornberger, *Scientific Thought in the American Colleges*, pp. 25-27; Morison, *Three Centuries of Harvard*, p. 79; JB Lon Hefferlin, *Dynamics of Academic Reform* (San Francisco: Jossey-Bass, 1969), p. 42.

24. Kingsley, *Yale College*, Vol. 1, pp. 62, 78; Warch, *School of the Prophets*, pp. 216-218; Edmund Morgan, *The Gentle Puritan: A Life of Ezra Stiles, 1727-1795* (Chapel Hill: University of North Carolina Press, for the Institute of Early American History and Culture, 1962), p. 319.

25. Richard Hofstadter and Walter P. Metzger, *The Development of*

Academic Freedom in the United States (New York: Columbia University Press, 1955), pp. 195-197.

26. Thomas Jefferson Wertenbaker, *Princeton, 1746-1896* (Princeton, N.J.: Princeton University Press, 1946), p. 95.

27. Hornberger, *Scientific Thought in the American Colleges*, p. 69; Humphrey, *From King's College to Columbia*, pp. 233-263; Cremin, *American Education*, p. 404; Edward Potts Cheyney, *History of the University of Pennsylvania, 1740-1940* (Philadelphia: University of Pennsylvania Press, 1940), p. 202; Hornberger, *Scientific Thought in the American Colleges*, p. 73.

28. Edward Eggleston, *The Transit of Civilization from England to America in the Seventeenth Century* (New York: Smith, 1933), p. 215 (originally published 1901); Morison, *Harvard College*, Vol. 1., pp. 85-86.

29. John Langdon Sibley, *Biographical Sketches of Graduates of Harvard University, in Cambridge, Massachusetts*, Vol. 1 (Cambridge, Mass.: Sever, 1873), p. 267; Morison, *Harvard College*, Vol. 2, p. 448, fn. 1.

30. Morison, *Harvard College*, Vol. 2., p. 448, fn. 1; William C. Lane, "Manuscript Laws of Harvard College," *Publications of the Colonial Society of Massachusetts*, 1923, *25* (April), 244-253; Warch, *School of the Prophets*, p. 198; Kelley, *Yale*, p. 42; Edwin C. Broome, *A Historical and Critical Discussion of College Admission Requirements* (New York: Macmillan, 1903), p. 23, fn. 8.

31. Robert Middlekauff, "A Persistent Tradition: The Classical Curriculum in Eighteenth-Century New England," *William and Mary Quarterly*, 3rd series, 1961, *18*, 56-60.

32. Morison, *Harvard College*, Vol. 1, p. 153.

33. Snow, *The College Curriculum*, p. 53; Broome, *A Historical and Critical Discussion of College Admission Requirements*, p. 23, fn. 10.

34. Morison, *Harvard College*, Vol. 1, p. 163.

35. Rollo LaVerne Lyman, *English Grammar in American Schools Before 1850*, U.S. Bureau of Education Bulletin No. 12, 1921 (Washington, D.C.: Government Printing Office, 1922), pp. 37-38.

36. Morison, *Three Centuries of Harvard*, p. 136.

37. Douglas Sloan, "Harmony, Chaos, and Consensus: The American College Curriculum," *Teachers College Record*, 1971, *78* (December), 241-242.

38. Morison, *Three Centuries of Harvard*, pp. 57-58; Abraham I. Katsh, *Hebrew Language Literature and Culture in American Institutions of Higher Learning* (New York: Payne Educational Sociology Foundation, 1950), pp. 2-6, 13; Warch, *School of the Prophets*, p. 200; Snow, *The College Curriculum*, p. 80.

39. Norman S. Fiering, "President Samuel Johnson and the Circle of Knowledge," *William and Mary Quarterly*, 3rd series, 1971, *28* (April), 228; Morgan, *The Gentle Puritan*, p. 320; Kelley, *Yale*, pp. 81-82.

40. Morison, *Three Centuries of Harvard*, pp. 89-90; Kelley, *Yale*, pp.

80-82; Kingsley, *Yale College,* Vol. 1, pp. 96-98; McLachlan, "The Choice of Hercules," in Lawrence Stone (Ed.), *The University in Society,* Vol. 2 (Princeton, N.J.: Princeton University Press, 1974), p. 460; Morgan, *The Gentle Puritan,* p. 385.

41. Warch, *School of the Prophets,* pp. 223-225; Kelley, *Yale,* p. 80.
42. Fiering, "President Samuel Johnson," p. 223.
43. Fiering, "President Samuel Johnson," p. 235.
44. Fiering, "President Samuel Johnson," pp. 223, 226.
45. Fiering, "President Samuel Johnson," p. 235.
46. Cremin, *American Education,* pp. 460-466.
47. G. Stanley Hall, "On the History of American College Textbooks and Teaching in Logic, Ethics, Psychology, and Allied Subjects," *Proceedings of the American Antiquarian Society,* new series, 1894, *9* (April), 145-147.
48. Thomas Clap, *An Essay on the Nature and Foundation of Moral Virtue and Obligation: Being a Short Introduction to the Study of Ethics, for the Use of the Students of Yale-College* (New Haven, Conn.: Mecom, 1765).
49. Published in New York by T. and J. Swords in 1795. See Humphrey, *From King's College to Columbia,* pp. 298-301.
50. Hall, "On the History of American College Textbooks and Teaching," pp. 152-158.
51. Morgan, *The Gentle Puritan,* pp. 64-68; Humphrey, *From King's College to Columbia,* p. 170.
52. Fiering, "President Samuel Johnson," p. 233.
53. Tucker, *Puritan Protagonist,* p. 80; Morgan, *The Gentle Puritan,* p. 391.
54. Hornberger, *Scientific Thought in the American Colleges,* pp. 45, 61.
55. Wertenbaker, *Princeton,* p. 97; Humphrey, *From King's College to Columbia,* p. 114.
56. Warch, *School of the Prophets,* pp. 64, 78, 198, 218; Cremin, *American Education,* pp. 215-218, 513-514; Humphrey, *From King's College to Columbia,* p. 106; William D. Carrell, "American College Professors, 1750-1800," *History of Education Quarterly,* 1968, *8* (Fall), 289-290.
57. Kingsley, *Yale College,* Vol. 2, pp. 495-496; Morgan, *The Gentle Puritan,* pp. 382-385; Warch, *School of the Prophets,* p. 245.
58. Morgan, *The Gentle Puritan,* p. 385.
59. Cremin, *American Education,* p. 203.
60. Warch, *School of the Prophets,* p. 10.
61. Warch, *School of the Prophets,* pp. 245-247.
62. Morison, *Three Centuries of Harvard,* p. 90.
63. Lucy Salmon, "The College Commencement," *Educational Review,* 1895, *9* (May), 437.
64. Kelley, *Yale,* pp. 81 ff.
65. Morgan, *The Gentle Puritan,* p. 394.
66. Morgan, *The Gentle Purtian,* p. 395.

67. Tucker, *Puritan Protagonist*, p. 77.

68. Tucker, *Puritan Protagonist*, p. 80; Milton Halsey Thomas (Ed.), "King's College Commencement in the Newspapers," *Columbia University Quarterly*, 1930, *22* (June), 236-237; David B. Davis, *The Problem of Slavery in the Age of Revolution, 1770–1823* (Ithaca, N.Y.: Cornell University Press, 1975), p. 302; Warch, *School of the Prophets*, pp. 216-217, 232.

69. Morgan, *The Gentle Puritan*, pp. 395-396.

70. James J. Walsh, *Education of the Founding Fathers of the Republic: Scholasticism in the Colonial Colleges, a Neglected Chapter in the History of American Education* (New York: Fordham University Press, 1935), p. 23; Joseph J. Ellis, *The New England Mind in Transition: Samuel Johnson of Connecticut, 1696–1772* (New Haven, Conn.: Yale University Press, 1973), pp. 232-233.

71. Morgan, *The Gentle Puritan*, pp. 394-399; John Rogers Williams, *Academic Honors in Princeton University, 1748–1902* (Princeton, N.J.: Princeton University Press, 1902), pp. xi-xii; Kingsley, *Yale College*, Vol. 1, p. 373; Walsh, *Education of the Founding Fathers of the Republic*, passim; Samuel Eliot Morison review of Walsh's book in *New England Quarterly*, 1935, *8* (September), 455-457; Hall, "On the History of American College Textbooks and Teaching," p. 148.

72. Snow, *The College Curriculum*, p. 58.

73. William Smith, *Discourses on Public Occasions in America* (2nd ed.; London: Millar, Wilson, and Becket and DeHondt, in the Strand; and Keith in Gracechurch Street, 1762), pp. 32-106; Theodore Hornberger, "A Note on the Probable Source of Provost Smith's Famous Curriculum for the College of Philadelphia," *Pennsylvania Magazine of History and Biography*, 1934, *58*, 370-377; Cheyney, *History of the University of Pennsylvania*, p. 82.

74. Smith, *Discourses*, pp. 32-106.

75. Hornberger, *Scientific Thought in the American Colleges*, p. 29; Cremin, *American Education*, pp. 381-383; Snow, *The College Curriculum*, pp. 67, 72-73; Cheyney, *History of the University of Pennsylvania*, pp. 71-81.

76. Humphrey, *From King's College to Columbia*, pp. 206-207; Morgan, *The Gentle Puritan*, pp. 323-324.

77. Morgan, *The Gentle Puritan*, pp. 381-382; Kelley, *Yale*, p. 111.

78. Herbert Baxter Adams, *The College of William and Mary*, U.S. Bureau of Education, Circulars of Information, No. 1 (Washington, D.C.: U.S. Government Printing Office, 1887), p. 39; E. W. Bagster-Collins, "History of Modern Language Teaching in the United States," in *Studies in Modern Language Teaching* (New York: Macmillan, 1930), pp. 50-51; Snow, *The College Curriculum*, pp. 73 ff.; Robert Polk Thomson, "Colleges in the Revolutionary South: The Shaping of a Tradition," *History of Education Quarterly*, 1970, *10* (Winter), 401; Roy J. Honeywell, *The Educational Work of Thomas Jefferson* (Cambridge, Mass.: Harvard University Press, 1931), pp. 54-56.

79. Snow, *The College Curriculum*, pp. 74-75.

80. Thomson, "Colleges in the Revolutionary South," p. 400; Steven J. Novak, *The Rights of Youth: American Colleges and Student Revolt, 1789–1815* (Cambridge, Mass.: Harvard University Press, 1977), pp. 96, 109, 114.

81. Humphrey, *From King's College to Columbia,* pp. 275-295; Carrell, "American College Professors," p. 290; Wertenbaker, *Princeton,* p. 123; Hugh Hawkins, *Between Harvard and America: The Educational Leadership of Charles W. Eliot* (New York: Oxford University Press, 1972), pp. 82-83.

82. Kelley, *Yale,* p. 100; W. H. Cowley, "European Influences upon American Higher Education," *Educational Record,* 1939, *20* (April), 171-173; Alfred J. Morrison (Ed.), *The College of Hampden-Sidney: Calendar of Board Minutes, 1776–1876* (Richmond: Hermitage Press, 1912), pp. 33, 35; Snow, *The College Curriculum,* p. 82; Bagster-Collins, "History of Modern Language Teaching," pp. 50-51; Broome, *A Historical and Critical Discussion of College Admission Requirements,* p. 55; Charles Hart Handschin, *The Teaching of Modern Languages in the United States,* U.S. Bureau of Education Bulletin No. 13 (Washington, D.C.: Government Printing Office, 1913), p. 19; Codman Hislop, *Eliphalet Nott* (Middletown, Conn.: Wesleyan University Press, 1971), pp. 115, 230; Novak, *The Rights of Youth,* pp. 106, 109, 114, 118, 121.

83. Humphrey, *From King's College to Columbia,* p. 93; Cremin, *American Education,* pp. 336-337; Warch, *School of the Prophets,* pp. 189, 197.

84. Warch, *School of the Prophets,* p. 188.

85. Snow, *The College Curriculum,* pp. 54-55.

86. Cremin, *American Education,* pp. 510-512; Joe W. Kraus, "The Development of a Curriculum in the Early American Colleges," *History of Education Quarterly,* 1961, *1* (June), 69-72; Warch, *School of the Prophets,* pp. 286-295; McLachlan, "The *Choice of Hercules*," pp. 486-491.

87. Warch, *School of the Prophets,* p. 297; Humphrey, *From King's College to Columbia,* p. 190.

88. Hawkins, *Between Harvard and America,* p. 80; Morgan, *The Gentle Puritan,* p. 48.

Chapter 3

1. John Howard Van Amringe and others, *A History of Columbia University, 1754–1904* (New York: Columbia University Press, 1904), pp. 89-90.

2. Van Amringe, *A History of Columbia University,* pp. 112-115; John S. Whitehead, *The Separation of College and State: Columbia, Dartmouth, Harvard, and Yale, 1776–1876* (New Haven, Conn.: Yale University Press, 1973), p. 105.

3. Douglas Sloan, "Harmony, Chaos, and Consensus: The American College Curriculum," *Teachers College Record,* 1971, *73,* 226.

4. Lawrence A. Cremin, *American Education: The Coloni-*

al Experience, 1607–1783 (New York: Harper & Row, 1970), p. 550.

5. Brooks Mather Kelley, *Yale: A History* (New Haven, Conn.: Yale University Press, 1974), p. 134.

6. Sloan, "Harmony, Chaos, and Consensus," p. 232.

7. Robert A. McCaughey, *Josiah Quincy, 1772–1864: The Last Federalist* (Cambridge, Mass.: Harvard University Press, 1974), pp. 179-180.

8. Leon B. Richardson, *History of Dartmouth College*, Vol. 1 (Hanover, N.H.: Dartmouth College, 1932), p. 265; George Franklin Smythe, *Kenyon College: Its First Century* (New Haven, Conn.: Yale University Press, for Kenyon College, 1924), p. 169.

9. Edwin A. Miles, "The Old South and the Classical World," *North Carolina Historical Review*, 1971, *48*, 258-275.

10. McCaughey, *Josiah Quincy*, p. 180.

11. Richardson, *History of Dartmouth College*, Vol. 1, pp. 365-366.

12. David B. Tyack, *George Ticknor and the Boston Brahmins* (Cambridge, Mass.: Harvard University Press, 1967), p. 101.

13. James McLachlan, "The *Choice of Hercules:* American Student Societies in the Early 19th Century," in Lawrence Stone (Ed.), *The University in Society*, Vol. 2 (Princeton, N.J.: Princeton University Press, 1974), p. 468.

14. McLachlan, "The *Choice of Hercules*," pp. 449-494.

15. McLachlan, "The *Choice of Hercules*," p. 487.

16. James McLachlan, *American Boarding Schools: A Historical Study* (New York: Scribner's, 1970), pp. 32-34; Theodore Sizer (Ed.), *The Age of the Academies* (New York: Teachers College, Columbia University, 1964), passim.

17. Thomas Jefferson Wertenbaker, *Princeton, 1746–1896* (Princeton, N.J.: Princeton University Press, 1946), p. 237; George Matthew Dutcher, *An Historical and Critical Survey of the Curriculum of Wesleyan University and Related Subjects* (Middletown, Conn.: Wesleyan University, 1948), p. 12; McLachlan, *American Boarding Schools*, pp. 92, 97.

18. McLachlan, *American Boarding Schools*, p. 318.

19. Frederick Rudolph, *The American College and University: A History* (New York: Knopf, 1962), pp. 47-67; Lester William Bartlett, *State Control of Private Incorporated Institutions of Higher Education* (New York: Teachers College, Columbia University, 1926), p. 70.

20. Rudolph, *The American College and University*, p. 219.

21. Frederick A. P. Barnard, *Analysis of Some Statistics of Collegiate Education: A Paper Read before the Trustees of Columbia College, New York, January 3, 1870, by the President of the College* (New York: Columbia University, 1870), passim.

22. Palmer Chamberlain Ricketts, *History of Rensselaer Polytechnic Institute, 1824–1914* (3rd ed.; New York: Wiley, 1934), p. 2; Dutcher, *An Historical and Critical Survey of the Curriculum of Wesleyan University*, p. 7; Walter P. Rogers, *Andrew D. White and the Modern University* (Ithaca, N.Y.: Cornell University Press, 1942), p. 28; Kelley, *Yale*, p. 129.

23. Kelley, *Yale*, p. 137.

24. Codman Hislop, *Eliphalet Nott* (Middletown, Conn.: Wesleyan University Press, 1971), p. 24.

25. Edward Potts Cheyney, *History of the University of Pennsylvania, 1740--1940* (Philadelphia: University of Pennsylvania Press, 1940), p. 205.

26. Earle D. Ross, *Democracy's College: The Land-Grant Movement in the Formative Stage* (Ames: Iowa State College Press, 1942), p. 11.

27. Sidney Forman, *West Point: A History of the United States Military Academy* (New York: Columbia University Press, 1950), pp. 23-60, 82-85; Stephen E. Ambrose, *Duty, Honor, Country: A History of West Point* (Baltimore, Md.: Johns Hopkins Press, 1966), pp. 87-146.

28. Ricketts, *History of Rensselaer Polytechnic Institute*, pp. xi-xii, 9-12, 43-45, 58-59, 85; Rudolph, *The American College and University*, pp. 229-231.

29. Daniel H. Calhoun, *The American Civil Engineer: Origins and Conflict* (Cambridge, Mass.: Technology Press, 1960), pp. ix, 46.

30. E. W. Bagster-Collins, "History of Modern Language Teaching in the United States," in *Studies in Modern Language Teaching* (New York: Macmillan, 1930), pp. 51-61.

31. Bagster-Collins, "History of Modern Language Teaching," p. 55.

32. Dutcher, *An Historical and Critical Survey of the Curriculum of Wesleyan University*, p. 14; Bagster-Collins, "History of Modern Language Teaching," p. 52; Willis Rudy, *The Evolving Liberal Arts Curriculum: A Historical Review of Basic Themes* (New York: Teachers College, Columbia University, 1960), p. 13.

33. McLachlan, *American Boarding Schools*, p. 75; Kelley, *Yale*, p. 159.

34. Richard J. Storr, *The Beginnings of Graduate Education in America* (Chicago: University of Chicago Press, 1953), pp. 29-30.

35. Melvin I. Urofsky, "Reforms and Response: The Yale Report of 1828," *History of Education Quarterly*, 1965, 5 (March), 62-63.

36. George P. Schmidt, *The Liberal Arts College* (New Brunswick, N.J.: Rutgers University Press, 1957), p. 186.

37. Kelley, *Yale*, p. 165.

38. Kelley, *Yale*, pp. 159, 168-169, 216; McCaughey, *Josiah Quincy*, p. 147.

39. *Reports on the Course of Instruction in Yale College: By a Committee of the Corporation and the Academical Faculty* (New Haven, Conn.: Howe, 1828), p. 3. Also published as "Original Papers in Relation to a Course of Liberal Education," *American Journal of Science and Arts*, 1829, *15*, 297-358. The 1828 pamphlet is the text used here.

40. *Reports . . . in Yale College*, p. 3.

41. *Reports . . . in Yale College*, p. 5.

42. *Reports . . . in Yale College*, p. 6.

43. *Reports . . . in Yale College*, pp. 6-7.

44. *Reports . . . in Yale College*, pp. 7-8.

45. *Reports . . . in Yale College*, p. 8.

46. *Reports . . . in Yale College*, p. 8; to which he added the attribution: "Cic." but, of course, no translation.

47. *Reports . . . in Yale College*, p. 8.

48. *Reports . . . in Yale College*, p. 10.

49. *Reports . . . in Yale College*, pp. 11-13.

50. *Reports . . . in Yale College*, pp. 14-16, 21-25.

51. *Reports . . . in Yale College*, pp. 19, 23.

52. *Reports . . . in Yale College*, p. 14.

53. *Reports . . . in Yale College*, p. 17.

54. *Reports . . . in Yale College*, p. 18.

55. *Reports . . . in Yale College*, p. 23.

56. *Reports . . . in Yale College*, p. 19.

57. *Reports . . . in Yale College*, p. 23.

58. *Reports . . . in Yale College*, p. 24.

59. *Reports . . . in Yale College*, pp. 27-30.

60. *Reports . . . in Yale College*, pp. 40, 42.

61. *Reports . . . in Yale College*, pp. 32-34, 37.

62. *Reports . . . in Yale College*, p. 36.

63. *Reports . . . in Yale College*, p. 39.

64. *Reports . . . in Yale College*, pp. 51, 55.

65. *Reports . . . in Yale College*, p. 56.

66. Daniel D. Barnard, *Address Delivered before the Adelphic Union Society of Williams College, Sept. 6, 1831* (Williamstown, Mass.: Banister, 1831); Alpheus Crosby, "Classical Study as a Part of a Liberal Education," *American Quarterly Observer*, 1833, *1* (October).

67. "Thoughts on the Study of Greek and Latin Languages," *New-England Magazine*, 1833, *5* (July, August, September).

68. *Addresses Delivered at the Inauguration of Middlebury College, March 18, 1839* (Middlebury, Vt.: Office of the People's Press, 1839), pp. 12-13, 47-56. See also Storr, *The Beginnings of Graduate Education in America*, pp. 33-34; *American Quarterly Register*, 1829, *1* (No. 8, April), 204-209; James Kent, *An Address Delivered at New Haven, before the Phi Beta Kappa Society, Sept. 13, 1831* (New Haven, Conn.: Howe, 1831).

69. James I. Osborne and Theodore G. Gronert, *Wabash College: The First Hundred Years, 1832-1932* (Crawfordsville, Ind.: Banta, 1932), p. 42; Louis Franklin Snow, *The College Curriculum in the United States* (New York: Teachers College, Columbia University, 1907), p. 145; R. Freeman Butts, *The College Charts Its Course: Historical Conceptions and Current Proposals* (New York: McGraw-Hill, 1939), p. 125; Schmidt, *The Liberal Arts College*, p. 57; Donald R. Come, "The Influence of Princeton on Higher Education in the South before 1825," *William and Mary Quarterly*, 3rd series, 1945, *2*, 359-396.

70. Snow, *The College Curriculum*, p. 142; Verne A. Stadtman, *The*

University of California, 1868-1968 (New York: McGraw-Hill, 1970), pp. 17-18; Richardson, *History of Dartmouth College*, Vol. 2, p. 429; Daniel Walker Hollis, *University of South Carolina*, Vol. 2 (Columbia: University of South Carolina Press, 1956), p. 12; Joseph D. Ibbotson and S. N. D. North, *Documentary History of Hamilton College* (Clinton, N.Y.: Hamilton College, 1922), p. 20; Allen E. Ragan, *A History of Tusculum College, 1794-1944* (Bristol, Tenn.: Tusculum College, 1945), p. 51.

71. Nevitt Sanford (Ed.), *The American College: A Psychological and Social Interpretation of the Higher Learning* (New York: Wiley, 1962), p. 426.

72. *Reports . . . in Yale College*, p. 31.

73. "Thoughts on the Study of the Greek and Latin Languages," *New-England Magazine*, 1833, 5 (July), 53.

74. Laurence Veysey, "Stability and Experiment in the American Undergraduate Curriculum," in Carl Kaysen (Ed.), *Content and Context: Essays on College Education* (New York: McGraw-Hill, 1973), p. 2.

75. Whitehead, *The Separation of College and State*, p. 129.

76. *Reports . . . in Yale College*, p. 8.

77. Tyack, *George Ticknor and the Boston Brahmins*, pp. 85-86; Samuel Eliot Morison, *Three Centuries of Harvard, 1636-1936* (Cambridge, Mass.: Harvard University Press, 1936), pp. 230-231; McLachlan, *American Boarding Schools*, p. 73.

78. Tyack, *George Ticknor and the Boston Brahmins*, pp. 95, 101-123.

79. Tyack, *George Ticknor and the Boston Brahmins*, p. 119.

80. Seymour Martin Lipset, "Political Controversies at Harvard, 1636 to 1974," in Seymour Martin Lipset and David Riesman, *Education and Politics at Harvard* (New York: McGraw-Hill, 1975), pp. 59, 65.

81. George Ticknor, *Remarks on Changes Lately Proposed or Adapted in Harvard University* (Boston: Cummings, Hilliard, 1825); *Reports . . . in Yale College*, p. 48 (Ticknor was also quoted on pp. 43, 46, 47).

82. McCaughey, *Josiah Quincy*, pp. 148, 169-170.

83. McCaughey, *Josiah Quincy*, p. 166.

84. Lipset, "Political Controversies at Harvard," p. 76.

85. McCaughey, *Josiah Quincy*, p. 178; Lipset, "Political Controversies at Harvard," p. 76; Tyack, *George Ticknor and the Boston Brahmins*, p. 123.

86. Leroy J. Halsey (Ed.), *The Works of Philip Lindsley, D.D.*, Vol. 1 (Philadelphia: Lippincott, 1866), pp. 375, 406; Wertenbaker, *Princeton*, p. 175; Rudolph, *The American College and University*, pp. 116-118.

87. James Torrey, *The Remains of the Rev. James Marsh, D.D., Late President, and Professor of Moral and Intellectual Philosophy, in the University of Vermont; with a Memoir of his Life* (Boston: Crocker and Brewster, 1843), pp. 77-85; [James Marsh], *Exposition of the System of Instruction and Discipline Pursued in the University of Vermont* (Burlington, Vt.?: Goodrich?, 1829), pp. 2-28; Rudolph, *The American College and University*, pp. 121-122.

88. [Marsh], *Exposition of the System of Instruction and Discipline Pursued in the University of Vermont*, pp. 6-7.

89. The proceedings in New York were fully recorded in *Journal of the Proceedings of a Convention of Literary and Scientific Gentlemen, Held in the Common Council Chamber of the City of New York, October 1830* (New York: Leavitt and Carvill, 1831). See also Storr, *The Beginnings of Graduate Education in America*, pp. 33-43; Theodore F. Jones (Ed.), *New York University, 1832-1932* (New York: New York University Press, 1933), pp. 6-35; Rudolph, *The American College and University*, pp. 128-130.

90. Storr, *The Beginnings of Graduate Education in America*, pp. 1-2.

91. "Report of the Commissioners Appointed to Fix the Site of the University of Virginia, Etc.," in Roy J. Honeywell, *The Educational Work of Thomas Jefferson* (Cambridge, Mass.: Harvard University Press, 1931), pp. 248-260; Philip Alexander Bruce, *History of the University of Virginia, 1819-1919*, Vol. 1 (New York: Macmillan, 1920), pp. 221-224, 322-331; Rudolph, *The American College and University*, pp. 124-130.

92. *Reports . . . in Yale College*, p. 21.

93. Bruce, *History of the University of Virginia*, Vol. 1, p. 331.

94. Bruce, *History of the University of Virginia*, Vol. 2, p. 140.

95. Honeywell, *The Educational Work of Thomas Jefferson*, pp. 130-133; Bruce, *History of the University of Virginia*, Vol. 3, pp. 244-255.

96. Jonas Viles and others, *The University of Missouri: A Centennial History* (Columbia: University of Missouri, 1939), p. 22; Rogers, *Andrew D. White and the Modern University*, p. 14; Hollis, *University of South Carolina*, Vol. 2, pp. 16, 27; Clarence Ray Aurner, *History of Education in Iowa*, Vol. 4 (Iowa City: State Historical Society of Iowa, 1916), p. 28; James F. Hopkins, *The University of Kentucky: Origins and Early Years* (Lexington: University of Kentucky Press, 1951), pp. 78-79; David Duncan Wallace, *History of Wofford College* (Nashville, Tenn.: Vanderbilt University Press, for Wofford College, 1951), pp. 94-95.

97. Bruce, *History of the University of Virginia*, Vol. 2, pp. 66-67.

98. Robert Samuel Fletcher, *A History of Oberlin College from its Foundation Through the Civil War*, Vol. 1 (Oberlin, Ohio: Oberlin College, 1943), pp. 364-368; Jack Morrison, *The Rise of the Arts on the American Campus* (New York: McGraw-Hill, 1973), p. 24.

99. *The Substance of Two Reports of the Faculty of Amherst College, to the Board of Trustees, with the Doings of the Board Thereon* (Amherst, Mass.: Carter and Adams, 1827); Russell Thomas, *The Search for a Common Learning: General Education, 1800-1960* (New York: McGraw-Hill, 1962), p. 15.

100. Frederick Rudolph, *Mark Hopkins and the Log: Williams College, 1836-1872* (New Haven, Conn.: Yale University Press, 1956), pp. 42-43.

101. Julian Ira Lindsay, *Tradition Looks Forward: The University of Vermont: A History, 1791-1904* (Burlington, Vt.: University of Vermont and State Agricultural College, 1954), p. 225; Thomas N. Hoover, *The History of*

Ohio University (Athens: Ohio University Press, 1954), pp. 64-65; Rudy, *The Evolving Liberal Arts Curriculum*, p. 24.

102. Dutcher, *An Historical and Critical Survey of the Curriculum of Wesleyan University*, p. 12; Walter Havighurst, *The Miami Years, 1809–1959* (New York: Putnam's, 1958), p. 45; Alfred J. Morrison (Ed.), *The College of Hampden-Sidney: Calendar of Board Minutes, 1776–1876* (Richmond, Va.: Hermitage Press, 1912), p. 98; Edwin C. Broome, *A Historical and Critical Discussion of College Admission Requirements* (New York: Macmillan, 1903), pp. 75 ff.; Butts, *The College Charts Its Course*, p. 135; Carl F. Price, *Wesleyan's First Century* (Middletown, Conn.: Wesleyan University, 1932), pp. 34 ff., 48.

103. The neglected story of Eliphalet Nott and Union is well told in Hislop, *Eliphalet Nott*, and Andrew Van Vranken Raymond (Ed.), *Union University: Its History, Influence, Characteristics and Equipment*, Vol. 1 (New York: Lewis, 1907).

104. Raymond, *Union University*, Vol. 1, p. 85; Hislop, *Eliphalet Nott*, pp. 167-168.

105. Hislop, *Eliphalet Nott*, p. 219.

106. Hislop, *Eliphalet Nott*, p. 223.

107. Hislop, *Eliphalet Nott*, pp. 209-217.

108. Hislop, *Eliphalet Nott*, pp. 226-227.

109. John Howard Van Amringe and others, *A History of Columbia University*, pp. 117-121; Hislop, *Eliphalet Nott*, pp. 221-230; Raymond, *Union University*, Vol. 1, p. 156.

110. Hislop, *Eliphalet Nott*, p. 232.

111. Hislop, *Eliphalet Nott*, pp. 230-231.

112. Francis Wayland, *Thoughts on the Present Collegiate System in the United States* (Boston: Gould, Kendall, & Lincoln, 1842), *Report to the Corporation of Brown University, on Changes in the System of Collegiate Education, Read March 28, 1850* (Providence, R.I.: Whitney, 1850), *The Education Demanded by the People of the U. States: A Discourse Delivered at Union College, Schenectady, July 25, 1854, on the Occasion of the Fiftieth Anniversary of the Presidency of Eliphalet Nott, D.D., LL.D.* (Boston: Phillips, Sampson, 1855).

113. Wayland, *Thoughts on the Present Collegiate System*, p. 41.

114. Wayland, *Thoughts on the Present Collegiate System*, p. 85.

115. Walter C. Bronson, *The History of Brown University, 1764–1914* (Providence, R.I.: Brown University, 1914), p. 314.

116. Bronson, *The History of Brown University*, p. 217; William Warren Sweet, *Indiana Asbury-DePauw University, 1837–1937: A Hundred Years of Higher Education in the Middle West* (New York: Abingdon Press, 1937), p. 87.

117. McLachlan, "The *Choice of Hercules*," pp. 467-468.

118. McLachlan, *American Boarding Schools*, p. 75.

119. Merrell R. Davis, "Emerson's 'Reason' and the Scottish

Philosophers," *New England Quarterly*, 1944, *17* (January), 219-221.
120. Tyack, *George Ticknor and the Boston Brahmins*, p. 93.
121. Kingsley, *Yale College*, Vol. 2, pp. 504-505.
122. Bronson, *The History of Brown University*, p. 204.
123. Tyack, *George Ticknor and the Boston Brahmins*, pp. 90-91; Wertenbaker, *Princeton*, p. 276; Kelley, *Yale*, pp. 166-167; Charles E. Ford, "Botany Texts: A Survey of Their Development in American Higher Education, 1643-1906," *History of Education Quarterly*, 1964, *4* (March), 62; Louis C. Hatch, *The History of Bowdoin College* (Portland, Maine: Loring, Short, & Harmon, 1927), pp. 53 ff.; Rudolph, *Mark Hopkins and the Log*, p. 51.
124. Richardson, *History of Dartmouth College*, Vol. 2., pp. 441-445.
125. Wertenbaker, *Princeton*, pp. 234-235.
126. George P. Schmidt, *The Old Time College President* (New York: Columbia University Press, 1930), pp. 108-145; Wilson Smith, "Apologia pro Alma Matre: The College as Community in Ante-Bellum America," in Stanley Elkins and Eric McKitrick (Eds.), *The Hofstadter Aegis: A Memorial* (New York: Knopf, 1974), passim; Wilson Smith, *Professors and Public Ethics: Studies of Northern Moral Philosophers before the Civil War* (Ithaca, N.Y.: Cornell University Press, 1956), passim.
127. Sloan, "Harmony, Chaos, and Consensus," p. 246.
128. Timothy Dwight, Jr., *President Dwight's Decisions of Questions Discussed by the Senior Class in Yale College in 1813 and 1814* (New York: Leavitt, 1833), p. i.
129. Dwight, *President Dwight's Decisions*, p. ii.
130. Dwight, *President Dwight's Decisions*, p. ii.
131. Dwight, *President Dwight's Decisions*, p. ii.
132. Dwight, *President Dwight's Decisions*, pp. 53-56.
133. Dwight, *President Dwight's Decisions*, pp. 74, 88, 103, 109, 122, 155, 177, 179.
134. Dwight, *President Dwight's Decisions*, pp. 240, 256, 305, 43.
135. Hislop, *Eliphalet Nott*, pp. 234-254.
136. Schmidt, *The Old Time College President*, pp. 138-139.
137. Hislop, *Eliphalet Nott*, p. 247.
138. This consideration of Mark Hopkins is adapted from my *Mark Hopkins and the Log*, pp. 45-52, with permission of Yale University Press.
139. Willis Rudy, *The College of the City of New York: A History, 1847-1947* (New York: City College Press, 1949), pp. 54-55.
140. Jonathan C. Messerli, *Horace Mann: A Biography* (New York: Knopf, 1972), p. 47.
141. Smythe, *Kenyon College*, p. 85; Lindsay, *Tradition Looks Forward*, p. 193; G. Wallace Chessman, *Denison: The Story of an Ohio College* (Granville, Ohio: Denison University, 1957), p. 76; Price, *Wesleyan's First Century*, p. 43; Rudolph, *Mark Hopkins and the Log*, pp. 144-155; Bronson, *The History of Brown University*, p. 181; Donald Fleming, *Science and Technology in Providence, 1760-1914: An Essay in the History of Brown Univer-*

sity in the Metropolitan Community (Providence, R.I.: Brown University, 1952), p. 29.

142. Paul T. Hartman, "Selected Student-Initiated Change at Harvard University, 1725-1925" (unpublished doctoral dissertation, Loyola University, 1975), passim.

143. Henry Davidson Sheldon, *The History and Pedagogy of American Student Societies* (New York: Appleton, 1901), p. 133.

144. Lowell Simpson, "The Little Republic: Undergraduate Literary Societies at Columbia, Dartmouth, Princeton, and Yale, 1753-1865" (unpublished doctoral dissertation, Teachers College, Columbia University, 1975), pp. 22 ff.; Rudolph, *The American College and University*, pp. 137-146.

145. McLachlan, "The *Choice of Hercules*," p. 472.

146. McLachlan, "The *Choice of Hercules*," pp. 478-483; Simpson, "The Little Republic," pp. 64, 126-128.

147. Simpson, "The Little Republic," pp. 128, 78, passim.

148. Hollis, *University of South Carolina*, Vol. 1, pp. 230-254; Havighurst, *The Miami Years*, pp. 76-78; Richardson, *History of Dartmouth College*, Vol. 2, p. 500; Rudolph, *Mark Hopkins and the Log*, pp. 162-163; Burton J. Bledstein, *The Culture of Professionalism: The Middle Class and the Development of Higher Education in America* (New York: Norton, 1976), pp. 259-268.

149. Kemp Plummer Battle, *History of the University of North Carolina*, Vol. 1 (Raleigh, N.C.: Edwards & Broughton, 1907), p. 477; James Albert Woodburn, *History of Indiana University, 1820-1902* (Bloomington: Indiana University, 1940), p. 303; Messerli, *Horace Mann*, pp. 44-53; Jonathan C. Messerli, "Horace Mann at Brown," *Harvard Educational Review*, 1963, *33* (Summer), 291; Anson Phelps Stokes, *Memorials of Eminent Yale Men*, Vol. 1 (New Haven, Conn.: Yale University Press, 1914), pp. 249-250; Simpson, "The Little Republic," pp. 65, 128; Wertenbaker, *Princeton*, pp. 203-204.

Chapter 4

1. Cornelius Howard Patton and Walter Taylor Field, *Eight O'clock Chapel: A Study of New England College Life* (Boston: Houghton Mifflin, 1927), p. 259; George R. Cutting, *Student Life at Amherst College* (Amherst, Mass.: Hatch & Williams, 1871), p. 129; E. Merton Coulter, *College Life in the Old South* (Athens: University of Georgia Press, 1951), p. 222; Walter Havighurst, *The Miami Years, 1809-1959* (New York: Putnam's, 1958), p. 151; Kemp Plummer Battle, *History of the University of North Carolina*, Vol. 1 (Raleigh, N.C.: Edwards & Broughton, 1907), p. 684.

2. Frederick Rudolph, *The American College and University: A History* (New York: Knopf, 1962), pp. 197-199.

3. Christopher Jencks and David Riesman, *The Academic Revolution* (New York: Doubleday, 1968), p. 92; Charles William Eliot, *A Late Harvest:*

Miscellaneous Papers Written Between Eighty and Ninety (Boston: Atlantic Monthly Press, 1924), p. 127.

4. James McLachlan, "American Colleges and the Transmission of Culture: The Case of the Mugwumps," in Stanley Elkins and Eric McKitrick (Eds.), *The Hofstadter Aegis: A Memorial* (New York: Knopf, 1974), pp. 184-206.

5. Laurence R. Veysey, *The Emergence of the American University* (Chicago: University of Chicago Press, 1965), p. 4.

6. Frederick A. P. Barnard, *Analysis of Some Statistics of Collegiate Education: A Paper Read before the Trustees of Columbia College, New York, January 3, 1870, by the President of the College* (New York: Columbia University, 1870), passim.

7. John S. Whitehead, *The Separation of College and State: Columbia, Dartmouth, Harvard, and Yale, 1776-1876* (New Haven, Conn.: Yale University Press, 1973), p. 124; Educational Policies Commission, *Higher Education in a Decade of Decision* (Washington, D.C.: National Education Association, 1957), p. 22.

8. Veysey, *The Emergence of the American University*, pp. 4-5.

9. Seymour Martin Lipset, "Political Controversies at Harvard, 1636 to 1974," in Seymour Martin Lipset and David Riesman, *Education and Politics at Harvard* (New York: McGraw-Hill, 1975), pp. 77-78; Clarence Ray Aurner, *History of Education in Iowa*, Vol. 4 (Iowa City: State Historical Society of Iowa, 1916), p. 172.

10. Samuel Eliot Morison, *Three Centuries of Harvard, 1636-1936* (Cambridge, Mass.: Harvard University Press, 1936), p. 287; James McLachlan, *American Boarding Schools: A Historical Study* (New York: Scribner's, 1970), p. 27.

11. Rudolph, *The American College and University*, pp. 231-233.

12. JB Lon Hefferlin, *Dynamics of Academic Reform* (San Francisco: Jossey-Bass, 1969), p. 30; William Lathrop Kingsley (Ed.), *Yale College: A Sketch of Its History*, Vol. 1 (New York: Henry Holt, 1879), pp. 150-152; Russell H. Chittenden, *History of the Sheffield Scientific School of Yale University, 1846-1922*, Vol. 1 (New Haven, Conn.: Yale University Press, 1928), pp. 52 ff.; Morison, *Three Centuries of Harvard*, p. 279; Brooks Mather Kelley, *Yale: A History* (New Haven, Conn.: Yale University Press, 1974), pp. 180-181; Charles F. Thwing, *A History of Higher Education in America* (New York: Appleton, 1906), p. 429.

13. Walter P. Rogers, *Andrew D. White and the Modern University* (Ithaca, N.Y.: Cornell University Press, 1942), p. 97.

14. Stanley M. Guralnick, *Science and the Ante-Bellum American College* (Philadelphia: The American Philosophical Society, 1975), p. ix; Douglas Sloan, "Harmony, Chaos, and Consensus: The American College Curriculum," *Teachers College Record*, 1971, *73* (December), 240.

15. William Warren Ferrier, *Origin and Development of the University of California* (Berkeley, Calif.: Sather Gate Book Shop, 1930), p. 258.

16. David Bishop Skillman, *The Biography of a College: Being the His-*

tory of the First Century of the Life of Lafayette College, Vol. 1 (Easton, Pa.: Lafayette College, 1932), pp. 279-285, 350.

17. Jencks and Riesman, *The Academic Revolution,* p. 229.

18. Merle Curti and Roderick Nash, *Philanthropy in the Shaping of American Higher Education* (New Brunswick, N.J.: Rutgers University Press, 1965), pp. 60-86; Nicholas Murray Butler (Ed.), *Monographs on Education in the United States,* Vol. 2 (Albany, N.Y.: Lyon, 1900), pp. 553 ff.

19. Palmer Chamberlain Ricketts, *History of Rensselaer Polytechnic Institute, 1824-1914* (3rd ed.; New York: Wiley, 1934), pp. 92-109; Richard G. Axt, *The Federal Government and Financing Higher Education* (New York: Columbia University Press, 1952), p. 59; Jesse Leonard Rosenberger, *Rochester, the Making of a University* (Rochester, N.Y.: University of Rochester, 1927), pp. 44-45; Leon Burr Richardson, *History of Dartmouth College,* Vol. 1 (Hanover, N.H.: Dartmouth College, 1932), pp. 422-427; Charles Henry Rammelkamp, *Illinois College: A Centennial History, 1829-1929* (New Haven, Conn.: Yale University Press, for Illinois College, 1928), pp. 168-169; G. Wallace Chessman, *Denison: The Story of an Ohio College* (Granville, Ohio: Denison University, 1957), p. 56; Battle, *History of the University of North Carolina,* Vol. 1, pp. 642-644; Aurner, *History of Education in Iowa,* Vol. 2, p. 22.

20. Rogers, *Andrew D. White and the Modern University,* p. 11; Thomas Jefferson Wertenbaker, *Princeton, 1746-1896* (Princeton, N.J.: Princeton University Press, 1946), pp. 307-308; Earle D. Ross, *Democracy's College: The Land-Grant Movement in the Formative Stage* (Ames: Iowa State College Press, 1942), p. 156; Frederick Rudolph, *Mark Hopkins and the Log: Williams College, 1836-1872* (New Haven, Conn.: Yale University Press, 1956), p. 141.

21. John William Draper, *The Indebtedness of the City of New York to Its University: An Address to the Alumni of the University of the City of New York, at Their Twenty-First Anniversary, 28th June, 1853* (New York: Association of the Alumni of the University of the City of New York, 1853), pp. 25, 19-20.

22. Sherman B. Barnes, "The Entry of Science and History in the College Curriculum, 1865-1914," *History of Education Quarterly,* 1964, *4* (March), 45; George E. Peterson, *The New England College in the Age of the University* (Amherst, Mass.: Amherst College Press, 1964), p. 72; Wertenbaker, *Princeton,* p. 287; Richard J. Storr, *The Beginnings of Graduate Education in America* (Chicago: University of Chicago Press, 1953), p. 73.

23. Henry Morton Bullock, *A History of Emory University* (Nashville, Tenn.: Parthenon Press, 1936), p. 142; Charles Elmer Allison, *A Historical Sketch of Hamilton College, Clinton, New York* (Yonkers, N.Y.: Hubley, 1889), pp. 35-38; Edwin Mims, *History of Vanderbilt University* (Nashville, Tenn.: Vanderbilt University Press, 1946), pp. 27-28; Arthur G. Beach, *A Pioneer College: The Story of Marietta* (Marietta, Ohio?: Privately printed, 1935), p. 88.

24. Andrew M. Greeley, *From Backwater to Mainstream: A Profile of*

Catholic Higher Education (New York: McGraw-Hill, 1969), p. 11; Sebastian A. Erbacher, *Catholic Higher Education for Men in the United States, 1850–1866* (Washington, D.C.: Catholic University of America, 1931), p. 116; Edward J. Power, *A History of Catholic Higher Education in the United States* (Milwaukee: Bruce, 1958), p. 56.

    25. Erbacher, *Catholic Higher Education for Men*, p. 87.

    26. Peterson, *The New England College*, pp. 122-123.

    27. Robert A. McCaughey, *Josiah Quincy, 1772–1864: The Last Federalist* (Cambridge, Mass.: Harvard University Press, 1974), p. 178.

    28. Bullock, *A History of Emory University*, p. 152.

    29. Walter C. Bronson, *The History of Brown University, 1764–1914* (Providence, R.I.: Brown University, 1914), p. 259; Francis Wayland, *Report to the Corporation of Brown University on Changes in the System of Collegiate Education, Read March 28, 1850* (Providence, R.I.: Whitney, 1850).

    30. Wilson Smith, "Apologia pro Alma Matre: The College as Community in Ante-Bellum America," in Stanley Elkins and Eric McKitrick (Eds.), *The Hofstadter Aegis: A Memorial* (New York: Knopf, 1974), p. 144; Theodore Rawson Crane, *Francis Wayland: Political Economist as Educator* (Providence, R.I.: Brown University Press, 1962), passim; Bronson, *The History of Brown University*, pp. 282-283.

    31. Wayland, *Report to the Corporation of Brown University*, p. 34.

    32. Wayland, *Report to the Corporation of Brown University*, pp. 25-26, 12-13.

    33. R. Freeman Butts, *The College Charts its Course: Historical Conceptions and Current Proposals* (New York: McGraw-Hill, 1939), pp. 148-149; Bronson, *The History of Brown University*, pp. 284-300, 322.

    34. Francis Wayland, *The Education Demanded by the People of the U. States: A Discourse Delivered at Union College, Schenectady, July 25, 1854, on the Occasion of the Fiftieth Anniversary of the Presidency of Eliphalet Nott, D.D., LL.D.* (Boston: Phillips, Sampson, 1855), pp. 12-22.

    35. Wayland, *The Education Demanded by the People of the U. States*, p. 25.

    36. *Reports on the Course of Instruction in Yale College: By a Committee of the Corporation and the Academical Faculty* (New Haven, Conn.: Howe, 1828), p. 29.

    37. Willis Rudy, *The Evolving Liberal Arts Curriculum: A Historical Review of Basic Themes* (New York: Teachers College, Columbia University, 1960), p. 31.

    38. Storr, *The Beginnings of Graduate Education in America*, pp. 112-117.

    39. Rudolph, *Mark Hopkins and the Log*, p. 185.

    40. Storr, *The Beginnings of Graduate Education in America*, pp. 94-111.

    41. Storr, *The Beginnings of Graduate Education in America*, pp. 82-93; Rudolph, *Mark Hopkins and the Log*, p. 185.

42. Edgar S. Furniss, *The Graduate School of Yale: A Brief History* (New Haven, Conn.: Yale University, 1965), p. 2.

43. Andrew D. White to Ezra Cornell, Dec. 5, 1872, quoted in Morris Bishop, *A History of Cornell* (Ithaca, N.Y.: Cornell University Press, 1962), pp. 43-44.

44. *Report of the Committee on Organization Presented to the Trustees of the Cornell University, October 21st, 1866* (Albany, N.Y.: Van Benthuysen, 1867); Rogers, *Andrew D. White and the Modern University*, p. 94; Waterman Thomas Hewett, *Cornell University: A History* (New York: University Publishing Society, 1905), Vol. 3, p. 3.

45. Rogers, *Andrew D. White and the Modern University*, p. 47.

46. Rogers, *Andrew D. White and the Modern University*, pp. 46-49; Veysey, *The Emergence of the American University*, p. 82.

47. Rudolph, *The American College and University*, p. 252.

48. Edward Danforth Eddy, Jr., *Colleges for Our Land and Time: The Land-Grant Idea in American Education* (New York: Harper & Row, 1957), p. x.

49. Rudolph, *The American College and University*, p. 252.

50. Rudolph, *The American College and University*, pp. 248-249.

51. Rudolph, *The American College and University*, pp. 253.

52. Rudolph, *The American College and University*, p. 249.

53. Rogers, *Andrew D. White and the Modern University*, pp. 54, 112; Bishop, *A History of Cornell*, pp. 40-43; *Report of the Committee on Organization*, p. 3.

54. *Report of the Committee on Organization*, pp. 3-4.

55. *Report of the Committee on Organization*, p. 4.

56. *Report of the Committee on Organization*, p. 5.

57. *Report of the Committee on Organization*, p. 5.

58. Bishop, *A History of Cornell*, p. 42.

59. *Report of the Committee on Organization*, p. 7.

60. *Report of the Committee on Organization*, p. 9.

61. *Report of the Committee on Organization*, p. 9.

62. *Report of the Committee on Organization*, p. 10.

63. *Report of the Committee on Organization*, p. 11.

64. *Report of the Committee on Organization*, pp. 21-22.

65. *Report of the Committee on Organization*, p. 21.

66. Veysey, *The Emergence of the American University*, pp. 16, 97; Rogers, *Andrew D. White and the Modern University*, p. 109.

67. *Account of the Proceedings at the Inauguration October 7th, 1868* (Ithaca, N.Y.: Cornell University Press, 1869), p. 18.

68. Rogers, *Andrew D. White and the Modern University*, pp. 163-168.

69. Andrew D. White, "Scientific and Industrial Education," *Popular Science Monthly*, 1874, 5 (June), 186.

70. Ross, *Democracy's College: The Land-Grant Movement in the Formative Stage*, pp. 122-128; Louis C. Hatch, *The History of Bowdoin College*

(Portland, Maine: Loring, Short, & Harmon, 1927), p. 146; James E. Pollard, *History of the Ohio State University: The Story of Its First Seventy-Five Years, 1873-1948* (Columbus: Ohio State University Press, 1952), pp. 74-76; James Albert Woodburn, *History of Indiana University, 1820-1902* (Bloomington: Indiana University, 1940), pp. 284-287; Orrin Leslie Elliott, *Stanford University: The First Twenty-Five Years* (Stanford, Calif.: Stanford University Press, 1937), p. 111.

71. *Report of the Committee on Organization*, p. 40.

72. Rudolph, *The American College and University*, p. 294; Bishop, *A History of Cornell*, p. 325; Albert Perry Brigham, *Present Status of the Elective System in American Colleges* (New York: Holt, 1897), p. 361.

73. S. Willis Rudy, *The College of the City of New York: A History, 1847-1947* (New York: City College Press, 1949), p. 191.

74. Thomas LeDuc, *Piety and Intellect at Amherst College, 1865-1912* (New York: Columbia University Press, 1946), p. 129; Rudolph, *Mark Hopkins and the Log*, pp. 161, 164.

75. Rogers, *Andrew D. White and the Modern University*, p. 187.

76. *Report of the Committee on Organization*, p. 39.

77. Rudolph, *The American College and University*, p. 316; Bishop, *A History of Cornell*, pp. 42, 57, 60, 89, 143-152.

78. Rudolph, *The American College and University*, p. 321.

79. Rudolph, *The American College and University*, pp. 317-318.

80. Jill Conway, "Perspectives on the History of Women's Education in the United States," *History of Education Quarterly*, 1974, *14* (Spring), 5-6.

81. Conway, "Perspectives," passim; Rogers, *Andrew D. White and the Modern University*, pp. 84-86.

82. Rogers, *Andrew D. White and the Modern University*, pp. 131-132.

83. Rogers, *Andrew D. White and the Modern University*, pp. 131-132.

84. Rogers, *Andrew D. White and the Modern University*, pp. 128-129.

85. Morison, *Three Centuries of Harvard*, p. 349.

86. Hewett, *Cornell University*, Vol. 1, p. 149.

87. Rogers, *Andrew D. White and the Modern University*, pp. 235, 74, 66.

88. Rudolph, *The American College and University*, p. 261.

89. Bishop, *A History of Cornell*, p. 191.

90. *North American Review*, 1867, *105* (July), 295-297; *Independent*, 1867, *19* (September 5), 4.

91. Douglas T. Miller, "The Transformation of Higher Education in America, 1865-1875, as Reflected in *The Nation*," *Educational Theory*, 1961, *11*, 187.

92. Miller, "The Transformation of Higher Education," p. 188.

93. Rogers, *Andrew D. White and the Modern University*, pp. 99-101.

94. "Editor's Easy Chair," *Harper's*, 1868, *38* (December), 144.

95. *New York Times*, June 3, 1873, p. 4; *New York Times*, April 11, 1874, p. 6.

96. "Cornell University," *Harper's Weekly,* 1889, *33* (June 8), 459.

97. Rudolph, *The American College and University,* pp. 339-344; Rogers, *Andrew D. White and the Modern University,* pp. 114, 173-174.

98. Rudolph, *The American College and University,* pp. 269-275.

99. Veysey, *The Emergence of the American University,* p. 159.

100. John C. French, *A History of the University Founded by Johns Hopkins* (Baltimore, Md.: Johns Hopkins Press, 1946), p. 32; Hugh Hawkins, *Pioneer: A History of the Johns Hopkins University, 1874–1889* (Ithaca, N.Y.: Cornell University Press, 1960), pp. 3-20.

101. Hawkins, *Pioneer,* pp. 60, 53.

102. Rudolph, *The American College and University,* p. 274.

103. Phillip W. Payton, "Origins of the Terms 'Major' and 'Minor' in American Higher Education," *History of Education Quarterly,* 1961, *1* (June), 57-61.

104. Veysey, *The Emergence of the American University,* p. 165; Dorothy Ross, *G. Stanley Hall: The Psychologist as Prophet* (Chicago: University of Chicago Press, 1972), pp. 186-230.

105. Morison, *Three Centuries of Harvard,* pp. 324-346; Kelley, *Yale,* pp. 237-238.

106. Noah Porter, *The American Colleges and the American Public* (New Haven, Conn.: Chatfield, 1870); *Addresses at the Inauguration of Professor Noah Porter, D.D., LL.D., as President of Yale College, Wednesday, October 11, 1871* (New York: Scribner's, 1871); Kelley, *Yale,* p. 206.

107. Porter, *The American Colleges and the American Public,* pp. 40-48, 55-56, 58.

108. Porter, *The American Colleges and the American Public,* pp. 60-66.

109. Timothy Dwight, *Yale College: Some Thoughts Respecting its Future* (New Haven, Conn.: Tuttle, Morehouse, and Taylor, 1871), p. 68.

110. Porter, *The American Colleges and the American Public,* pp. 71, 77; *Addresses at the Inauguration of Professor Noah Porter,* p. 45.

111. Porter, *The American Colleges and the American Public,* pp. 30, 220, 224.

112. Porter, *The American Colleges and the American Public,* p. 36.

113. Porter, *The American Colleges and the American Public,* p. 99.

114. Porter, *The American Colleges and the American Public,* p. 74.

115. Lyman H. Bagg, *Four Years at Yale* (New Haven, Conn.: Chatfield, 1871), passim.

116. Bagg, *Four Years at Yale,* pp. 563-564; Kelley, *Yale,* pp. 263-264.

117. Kelley, *Yale,* pp. 249-250.

118. Kelley, *Yale,* pp. 174-175; George Wilson Pierson, *Yale College: An Educational History, 1871–1921* (New Haven, Conn.: Yale University Press, 1952), pp. 69-73.

119. Robert A. McCaughey, "The Transformation of American Aca-

demic Life: Harvard University, 1821-1892," *Perspectives in American History*, 1974, *8*, 267-268.

120. Charles W. Eliot, "The New Education. Its Organization," *Atlantic Monthly*, 1869, *23*, 203-220, 358-367.

121. Morison, *Three Centuries of Harvard*, pp. 324-326.

122. *Addresses at the Inauguration of Charles William Eliot as President of Harvard College, Tuesday, October 19, 1869* (Cambridge, Mass.: Sever and Francis, 1869), pp. 40-41.

123. *Addresses at the Inauguration of Charles William Eliot*, pp. 19-20.

124. Eliot, "The New Education. Its Organization," p. 215; *Addresses at the Inauguration of Charles William Eliot*, p. 30.

125. *Addresses at the Inauguration of Charles William Eliot*, p. 29.

126. *Addresses at the Inauguration of Charles William Eliot*, p. 42.

127. *Addresses at the Inauguration of Charles William Eliot*, p. 40.

128. Eliot, "The New Education. Its Organization," p. 218.

129. McCaughey, "The Transformation of American Academic Life," p. 274; Hugh Hawkins, *Between Harvard and America: The Educational Leadership of Charles W. Eliot* (New York: Oxford University Press, 1972), pp. 4, 93; Lipset, "Political Controversies at Harvard," p. 81.

130. Hawkins, *Between Harvard and America*, p. 59; Butts, *The College Charts its Course*, p. 177; *Addresses at the Inauguration of Charles William Eliot*, pp. 41-42.

131. Walter Crosby Eells, *Academic Degrees: Earned and Honorary Degrees Conferred by Institutions of Higher Education in the United States*, U.S. Office of Education Bulletin No. 28, 1961 (Washington, D.C.: U.S. Government Printing Office, 1960), p. 24; George Matthew Dutcher, *An Historical and Critical Survey of the Curriculum of Wesleyan University and Related Subjects* (Middletown, Conn.: Wesleyan University, 1948), p. 12.

132. Eells, *Academic Degrees*, pp. 94, 150, 176, 114.

133. Burton Dorr Myers, *History of Indiana University, 1902-1937* (Bloomington: Indiana University, 1952), p. 486; W. Freeman Galpin, *Syracuse University: The Pioneer Days* (Syracuse, N.Y.: Syracuse University Press, 1952), p. 40; Chessman, *Denison*, p. 116; Richardson, *History of Dartmouth College*, Vol. 2, p. 596; Pollard, *History of the Ohio State University*, p. 53; John Hugh Reynolds and David Yancey Thomas, *History of the University of Arkansas* (Fayetteville: University of Arkansas, 1910), p. 114; Ross, *Democracy's College*, pp. 159-161; Bronson, *The History of Brown University*, p. 448.

134. Eells, *Academic Degrees*, pp. 37-41.

135. Wilson Smith, *Professors and Public Ethics: Studies of Northern Moral Philosophers Before the Civil War* (Ithaca, N.Y.: Cornell University Press, 1956), p. 203.

136. Sheldon M. Stern, in Paul Buck (Ed.), *Social Sciences at Harvard, 1860-1920: From Inculcation to the Open Mind* (Cambridge, Mass.: Harvard University Press, 1965), pp. 180 ff.; Robert L. Church, "Economists as

Experts: The Rise of an Academic Profession in America 1870–1917," in Lawrence Stone (Ed.), *The University in Society*, Vol. 2 (Princeton, N.J.: Princeton University Press, 1974), pp. 574-577, 593-596.

137. Rudolph, *Mark Hopkins and the Log*, p. 128; Peterson, *The New England College in the Age of the University*, p. 70.

138. *Addresses at the Inauguration of Charles William Eliot*, p. 30; Pierson, *Yale College*, p. 299; Skillman, *The Biography of a College*, Vol. 1, pp. 227-234.

139. Frank Aydelotte, *The Oxford Stamp and Other Essays* (New York: Oxford University Press, 1917), pp. 176-196.

140. *Addresses at the Inauguration of Charles William Eliot*, p. 64; Wertenbaker, *Princeton*, p. 55; LeDuc, *Piety and Intellect at Amherst College*, p. 91; Eliot, *A Late Harvest*, pp. 95-96.

141. Hatch, *The History of Bowdoin College*, pp. 447-454.

142. Kingsley, *Yale College*, Vol. 1, p. 141; Kingsley, *Yale College*, Vol. 2, pp. 153-154; Pierson, *Yale College*, p. 49; Bronson, *The History of Brown University*, p. 375; Elizabeth M. Farrand, *History of the University of Michigan* (Ann Arbor, Mich.: Register Publishing House, 1885), p. 118; Julian Ira Lindsay, *Tradition Looks Forward: The University of Vermont: A History, 1791–1904* (Burlington: University of Vermont and State Agricultural College, 1954), p. 235; Allan Nevins, *Illinois* (New York: Oxford University Press, 1917), p. 74; William Warren Ferrier, *Origin and Development of the University of California*, pp. 427-430; Wertenbaker, *Princeton 1746–1896*, p. 309.

143. Rudolph, *Mark Hopkins and the Log*, pp. 80-81.

144. Aurner, *History of Education in Iowa*, Vol. 4., p. 40; Farrand, *History of the University of Michigan*, p. 98.

145. Jack Morrison, *The Rise of the Arts on the American Campus* (New York: McGraw-Hill, 1973), pp. 26-27; Kingsley, *Yale College*, Vol. 2, pp. 140-152; Pierson, *Yale College*, p. 52; Galpin, *Syracuse University*, p. 102.

146. Galpin, *Syracuse University*, pp. 103-117; Morison, *Three Centuries of Harvard*, p. 352; Butler, *Monographs on Education in the United States*, Vol. 2, pp. 721-722; Robert Lincoln Kelly, *The American Colleges and the Social Order* (New York: Macmillan, 1940), p. 233; Morrison, *The Rise of the Arts on the American Campus*, pp. 32-33.

147. Morison, *Three Centuries of Harvard*, p. 352; Saul Sack, "Liberal Education: What Was It? What Is It?" *History of Education Quarterly*, 1962, 2 (December), 221.

148. Hatch, *The History of Bowdoin College*, p. 453.

149. Charles Burt Sumner, *The Story of Pomona College* (Boston: Pilgrim Press, 1914), pp. 103-115; Frank P. Brackett, *Granite and Sagebrush: Reminiscences of the First Fifty Years of Pomona College* (Los Angeles: Ward Richie Press, 1944), pp. 194-201.

150. Kelley, *Yale*, pp. 251-252; McCaughey, "The Transformation of American Academic Life," p. 277.

151. *Addresses at the Inauguration of Charles William Eliot*, p. 42; Porter, *The American Colleges and the American Public*, pp. 119-133, 136; Rogers, *Andrew D. White and the Modern University*, p. 135; Patton and Field, *Eight O'Clock Chapel*, pp. 48-49; Herbert Baxter Adams, *Seminary Libraries and University Extension* (Baltimore, Md.: Johns Hopkins University, 1887), pp. 7-12; Jurgen Herbst, *The German Historical School in American Scholarship: A Study in the Transfer of Culture* (Ithaca, N.Y.: Cornell University Press, 1965), p. 35; Henry Adams, *The Education of Henry Adams: An Autobiography* (Boston: Houghton Mifflin, 1918), p. 303.

152. Hawkins, *Between Harvard and America*, p. 16; Vernon Rosco Carstensen, "The History of the State University of Iowa: The Collegiate Department from the Beginning to 1878," in *University of Iowa Studies in the Social Sciences, Abstracts in History III*, 1938, 10 (February), 110; Aurner, *History of Education in Iowa*, Vol. 4, p. 178; Bullock, *A History of Emory University*, p. 180.

153. Rogers, *Andrew D. White and the Modern University*, p. 38; Wayland, *Thoughts on the Present Collegiate System*, p. 50.

154. Mary Lovett Smallwood, *An Historical Study of Examinations and Grading Systems in Early American Universities* (Cambridge, Mass.: Harvard University Press, 1935), passim.

155. Smallwood, *An Historical Study of Examinations and Grading Systems*, pp. 14-15.

156. Hawkins, *Between Harvard and America*, p. 15; Morison, *Three Centuries of Harvard*, pp. 298-300; Smallwood, *An Historical Study of Examinations and Grading Systems*, pp. 15-16; Rudolph, *Mark Hopkins and the Log*, pp. 223-224; Kelley, *Yale*, p. 174; Skillman, *The Biography of a College*, Vol. 1, p. 389; David Duncan Wallace, *History of Wofford College* (Nashville, Tenn.: Vanderbilt University Press, for Wofford College, 1951), p. 93.

157. Smallwood, *An Historical Study of Examinations and Grading Systems*, pp. 41-43.

158. Morison, *Three Centuries of Harvard*, p. 260.

159. Rudolph, *The American College and University*, p. 348; Smallwood, *An Historical Study of Examinations and Grading Systems*, pp. 50-52.

160. James M. McPherson, "The New Puritanism: Values and Goals of Freedmen's Education in America," in Lawrence Stone (Ed.), *The University in Society*, Vol. 2 (Princeton, N.J.: Princeton University Press, 1974), p. 624.

161. Thomas Jesse Jones (Ed.), *Negro Education: A Study of the Private and Higher Schools for Colored People in the United States*, Vol. 2 (New York: Arno Press, 1969), pp. 16-17; Dwight Oliver Wendell Holmes, *The Evolution of the Negro College* (New York: Teachers College, Columbia University, 1934), p. 54; Rayford W. Logan, *Howard University: The First Hundred Years, 1867-1967* (New York: New York University Press, 1969), pp. 26, 7.

162. Logan, *Howard University*, pp. 3-18.

163. McPherson, "The New Puritanism," p. 615.

164. Jones, *Negro Education*, Vol. 2, p. 16; Henry Allen Bullock, *A History of Negro Education in the South* (Cambridge, Mass.: Harvard University Press, 1967), p. 188.

165. Bullock, *A History of Negro Education in the South*, p. 159.

166. Holmes, *The Evolution of the Negro College*, pp. 113-114.

167. McPherson, "The New Puritanism," p. 635.

168. Earl J. McGrath, *The Graduate School and the Decline of Liberal Education* (New York: Teachers College, Columbia University, 1959), p. 11.

169. Michael R. Harris, *Five Counter-Revolutionists in Higher Education* (Corvallis: Oregon State University Press, 1970), p. 13.

170. Harris, *Five Counter-Revolutionists in Higher Education*, p. 31.

171. Sheldon, *The History and Pedagogy of American Student Societies*, pp. 134-135.

Chapter 5

1. Kermit Vanderbilt, *Charles Eliot Norton: Apostle of Culture in a Democracy* (Cambridge, Mass.: Harvard University Press, 1959), p. 136.

2. Madison Kuhn, *Michigan State: The First Hundred Years* (East Lansing, Mich.: Michigan State University Press, 1955), p. 23.

3. James McLachlan, "American Colleges and the Transmission of Culture: The Case of the Mugwumps," in Stanley Elkins and Eric McKitrick (Eds.), *The Hofstadter Aegis: A Memorial* (New York: Knopf, 1974), pp. 188, 193.

4. Educational Policies Commission, *Higher Education in a Decade of Decision* (Washington, D.C.: National Education Association, 1957), p. 22.

5. Lester William Bartlett, *State Control of Private Incorporated Institutions of Higher Education* (New York: Teachers College, Columbia University, 1926), p. 2.

6. McLachlan, "American Colleges and the Transmission of Culture," p. 185.

7. McLachlan, "American Colleges and the Transmission of Culture," p. 185.

8. Robert A. McCaughey, "The Transformation of American Academic Life: Harvard University, 1821-1892," *Perspectives in American History*, 1974, *8*, 287, 273-274, 292.

9. McCaughey, "The Transformation of American Academic Life," pp. 290, 308.

10. McCaughey, "The Transformation of American Academic Life," p. 174.

11. McCaughey, "The Transformation of American Academic Life," p. 246.

12. Samuel Eliot Morison, *Three Centuries of Harvard, 1636-1936* (Cambridge, Mass.: Harvard University Press, 1936), pp. 372-373.

13. Christopher Jencks and David Riesman, *The Academic Revolution* (New York: Doubleday, 1968), p. 13.

14. Jurgen Herbst, *The German Historical School in American Scholarship: A Study in the Transfer of Culture* (Ithaca, N.Y.: Cornell University Press, 1965), p. 8.

15. Walton C. John, *Graduate Study in Universities and Colleges in the United States*, Office of Education Bulletin No. 20, 1934 (Washington, D.C.: U.S. Government Printing Office, 1935), pp. 62-63.

16. Mary O. Furner, *Advocacy & Objectivity: A Crisis in the Professionalization of American Social Science, 1865-1905* (Lexington: University Press of Kentucky, 1975), passim.

17. Claude M. Fuess, *The College Board: Its First Fifty Years* (New York: Columbia University Press, 1950), pp. 6-17.

18. Joseph Lindsey Henderson, *Admission to College by Certificate* (New York: Teachers College, Columbia University, 1912), p. 3.

19. Fuess, *The College Board*, p. 7.

20. Dwight C. Miner (Ed.), *A History of Columbia College on Morningside* (New York: Columbia University Press, 1954), p. 35.

21. James McLachlan, *American Boarding Schools: A Historical Study* (New York: Scribner's, 1970), pp. 121 ff., 193; Henry M. McCracken and others, *New York University* (Boston: Herndon, 1901), p. 5.

22. Orrin Leslie Elliott, *Stanford University: The First Twenty-Five Years* (Stanford, Calif.: Stanford University Press, 1937), p. 498.

23. Henderson, *Admission to College by Certificate*, p. 86.

24. Henderson, *Admission to College by Certificate*, pp. 89-90; George Wilson Pierson, *Yale College: An Educational History, 1871-1921* (New Haven, Conn.: Yale Univerity Press, 1952), p. 390.

25. James I. Osborne and Theodore G. Gronert, *Wabash College; The First Hundred Years, 1832-1932* (Crawfordsville, Ind.: Banta, 1932), pp. 219-221.

26. Henderson, *Admission to College by Certificate*, pp. 24-28.

27. Henderson, *Admission to College by Certificate*, pp. 41-44, 49, 52-82; Burke A. Hinsdale, *History of the University of Michigan* (Ann Arbor: University of Michigan, 1906), p. 60; Harold S. Wechsler, *The Qualified Student: A History of Selective College Admission in America* (New York: Wiley, 1977), pp. 16-61.

28. Allan Nevins, *Illinois* (New York: Oxford University Press, 1917), pp. 87-88; Vernon Rosco Carstensen, "The History of the State University of Iowa: The Collegiate Department from the Beginning to 1878," *University of Iowa Studies in the Social Sciences, Abstracts in History III*, 1938, *10* (February), 103-105; Edwin Mims, *History of Vanderbilt University* (Nashville, Tenn.: Vanderbilt University Press, 1946), pp. 89-90; Daniel Walker Hollis, *University of South Carolina*, Vol. 2 (Columbia: University of South Carolina Press, 1956), pp. 176-177; Thomas N. Hoover, *The History of Ohio University* (Athens: Ohio University Press, 1954), p. 155.

29. Edwin C. Broome, *A Historical and Critical Discussion of College Admission Requirements* (New York: Macmillan, 1903), pp. 116 ff.;

Henderson, *Admission to College by Certificate*, p. 82; William Warren Ferrier, *Origin and Development of the University of California* (Berkeley, Calif.: Sather Gate Book Shop, 1930), p. 382; Philip Alexander Bruce, *History of the University of Virginia*, Vol. 4 (New York: Macmillan, 1920-1922), p. 237.

30. William H. Powers (Ed.), *A History of South Dakota State College* (Brookings: South Dakota State College, 1931), p. 72; Louis G. Geiger, *University of the Northern Plains: A History of the University of North Dakota, 1883-1958* (Grand Forks: University of North Dakota Press, 1958), p. 69; Jencks and Riesman, *Academic Revolution*, p. 29; John Hugh Reynolds and David Yancey Thomas, *History of the University of Arkansas* (Fayetteville: University of Arkansas, 1910), p. 195; Hollis, *University of South Carolina*, Vol. 2, p. 268 ff.

31. Osborne and Gronert, *Wabash College*, p. 231.

32. McLachlan, *American Boarding Schools*, pp. 7-12, 136 ff.; Thomas Jefferson Wertenbaker, *Princeton, 1746-1896* (Princeton, N.J.: Princeton University Press, 1946), pp. 313-315.

33. McLachlan, *American Boarding Schools*, p. 206.

34. Broome, *A Historical and Critical Discussion of College Admission Requirements*, pp. 17-39, 43.

35. Broome, *A Historical and Critical Discussion of College Admission Requirements*, p. 62.

36. Broome, *A Historical and Critical Discussion of College Admission Requirements*, pp. 45-59 ff.

37. Broome, *A Historical and Critical Discussion of College Admission Requirements*, pp. 55-57, 82.

38. Broome, *A Historical and Critical Discussion of College Admission Requirements*, pp. 66-68.

39. Broome, *A Historical and Critical Discussion of College Admission Requirements*, pp. 128-129; Fuess, *The College Board*, pp. 9-10.

40. Theodore Sizer, *Secondary Schools at the Turn of the Century* (New Haven, Conn.: Yale University Press, 1964), passim; Edward A. Krug, *The Shaping of the American High School, 1880-1920* (Madison: University of Wisconsin Press, 1969), pp. 18-92; Hugh Hawkins, *Between Harvard and America: The Educational Leadership of Charles W. Eliot* (New York: Oxford University Press, 1972), pp. 224-262; Fuess, *The College Board*, pp. 12-14; McLachlan, *American Boarding Schools*, p. 281; Wechsler, *The Qualified Student*, pp. 82-112.

41. Hawkins, *Between Harvard and America*, p. 239.

42. Fuess, *The College Board*, pp. 26-29; Broome, *A Historical and Critical Discussion of Admission Requirements*, p. 141; Frederick Rudolph, *The American College and University: A History* (New York: Knopf, 1962), pp. 436-438.

43. Hawkins, *Between Harvard and America*, p. 171; Broome, *A Historical and Critical Discussion of Admission Requirements*, pp. 99-100, 62.

44. Ernest Victor Hollis, *Philanthropic Foundations and Higher Education* (New York: Columbia University Press, 1938), pp. 130-131.

45. Dwight Oliver Wendell Holmes, *The Evolution of the Negro College* (New York: Teachers College, Columbia University, 1934), p. vi; James M. McPherson, "The New Puritanism: Values and Goals of Freedmen's Education in America," in Lawrence Stone (Ed.), *The University in Society*, Vol. 2 (Princeton, N.J.: Princeton University Press, 1974), pp. 621, 632.

46. Holmes, *The Evolution of the Negro College*, pp. 150-154; John W. Davis, *Land-Grant Colleges for Negroes* (Institute, W. Va.: West Virginia State College, 1934), p. 13.

47. Henry Allen Bullock, *A History of Negro Education in the South* (Cambridge, Mass.: Harvard University Press, 1967), pp. 163-166; McPherson, "The New Puritanism," p. 635.

48. Bullock, *A History of Negro Education in the South*, pp. 33, 80, 85; McPherson, "The New Puritanism," pp. 621, 632.

49. Allan Nevins, *The Emergence of Modern America* (New York: Macmillan, 1927), p. 280; Thomas Woody, *A History of Women's Education in the United States*, Vol. 2 (New York: Science Press, 1929), pp. 182-185.

50. Mabel Newcomer, *A Century of Higher Education for American Women* (New York: Harper & Row, 1959), pp. 78-90; Woody, *A History of Women's Education in the United States*, Vol. 2, pp. 193-194; Earle D. Ross, *Democracy's College: The Land-Grant Movement in the Formative Stage* (Ames: Iowa State College Press, 1942), pp. 156-158; Charles F. Thwing, *American Colleges: Their Students and Work* (New York: Putnam's, 1878), pp. 17-18.

51. Jill Conway, "Perspectives on the History of Women's Education in the United States," *History of Education Quarterly*, 1974, *14* (Spring), 8; Newcomer, *A Century of Higher Education for Women*, p. 99; Roberta Wein, "Women's Colleges and Domesticity, 1875-1918," *History of Education Quarterly*, 1974, *14* (Spring), 31-48; Elaine Kendall, *"Peculiar Institutions": An Informal History of the Seven Sisters Colleges* (New York: Putnam's, 1975), pp. 132-143.

52. Philip Gleason, "American Catholic Higher Education: A Historical Perspective," in Robert Hassenger (Ed.), *The Shape of Catholic Higher Education* (Chicago: University of Chicago Press, 1967), p. 25.

53. Edward J. Power, *A History of Catholic Higher Education in the United States* (Milwaukee: Bruce, 1958), p. 84; Arthur J. Hope, *Notre Dame: One Hundred Years Later* (Notre Dame, Ind.: Notre Dame University Press, 1943), p. 198.

54. Thomas Gaffney Taaffe, *A History of St. John's College, Fordham, New York* (New York: Catholic Publication Society, 1891), pp. 74, 112 ff.

55. Jencks and Riesman, *Academic Revolution*, p. 365.

56. Gleason, "American Catholic Higher Education," pp. 25-39, 46.

57. James Axtell, "The Death of the Liberal Arts College," *History of Education Quarterly*, 1971, *11* (Winter), 347.

58. William Rainey Harper, *The Prospects of the Small College* (Chicago: University of Chicago Press, 1900), pp. 31-38; Leon B. Richardson, *A Study of the Liberal College: A Report to the President of Dartmouth College* (Hanover, N.H.: Dartmouth College, 1924), p. 15.

59. Laurence R. Veysey, *The Emergence of the American University* (Chicago: University of Chicago Press, 1965), p. 55; John C. Schwab, "The Yale College Curriculum, 1701-1901," *Educational Review*, 1901, *22* (June), 10-11; Harlow Gale, "A Yale Education Versus Culture," *Pedagogical Seminary*, 1902, *9*, 3-15.

60. Veysey, *The Emergence of the American University*, pp. 51-54.

61. Hawkins, *Between Harvard and America*, p. 202; Brooks Mather Kelley, *Yale: A History* (New Haven, Conn.: Yale University Press, 1974), p. 293; John S. Whitehead, *The Separation of College and State: Columbia, Dartmouth, Harvard, and Yale, 1776-1876* (New Haven, Conn.: Yale University Press, 1973), p. 110; Veysey, *The Emergence of the American University*, pp. 13-14.

62. George E. Peterson, *The New England College in the Age of the University* (Amherst, Mass.: Amherst College Press, 1964), pp. 27-51; Thomas Humphrey Jackson, "Redefining the Whole Man: The Little Three and the Liberal Arts Ideal, 1908-1923" (unpublished honors thesis, Williams College, 1972), pp. 1-105; McLachlan, *American Boarding Schools*, p. 15; Thomas LeDuc, *Piety and Intellect at Amherst College, 1865-1912* (New York: Columbia University Press, 1946), p. 150.

63. Michael McGiffert, *The Higher Learning in Colorado: An Historical Study, 1860-1940* (Denver: Swallow, 1964), p. 47.

64. Vanderbilt, *Charles Eliot Norton*, pp. 123, 132.

65. Vanderbilt, *Charles Eliot Norton*, p. 119.

66. Veysey, *The Emergence of the American University*, p. 175; Earl J. McGrath, *The Graduate School and the Decline of Liberal Education* (New York: Teachers College, Columbia University, for the Institute of Higher Education, 1959), p. 21.

67. Veysey, *The Emergence of the American University*, p. 136.

68. Herbst, *The German Historical School in American Scholarship*, p. 142; Powers, *A History of South Dakota State College*, p. 29; Ferrier, *Origin and Development of the University of California*, pp. 438-439.

69. Josiah Royce, "Present Ideals of American University Life," *Scribner's Magazine*, 1891, *10* (September), 387.

70. Royce, "Present Ideals," p. 387.

71. Royce, "Present Ideals," p. 387.

72. Michael J. L. O'Connor, *Origins of Academic Economics in the United States* (New York: Columbia University Press, 1944), pp. 2-4, 277-289.

73. McLachlan, "American Colleges and the Transmission of Culture," p. 201; JB Lon Hefferlin, *Dynamics of Academic Reform* (San Francisco: Jossey-Bass, 1969), p. 37; Robert L. Church, in Paul Buck (Ed.), *Social Sciences at Harvard, 1860-1920: From Inculcation to the Open Mind* (Cambridge, Mass.: Harvard University Press, 1965), pp. 13, 32-36, 51, 69.

74. Sherman B. Barnes, "The Entry of Science and History in the College Curriculum, 1865–1914," *History of Education Quarterly*, 1964, *4* (March), 39; Carol F. Baird, in Paul Buck (Ed.), *Social Sciences at Harvard, 1860–1920: From Inculcation to the Open Mind* (Cambridge, Mass.: Harvard University Press, 1965), pp. 132-135, 171.

75. Sheldon M. Stern, in Paul Buck (Ed.), *Social Sciences at Harvard, 1860–1920: From Inculcation to the Open Mind* (Cambridge, Mass.: Harvard University Press, 1965), pp. 205-207.

76. Pierson, *Yale College*, pp. 88-89; Walter C. Bronson, *The History of Brown University, 1764–1914* (Providence, R.I.: Brown University, 1914), p. 430.

77. Veysey, *The Emergence of the American University*, pp. 323-324, 59.

78. Nicholas Murray Butler (Ed.), *Monographs on Education in the United States*, Vol. 2 (Albany, N.Y.: Lyon, 1900), pp. 473, 495.

79. Butler, *Monographs on Education*, pp. 473, 507.

80. Butler, *Monographs on Education*, pp. 473, 490.

81. Butler, *Monographs on Education*, pp. 490, 495, 507.

82. *General Education in a Free Society: Report of the Harvard Committee* (Cambridge, Mass.: Harvard University Press, 1945), p. 23; Jencks and Riesman, *The Academic Revolution*, p. 232; Hinsdale, *History of the University of Michigan*, pp. 82-84.

83. Monte A. Calvert, *The Mechanical Engineer in America, 1830–1910: Professional Culture in Conflict* (Baltimore, Md.: Johns Hopkins Press, 1967), pp. 87-105; Samuel Eliot Morison (Ed.), *The Development of Harvard University Since the Inauguration of President Eliot, 1869–1929* (Cambridge, Mass.: Harvard University Press, 1930), pp. 413-450, 533-548; Merle Curti and Vernon Carstensen, *The University of Wisconsin: A History, 1848–1925*, Vol. 2 (Madison: University of Wisconsin Press, 1949), pp. 444-479; Jonas Viles and others, *The University of Missouri: A Centennial History* (Columbia: University of Missouri, 1939), pp. 411-434.

84. McGiffert, *The Higher Learning in Colorado: An Historical Study, 1860–1940*, p. 54; Rogers, *Andrew D. White and the Modern University*, p. 99; Jesse Leonard Rosenberger, *Rochester, the Making of a University* (Rochester, N.Y.: University of Rochester, 1927), p. 176; Julius Terrass Willard, *History of the Kansas State College of Agriculture and Applied Science* (Manhattan: Kansas State College Press, 1940), p. 28.

85. James Albert Woodburn, *History of Indiana University, 1820–1902* (Bloomington: Indiana University, 1940), p. 283; Willis Rudy, *The College of the City of New York: A History, 1847–1947* (New York: City College Press, 1949), p. 165.

86. Hawkins, *Between Harvard and America*, pp. 173-174; R. Freeman Butts, *The College Charts its Course: Historical Conceptions and Current Proposals* (New York: McGraw-Hill, 1939), pp. 231-250.

87. Willis Rudy, *The Evolving Liberal Arts Curriculum: A Historical Review of Basic Themes* (New York: Teachers College, Columbia University, 1960), p. 31.

88. Woodburn, *History of Indiana University*, p. 300; Veysey, *The Emergence of the American University*, p. 195; Albert Perry Brigham, *Present Status of the Elective System in American Colleges* (New York: Holt, 1897), p. 362; Louis C. Hatch, *The History of Bowdoin College* (Portland, Maine: Loring, Short, & Harmon, 1927), p. 187.

89. Veysey, *The Emergence of the American University*, p. 234; Rudy, *The Evolving Liberal Arts Curriculum*, p. 43; Pierson, *Yale College*, p. 200.

90. William Torrey Harris, "Equivalents in a Liberal Course of Study," in *The Addresses and Journals of Proceedings of the National Educational Association* (Salem, Ohio: National Educational Association, 1880), p. 173.

91. Harris,"Equivalents in a Liberal Course of Study," p. 173.

92. Paul R. Shipman, "The Classics that Educate Us," *Popular Science Monthly*, 1880, *17* (June), 146-149.

93. Charles Francis Adams, Jr., *A College Fetich: An Address Delivered Before the Harvard Chapter of the Fraternity of the Phi Beta Kappa, in Sanders Theatre, Cambridge, June 28, 1883* (3rd ed.; Boston: Lee and Shepard, 1884), pp. 12, 38, 55.

94. Vanderbilt, *Charles Eliot Norton*, p. 137.

95. Adams, *A College Fetich*, pp. 14, 28-29.

96. Adams, *A College Fetich*, p. 20.

97. Adams, *A College Fetich*, p. 20; LeDuc, *Piety and Intellect at Amherst College*, pp. 62-63; William Graham Sumner, "Our Colleges Before the Country," *Princeton Review*, 3rd series, 1884, *13* (March), 127-140.

98. John Bascom, "The Part Which the Study of Language Plays in a Liberal Education," *Journal of Proceedings and Addresses of the National Educational Association, Session of the Year 1884, at Madison, Wisconsin* (Boston: National Educational Association, 1885), pp. 273-274.

99. Andrew P. Peabody, "The Study of Greek," appendix to Daniel H. Chamberlain, *Not "A College Fetish": An Address in Reply to the Address of Charles Francis Adams, Jr.* (Boston: Small, 1884), p. 92; Clarence King, "Artium Magister," *North American Review*, 1888, *147* (October), 370-373.

100. William G. Frost, "Greek Among Required Studies," *Bibliotheca Sacra*, 1885, *165* (April), 336; Sumner, "Our Colleges Before the Country," p. 132; Albert S. Bolles, "What Instruction Should be Given in our Colleges?" *Atlantic Monthly*, 1883, *52* (November), 687; Chamberlain, *Not "A College Fetish,"* pp. 32-33; George P. Fisher, "The Study of Greek," appendix to Daniel H. Chamberlain, *Not "A College Fetish": An Address in Reply to the Address of Charles Francis Adams, Jr.* (Boston: Small, 1884), pp. 73-76.

101. Noah Porter, "Greek and a Liberal Education," *Princeton Review*, 2nd series, 1884, *60* (September), 203-206.

102. Domis E. Pluggé, *History of Greek Play Production in American Colleges and Universities from 1881 to 1936* (New York: Teachers College, Columbia University, 1938), pp. 1-5, 14-16, 30-31.

103. McGiffert, *The Higher Learning in Colorado*, pp. 55-58, 74-75.

104. McGiffert, *The Higher Learning in Colorado*, p. 49.

105. Veysey, *The Emergence of the American University*, pp.

111, 79; Jencks and Riesman, *The Academic Revolution*, pp. 263 ff.

106. McLachlan, *American Boarding Schools*, passim.

107. Russell Thomas, *The Search for a Common Learning: General Education, 1800-1960* (New York: McGraw-Hill, 1962), p. 12; Rudy, *The Evolving Liberal Arts Curriculum*, p. 34; Kelley, *Yale*, p. 287; Samuel Bradford Doten, *An Illustrated History of the University of Nevada* (Reno: University of Nevada, 1924), p. 57.

108. Kelley, *Yale*, p. 294.

109. Veysey, *The Emergence of the American University*, pp. 180 ff.

110. Veysey, *The Emergence of the American University*, p. 191.

111. Hawkins, *Between Harvard and America*, pp. 264 ff.; Veysey, *The Emergence of the American University*, pp. 221-227.

112. Veysey, *The Emergence of the American University*, p. 197.

113. Veysey, *The Emergence of the American University*, pp. 201, 216.

114. Veysey, *The Emergence of the American University*, p. 233.

115. Patton and Field, *Eight O'Clock Chapel*, pp. 86-97.

116. Charles Francis Adams, Jr., *Three Phi Beta Kappa Addresses* (Boston: Houghton Mifflin, 1907), p. 115.

117. George Wilson Pierson, "The Elective System and the Difficulties of College Planning, 1870-1940," *Journal of General Education*, 1950, *4*, (April), 165.

118. Pierson, *Yale College*, p. 46.

119. Butts, *The College Charts Its Course*, pp. 159-171.

120. Pierson, "The Elective System," pp. 171-174.

121. Pierson, "The Elective System," pp. 171-174.

122. Frederick Rudolph, *Mark Hopkins and the Log: Williams College, 1836-1872* (New Haven, Conn.: Yale University Press, 1962), pp. 149, 221.

123. Pierson, "The Elective System," pp. 171-174.

124. Pierson, "The Elective System," p. 168.

125. Pierson, "The Elective System," p. 166.

126. Charles W. Eliot, *University Administration* (Boston: Houghton Mifflin, 1908), p. 150.

127. George Wilson Pierson, *Yale: The University College, 1921-1937* (New Haven, Conn.: Yale University Press, 1955), pp. 36-37.

128. Wertenbaker, *Princeton*, pp. 304-307.

129. Butts, *The College Charts Its Course*, pp. 175 ff.; Hawkins, *Between Harvard and America*, pp. 95-96; Wertenbaker, *Princeton*, p. 293; *Inauguration of James McCosh, D.D., LL.D., as President of the College of New Jersey, Princeton, October 27, 1868* (New York: Carter, 1868), pp. 45, 47, 53, 59, 7-75.

130. James McCosh, *The New Departure in Education: Being a Reply to President Eliot's Defence of it in New York, February 24, 1885* (New York: Scribner's, 1885), pp. 12, 7-9, 18, 22, 21.

131. John C. Schwab, "The Yale College Curriculum, 1701-1901,"

Educational Review, 1901, *22* (June), 15; Kelley, *Yale*, pp. 266-292; Butts, *The College Charts Its Course*, p. 240; Brigham, *Present Status of the Elective System*, p. 361.

132. William T. Foster, *Administration of the College Curriculum* (Boston: Houghton Mifflin, 1911), pp. 140-142.

133. Butts, *The College Charts Its Course*, pp. 240-242; Pierson, *Yale College*, p. 264; Veysey, *The Emergence of the American University*, pp. 118-120.

134. Thomas, *The Search for a Common Learning*, pp. 18-19.

135. Laurence Veysey, "Stability and Experiment in the American Undergraduate Curriculum," in Carl Kaysen (Ed.), *Content and Context: Essays on College Education* (New York: McGraw-Hill, 1973), p. 3; Douglas Sloan, "Harmony, Chaos, and Consensus: The American College Curriculum," *Teachers College Record*, 1971, *73* (December), 249.

136. *The University of Chicago Official Bulletin No. 1* (4th ed.; Chicago: University of Chicago, 1891), passim.

137. Thomas Wakefield Goodspeed, *A History of the University of Chicago Founded by John D. Rockefeller: The First Quarter-Century* (Chicago: University of Chicago Press, 1916), pp. 264, 136, 139; Richard J. Storr, *Harper's University: The Beginnings: A History of the University of Chicago* (Chicago: University of Chicago Press, 1966), passim; *The University of Chicago Official Bulletin No. 1*, pp. 7-8.

138. *The University of Chicago Official Bulletin No. 1*, pp. 9-11.

139. *The University of Chicago Official Bulletin No. 1*, p. 11.

140. *The University of Chicago Official Bulletin No. 1*, pp. 12-13; Goodspeed, *A History of the University of Chicago*, p. 140; Storr, *Harper's University*, pp. 113-146.

141. Rudolph, *The American College and University*, pp. 350-351.

142. Goodspeed, *A History of the University of Chicago*, p. 369; *Nation*, 1892, *55* (October 6), 255-256.

143. *Report of the Committee on Organization, Presented to the Trustees of the Cornell University, October 21st, 1866* (Albany, N.Y.: Van Benthuysen, 1867), p. 18; W. Carson Ryan, *Studies in Early Graduate Education: The Johns Hopkins, Clark University, The University of Chicago* (New York: Carnegie Foundation for the Advancement of Teaching, Bulletin No. 30, 1939), p. 126; Goodspeed, *A History of the University of Chicago*, pp. 145-146.

144. Robert Herrick, "The University of Chicago," *Scribner's Magazine*, 1895, *18* (October), 404-409.

145. *The Decennial Publications of the University of Chicago* (Chicago: University of Chicago Press, 1903), 1st series, pp. 78, 67-68, xcv-xcvi; Storr, *Harper's University*, p. 306.

146. Veysey, *The Emergence of the American University*, passim; Lyman Abbott, "William Rainey Harper," *Outlook*, 1906, *82* (January 20), 110-111.

147. Robert Herrick, *Chimes* (New York: Macmillan, 1926); Amos Alonzo Stagg, *Touchdown!* (New York: Longmans Green, 1927); *All Our Years: The Autobiography of Robert Morss Lovett* (New York: Viking, 1948); Thorstein Veblen, *The Higher Learning in America: A Memorandum on the Conduct of Universities by Business Men* (New York: Huebsch, 1918).

148. Goodspeed, *A History of the University of Chicago*, p. 322.

149. Broome, *A Historical and Critical Discussion of College Admission Requirements*, p. 82; Louis Franklin Snow, *The College Curriculum in the United States* (New York: Teachers College, Columbia University, 1907), p. 174; Veysey, *The Emergence of the American University*, p. 114.

Chapter 6

1. Frederick Paul Keppel, *Columbia* (New York: Oxford University Press, 1914), p. 146; John Dewey, "Academic Freedom," *Educational Review*, 1902, 22 (January), 2; Frederick Rudolph, *The American College and University: A History* (New York: Knopf, 1962), p. 347.

2. Laurence R. Veysey, *The Emergence of the American University* (Chicago: University of Chicago Press, 1965), p. 283.

3. Walter C. Bronson, *The History of Brown University, 1764–1914* (Providence, R.I.: Brown University, 1914), p. 489; Jurgen Herbst, *The German Historical School in American Scholarship: A Study in the Transfer of Culture* (Ithaca, N.Y.: Cornell University Press, 1965), p. 50.

4. Michael R. Harris, *Five Counter-Revolutionists in Higher Education* (Corvallis: Oregon State University Press, 1970), pp. 122 ff.; Abraham Flexner, *Universities: American, English, German* (New York: Oxford University Press, 1968, originally published 1930), pp. 39-72.

5. Willis Rudy, *The Evolving Liberal Arts Curriculum: A Historical Review of Basic Themes* (New York: Teachers College, Columbia University, 1960), pp. 19, 15.

6. George Wilson Pierson, *Yale College: An Educational History, 1871–1921* (New Haven, Conn.: Yale University Press, 1952), p. 206; Hugh Hawkins, *Between Harvard and America: The Educational Leadership of Charles W. Eliot* (New York: Oxford University Press, 1972), pp. 116-119; Samuel Eliot Morison, *Three Centuries of Harvard, 1636–1936* (Cambridge, Mass.: Harvard University Press, 1946), pp. 370-371; Veysey, *The Emergence of the American University*, pp. 267-271.

7. Thomas Wakefield Goodspeed, *A History of the University of Chicago Founded by John D. Rockefeller: The First Quarter Century* (Chicago: University of Chicago Press, 1916), p. 463.

8. Joseph Ben-David, *American Higher Education: Directions Old and New* (New York: McGraw-Hill, 1972), p. 57.

9. Willis Rudy, "The 'Revolution' in American Higher Education, 1865–1900," *Harvard Educational Review*, 1951, 21 (Summer), 162.

10. Rudy, "The 'Revolution' in American Higher Education," p. 162.

11. Brooks Mather Kelley, *Yale: A History* (New Haven, Conn.: Yale University Press, 1974), p. 343; Dwight C. Miner (Ed.), *A History of Columbia College on Morningside* (New York: Columbia University Press, 1954), p. 32.

12. Sidney Forman, *West Point: A History of the United States Military Academy* (New York: Columbia University Press, 1950), pp. 162-163; Veysey, *The Emergence of the American University*, p. 250.

13. Hawkins, *Between Harvard and America*, p. 99.

14. Rudolph, *The American College and University*, pp. 289-290; Veysey, *The Emergence of the American University*, p. 272.

15. Pierson, *Yale College*, pp. 245-246; Earl J. McGrath, *The Graduate School and the Decline of Liberal Education* (New York: Teachers College, Columbia University, for the Institute of Higher Education, 1959), p. 22; Hawkins, *Between Harvard and America*, pp. 274-275.

16. Francis Wayland, *The Education Demanded by the People of the U. States: A Discourse Delivered at Union College, Schenectady, July 25, 1854, on the Occasion of the Fiftieth Anniversary of the Presidency of Eliphalet Nott, D.D., LL.D.* (Boston: Phillips, Sampson, 1855), pp. 8-9; *Addresses at the Inauguration of Charles William Eliot as President of Harvard College, Tuesday, October 19, 1869* (Cambridge, Mass.: Sever and Francis, 1869), pp. 39-40.

17. Agatho Zimmer, *Changing Concepts of Higher Education in America Since 1700* (Washington, D.C.: Catholic University of America, 1938), p. 44.

18. Charles Henry Rammelkamp, *Illinois College: A Centennial History, 1829–1929* (New Haven, Conn.: Yale University Press, for Illinois College, 1928), pp. 383-384.

19. Edwin E. Slosson, *Great American Universities* (New York: Macmillan, 1910), p. 17.

20. Christopher Jencks and David Riesman, *The Academic Revolution* (New York: Doubleday, 1968), p. 77; Educational Policies Commission, *Higher Education in a Decade of Decision* (Washington, D.C.: National Education Association, 1957), p. 22; George Wilson Pierson, *Yale: The University College, 1921–1937* (New Haven, Conn.: Yale University Press, 1955), p. 616; *U.S. Commissioner of Education, Report: 1910* (Washington, D.C.: U.S. Government Printing Office, 1910), pp. 856-858.

21. Richard Hofstadter, *Anti-Intellectualism in American Life* (New York: Knopf, 1963), p. 334.

22. Rudy, "The 'Revolution' in American Higher Education," p. 164; Habib Amin Kurani, *Selecting the College Student in America: A Study of Theory and Practice* (New York: Teachers College, Columbia University, 1931), p. 99; Ivol Spafford and others, *Building a Curriculum for General Education* (Minneapolis: University of Minnesota Press, 1943), p. 10; Robert L. Duffus, *Democracy Enters College: A Study of the Rise and Decline of the Academic Lockstep* (New York: Scribner's, 1936), p. 1.

23. Julius Terrass Willard, *History of the Kansas State College of Agri-*

culture and Applied Science (Manhattan: Kansas State College Press, 1940), p. 152; Ernest Victor Hollis, Philanthropic Foundations and Higher Education (New York: Columbia University Press, 1938), pp. 132-133.

24. Louis G. Geiger, University of the Northern Plains: A History of the University of North Dakota, 1883-1958 (Grand Forks: University of North Dakota Press, 1958), pp. 213-214; Daniel Walker Hollis, University of South Carolina, Vol. 2 (Columbia: University of South Carolina, 1956), pp. 268-269.

25. Seymour Martin Lipset, "Political Controversies at Harvard 1636 to 1974," in Seymour Martin Lipset and David Riesman, Education and Politics at Harvard (New York: McGraw-Hill, 1975), p. 106; Burton R. Clark, The Distinctive College: Antioch, Reed and Swarthmore (Chicago: Aldine, 1970), p. 99.

26. Russell Thomas, The Search for a Common Learning: General Education, 1800-1960 (New York: McGraw-Hill, 1962), p. 41.

27. John Howard Van Amringe and others, A History of Columbia University, 1754-1904 (New York: Columbia University Press, 1904), p. 170; Leon Burr Richardson, History of Dartmouth College, Vol. 2 (Hanover, N.H.: Dartmouth College, 1932), p. 700; Theodore F. Jones (Ed.), New York University: 1832-1932 (New York: New York University Press, 1933), p. 226; Pierson, Yale College, p. 194; John O. Lyons, The College Novel in America (Carbondale: Southern Illinois University Press, 1962), pp. 15-16.

28. Pierson, Yale College, pp. 408, 510; Pierson, Yale, pp. 43, 46; Pierson, "The Elective System and the Difficulties of College Planning, 1870-1940," Journal of General Education, 1950, 4 (April), 169.

29. Leon B. Richardson, A Study of the Liberal College: A Report to the President of Dartmouth College (Hanover, N.H.: Dartmouth College, 1924), p. 168; Pierson, Yale, p. 318; James I. Osborne and Theodore G. Gronert, Wabash College: The First Hundred Years, 1832-1932 (Crawfordsville, Ind.: Banta, 1932), p. 298; Saul Sack, "Liberal Education: What Was It? What Is It?" History of Education Quarterly, 1962, 2 (December), 219.

30. Pierson, Yale, p. 315.

31. Charles W. Eliot, "The Case Against Compulsory Latin," Atlantic Monthly, 1917, 119 (March), 357-358.

32. Rudy, The Evolving Liberal Arts College, pp. 46, 28.

33. Geiger, University of the Northern Plains, p. 207; Dixon Ryan Fox, Union College: An Unfinished History (Schenectady: Union College, 1945), p. 40.

34. Rudy, The Evolving Liberal Arts College, pp. 60, 87.

35. Walter Crosby Eells, Academic Degrees: Earned and Honorary Degrees Conferred by Institutions of Higher Education in the United States, U.S. Office of Education Bulletin No. 28 (Washington, D.C.: U.S. Government Printing Office, 1960), p. 154.

36. Robert Maynard Hutchins, The Higher Learning in America (New Haven, Conn.: Yale University Press, 1936), p. 5.

37. Edwin G. Knepper, History of Business Education in the United

States (Bowling Green, Ohio: Edwin G. Knepper, 1941), pp. 43-44, 71, 108-110.

38. Knepper, *History of Business Education*, pp. 111-112, 190; Jones, *New York University*, pp. 182-184.

39. Rudy, *The Evolving Liberal Arts Curriculum*, pp. 12, 46, 28-29, 78; Miner, *A History of Columbia College on Morningside*, pp. 31-32.

40. Richardson, *History of Dartmouth College*, Vol. 2, pp. 736-737.

41. Noah Porter, "Greek and a Liberal Education," *Princeton Review*, 2nd series, 1884, *60* (September), 217.

42. Slosson, *Great American Universities*, p. 60.

43. Pierson, *Yale College*, pp. 213, 222. Kelley; *Yale*, p. 344.

44. Lipset, "Political Controversies at Harvard," p. 115; Arthur G. Beach, *A Pioneer College: The Story of Marietta* (Privately printed, 1935), p. 276; George E. Peterson, *The New England College in the Age of the University* (Amherst, Mass.: Amherst College Press, 1964), p. 178.

45. Eells, *Academic Degrees*, pp. 181, 187.

46. Pierson, *Yale College*, pp. 249-250.

47. Pierson, *Yale College*, p. 228.

48. Carnegie Foundation for the Advancement of Teaching, *Annual Report of the President and Treasurer*, Vol. 3 (1908), pp. 94-102; Fred J. Kelly and others, *Collegiate Accreditation by Agencies Within States*, U.S. Office of Education Bulletin No. 3 (Washington, D.C.: U.S. Government Printing Office, 1940), pp. 8-10, 20-26; Peter E. Hogan, *The Catholic University of America, 1896-1903: The Rectorship of Thomas J. Conaty* (Washington, D.C.: Catholic University of America Press, 1949), p. 72; Lester William Bartlett, *State Control of Private Incorporated Institutions of Higher Education* (New York: Teachers College, Columbia University, 1926), pp. 4 ff.

49. Kelly, *Collegiate Accreditation by Agencies Within States,* pp. 13-18.

50. Kelly, *Collegiate Accreditation by Agencies Within States*, pp. 20-26; Duffus, *Democracy Enters College*, pp. 57 ff.; Carnegie Foundation for the Advancement of Teaching, *Annual Report* (1908), p. 102.

51. Hollis, *Philanthropic Foundations and Higher Education*, pp. 303-306.

52. Hollis, *Philanthropic Foundations and Higher Education*, pp. 128 ff., 194-196; Howard J. Savage, *Fruit of an Impulse: Forty-Five Years of the Carnegie Foundation, 1905-1950* (New York: Harcourt Brace Jovanovich, 1953), p. 43; Claude Charleton Bowman, *The College Professor in America: An Analysis of Articles Published in the General Magazines, 1890-1938* (Philadelphia: Claude Charleton Bowman, 1938), pp. 57-63.

53. Carnegie Foundation for the Advancement of Teaching, *Annual Report* (1906), pp. 21-22.

54. Carnegie Foundation for the Advancement of Teaching, *Annual Report* (1906), pp. 66, 79.

55. Carnegie Foundation for the Advancement of Teaching, *Annual Report* (1906), pp. 66, 79.

330 *(For pages 223-230) Notes*

56. Savage, *Fruit of an Impulse*, p. 103.
57. Philip Alexander Bruce, *History of the University of Virginia, 1819-1919*, Vol. 5 (New York: Macmillan, 1922), p. 110; Zimmer, *Changing Concepts of Higher Education in America Since 1700*, pp. 107-113; Frederick James Kelly and others, *The Influence of Standardizing Agencies in Education* (St. Paul: University of Minnesota, 1928), pp. 7-8, 21; Hollis, *Philanthropic Foundations and Higher Education*, p. 137.
58. Hollis, *Philanthropic Foundations and Higher Education*, p. 36.
59. Dwight Oliver Wendell Holmes, *The Evolution of the Negro College* (New York: Teachers College, Columbia University, 1934), pp. 172-176.
60. Hollis, *Philanthropic Foundations and Higher Education*, pp. 133-134.
61. Hollis, *Philanthropic Foundations and Higher Education*, pp. 157-158.
62. Savage, *Fruit of an Impulse*, p. 92; Carnegie Foundation for the Advancement of Teaching, *Annual Report* (1909), p. 161.
63. Duffus, *Democracy Enters College*, pp. 69-71.
64. Carnegie Foundation for the Advancement of Teaching, *Annual Report* (1908), pp. 148-149; Hollis, *Philanthropic Foundations and Higher Education*, passim.
65. Jencks and Riesman, *Academic Revolution*, pp. 168 ff.; Veysey, *The Emergence of the American University*, p. 330.
66. Hollis, *Philanthropic Foundations and Higher Education*, pp. 32, 274.
67. Merle Curti and Roderick Nash, *Philanthropy in the Shaping of American Higher Education* (New Brunswick, N.J.: Rutgers University Press, 1965), passim.
68. Veysey, *The Emergence of the American University*, p. 114.
69. Lipset, "Political Controversies at Harvard," p. 129.
70. Hawkins, *Between Harvard and America*, p. 103.
71. John C. Schwab, "The Yale College Curriculum, 1701-1901," *Educational Review*, 1901, *22* (June), 16-17; Hawkins, *Between Harvard and America*, pp. 100-101; George Matthew Dutcher, *An Historical and Critical Survey of the Curriculum of Wesleyan University and Related Subjects* (Middletown, Conn.: Wesleyan University, 1948), p. 28.
72. Hawkins, *Between Harvard and America*, p. 283.
73. S. Willis Rudy, *The College of the City of New York: A History, 1847-1947* (New York: City College Press, 1949), p. 321.
74. Thomas, *The Search for a Common Learning*, p. 54.
75. Morison, *Three Centuries of Harvard*, p. 441.
76. Laurence Veysey, "Stability and Experiment in the American Undergraduate Curriculum," in Carl Kaysen (Ed.), *Content and Context: Essays on College Education* (New York: McGraw-Hill, 1973), p. 36.
77. William T. Foster, *Administration of the College Curriculum* (Boston: Houghton Mifflin, 1911), pp. 204-209.

78. William C. DeVane, *Higher Education in Twentieth-Century America* (Cambridge, Mass.: Harvard University Press, 1965), p. 25.

79. Walter Pilkington, *Hamilton College, 1812-1962* (Clinton, N.Y.: Hamilton College, 1962), p. 249.

80. Pierson, *Yale College*, pp. 311, 338; Frank Aydelotte, *Breaking the Academic Lock Step: The Development of Honors Work in American Colleges and Universities* (New York: Harper & Row, 1944), pp. 30-44; JB Lon Hefferlin, *Dynamics of Academic Reform* (San Francisco: Jossey-Bass, 1969), p. 43; Clark, *The Distinctive College*, p. 93; Frances Blanshard, *Frank Aydelotte of Swarthmore* (Middletown, Conn.: Wesleyan University Press, 1970), pp. 188, 212, 221, 260.

81. Aydelotte, *Breaking the Academic Lock Step*, pp. 7-8.

82. DeVane, *Higher Education in Twentieth-Century America*, pp. 66-67.

83. Pierson, *Yale*, p. 192.

84. Pierson, *Yale*, pp. 333 ff.; Veysey, "Stability and Experiment," pp. 11-12; Rudy, *The Evolving Liberal Arts Curriculum*, pp. 73, 103; Carl F. Price, *Wesleyan's First Century* (Middletown, Conn.: Wesleyan University, 1932), p. 194; Dutcher, *An Historical and Critical Survey of the Curriculum of Wesleyan University*, pp. 40-41; Richardson, *History of Dartmouth College*, Vol. 2, p. 787.

85. Burton Dorr Myers, *History of Indiana University, 1902-1937* (Bloomington: Indiana University, 1952), p. 497; Dutcher, *An Historical and Critical Survey of the Curriculum of Wesleyan University*, p. 39.

86. Richardson, *A Study of the Liberal College*, pp. 159-161.

87. Clarence F. Birdseye, *Individual Training in Our Colleges* (New York: Macmillan, 1907), p. 175.

88. Veysey, *The Emergence of the American University*, p. 144.

89. Pierson, *Yale College*, p. 115; DeVane, *Higher Education in Twentieth-Century America*, p. 9.

90. Veysey, *The Emergence of the American University*, p. 339; Birdseye, *Individual Training in Our Colleges*, pp. 176, 397-407.

91. Birdseye, *Individual Training in Our Colleges*, p. 404; Slosson, *Great American Universities*, p. 19; Charles W. Eliot, *University Administration* (Boston: Houghton Mifflin, 1908), pp. 174-213.

92. Veysey, *The Emergence of the American University*, p. 297; Slosson, *Great American Universities*, p. 50.

93. Pierson, *Yale College*, p. 240.

94. Slosson, *Great American Universities*, p. 66.

95. Kelley, *Yale*, p. 302.

96. Henry Wilkinson Bragdon, *Woodrow Wilson: The Academic Years* (Cambridge, Mass.: Harvard University Press, 1967), pp. 305-307, 359 ff.; Slosson, *Great American Universities*, pp. 80-85; Bliss Perry, *And Gladly Teach: Reminiscences* (Boston: Houghton Mifflin, 1935), pp. 126-159.

97. Slosson, *Great American Universities*, p. 75.

98. Veysey, *The Emergence of the American University*, p. 242.

99. Duffus, *Democracy Enters College*, p. 73; Morison, *Three Centuries of Harvard*, p. 446; Edward Safford Jones, *Comprehensive Examinations in American Colleges* (New York: Macmillan, 1933), p. 419.

100. Pierson, *Yale College*, p. 347.

101. Charles Tabor Fitts and Fletcher Harper Swift, *The Construction of Orientation Courses for Freshmen* (Berkeley: University of California Press, 1928), pp. 154-161.

102. Miner, *A History of Columbia College on Morningside*, pp. 46-47, 53; Daniel Bell, *The Reforming of General Education: The Columbia College Experience in Its National Setting* (New York: Columbia University Press, 1966), pp. 12-26; Russell Thomas, *The Search for a Common Learning*, pp. 69, 76; Carol S. Gruber, *Mars and Minerva: World War I and the Uses of the Higher Learning in America* (Baton Rouge: Louisiana State University Press, 1976), pp. 237-244.

103. Merle Curti and Vernon Carstensen, *The University of Wisconsin: A History, 1848-1925*, Vol. 2 (Madison: University of Wisconsin Press, 1949), p. 319; Fitts and Swift, *The Construction of Orientation Courses for Freshmen*, pp. 161 ff.

104. Fitts and Swift, *The Construction of Orientation Courses for Freshmen*, pp. 180 ff.

105. Veysey, *The Emergence of the American University*, pp. 255-256.

106. Wilson Smith, "Apologia pro Alma Matre: The College as Community in Ante-Bellum America," in Stanley Elkins and Eric McKitrick (Eds.), *The Hofstadter Aegis: A Memorial* (New York: Knopf, 1974), pp. 129-130; Thomas LeDuc, *Piety and Intellect at Amherst College, 1865-1912* (New York: Columbia University Press, 1946), p. 138.

107. Pierson, *Yale College*, p. 359; Pierson, *Yale*, p. 153.

108. Harris, *Five Counter-Revolutionists in Higher Education*, pp. 77, 61.

109. Birdseye, *Individual Training in Our Colleges*, p. 194.

110. Thomas Woody, *A History of Women's Education in the United States*, Vol. 2 (New York: Science Press, 1929), pp. 317-318; Orin Leslie Elliott, *Stanford University: The First Twenty-Five Years* (Stanford, Calif.: Stanford University Press, 1937), p. 476.

111. Veysey, *The Emergence of the American University*, pp. 187-188 ff.

112. Clark, *The Distinctive College*, pp. 8-9.

113. Clark, *The Distinctive College*, pp. 92-95 ff.

114. Clark, *The Distinctive College*, p. 116.

115. Hefferlin, *Dynamics of Academic Reform*, pp. 23-24; Algo D. Henderson and Dorothy Hall, *Antioch College: Its Design for Liberal Education* (New York: Harper & Row, 1946), pp. viii, 4, 1-63; Arthur E. Morgan, "The Antioch Plan," *Journal of Higher Education*, 1930, *1* (December), 497-502; Clark, *The Distinctive College*, p. 45.

116. Clark, *The Distinctive College*, pp. 171-200.

117. G. Stanley Hall, "On the History of American College Textbooks and Teaching in Logic, Ethics, Psychology, and Allied Subjects," *Proceedings of the American Antiquarian Society*, new series, 1894, 9 (April), 157.

118. McGrath, *The Graduate School and the Decline of Liberal Education*, p.11.

Chapter 7

1. JB Lon Hefferlin, *Dynamics of Academic Reform* (San Francisco: Jossey-Bass, 1969), pp. 55-56.

2. Willis Rudy, *The Evolving Liberal Arts Curriculum: A Historical Review of Basic Themes* (New York: Teachers College, Columbia University, 1960), p. 89.

3. Rudy, *The Evolving Liberal Arts Curriculum*, p. 42.

4. George Wilson Pierson, *Yale: The University College, 1921-1937* (New Haven, Conn.: Yale University Press, 1955), p. 331.

5. G. Wallace Chessman, *Denison: The Story of an Ohio College* (Granville, Ohio: Denison University, 1957), p. 396.

6. Rudy, *The Evolving Liberal Arts Curriculum*, p. 103.

7. Rudy, *The Evolving Liberal Arts Curriculum*, p. 101; Louis G. Geiger, *University of the Northern Plains: A History of the University of North Dakota, 1883-1958* (Grand Forks: University of North Dakota Press, 1958), p. 429.

8. Rudy, *The Evolving Liberal Arts Curriculum*, p. 46.

9. William C. DeVane, *Higher Education in Twentieth-Century America* (Cambridge, Mass.: Harvard University Press, 1965), p. 7.

10. Brooks Mather Kelley, *Yale: A History* (New Haven, Conn.: Yale University Press, 1974), p. 5.

11. Pierson, *Yale*, p. 285.

12. John R. Thelin, "Life and Learning in Southern California: Private Colleges in the Popular Culture," *History of Education Quarterly*, 1975, 15 (Spring), 113.

13. David D. Henry, *Challenges Past, Challenges Present: An Analysis of American Higher Education Since 1930* (San Francisco: Jossey-Bass, 1975), p. 33.

14. James E. Pollard, *History of the Ohio State University: The Story of the First Seventy-Five Years, 1873-1948* (Columbus: Ohio State University Press, 1952), p. 309; Kent Sagendorph, *Michigan: The Story of the University* (New York: Dutton, 1948), pp. 312-315.

15. Hefferlin, *Dynamics of Academic Reform*, p. 59.

16. David Riesman, "Educational Reform at Harvard College: Meritocracy and Its Adversaries," in Seymour Martin Lipset and David Riesman, *Education and Politics at Harvard* (New York: McGraw-Hill, 1975), p. 344.

17. Hefferlin, *Dynamics of Academic Reform*, pp. 119, 141.

18. Robert Blackburn and others, *Changing Practices in Undergradu-*

ate Education (Berkeley, Calif.: Carnegie Council on Policy Studies in Higher Education, 1976), pp. 33-35; Arthur Levine and John Weingart, *Reform of Undergraduate Education* (San Francisco: Jossey-Bass, 1973), pp. 64-74.

19. Levine and Weingart, *Reform of Undergraduate Education,* p. 58.

20. Kelley, *Yale,* p. 410.

21. Riesman, "Educational Reform at Harvard College," p. 325.

22. Levine and Weingart, *Reform of Undergraduate Education,* pp. 75-109.

23. Rudy, *The Evolving Liberal Arts Curriculum,* p. 75.

24. David Truman, in introduction to Daniel Bell, *The Reforming of General Education: The Columbia College Experience in Its National Setting* (New York: Columbia University Press, 1966), p. ix.

25. Russell Thomas, *The Search for a Common Learning: General Education, 1800–1960* (New York: McGraw-Hill, 1962), p. 96; Kelley, *Yale,* p. 387; Christopher Jencks and David Riesman, *The Academic Revolution* (New York: Doubleday, 1968), p. 248.

26. Levine and Weingart, *Reform of Undergraduate Education,* pp. 25-29.

27. Thomas, *The Search for a Common Learning,* pp. 97 ff.

28. Blackburn and others, *Changing Practices in Undergraduate Education,* p. 41.

29. Pierson, *Yale,* pp. 51-52; Kelley, *Yale,* p. 389.

30. Levine and Weingart, *Reform of Undergraduate Education,* pp. 50-51.

31. Thomas, *The Search for a Common Learning,* p. 277.

32. Richard Hofstadter and C. DeWitt Hardy, *The Development and Scope of Higher Education in the United States* (New York: Columbia University Press, 1952), p. 55.

33. Thomas, *The Search for a Common Learning,* pp. 80-81 ff.

34. Dwight C. Miner (Ed.), *A History of Columbia College on Morningside* (New York: Columbia University Press, 1954), pp. 60-61; Harry J. Carman, "Reminiscences of Thirty Years," *Journal of Higher Education,* 1951, *22* (March), 115-122, 168-169, passim.

35. Henry D. Sheldon, *History of University of Oregon* (Portland: Binfords & Mort, 1940), p. 237.

36. Chessman, *Denison,* pp. 397-402.

37. George Matthew Dutcher, *An Historical and Critical Survey of the Curriculum of Wesleyan University and Related Subjects* (Middletown, Conn.: Wesleyan University, 1948), pp. 56-63.

38. *General Education in a Free Society: Report of the Harvard Committee* (Cambridge, Mass.: Harvard University Press, 1945).

39. *General Education in a Free Society,* p. 50.

40. *General Education in a Free Society,* p. 51.

41. *General Education in a Free Society,* p. 244.

42. Kelley, *Yale,* p. 409.

43. Rudy, *The Evolving Liberal Arts Curriculum,* p. 53.

44. Arnold B. Arons, "The Amherst Program," *Journal of Higher Education,* 1955, *26* (February), 75-81.

45. Daniel Bell, *The Reforming of General Education: The Columbia College Experience in Its National Setting* (New York: Columbia University Press, 1966), pp. 38-50; Riesman, "Educational Reform at Harvard College," pp. 345-349; Jencks and Riesman, *The Academic Revolution,* pp. 493, 497.

46. Riesman, "Educational Reform at Harvard College," pp. 346-347.

47. Kelley, *Yale,* p. 450.

48. Levine and Weingart, *Reform of Undergraduate Education,* pp. 21-25.

49. Levine and Weingart, *Reform of Undergraduate Education,* pp. 38-51.

50. Thomas, *The Search for a Common Learning,* p. 283.

51. Charles McArthur, "Personalities of Public and Private School Boys," *Harvard Educational Review,* 1954, *24* (Fall), 258.

52. Thomas, *The Search for a Common Learning,* p. 290.

53. Levine and Weingart, *Reform of Undergraduate Education,* p. 50.

54. Howard Mumford Jones, "Undergraduates on Apron Strings," *Atlantic Monthly,* 1955, *196* (October), 45.

55. Jones, "Undergraduates," pp. 45, 47.

56. Joseph Ben-David, *American Higher Education: Directions Old and New* (New York: McGraw-Hill, 1972), p. 65.

57. Henry, *Challenges Past, Challenges Present,* pp. 71-79; Laurence Veysey, "Stability and Experiment in the American Undergraduate Curriculum," in Carl Kaysen (Ed.), *Content and Context: Essays on College Education* (New York: McGraw-Hill, 1973), pp. 30-31.

58. Mina Rees, "Efforts of the Mathematical Community to Improve the Mathematics Curriculum," in Logan Wilson (Ed.), *Emerging Patterns in American Higher Education* (Washington, D.C.: American Council on Education, 1965), pp. 229-230; Henry, *Challenges Past, Challenges Present,* pp. 118 ff.; Hefferlin, *Dynamics of Academic Reform,* pp. 37-38.

59. Wilbur Fisk, *The Science of Education: An Inaugural Address, Delivered at the Opening of the Wesleyan University, Sept. 21, 1831* (New York: M'Elrath & Bangs, 1832), p. 13.

60. Kelley, *Yale,* p. 343.

61. Dutcher, *An Historical and Critical Survey of the Curriculum of Wesleyan University,* p. 43; George Wilson Pierson, *Yale College: An Educational History, 1871-1921* (New Haven, Conn.: Yale University Press, 1952), pp. 224-226.

62. Jesse Leonard Rosenberger, *Rochester, the Making of a University* (Rochester, N.Y.: University of Rochester, 1927), pp. 301-303; Walter

Havighurst, *The Miami Years, 1809–1959* (New York: Putnam's, 1958), p.
190; Robert Lincoln Kelly, *The American Colleges and the Social Order*
(New York: Macmillan, 1940), pp. 222-225, 234, 240.

63. Jack Morrison, *The Rise of the Arts on the American Campus* (New
York: McGraw-Hill, 1973), pp. 9-10.

64. Morrison, *The Rise of the Arts,* p. 14.

65. Morrison, *The Rise of the Arts,* pp. 15-18.

66. Veysey, *The Emergence of the American University,* p. 25.

67. Bob Knott, "What is a Competence-Based Curriculum in the Liberal Arts?" *Journal of Higher Education,* 1975, *46* (January-February), 27-28.

68. Knott, "What is a Competence-Based Curriculum?" pp. 28-29.

69. Knott, "What is a Competence-Based Curriculum?" passim; Levine
and Weingart, *Reform of Undergraduate Education,* p. 53.

70. Veysey, "Stability and Experiment," pp. 30-31.

71. Jencks and Riesman, *The Academic Revolution,* p. 285.

72. Clifton Fadiman in Robert M. Hutchins, "The Intellectual Community," *The Center Magazine,* 1977, *10* (January-February), 5-6.

73. Verne A. Stadtman, *The University of California, 1868–1968* (New
York: McGraw-Hill, 1970), pp. 381-382, 412-420, 474-495.

74. Clark Kerr, *The Uses of the University* (Cambridge, Mass.: Harvard
University Press, 1963).

75. David Riesman and Verne A. Stadtman (Eds.), *Academic Transformation: Seventeen Institutions Under Pressure* (New York: McGraw-Hill,
1973), p. 441; Levine and Weingart, *Reform of Undergraduate Education,* pp.
143-144.

76. Seymour Martin Lipset, "Political Controversies at Harvard 1636 to
1974," in Seymour Martin Lipset and David Riesman, *Education and Politics
at Harvard* (New York: McGraw-Hill, 1975), pp. 217, 223.

77. Levine and Weingart, *Reform of Undergraduate Education,*
passim.

78. Levine and Weingart, *Reform of Undergraduate Education,* p. 8.

79. Veysey, "Stability and Experiment," pp. 10-11.

80. Frederick Rudolph, *The American College and University: A History* (New York: Knopf, 1962), p. 458; Martin Duberman, *Black Mountain:
An Exploration in Community* (New York: Dutton, 1972), pp. 1-10.

81. Louis Tomlinson Benezet, *General Education in the Progressive
College* (New York: Teachers College, Columbia University, 1943), pp. 108-
111.

82. Benezet, *General Education in the Progressive College,* pp. 50-51,
74-76, 137-144.

83. Robert L. Leigh, "The Bennington College Program," *Journal of
Higher Education,* 1930, *1* (December), 520-524; Barbara Jones, *Bennington
College: The Development of an Educational Idea* (New York: Harper &
Row, 1946), passim.

84. Gerald Grant and David Riesman, "An Ecology of Academic

Reform," *Daedalus*, 1975, *104* (Winter) of *Proceedings of the American Academy of Arts and Sciences—American Higher Education: Toward an Uncertain Future*, Vol. 2, 171.

85. Michael R. Harris, *Five Counter-Revolutionists in Higher Education* (Corvallis: Oregon State University Press, 1970), p. 164.

86. Alexander Meiklejohn, *The Experimental College* (Madison: University of Wisconsin, 1928), pp. 1-6, 8, 20, 67-68 ff.

87. Veysey, "Stability and Experiment," p. 56.

88. Ivol Spafford and others, *Building a Curriculum for General Education: A Description of the General College Program* (Minneapolis: University of Minnesota Press, 1943), pp. ix, 1-9, 24; James Gray, *The University of Minnesota, 1851-1951* (Minneapolis: University of Minnesota Press, 1951), pp. 308-322.

89. Thomas, *The Search for a Common Learning*, pp. 83-87; Bell, *The Reforming of General Education*, pp. 26-38; Harris, *Five Counter-Revolutionists in Higher Education*, pp. 155-156.

90. Thomas, *The Search for a Common Learning*, p. 86.

91. Thomas, *The Search for a Common Learning*, p. 83; Robert M. Hutchins, "The University of Chicago and the Bachelor's Degree," *Educational Record*, 1942, *23*, 57 ff.; Hutchins, "The Intellectual Community," pp. 5-6.

92. Robert Maynard Hutchins, *The Higher Learning in America* (New Haven, Conn.: Yale University Press, 1936), p. 66.

93. Harry David Gideonse, *The Higher Learning in a Democracy: A Reply to President Hutchins' Critique of the American University* (New York: Farrar & Rinehart, 1937), p. 33.

94. Hefferlin, *Dynamics of Academic Reform*, p. 24; Levine and Weingart, *Reform of Undergraduate Education*, pp. 38-51; Thomas, *The Search for a Common Learning*, pp. 230-250.

95. Hutchins, "The Intellectual Community," p. 6.

96. Keith W. Olson, *The G.I. Bill, the Veterans, and the Colleges* (Lexington: University Press of Kentucky, 1974), p. 59.

97. Olson, *The G.I. Bill*, p. 33.

98. Olson, *The G.I. Bill*, p. 25.

99. Olson, *The. G.I. Bill*, p. 36.

100. Roscoe H. Eckelberry, *The History of the Municipal University in the United States*, U.S. Office of Education Bulletin No. 2 (Washington, D.C.: U.S. Government Printing Office, 1932), p. 7; Parke R. Kolbe, *Urban Influences on Higher Education in England and the United States* (New York: Macmillan, 1928), p. 138.

101. M. M. Chambers, "Diversify the Colleges," *Journal of Higher Education*, 1960, *31* (January), 10.

102. Earl J. McGrath, *The Predominantly Negro Colleges and Universities in Transition* (New York: Teachers College, Columbia University, 1965), pp. 66-70.

103. Hefferlin, *Dynamics of Academic Reform*, p. 23; S. Willis Rudy, *The College of the City of New York: A History, 1847–1947* (New York: City College Press, 1949), p. 447; Henry, *Challenges Past, Challenges Present*, p. 68.

104. Veysey, *The Emergence of the American University*, p. 338.

105. *"The Open-Door Colleges": Policies for Community Colleges: A Special Report and Recommendations by the Carnegie Commission on Higher Education* (New York: McGraw-Hill, 1970); B. Lamar Johnson, *General Education in Action* (Washington, D.C.: American Council on Education, 1952); B. Lamar Johnson, *Islands of Innovation Expanding: Changes in the Community College* (Beverly Hills, Calif.: Glencoe Press, 1969); Leland L. Medsker and Dale Tillery, *Breaking the Access Barriers: A Profile of Two-Year Colleges* (New York: McGraw-Hill, 1971).

106. L. Steven Zwerling, *The Crisis of the Community College: Second Best* (New York: McGraw-Hill, 1976), pp. 234-236.

107. Jencks and Riesman, *The Academic Revolution*, pp. 481-492.

108. Rudy, *The Evolving Liberal Arts Curriculum*, p. 57.

109. Levine and Weingart, *Reform of Undergraduate Education*, pp. 50-51.

110. Levine and Weingart, *Reform of Undergraduate Education*, p. 72.

111. Nevitt Sanford (Ed.), *The American College: A Psychological and Social Interpretation of the Higher Learning* (New York: Wiley, 1962), p. 422.

112. Hefferlin, *Dynamics of Academic Reform*, pp. 64-66.

Bibliography

Because the chapter notes provide full citations of studies useful to a consideration of particular subjects and because the bibliography of my general history of higher education in the United States—*The American College and University: A History* (New York: Knopf, 1962), pp. 497-516—contains an extensive guide to materials published before 1960, this bibliography is limited to books and articles first published in 1960 and later. Limiting this bibliography in this way, in addition to avoiding repetition of the bibliography of my earlier work, provides some sense of the directions in which the history of higher education in the United States has moved in recent years. It also makes clear how much the present work is indebted to recent scholarship.

Books

Altbach, Philip G. *Student Politics in America: A Historical Analysis.* New York: McGraw-Hill, 1974.

Altman, Robert A. *The Upper Division College.* San Francisco: Jossey-Bass, 1970.

Ambrose, Stephen E. *Duty, Honor, Country: A History of West Point.* Baltimore, Md.: Johns Hopkins Press, 1966.

Barnard, John. *From Evangelicalism to Progressivism at Oberlin College, 1866-1917.* Columbus: Ohio State University Press, 1969.

Bell, Daniel. *The Reforming of General Education: The Columbia College Experience in Its National Setting.* New York: Columbia University Press, 1966.

Ben-David, Joseph. *American Higher Education: Directions Old and New.* New York: McGraw-Hill, 1972.

Berelson, Bernard. *Graduate Education in the United States.* New York: McGraw-Hill, 1960.

Billington, Ray Allen. *Frederick Jackson Turner: Historian, Scholar, Teacher.* New York: Oxford University Press, 1973.

Bishop, Morris. *A History of Cornell.* Ithaca, N.Y.: Cornell University Press, 1962.

Blackburn, Robert, and others. *Changing Practices in Undergraduate Education.* Berkeley, Calif.: Carnegie Council on Policy Studies in Higher Education, 1976.

Blanshard, Frances. *Frank Aydelotte of Swarthmore.* Middletown, Conn.: Wesleyan University Press, 1970.

Bledstein, Burton J. *The Culture of Professionalism: The Middle Class and the Development of Higher Education in America.* New York: Norton, 1976.

Blocker, Clyde E., Plummer, Robert H., and Richardson, Richard C., Jr. *The Two-Year College: A Social Synthesis.* Englewood Cliffs, N.J.: Prentice-Hall, 1965.

Bowles, Frank, and DeCosta, Frank A. *Between Two Worlds: A Profile of Negro Higher Education.* New York: McGraw-Hill, 1971.

Bragdon, Henry Wilkinson. *Woodrow Wilson: The Academic Years.* Cambridge, Mass.: Harvard University Press, 1967.

Brunner, Henry S. *Land-Grant Colleges and Universities, 1862–1962.* U.S. Office of Education Bulletin No. 13. Washington, D.C.: U.S. Government Printing Office, 1962.

Buck, Paul (Ed.). *Social Sciences at Harvard, 1860–1920: From Inculcation to the Open Mind.* Cambridge, Mass.: Harvard University Press, 1965.

Bullock, Henry Allen. *A History of Negro Education in the South.* Cambridge, Mass.: Harvard University Press, 1967.

Calhoun, Daniel H. *The American Civil Engineer: Origins and Conflict.* Cambridge, Mass.: Technology Press, 1960.

Calhoun, Daniel H. *Professional Lives in America: Structure and Aspiration, 1750–1850.* Cambridge, Mass.: Harvard University Press, 1965.

Calhoun, Daniel H. *The Intelligence of a People.* Princeton, N.J.: Princeton University Press, 1973.

Calvert, Monte A. *The Mechanical Engineer in America, 1830–1910: Professional Culture in Conflict.* Baltimore, Md.: Johns Hopkins Press, 1967.

Carnegie Commission on Higher Education. *"The Open-Door Colleges"; Policies for Community Colleges.* New York: McGraw-Hill, 1970.

Carnegie Commission on Higher Education. *Less Time, More Options: Education Beyond the High School.* New York: McGraw-Hill, 1971.

Carnegie Commission on Higher Education. *Reform on Campus: Changing Students, Changing Academic Programs.* New York: McGraw-Hill, 1972.

Carnegie Commission on Higher Education. *College Graduates and Jobs: Adjusting to a New Labor Market Situation.* New York: McGraw-Hill, 1973.

Carnegie Commission on Higher Education. *The Purpose and Performance of Higher Education in the United States.* New York: McGraw-Hill, 1973.

Cary, Harold W. *The University of Massachusetts: A History of One Hundred Years.* Amherst: University of Massachusetts, 1962.

Church, Robert L. "Economists as Experts: The Rise of an Academic Profession in America, 1870–1917." In Lawrence Stone (Ed.), *The University in Society.* Vol. 2. Princeton, N.J.: Princeton University Press, 1974.

Church, Robert L., and Sedlak, Michael W. *Education in the United States: An Interpretive History.* New York: Free Press, 1976.

Clark, Burton R. *The Distinctive College: Antioch, Reed and Swarthmore.* Chicago: Aldine, 1970.

Crane, Theodore Rawson. *Francis Wayland: Political Economist as Educator.* Providence, R.I.: Brown University Press, 1962.

Cremin, Lawrence A. *American Education: The Colonial Experience, 1607–1783.* New York: Harper & Row, 1970.

Curti, Merle, and Nash, Roderick. *Philanthropy in the Shaping of American Higher Education.* New Brunswick, N.J.: Rutgers University Press, 1965.

Daniels, George H. *American Science in the Age of Jackson.* New York: Columbia University Press, 1968.

Dennis, Lawrence E., and Kaufman, Joseph F. (Eds.). *The College and the Student.* Washington, D.C.: American Council on Education, 1966.

DeVane, William C. *Higher Education in Twentieth-Century America.* Cambridge, Mass.: Harvard University Press, 1965.

Duberman, Martin. *Black Mountain: An Exploration in Community.* New York: Dutton, 1972.

Dunbar, Willis F. *The Michigan Record in Higher Education.* Detroit: Wayne State University Press, 1963.

Dyer, John Percy. *Tulane: The Biography of a University, 1834–1965.* New York: Harper & Row, 1966.

Eells, Walter Crosby. *Academic Degrees: Earned and Honorary Degrees Conferred by Institutions of Higher Education in the United States.* U.S. Office of Education Bulletin No. 28. Washington, D.C.: U.S. Government Printing Office, 1960.

Ellis, Joseph J. *The New England Mind in Transition: Samuel Johnson of Connecticut, 1696–1772.* New Haven, Conn.: Yale University Press, 1973.

Eschenbacher, Herman F. *The University of Rhode Island.* New York: Appleton-Century-Crofts, 1967.

Foster, Margery Somers. *"Out of Small Beginnings . . .": An Economic History of Harvard College in the Puritan Period (1636 to 1712).* Cambridge, Mass.: Harvard University Press, 1962.

Furner, Mary O. *Advocacy & Objectivity: A Crisis in the Professionalization of American Social Science, 1865–1905.* Lexington: University Press of Kentucky, 1975.

Furniss, Edgar S. *The Graduate School of Yale: A Brief History.* New Haven, Conn.: Yale University Press, 1965.

Gatewood, Willard B. *Preachers, Pedagogues and Politicians: The Evolution*

Controversy in North Carolina, 1920–1927. Chapel Hill: University of North Carolina Press, 1966.

Gleazer, Edmund J. *Project Focus: A Forecast Study of Community Colleges.* New York: McGraw-Hill, 1973.

Greeley, Andrew M. *From Backwater to Mainstream: A Profile of Catholic Higher Education.* New York: McGraw-Hill, 1969.

Gruber, Carol S. *Mars and Minerva: World War I and the Uses of the Higher Learning in America.* Baton Rouge: Louisiana State University Press, 1976.

Guralnick, Stanley M. *Science and the Ante-Bellum American College.* Philadelphia: American Philosophical Society, 1975.

Handlin, Oscar, and Handlin, Mary F. *The American College and American Culture: Socialization as a Function of Higher Education.* New York: McGraw-Hill, 1970.

Harris, Michael R. *Five Counter-Revolutionists in Higher Education.* Corvallis: Oregon State University Press, 1970.

Harris, Seymour (Ed.). *Higher Education in the United States: The Economic Problems.* Cambridge, Mass.: Harvard University Press, 1960.

Harris, Seymour. *The Economics of Harvard.* New York: McGraw-Hill, 1970.

Hassenger, Robert (Ed.). *The Shape of Catholic Higher Education.* Chicago: University of Chicago Press, 1967.

Hawkins, Hugh. *Pioneer: A History of the Johns Hopkins University, 1874–1889.* Ithaca, N.Y.: Cornell University Press, 1960.

Hawkins, Hugh. *Between Harvard and America: The Educational Leadership of Charles W. Eliot.* New York: Oxford University Press, 1972.

Hefferlin, JB Lon. *Dynamics of Academic Reform.* San Francisco: Jossey-Bass, 1969.

Henry, David D. *Challenges Past, Challenges Present: An Analysis of American Higher Education Since 1930.* San Francisco: Jossey-Bass, 1975.

Herbst, Jurgen. *The German Historical School in American Scholarship: A Study in the Transfer of Culture.* Ithaca, N.Y.: Cornell University Press, 1965.

Hislop, Codman. *Eliphalet Nott.* Middletown, Conn.: Wesleyan University Press, 1971.

Hofstadter, Richard. *Anti-Intellectualism in American Life.* New York: Knopf, 1963.

Hofstadter, Richard, and Smith, Wilson. *American Higher Education: A Documentary History.* 2 vols. Chicago: University of Chicago Press, 1962.

Howe, Daniel Walker. *The Unitarian Conscience: Harvard Moral Philosophy, 1805–1861.* Cambridge, Mass.: Harvard University Press, 1970.

Humphrey, David C. *From King's College to Columbia, 1746–1800.* New York: Columbia University Press, 1976.

Jencks, Christopher, and Riesman, David. *The Academic Revolution.* New York: Doubleday, 1968.

Johnson, B. Lamar. *Islands of Innovation Expanding: Changes in the Community College.* Beverly Hills: Glencoe Press, 1969.

Kaysen, Carl (Ed.). *Content and Context: Essays on College Education.* New York: McGraw-Hill, 1973.

Keeton, Morris T. *Models and Mavericks: A Profile of Private Liberal Arts Colleges.* New York: McGraw-Hill, 1971.

Kelley, Brooks Mather. *Yale: A History.* New Haven, Conn.: Yale University Press, 1974.

Kendall, Elaine. *"Peculiar Institutions": An Informal History of the Seven Sisters Colleges.* New York: Putnam's, 1975.

Kerr, Clark. *The Uses of the University.* Cambridge, Mass.: Harvard University Press, 1963.

Knapp, Robert H. *The Origins of American Humanistic Scholars.* Englewood Cliffs, N.J.: Prentice-Hall, 1964.

Krug, Edward A. *The Shaping of the American High School, 1880–1920.* Madison: University of Wisconsin Press, 1969. (Originally published 1964.)

Krug, Edward A. *The Shaping of the American High School, 1920–1941.* Madison: University of Wisconsin Press, 1972.

Levine, Arthur, and Weingart, John. *Reform of Undergraduate Education.* San Francisco: Jossey-Bass, 1973.

Lipset, Seymour Martin, and Riesman, David. *Education and Politics at Harvard.* New York: McGraw-Hill, 1975.

Logan, Rayford W. *Howard University: The First Hundred Years, 1867–1967.* New York: New York University Press, 1969.

Lyons, John O. *The College Novel in America.* Carbondale: Southern Illinois University Press, 1962.

McCaughey, Robert A. *Josiah Quincy 1772–1864: The Last Federalist.* Cambridge, Mass.: Harvard University Press, 1974.

McCormick, Richard P. *Rutgers: A Bicentennial History.* New Brunswick, N.J.: Rutgers University Press, 1966.

McGiffert, Michael. *The Higher Learning in Colorado: An Historical Study, 1860–1940.* Denver: Swallow, 1964.

McGrath, Earl J. *The Predominantly Negro Colleges and Universities in Transition.* New York: Teachers College, Columbia University, 1965.

McLachlan, James. *American Boarding Schools: A Historical Study.* New York: Scribner's, 1970.

McLachlan, James. "American Colleges and the Transmission of Culture: The Case of the Mugwumps." In Stanley Elkins and Eric McKitrick (Eds.), *The Hofstadter Aegis: A Memorial.* New York: Knopf, 1974.

McLachlan, James. "The *Choice of Hercules:* American Student Societies in the Early 19th Century." In Lawrence Stone (Ed.), *The University in Society.* Vol. 2. Princeton, N.J.: Princeton University Press, 1974.

McPherson, James W. "The New Puritanism: Values and Goals of Freedmen's Education in America." In Lawrence Stone (Ed.), *The University in Society*. Vol. 2. Princeton, N.J.: Princeton University Press, 1974.

Mayhew, Lewis B. *The Carnegie Commission on Higher Education: A Critical Analysis of the Reports and Recommendations*. San Francisco: Jossey-Bass, 1973.

Medsker, Leland L. *The Junior College: Progress and Prospect*. New York: McGraw-Hill, 1960.

Medsker, Leland L., and Tillery, Dale. *Breaking the Access Barriers: A Profile of the Two-Year Colleges*. New York: McGraw-Hill, 1971.

Messerli, Jonathan. *Horace Mann: A Biography*. New York: Knopf, 1972.

Middlekauf, Robert. *Accents and Axioms: Secondary Education in Eighteenth-Century New England*. New Haven, Conn.: Yale University Press, 1963.

Miller, Russell E. *Light on the Hill: A History of Tufts College, 1852–1952*. Boston: Beacon Press, 1966.

Morgan, Edmund S. *The Gentle Puritan: A Life of Ezra Stiles, 1727–1795*. Chapel Hill: University of North Carolina Press, 1962.

Morrison, Jack. *The Rise of the Arts on the American Campus*. New York: McGraw-Hill, 1973.

Nevins, Allan. *The State Universities and Democracy*. Urbana: University of Illinois Press, 1962.

Novak, Steven J. *The Rights of Youth: American Colleges and Student Revolt, 1798–1815*. Cambridge, Mass.: Harvard University Press, 1977.

Olson, Keith W. *The G.I. Bill, the Veterans, and the Colleges*. Lexington: University Press of Kentucky, 1974.

Peterson, George E. *The New England College in the Age of the University*. Amherst, Mass.: Amherst College Press, 1964.

Pilkington, Walter. *Hamilton College, 1812–1962*. Clinton, N.Y.: Hamilton College, 1962.

Porter, Earl W. *Trinity and Duke, 1892–1924: Foundations of Duke University*. Durham, N.C.: Duke University Press, 1964.

Raushenbush, Esther. *The Student and His Studies*. Middletown, Conn.: Wesleyan University Press, 1964.

Riesman, David, and Stadtman, Verne A. (Eds.). *Academic Transformation: Seventeen Institutions Under Pressure*. New York: McGraw-Hill, 1973.

Ross, Dorothy. *G. Stanley Hall: The Psychologist as Prophet*. Chicago: University of Chicago Press, 1972.

Rudolph, Frederick. *The American College and University: A History*. New York: Knopf, 1962.

Rudy, Willis. *The Evolving Liberal Arts Curriculum: A Historical Review of Basic Themes*. New York: Teachers College, Columbia University, 1960.

Sanford, Nevitt (Ed.). *The American College: A Psychological and Social Interpretation of the Higher Learning*. New York: Wiley, 1962.

Selden, William K. *Accreditation: A Struggle Over Standards in Higher Education*. New York: Harper & Row, 1960.

Sellers, Charles Coleman. *Dickinson College: A History.* Middletown, Conn.: Wesleyan University Press, 1973.

Simons, William E. *Liberal Education in the Service Academies.* New York: Teachers College Press, 1965.

Sizer, Theodore R. *Secondary Schools at the Turn of the Century.* New Haven, Conn.: Yale University Press, 1964.

Sloan, Douglas. *The Scottish Enlightenment and the American College Ideal.* New York: Teachers College Press, 1971.

Smith, Wilson. "Apologia pro Alma Matre: The College as Community in Ante-Bellum America." In Stanley Elkins and Eric McKitrick (Eds.), *The Hofstadter Aegis: A Memorial.* New York: Knopf, 1974.

Solberg, Winton U. *The University of Illinois, 1867-1894: An Intellectual and Cultural History.* Urbana: University of Illinois Press, 1968.

Stadtman, Verne A. *The University of California, 1868-1968.* New York: McGraw-Hill, 1970.

Stephens, Frank F. *A History of the University of Missouri.* Columbia: University of Missouri Press, 1962.

Stocking, George W., Jr. *Race, Culture, and Evolution: Essays in the History of Anthropology.* New York: Free Press, 1968.

Storr, Richard J. *Harper's University: The Beginnings: A History of the University of Chicago.* Chicago: University of Chicago Press, 1966.

Taylor, Harold. *Students Without Teachers: The Crisis in the University.* New York: McGraw-Hill, 1969.

Taylor, Harold. *The World as Teacher.* New York: Doubleday, 1969.

Thomas, Russell. *The Search for a Common Learning: General Education, 1800-1960.* New York: McGraw-Hill, 1962.

Trow, Martin. *Problems in the Transition from Elite to Mass Higher Education.* Berkeley, Calif.: Carnegie Commission on Higher Education, 1973.

Trow, Martin (Ed.). *Teachers and Students: Aspects of American Higher Education.* New York: McGraw-Hill, 1975.

Tucker, Louis L. *Puritan Protagonist: President Thomas Clap of Yale College.* Chapel Hill: University of North Carolina Press, 1962.

Tyack, David B. *George Ticknor and the Boston Brahmins.* Cambridge, Mass.: Harvard University Press, 1967.

Tyack, David B. *The One Best System: A History of American Urban Education.* Cambridge, Mass.: Harvard University Press, 1974.

Veysey, Laurence. *The Emergence of the American University.* Chicago: University of Chicago Press, 1965.

Warch, Richard. *School of the Prophets: Yale College, 1701-1740.* New Haven, Conn.: Yale University Press, 1973.

Wechsler, Harold S. *The Qualified Student: A History of Selective College Admission in America.* New York: Wiley, 1977.

Whitehead, John S. *The Separation of College and State: Columbia, Dartmouth, Harvard, and Yale, 1776-1876.* New Haven, Conn.: Yale University Press, 1973.

Wilson, Logan (Ed.). *Emerging Patterns in American Higher Education.* Washington, D.C.: American Council on Education, 1965.

Zwerling, L. Steven. *The Crisis of the Community College: Second Best.* New York: McGraw-Hill, 1976.

Articles

Allmendinger, David F., Jr. "New England Students and the Revolution in Higher Education, 1800–1900." *History of Education Quarterly,* 1971, *11* (Winter), 381–389.

Axtell, James. "The Death of the Liberal Arts College." *History of Education Quarterly,* 1971, *11* (Winter), 339–352.

Barnes, Sherman B. "The Entry of Science and History in the College Curriculum, 1865–1914." *History of Education Quarterly,* 1964, *4* (March), 44–58.

Carrell, William D. "American College Professors, 1750–1800." *History of Education Quarterly,* 1968a, *8* (Fall), 289–305.

Carrell, William D. "Biographical List of American College Professors to 1800." *History of Education Quarterly,* 1968b, *8* (Fall), 358–374.

Clement, Rufus E. "The Historical Development of Higher Education for Negro Americans." *Journal of Negro Education,* 1966, *35* (Fall), 299–305.

Cohen, Sheldon S. "Benjamin Trumbull, The Years at Yale 1755–1759." *History of Education Quarterly,* 1966, *6* (Winter), 33–48.

Cohen, Sheldon S. "The Yale College Journal of Benjamin Trumbull." *History of Education Quarterly,* 1968, *8* (Fall), 375–385.

Conway, Jill. "Perspectives on the History of Women's Education in the United States." *History of Education Quarterly,* 1974, *14* (Spring), 1–12.

Eells, Walter Crosby. "First Degrees in Music." *History of Education Quarterly,* 1961, *1* (March), 35–40.

Faherty, William Barnaby. "Nativism and Midwestern Education: The Experience of Saint Louis University, 1832–1856." *History of Education Quarterly,* 1968, *8* (Winter), 447–458.

Fiering, Norman S. "President Samuel Johnson and the Circle of Knowledge." *William and Mary Quarterly,* 3rd series, 1971, *28* (April), 199–236.

Florer, John H. "Major Issues in the Congressional Debate of the Morrill Act of 1862." *History of Education Quarterly,* 1968, *8* (Winter), 459–478.

Ford, Charles E. "Botany Texts: A Survey of Their Development in American Higher Education, 1643–1906." *History of Education Quarterly,* 1964, *4* (March), 59–71.

Gerhard, Dietrich. "Development and Structure of Continental European and American Universities—A Comparison." *Jahrbuch für Amerikastudien,* 1967, *12,* 19–35.

Grant, Gerald, and Riesman, David. "An Ecology of Academic Reform." *Daedalus,* 1975, *104* (Winter) of *Proceedings of the American Academy of*

Arts and Sciences—American Higher Education: Toward an Uncertain Future," Vol. 2, 166-191.

Hawkins, Hugh. "The University-Builders Observe the Colleges." *History of Education Quarterly,* 1971, *11* (Winter), 353-362.

Herbst, Jurgen. "The First Three American Colleges: Schools of the Reformation." *Perspectives in American History,* 1974, *8,* 5-54.

Humphrey, David C. "Colonial Colleges and English Dissenting Academies: A Study in Transatlantic Culture." *History of Education Quarterly,* 1972, *12* (Summer), 184-197.

Humphrey, David C. "British Influences on Eighteenth Century American Education." *History of Education Quarterly,* 1973, *13* (Spring), 65-72.

Johnson, William R. "Professors in Process: Doctors and Teachers in American Culture." *History of Education Quarterly,* 1975, *15* (Summer), 185-199.

Kraus, Joe W. "The Development of a Curriculum in the Early American Colleges." *History of Education Quarterly,* 1961, *1* (June), 64-76.

Lazerson, Marvin. "F. A. P. Barnard and Columbia College: Prologue to a University." *History of Education Quarterly,* 1966, *6* (Winter), 49-64.

McCaughey, Robert A. "The Transformation of American Academic Life: Harvard University, 1821-1892." *Perspectives in American History,* 1974, *8,* 237-332.

Messerli, Jonathan C. "Horace Mann at Brown." *Harvard Educational Review,* 1963, *33* (Summer), 285-311.

Miles, Edwin A. "The Old South and the Classical World." *North Carolina Historical Review,* 1971, *48* (July), 258-275.

Miles, Edwin A. "The Young American Nation and the Classical World." *Journal of the History of Ideas,* 1974, *35* (April-June), 259-274.

Naylor, Natalie A. "The Ante-Bellum College Movement: A Reappraisal of Tewksbury's *The Founding of American Colleges and Universities.*" *History of Education Quarterly,* 1973, *13* (Fall), 261-274.

Paulston, Roland G. "French Influence in American Institutions of Higher Learning, 1784-1825." *History of Education Quarterly,* 1968, *8* (Summer), 229-245.

Payton, Phillip W. "Origins of the Terms 'Major' and 'Minor' in American Higher Education." *History of Education Quarterly,* 1961, *1* (June), 57-63.

Phillips, J. O. C. "The Education of Jane Addams." *History of Education Quarterly,* 1974, *14* (Spring), 49-68.

Potts, David B. "American Colleges in the Nineteenth Century: From Localism to Denominationalism." *History of Education Quarterly,* 1971, *11* (Winter), 363-380.

Sack, Saul. "Liberal Education: What Was It? What Is It?" *History of Education Quarterly,* 1962, *3* (December), 210-224.

Schudson, Michael S. "Organizing the 'Meritocracy': A History of the College Entrance Examination Board." *Harvard Educational Review*, 1972, *42* (February), 54–69.

Sloan, Douglas. "Harmony, Chaos, and Consensus: The American College Curriculum." *Teachers College Record*, 1971, *73* (December), 221–251.

Story, Ronald. "Harvard Students, the Boston Elite, and the New England Preparatory System, 1800–1870." *History of Education Quarterly*, 1975, *15* (Fall), 281–298.

Thelin, John R. "Life and Learning in Southern California: Private Colleges in the Popular Culture." *History of Education Quarterly*, 1975, *15* (Spring), 111–117.

Urofsky, Melvin I. "Reforms and Response: The Yale Report of 1828." *History of Education Quarterly*, 1965, *5* (March), 53–67.

Wein, Roberta. "Women's Colleges and Domesticity, 1875–1918." *History of Education Quarterly*, 1974, *14* (Spring), 31–48.

Name Index

Subject Index

Elective system *(cont.)*
tionalism and, 217-218; disillusionment with, 227, 243; in German universities, 206-207; in the high school,
211-212; as instrument of reform, 178,
191-196, 206-208; rate of change in,
246
Elites, education for, 15-17, 29, 101-102,
162-163, 179, 181, 189, 199
Emory, 108, 145
Engineering, 20, 106-107, 110, 138
England, 3, 25-53 *passim*, 63
English language, 36-39, 45, 47, 53, 140,
212
English literature, 134, 140
Enrollments: in business/commercial
courses, 216; elective system and, 209,
210-211; high school, 212-213; history
of, 101-102, 110, 152, 172-173, 210-211;
lecture system and, 233
Esthetics, 140-143, 265-268
Ethics. *See* Moral philosophy
European intellectual movements, in
colonial colleges, 33-34
Evolution, 107-108
Examinations: at classical colleges, 16,
145-148; comprehensive, 235-236, 278-
279; for honors degrees, 231
Experimental institutions, 274-275, 277
Extension courses, 197, 199
Extracurriculum: the arts in, 141-142; in
disarray, 150, 206, 233-234; professorship, 205; student development of, 12-
13, 90, 94-98, 134, 218

Faculties: authority of, 18; as internal
police force, 121
Faculty psychology, 68-69, 88, 146, 209-
210
Faculty-student relationship, 121
Film, 267
Fine arts, 140-144, 265-268
Fisk University, 168
Ford Foundation, 265
Fordham, 171
Foreign languages. *See* Hebrew lan-
guage; Languages; Latin language;
Modern languages; *etc.*

Form versus content, 226, 241
Foundations, 221-227, 264. *See also*
Carnegie Foundation; Ford Founda-
tion; *etc.*
Fraternities, 95, 282
French influence, 51-52
French language, 51-52
Freshman years, variety in, 19

General education, 118-119, 150, 236-239,
241, 252-264, 273, 276-277, 288; at
Chicago, 278-279; through great
books, 280; Harvard Report on, 257-
259, 261, 262; lack of science in, 255-
256, 265
General Education Board, 221, 224, 226,
230, 235, 241
Geology, 17
German universities, 10-11, 113-114, 144-
145, 155-156, 206-207
G.I. Bill of Rights, 282-283, 284
Goddard College, 275
Government, and higher education, 220-
221, 264
Grading systems: of classical college, 145-
148; standards and, 15-16
Graduate instruction, 80-81, 130, 175,
199-200
Great books concept, 280
Great Depression, 248, 278
Greece, ancient, 29-30, 37-38
Greek language, 30-32, 37, 38, 50-57 *pas-
sim*, 72, 180-188, 209, 210, 213-214
Guidance and testing services, 251-252

Hamilton College, 108, 230
Hampden-Sidney College, 51
Hampton, 149
Hampton Institute, 168
Harvard: admission standards, 167, 181;
the arts at, 140-141, 143; enrollments,
102, 233; criticisms of curriculum at,
184-186; degrees, 10, 31-33, 138, 173,
205, 214, 246; duration of course of
study, 205-206; elective system at, 135-
137, 191, 194-196, 206-208, 227, 228,
229; examinations and grading, 16,
146-148, 235-236; faculty, 144, 175;